Distributed Object-Oriented Data-Systems Design

Prabhat K. Andleigh
Michael R. Gretzinger

Prentice Hall
Englewood Cliffs, New Jersey 07632

Library of Congress Cataloging-in-Publication Data

Andleigh, Prabhat K.
   Distributed object oriented data-systems design/Prabhat K.
Andleigh, Michael R. Gretzinger.
      p.   cm.
   Includes bibliographical references and index.
   ISBN 0-13-174913-7
   1. System design.   2. Object-oriented data bases.   3. Distributed
data bases.   I. Gretzinger, Michael R., 1961–   .   II. Title.
   QA76.9.S88A528   1992   91-41274
005.75'8—dc20   CIP

Editorial/production supervision and
    interior design: Laura A. Huber
Cover design: Wanda Lubelska
Prepress buyer: Mary Elizabeth McCartney
Manufacturing buyer: Susan Brunke
Acquistions editor: Paul W. Becker

© 1992 by Prentice-Hall, Inc.
A Simon & Schuster Company
Englewood Cliffs, New Jersey 07632

The publisher offers discounts on this book when ordered
in bulk quantities. For more information, write:
    Special Sales/Professional Marketing
    Prentice-Hall, Inc.
    Professional & Technical Reference Division
    Englewood Cliffs, New Jersey 07632

Printed in the United States of America

10 9 8 7 6 5 4 3 2 1

ISBN 0-13-174913-7

PRENTICE-HALL INTERNATIONAL (UK) LIMITED, *London*
PRENTICE-HALL OF AUSTRALIA PTY. LIMITED, *Sydney*
PRENTICE-HALL CANADA INC., *Toronto*
PRENTICE-HALL HISPANOAMERICANA, S.A., *Mexico*
PRENTICE-HALL OF INDIA PRIVATE LIMITED, *New Delhi*
PRENTICE-HALL OF JAPAN, INC., *Tokyo*
SIMON & SCHUSTER ASIA PTE. LTD., *Singapore*
EDITORA PRENTICE-HALL DO BRASIL, LTDA., *Rio de Janeiro*

To our parents for their love and sacrifices, to our families and friends for their encouragement, and to Deepa, Vinnie, Vaibhav and Vipur for their patience, understanding and support.

Contents

PREFACE   *xiii*

Part I Advanced Information Management Systems   **1**

1 CONTEMPORARY INFORMATION SYSTEMS   **4**

    1.1   Introduction 4

    1.2   The Open OLTP Environment 6

    1.3   Distributed Database Architectures 7

    1.4   Design Issues for Distributed Database
            Architectures 10

    1.5   Advanced User Interfaces 16

    1.6   Object Orientation 21

    1.7   Summary 22

    1.8   Exercises 22

2 RELATIONAL DATABASE SYSTEMS   **23**

    2.1   Introduction 23

    2.2   Basic Definitions and Concepts of the Relational
            Model 26

2.3   Relational Algebra   26

2.4   Foundation Rules of the Relational Model   31

2.5   Data Independence   45

2.6   Integrated Data Dictionary   46

2.7   Transaction Management   47

2.8   Limitations of Record-based Information
        Models   49

2.9   Summary   52

2.10   Exercises   53

3   OBJECT-ORIENTED DATABASE MANAGEMENT   55

3.1   Introduction   55

3.2   Definition of Objects   59

3.3   Review of Key Object-oriented Programming
        Concepts   60

3.4   Object Orientation for Database Systems   87

3.5   Relational Extensions to Object-oriented Database
        Systems   96

3.6   Object Orientation in Relational Databases   98

3.7   Uses for Object-oriented Databases   100

3.8   Summary   102

3.9   Exercises   103

Part II Contemporary Information Systems Design
         Methodology   105

4   INFORMATION ENGINEERING SURVEY OF
    DEPICTION TECHNIQUES   107

4.1   Information Engineering Methodology   108

4.2   Normalization   110

4.3   Entity Relationship Diagrams   115

4.4   Data-flow Diagrams   120

4.5   Information Analysis   125

4.6   Semantic Networks   129

4.7   Frame Diagrams   134

4.8   Frame-object Analysis Diagrams   136

4.9   Summary   143

4.10   Exercises   143

**5 SYSTEMS DESIGN METHODOLOGY FOR
OBJECT-ORIENTED SYSTEMS   145**

5.1   Advanced Information Systems Design   146

5.2   Design Methodology: Object Oriented versus
Relational   147

5.3   Object-oriented Design Methodology   148

5.4   Advanced Object-oriented Design   160

5.5   Key Features of ODMSs   163

5.6   Summary   164

5.7   Exercises   164

6 EFFECTIVE PROJECT DESIGN MANAGEMENT   166

6.1   Requirements Analysis   167

6.2   Knowledge Engineering and Use of Functional
Experts   168

6.3   Prototyping   170

6.4   Designing Application Solutions   173

6.5   Business Rules Programming   174

6.6   Testing an Advanced Information System   175

6.7   Effective Use of CASE Tools   176

6.8   Summary   182

6.9   Exercises   182

Part III   Advanced Information Systems Design   **185**

7   ADVANCED DESIGN FOR DATA DICTIONARY   **189**

    7.1   Data Dictionary   190

    7.2   Conceptual Database Schema Definition   191

    7.3   Data-dictionary-enforced Integrity Issues   194

    7.4   Deficiencies of RDBMS Data Dictionaries   195

    7.5   Database Integrity for Distributed Objects   196

    7.6   Data Dictionary for an Object-oriented Database   198

    7.7   Summary   199

    7.8   Exercises   200

8   ADVANCED DATA MODELING   **201**

    8.1   Introduction   201

    8.2   System Design Methodology   203

    8.3   Fundamental Design Issues   205

    8.4   Business Information Model   206

    8.5   Architectural Recommendation and Technology Feasibility   209

    8.6   Modeling and Information System   210

    8.7   Information System Model   212

    8.8   Object Model   229

    8.9   Implementing an Object Model   246

    8.10   Summary   248

    8.11   Exercises   250

9   OBJECT-ORIENTED DESIGN   **251**

    9.1   Object Definition   252

    9.2   Assigning Datatypes to Objects   253

    9.3   Creating Object Methods   260

    9.4   Implementing Object Classes   267

9.5   Object Use and Manipulation   270

9.6   Summary   272

9.7   Exercises   273

10 DISTRIBUTED SYSTEMS ISSUES   **274**

10.1   Distributed Systems   276

10.2   Information Resource Management   278

10.3   Data Distribution by Corporate Hierarchy   280

10.4   Distributed Database System Architectures   282

10.5   Data Integrity in a Distributed Environment   288

10.6   Distributed Database Management   298

10.7   Summary   305

10.8   Exercises   305

11 DESIGNING FOR PERFORMANCE   **307**

11.1   Performance Issues and Monitoring for
        Performance   308

11.2   Role of Indexes in Database Physical
        Design   311

11.3   Denormalization and Re-structuring of
        Databases   316

11.4   Object Design Techniques for Performance
        Realization   318

11.5   Summary   320

11.6   Exercises   320

**Part IV Design Approaches to Advanced Information
          Systems**   **323**

12 ADVANCED USER INTERFACES   **325**

12.1   GUIs/Multimedia User Interfaces   327

12.2   Characteristics of Programming Tools for
        GUIs   330

12.3   Simultaneous Multimedia Output   332

12.4   Multidimensional Pointing Device   332

12.5   Use of Natural Language Interfaces   333

12.6   Voice Command Recognition and Voice
        Synthesis   334

12.7   Use of SQL for Nonalphanumeric Data   334

12.8   Summary   335

12.9   Exercises   335

13 RAPID DEVELOPMENT METHODOLOGIES   336

13.1   Advanced Application Builders   337

13.2   Advanced CASE-based Systems   343

13.3   Expert-systems-based Development Tools   343

13.4   Summary   344

13.5   Exercises   344

**14 DESIGN ISSUES FOR IMAGING, CAD/CAM/CAE,
      AND CARTOGRAPHY**   345

14.1   Requirements for Imaging   346

14.2   Data Structures for CAD/CAM/CAE and GIS
        349

14.3   Integration of Advanced Technologies   352

14.4   Design Issues for ODMS-based CAD/CAM and
        GIS Systems   357

14.5   Summary   360

14.6   Exercises   360

Part V   Object-oriented Design Example   361

15 DESIGNING A FINANCIAL APPLICATION   364

15.1   Business Model for the International Trading
        Corporation   365

15.2   Business Information Model for ITC   366

Contents

15.3   Architectural Recommendation and Technology Feasibility   376

15.4   Summary   380

15.5   Exercises   381

16   DATA MODELING AND DESIGN   **382**

16.1   Information System Model   383

16.2   Object Model   405

16.3   System Design   421

16.4   Benefits of Object-oriented Design Approach   462

16.5   Summary   463

16.6   Exercises   464

GLOSSARY OF DATABASE TERMS   **466**

BIBLIOGRAPHY AND REFERENCES   **484**

INDEX   **486**

Preface

This is a book about advanced distributed information systems; what constitutes an advanced distributed information system and how to design and implement one. As computers have become more integrated into the workplace and society, there has been a growing need to store and manipulate increasingly complex data and to develop more sophisticated ways of presenting information to users.

Users of computer systems in businesses are getting to be more and more sophisticated. Furthermore, businesses have networked systems that span facilities, cities, and nations and have integrated applications running on these networks. There is a growing need to manage widely distributed data in a timely and effective manner.

A very important aspect of a contemporary information system is the underlying data management system and how it handles diverse and complex datatypes, high data volumes, data integrity under access from distributed users, and updates from distributed sources of data. Another major aspect of contemporary information systems is managing advanced applications that are based on multimedia user interfaces, widely distributed data sources, and multiple concurrent users. As we see it, there are three major components in a modern information system:

1. An object-oriented data management system that provides fast and flexible access to many classes of data objects.

2. A distributed environment supporting multiple workstations connected to a local or wide-area network, with one or more database servers providing transparent access to multiple data sources.

3. An advanced user interface provided by a graphics workstation or PC with the capability of integrating text, graphics, pictures, and possibly sound and video.

These three components form one group of topics for discussion in this book. We believe that the migration of relational databases to include object datatypes and object-oriented databases featuring greater relational database-like controls are movements that are bringing the two technologies closer together. For some length of time, the two environments, relational and object oriented, will coexist on networks, until database systems emerge that have a very flexible and tunable personality that can fully address the needs for object orientation, as well as rigorous relational control for advanced systems. In any case, a study of relational systems is as important as a study of object-oriented systems for contemporary information systems design.

Readers are assumed to be students of data processing or to have a professional interest in information systems, especially in the design of contemporary information systems. We expect that the readers will have some understanding of the C language (although that is not really necessary for understanding the examples) and some knowledge of SQL programming (and, again, that is not necessary but it is beneficial).

Another major emphasis of the book is the presentation and evaluation of application design and development methodologies. A detailed presentation includes data modeling and the development of a conceptual database design for an object-oriented database system. We will also show how to convert the design to produce efficient, flexible, and extensible applications. Object-oriented systems design is an important element of this presentation.

This book is divided into five major parts that present relevant technologies, development methodologies, data modeling, and design in a congruous manner. Part I concentrates on our definition of an advanced information system and the presentation of the prominent design features of the two principal contemporary technologies for information systems: relational and object-oriented database systems. Part II presents a design methodology to prepare the user for an advanced information system design discussion presented in Part III. Part III describes a methodology for advanced data modeling and presents a step by step approach to application design. Part IV evaluates design issues for advanced user interfaces and multimedia storage and retrieval. Part V presents a real-life example of how a financial system can be designed using object-oriented techniques. The progression in these parts, especially Parts I, II, and III, is important. These three parts are informative as well as tutorial in nature, especially when approached in that sequence.

At a detailed level, the contents of the five parts are as follows:

Part I   Advanced Information Management Systems
Chapter 1 presents our basic definition of the notable design features relevant to advanced information systems. In Chapter 2 we present a review of relational database concepts, and in Chapter 3 a review of object-oriented programming principles. These two chapters may be viewed as a review of these two important technologies.

Part II   Contemporary Information Systems Design Methodologies
Part II is concerned primarily with data modeling. Chapter 4 compares a number of data modeling diagramming techniques that are currently in use and presents our own adaptation that we believe is crucial for advanced information systems design. This is followed, in Chapter 5, by a presentation of how classes of objects are derived from a data model and how this model may be converted into an object-oriented design. Chapter 6 is a presentation of project design management issues and application prototyping, especially for object-oriented systems.

Part III   Advanced Information Systems Design
Part III presents a detailed study of the advanced information system design process. In Chapter 7, we discuss the components and use of advanced data dictionaries. Chapter 8 presents a methodology for advanced data modeling with emphasis on modeling object-oriented systems. Chapter 9 offers a step by step approach to application design based on an object-oriented database. Chapters 10 and 11 discuss the technology of distributed object-oriented database systems and the issues involved in applying an object-oriented design to the implementation of an application in such an environment.

Part IV   Design Approaches to Advanced Information Systems
In Chapters 12, 13, and 14 we present issues relevant to advanced information systems. These issues include advanced graphical user interfaces, multimedia systems, and advanced integrated applications concepts such as CAD/CAM and cartography.

Part V   Object-Oriented Design Example
In Part V we present a complete example of an object-oriented application design. This example uses the concepts and methodologies presented in the first four parts and will help the reader understand and put to immediate use the knowledge gained from this book.

In addition, a glossary of terms is provided for reference, along with a complete detailed index.

The exercises at the end of each chapter encourage readers to apply what they have learned through actual design and implementation. References, where applicable, are identified in footnotes.

A number of new concepts and methodologies are being presented in this book. The authors hope that the reader will enjoy exploring them and building on them as much as the authors enjoyed developing them. We will find it especially rewarding if we have succeeded in promoting new ideas and avenues in the advancement of database management technology.

Acknowledgments   Producing a book is a team effort. A number of people contributed their time and effort in reviewing the contents and bringing this book into production. We would like to thank everyone who contributed to this effort by sharing their time and taking interest in our work and encouraging us to continue.

In particular, we would like to thank Rakesh Kamdar for reviewing this book and his helpful comments. The effort put in by Timothy P. Hayes in performing a very detailed review and using his hands-on object-oriented design knowledge for critiquing the text for its final cleanup is greatly appreciated. We would also like to thank Dr. Suresh C. Mathur for his expert comments.

Our special thanks go to Mr. Paul Becker, our editor, for his patience, guidance, and encouragement at all times, as well as for steering this book through to production. We also acknowledge the efforts of Bi-Comp, Inc. and William Thomas for their painstaking efforts in typesetting and copy editing this text.

Last, but not least, we would like to thank our families and friends, who inspired and encouraged us throughout and demonstrated a high level of patience during our preoccupation in putting this text together. In particular we would like to thank Deepa Andleigh for her support and understanding, and Vaibhav and Vipur Andleigh for their patience through a year of lost holidays and weekends.

Prabhat K. Andleigh
Michael R. Gretzinger

1

ADVANCED INFORMATION MANAGEMENT SYSTEMS

Databases have progressed hand in hand with the evolution of the computer industry from its inception. They continue to improve on their original goal to store and organize data for rapid and flexible access. These basic information systems requirements have not changed. Nonetheless, the system architectures have changed significantly and the development tool enhancements have made it possible to develop increasingly complex applications. While the proprietary mainframes of the 1960s featured simple file handling systems, the requirements changed as computer system usage became more widespread in the mid 1960s and early 1970s. Users started demanding support for a wider variety of applications, and the mid 1960s saw the first generation of database management systems. The late 1970s marked the start of the relational model for data management for commercial use.

The mainframes of the 1960s, often called the second-generation systems, were programmed primarily in Assembler, COBOL, and FORTRAN languages. Data management was designed to conserve memory space and processing load; that is, data was organized along clearly defined access paths. Initial implementations used file managers that replaced punched cards for data storage. However, two evolving data management models met the memory and performance requirements: the *hierarchical* and the *network* model.

In the *hierarchical* model, data is organized in an inverted tree structure and is accessed from the top to the bottom in a series of nodes similar to branches in a tree. The inverted tree structure provides clearly defined and fixed paths for accessing the data by traversing the branches of the tree. The rigidity of the structure has some disadvantages in that new access paths, not defined at the outset, may be complicated or even impossible to achieve. Modification of the data base structure is a very complex task.

The *network* model traded off some of the high-access performance for flexibility in organizing and accessing the data. As in a hierarchical model, the data is organized in an inverted tree. The greater flexibility is achieved by allowing a node to be connected to more than one branch. Records are linked by predefined pointers. Equal or better performance, as compared to the hierarchical model, was achieved by maintaining permanent pointers linking records. The complexity of the data structure made queries more complex and modification and ad hoc queries more complicated. Typically, the data retrieval language was COBOL for these systems. The network model of data management was used by the MIS departments for large-scale batch processing.

The minicomputers of the late 1970s and the early 1980s brought processing out of the MIS centers to the departmental processing arena, and with it the need for interactive and more flexible data management. The relational model promised a structure that met these new requirements. Structurally different from the inverted trees of the hierarchical and network models, data in the relational model is stored in tables consisting of columns and rows. Links between data records are largely established as needed on an ad hoc basis. The rows of a table represent records and the columns within a table represent the fields in a record. Different types of records are stored in separate tables. Some frequently used connections between tables can be predefined, while others can be established at the time of the query. This model achieved the desired flexibility and ease of use, but at a cost. The relational model requires a higher level of processing to establish connections and access data. Consequently, system requirements for processor and memory are higher to achieve the same level of overall performance.

The developments of the 1980s have also seen the demand for portability of application software and the advent of the fourth-generation languages (4GLs). The modern 4GLs are based on IBM's industry standard Structured Query Language (SQL), a higher-level language that has the capability to perform complex queries using simple English-like statements.

Powerful tools such as 4GLs, windowing systems, and report writers are making relational database management systems (RDBMSs) more flexible and easier to use. Additionally, graphics, distributed RDBMSs, and free-form text retrieval systems are addressing the enterprise needs to integrate all computing requirements. Technology will continue to spur development and the demand for more powerful and flexible distributed RDBMSs.

One such important requirement is the handling of all data as objects such that the properties of the data remain with it in all forms of its existence. Object-oriented database management systems (ODMSs), in support of these requirements, promise a more natural relationship between information and the processing of that information, thereby offering greater flexibility and better maintainability.

The first chapter in this part discusses the key requirements of distributed database architectures, advanced user interfaces, and object orientation for database management systems. These requirements play an important role in the design of a contemporary information system for enterprise-wide data management system applications. These features collectively define what we call an *advanced information system*. The second and third chapters review the principal concepts of relational database management systems and object-oriented systems. Both technologies continue to play an important role in the enterprise-wide information systems.

1

Contemporary
Information Systems

1.1 INTRODUCTION

A generation of database designers and administrators grew up believing that the salvation for database administrators could be found in a single database that served all purposes. The roots of this belief in the 1970s came from the need to manage the complexities of multiple master files and accompanying data redundancy. Maintaining proper synchronization across all files was a daunting task.

Single databases did make noticeable headway, but the boom in information processing and the capabilities to link systems via LANs dramatically changed the vision of the database designers in the 1980s. Distributed network computing started out with the concept of a centralized shared database accessed by a large number of users across an enterprise. Increasing storage requirements and changing technologies had a direct impact on distributed computing. Information systems graduated from a batch mode of operation to a fully interactive mode of operation.

Heavy demands on database servers, geographic distribution of users across towns, cities, states, countries, and continents sharing the same data, and increasing processing resources closer to the users have caused a dramatic shift in the manner in which databases are being used. Consequently, the development of database management systems has undergone rapid evolution. Decentralization is a major step forward in bringing the data closer to the user and providing improved performance, while still maintaining the communications links for uniform access to all data across the enterprise.

User interface technologies commonly available in the personal computer environment, such as windows and pointing devices, have found a home in the contemporary information system. Graphical user interfaces (GUIs) such as Apple MacIntosh, × Windows, and other similar implementations have made a significant impact on the design of information systems. Multiple windows on a user screen opened the way for a user to run multiple applications at the same time. A user can make changes to the database in one window and review the impact of the changes in another window. The flexibility and the power of a windows environment are limited only by the imagination and the resources available to the application developer and the user.

The imagination of developers and users is by no means limited to alphanumeric data. Multimedia databases are not only within the realm of imagination, but are commonly available. A wide variety of peripheral devices is now available for high-quality data input, including document images, live video images, graphics, voice (or audio), and free-form text created by word processors or editors. It is not enough for the multimedia database to act as an electronic file cabinet for this variety of information types. Beyond the basic search and retrieval functions, a multimedia database must support its variety of information types with essentially all of the capabilities traditional databases apply to alphanumeric data. And this must be done at a performance level not too different from the performance level expected of the traditional databases. This implies that all information—alphanumeric, free-form text, graphic, and voice—must be made an integral part of the database management framework. The following lists some of the considerable challenges faced by distributed multimedia database management systems:

1. The sheer size of the data objects that must be handled is very large. Whereas typical alphanumeric fields vary from 1 to 100 bytes, image and voice data may require 50 kilobytes to several megabytes.
2. There is no information in the multimedia data fields that the database can interpret.
3. The entities are too unwieldy for conventional database mechanisms to cope with.
4. There is no guarantee that the user workstation can cope with the retrieved information. For example, compressed document image data may need special processing and special display attributes before it can be displayed correctly.

At the very outset, users must have the capability to retrieve and view multiple components of information at one time. This implies that they must have the capability to operate in a multiple window environment so that alphanumeric data and an image or a video can be viewed side by side.

A number of graphical user interface (GUI) techniques have been employed to address the needs for multimedia data display. It is essential to understand the architecture and operation of these GUIs to visualize the impact on a corporate information system. X Windows (and its derivatives such as OSF Motif) is one such GUI that has won a large following. These technologies are the driving force behind the emerging requirements for advanced information systems.

In this chapter, we will raise a number of design issues that we believe are crucial for contemporary advanced information systems. Brief discussions provide an overview of the concepts and the issues and set the stage for more detailed discussions in later chapters. We admit that this approach introduces a number of new concepts that may be unfamiliar to the reader. At the same time, we believe that this backdrop will help the users to understand the sequence of presentation in the rest of the chapters much better.

The increasing use of multimedia data objects brought into focus a limitation of the existing database structures—hierachical, network, and relational. In all these cases, field lengths are generally fixed (except variable length character fields in some implementations), and the database system interprets the contents of these fields. Data objects such as voice, image, long text fields (hypertext), and binary files cannot be stored in the traditional field datatypes. The need to store and manage multimedia data objects in a database has given rise to object orientation in database storage. Object orientation is realized in relational databases as a special datatype and as objects in an object-oriented database.

In this chapter, we will explore the objectives of enterprise-wide contemporary information systems, especially as they relate to on-line transaction processing, distributed database architectures, advanced user interfaces, and object orientation.

1.2 THE OPEN OLTP ENVIRONMENT

Systems have been implemented using centralized databases even when other functions have been distributed. The need to support data on line for hundreds of user nodes in a network and the emerging communications trends have given rise to on-line transaction processing (OLTP) based on open architectures.

The key trends that are pushing the industry toward open OLTP environments are the following:

1. High performance network protocols.
2. Convergence of firmware and device driver functions into structural products that support a wide variety of protocols and communications and networking media (such as twisted pair, coaxial cable, fiber optic cable, and so on).

3. Convergence of upper layer applications at industry standard interfaces (such as TLI for TCP/IP, OSI, and so on).

4. Module design that lends itself to flexible protocol stacking, allowing a variety of options for mixing and matching protocols.

The integration of database systems technology and a network environment leads to a new class of problems and consequently new means to solve these problems. An important aspect of this is the need for network-wide definition (or directory) of the location and characteristics of data objects. This definition should include the details about how information is partitioned and if it is replicated on different nodes of a network. When a user requests access to data (commonly known as a *query*), the local node must determine where the data is located, if the data is on a remote node, and if the user has permissions to access the data. If data is on a remote node, the user node must determine if the remote node is of a compatible type and if any data translation is required. The data may also require special formatting or processing due to different display technologies.

The local node that we just described and that we call a *client* performs the following functions:

1. *Analyzing a database query* to determine if data is to be transferred from a local server or from a remote server.

2. *Retrieving routing information* from network data directly to determine routing through the network for remote data.

3. *Coordinating multiple queries* from different nodes in the network for complex multiple action queries.

4. *Translating data* from remote nodes that are incompatible.

5. *Processing data* locally according to processing specified for that object class and preparing it for display.

6. *Presenting the data* to the user in the appropriate display format and interacting with the user for updates.

1.3 DISTRIBUTED DATABASE ARCHITECTURES

Ceri[1] and Pellagoti defined distributed database systems in 1984 as a collection of data distributed across many computers running a number of different applications over a communications network. A local area network (LAN) provides data access to applications within a site, while a wide area network (WAN) provides data access to a number of geographically dispersed sites.

---

[1] Stefano Ceri and Guiseppe Pellagoti, *Distributed Databases: Principles and Systems.* New York: McGraw-Hill Book Co., 1984.

Major characteristics of a distributed system include the following:

1. Clustered or networked systems
2. Distributed database servers
3. Clustered disk configurations (disk shadowing)
4. Public/private workstations and terminals

In a distributed system, as we define it here, not only is the data distributed, but also access to the data is distributed, consisting of a wide variety of workstations, terminals, and other computer systems. LANs and very high speed specialized links such as the DEC VAX clusters provide a communications environment that supports both distributed data and distributed access. A database server that supports a number of distributed clients across a LAN addresses only one part of our definition of a fully distributed architecture.

The simplest form of a distributed application is based on the client/server architecture mode with a single server. More complex environments consist of multiple database servers distributed over a LAN. Let us review here the basic client/server distributed architecture and analyze the design issues related to the operation of databases.

1.3.1 Client/Server Architectures

The *client/server model* is based on the concept of distributed processing, with the front end (or the user application) being the client and the back end (the database access and manipulation), the server. The functions performed by the server include the following:

1. Centralized data management
2. Data integrity and database consistency
3. Database security
4. Concurrent operations (for multiuser access)
5. Centralized processing (for example, stored procedures)

The client is responsible for handling user-specific database access tasks, and the server is responsible for managing shared data. The applications functions run on the client machines (usually a workstation), and the data access and manipulation functions run on one or more server machines. The functions performed by the client include the following:

1. Customized user interface
2. Front-end processing of data
3. Initiation of the server remote procedure calls
4. Access to a database server across a LAN

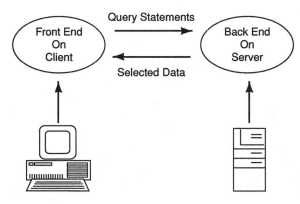

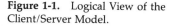

Figure 1-1. Logical View of the Client/Server Model.

Figure 1-1 shows a generic logical view of the client/server model for database systems.

The client/server architecture allows running an application on one computer while running the database on another computer. For example, the client side could handle number crunching and customized screens for the display of data, while the server fields the requests for selected data items.

Database server software is normally designed to be portable to a variety of processors and, in some cases, operating systems. Similarly, it is designed to function in a variety of networking environments, either independently or in concert with other database servers. When multiple database servers are connected in the same LAN or WAN, they can be set up to act as one logical database with its components distributed on a number of servers. In this manner, the client/server architecture facilitates setting up enterprise-wide connectivity. The common logical database can be managed at each server site through the system administration facilities provided by the database.

The client/server architecture offers a flexible, expandable, and cost-effective solution to complex shared database applications. The server is customized for providing CPU-intensive database access, while the clients are customized for interactive display-intensive tasks. System expandability is achieved easily as long as the server has spare capacity to handle a larger number of clients. The clients, in typical configurations, can be system architectures different from that of the server. A mix of architectures can be used with the same server, thereby giving the user the opportunity to select the client architecture most appropriate for the application. The client architecture can be based on a variety of user interfaces, including graphical user interfaces.

1.3.2 Database Servers Distributed over Networks

Managing distributed database servers (that is, systems with the capability to distribute the data across a number of processing nodes in a network) is a more complex requirement that presents an architectural challenge for database application developers, as well as for application designers. Distributed data must be accessible transparently by all applications. Database control mechanisms should successfully address relational integrity, database integrity, and network security requirements. An independent, but related, feature of a distributed database, called *replication*, is the ability to maintain duplicate copies of data at multiple nodes in the network for achieving high performance. A distributed database system should be capable of optimizing distributed queries as well as simultaneous updates to multiple servers to achieve acceptable performance. The database system should automatically determine, on a dynamic basis, which copies are to be used for queries and which copies for updates without losing data synchronization among the copies. An update is the more involved of the two and requires a strategy that ensures that all distributed data components remain synchronized at all times (or at least within a very short, predictable time duration). Flexibility in maintaining multiple copies is essential for successful functioning of a truly distributed and redundant database system.

Another important consideration for distributed data servers is ensuring high reliability and availability of the data. Maintaining multiple copies also addresses the issue of recovery from disk hardware or file system failures.

We have now seen that there are a number of important design considerations that affect the functioning and performance of a distributed database information system. Let us look at these design issues for distributed database architectures in greater detail in the following sections.

1.4 DESIGN ISSUES FOR DISTRIBUTED DATABASE ARCHITECTURES

The very nature of distributed systems imposes a number of design considerations for reliable and secure management of critical business information. A number of design issues require close examination and evaluation in the design of a complex advanced information system for a distributed environment. These design issues include the following:

1. Location transparency for distributed access
2. Performance and distributed query optimization
3. Database security
4. Transaction management and integrated concurrency control
5. Communications structure for distributed commit protocol
6. Localized failures

In the following sections, we will analyze these issues and develop a framework for the major design issues for complex contemporary information systems.

1.4.1 Location Transparency for Distributed Access

Location transparency is the capability of managing a database such that that data is distributed across a number of network nodes known as database servers. The database system automatically determines how data should be combined from these different nodes for a query or how a distributed update should be addressed. In other words, location transparency manifests a single logical view of data distributed among multiple servers; the database system automatically locates and combines user-requested data elements in a manner transparent to the user. A key benefit of this single, logical view of the database is that users can access the database from any node on the network without any change in the data access parameters.

The concept of location transparency can be extended beyond the database system to cover user programs and other files in the system. Location transparency further implies that users should be able to log on from any workstation or terminal and be able to gain access to their applications programs and related data. In addition, their custom working environment should be duplicated (or adapted depending on the class of the workstation or terminal) on whichever workstation they log on.

Users may need the capability to create and edit personal databases consisting of random text and images for organized retrieval and integration into the primary database at a later time. These personal databases can be the temporary repositories for data feeds received from dial-up automated news reports, stock trades, corporate information, and so on.

We can summarize by stating that the following characterize location transparency:

1. A single logical view of the database system.
2. Ability to operate from any workstation in the network with the same working environment and privileges.
3. Ability to move from one workstation to another without resetting access paths for database elements.

1.4.2 Performance and Distributed Query Optimization

Fast transparent access to remote database files requires fast LANs and WANs. Response times become particularly significant for remote database file access, especially in the case of a distributed query that requires combining data from a number of database servers. In the case of object-oriented databases, executables for methods (note that they are part of objects) residing on remote database servers have notable response time considerations due to privilege checking and data downloading procedures. An important design issue is where and how local copies of data objects are created and how they are kept synchronized with the master copy. In fact, in an ideal design, an architectural entity will be responsible for determining when (based on performance parameters) local copies should be created and used.

Combining data elements from multiple tables in relational databases (*joins*) and operations that require combining attributes from multiple objects classes (as an atomic operation) are complex operations, especially if the data objects are distributed among multiple database servers. In both cases, significant performance improvement can be achieved by managing the sequence of operations in an optimized manner, a process known as *query optimization*.

Query optimization. Query optimization, in both nondistributed as well as distributed environments, has been a subject for significant research and development. Concepts of artificial intelligence and back-end expert systems have been utilized for query optimization. Primary tasks in query optimization are access path selection for joins and developing an optimal plan for joining n relations.

While most research has been performed on optimizing relational databases, query optimization has not been a subject of major importance for object-oriented database systems. However, as object-oriented database systems continue to make headway in mainstream database applications, performance optimization of operations in an object-oriented database will be viewed with increasing importance.

Query execution plan. A query execution plan describes the internal sequence of operations for executing a query. For relational databases, depending on the implementation, it is either in the form of a tree, where the leaf nodes represent tables and nonleaf nodes represent operations, or it is in a canonical form (for example, in INGRES). The tree form or the canonical form is created by parsing and compiling the query into the internal representation. This step reduces the query into an abstract view of the high-level operations (such as join, projection, sort, and so on). The following describes the steps for creating the internal representation.

1. Convert the query into an internal representation.
2. Convert the representation into its canonical form.
3. Choose possible low-level processing methods.
4. Generate all possible plans.
5. Evaluate and choose the optimal plan.

Object-oriented systems do not lend themselves easily to traditional approaches to query optimization due to their inherent lack of a tightly defined structure. Artificial intelligence (AI) techniques, used frequently for query optimization in relational database systems, are fostering advanced query optimization approaches for object-oriented database systems.

Use of AI techniques.   Some query optimizers, in addition to syntactic analysis, perform semantic analysis. *Semantic analysis* is especially useful in a distributed query because, no matter how the query is structured, it is always reduced to the same canonical structure containing an identical join order. Very often, AI techniques are required for "intelligent" semantic analysis.

Heuristics can be used to evaluate execution plans without really performing a detailed cost analysis on them. This, obviously, saves processing time and affords the opportunity to determine the most promising paths in greater detail. In a distributed server, the number of potential execution plans can increase dramatically as the number of network nodes involved in the query increases. Heuristic elimination of unpromising execution plans reduces the task to a more manageable level.

Another important feature of AI systems is the capability to learn. An optimizer based on AI techniques can be implemented with a capability to learn from the following parameters:

1. Query statistics
2. Usage patterns
3. Frequency and quantity of updates
4. Impact of the organization of data

In conventional relational database management systems, even if the optimizer does manage to learn from these parameters, it may not be able to relocate data very easily due to the inherently rigid structure of a relational database. This, however, is not so in an object-oriented database. Due to encapsulation (a data abstraction that combines data, operations, preconditions, and constraints within the object), objects have a greater freedom to move. Consequently, AI-based optimizers present unquestionably greater benefits when applied to object-oriented databases.

Query optimization for distributed systems.   We have touched on a number of issues pertinent to query optimization in a distributed database server environment. Let us summarize the principal issues here as follows:

1. Is the optimization capability restricted to individual nodes (local) or can it optimize a distributed query globally?
2. If optimization is global, can the optimizer evaluating a query assess execution plans on a remote node and select the most effective subexecution plan for the part of the query executed on the remote node?
3. Are execution plans cataloged and/or stored locally or globally?
4. Can remote execution plans be performed in parallel and, if not, can the optimizer determine the most efficient execution order?
5. Can the optimizer determine the most efficient join order that would produce the same results every time? Are these results predictable?

We are still in the formative stage of defining the issues that are significant for advanced information systems. Query optimization for a distributed database is a very complex task. We will not attempt to provide a solution here. The approaches to addressing query optimization in distributed databases are addressed in later chapters. It is sufficient at this time to analyze the issues, and we encourage the reader to expand upon the list noted above and to gain a better understanding of other related issues that must be addressed. Comprehending how query optimization works is very important for the application designers and developers. Developers must take into account a number of query optimization issues.

1.4.3 Distributed Commit Protocols

To maintain consistency in a distributed database environment, one important requirement is that the transactions be executed atomically. The two-phase commit protocol and its variations are the well-known protocols employed for this purpose. Generally called *distributed commit* protocols, these protocols are characterized by successive sequences of message exchanges to ensure that all components of a distributed database that need to be updated by the transaction in progress are completed. The *atomic* requirement for a transaction implies that all actions required for completion of the transaction must be performed in entirety, or no action should be performed at all. If successfully completed, the transaction is said to be *committed*. If the transaction fails at any step, it is *aborted*. The distributed functions must take databases as well as network failures into account to ensure that the consistency (or integrity) of the database is not adversely affected. Replicating copies of the database at each node greatly simplifies this process. However, it significantly complicates the process of keeping the entire database synchronized at all times.

1.4.4 Database Security

To ensure security, users must log on to a database server explicitly before accessing data resident at the server. In a data network consisting of multiple database servers, this log-on requirement could become very cumbersome because users would have to log on to every server in turn to access data. A distributed database environment has to be designed to facilitate a security mechanism that is complete and convenient for the users. The key to maintaining the security of a distributed access database system is proper *authentication* at all levels. Authentication is a generic problem for all applications and services in a distributed environment. Ideally, there should be a generalized scheme for authentication. A user logs on once into the network environment by *username* and *password*. At this point, the issue of authentication comes into play. An administrative database would provide a list of services that each user is authorized to use. A hierarchy of services may be defined so that in the case of a database service the user may be authorized to use a particular server or servers (or the database service in general), and the user may be allowed access to particular objects within the database.

One method of identifying authorized users to network services is to generate *tickets* when a user is approved for each service that the user is authorized to access. These tickets are supplied to the service provider when the initial connection is requested by the user. The approach to authentication must provide a fine balance between additional actions performed by the user and the depth of security necessary for the organization. Thought has to be given to what actions users can perform from local terminals (being considered more protected than remote terminals) and reduced capabilities for remote dial-ups. Similarly, the abilities to copy data to remote workstations or other nodes on a network have to be taken into account.

We can summarize the security requirements for a distributed database as follows:

1. All users on the system must have log-on and password security.
2. All access to database servers is controlled by access security via password checks.
3. Users should not have to log on repeatedly to access data on a number of different database servers.
4. Users should be able to access data from multiple database servers at the same time.
5. A single query should be able to access data from multiple database servers at the same time.

A network-wide *access name server* can maintain an on-line distributed database of the log ons and passwords for every user, along with the servers these users can access. Similarly, each server maintains a list of all users who can access data on that server. Under this scheme, a distributed query is checked against the access name server to determine if the user has access to all servers. Only on access confirmation is the query attempted.

1.4.5 Transaction Management and Integrated Concurrency Control

Transactions are defined in database applications to ensure orderly updates of all related data at the same time. Two transactions in progress at the same time that update the same sets of data may leave the database in a very inconsistent state. *Transaction management* protects users from side effects caused by interference between their own transaction and transactions initiated by other users. Managing a transaction via a user-defined function or a stored procedure may ensure that the complete transaction is executed before another change to the database.

Locking of tables using explicit *lock* commands should be used sparingly and carefully due to the potential of network interruptions. A table lock, or even a temporary lock, may cause many users to be denied access to data for long periods, especially when the data has been locked by a user not active any more. Transaction management and locking schemes go hand in hand for good, effective concurrency management.

In an object environment, updates are performed on each specific object through the *operations* or *methods* (routines included as a part of the object specification) defined for each object's class (methods are defined in detail in Chapter 3). Transactions are performed within a *method*. A large transaction that modifies many objects (*nested transactions*) is built in a modular manner by implementing a *method* of the large object such that it calls the lower-level object methods. Ideally, all object methods should exist in the same data server.

In a distributed application with frequent updates from many users, it may be necessary to update specific versions of objects. For example, a user reads information from the database and decides to update a particular element of the object. If this object is modified by another user (assuming that locking is not applied due to version update mode) during the interval, one of the changes is lost inadvertently. The database should really be able to track both changes in progress and be able to inform the concurrent users when the object is changed. This allows the users to look at the object again to determine if a new change is required. This problem becomes more acute if objects change very frequently.

1.4.6 Localized Failures

Localized failures imply that, if a node fails or the database becomes inaccessible at one node, other nodes in the network can continue to operate via local copies of the database, or a master copy is still available. A key design issue to be noted here is proper and complete resynchronization of the databases on recovery of the failed network node. Resynchronization requires all legitimate updates that took place while the local copy of the database was out of service be applied in the proper sequence. Before the updates are applied, the local database may need to run recovery so that all transactions not completed are backed off. The local transaction log has to be compared with the update log to ensure that the distributed database components remain synchronized.

1.5 ADVANCED USER INTERFACES

The Apple MacIntosh graphical user interface systems created a new generation of users who felt comfortable in using a point and click approach to interacting with a computer, rather than a job control language (JCL) or a command line interface (CLI). The graphical interface made a computer more accessible for nontechnical users who found command-driven interfaces too cumbersome. The graphical interface was more intuitive and prompted the user to make a choice, rather than remembering what they should search for. Multiple windows made it easy to remember the intermediate steps and retrace through these steps. The windows-based graphical user interface transcended computer systems and operating systems and appeared on PC-DOS/MS-DOS based systems. A new generation of users demanding windows-based graphical user interfaces was born.

Another activity, based on the same original research, had been taking place separately; this research would have a major impact on multiuser departmental systems and ultimately on mainframes. In 1982, Paul Asente and Brian Reid of Stanford University developed the W Window system. A precursor to X, W Windows was a synchronous, networked system designed to run under the Stanford V operating system. A year later, the two researchers ported it to the UNIX system at the DEC Western Research Lab. They also gave a port to Jim Gettys and Robert Scheifler, who transformed W into an asynchronous system in 1983. They named this system after the next letter in the alphabet, X. By 1985, engineers at both DEC and MIT were pursuing X Windows development, and MIT released the first public version of X Windows later in that year for the VAXstation II. The X Consortium at MIT (an agency of the MIT Office of Technology) has owned the responsibility for continued development and distribution of X Windows, and X11R4 was released in 1990.

The X Windows concepts are important for our design considerations because X Windows represents the first major advance in a user interface that can concurrently support a number of applications based on a variety of operating platforms. It presents an ideal solution for the needs of multiple users accessing a number of applications distributed around the enterprise. With a number of RDBMSs supporting X Windows, the use of X Windows for business applications is a significant event that bears close scrutiny from an application designer's perspective. Using X Windows and supporting tool kits presents opportunities for the design of complex applications in a manner that makes them simple for the user; a user can perform a number of tasks concurrently and view data from a variety of perspectives. Data can be updated in one view while being viewed from different perspectives in other windows. Careful design allows the user to immediately determine the impact of an update from the other perspectives important for the business enterprise. In that sense, it becomes an excellent modeling tool. For example, the user can view the change in the profitability from a product line as the sales mix or pricing is changed.

While the X Windows class of graphical user interfaces represents significant opportunities, it also presents a challenge in the level of design complexity for a set of related but distributed applications using a distributed database. We will first briefly review the architecture and key features of the X Windows graphical user interface to develop the basic foundations for the capabilities that are available for application design. And then we will see how these capabilities are applied to business information systems. A more detailed treatment of applica-

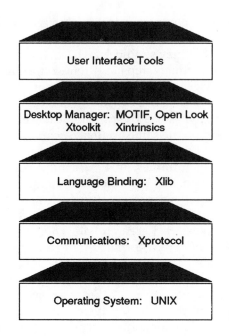

Figure 1-2. X Windows Architecture.

tion design using multitasking graphical user interfaces is presented in Chapter 12.

It should also be noted that X Windows provides an excellent base for object-oriented programming. Chapter 15 presents a detailed design walk-through of an object-oriented program using X Windows. But first let us review the X Windows architecture as a multitasking representative graphical user interface. Figure 1-2 describes the architecture of the X Windows system.

1.5.1 Design Impact of Graphical User Interfaces

A number of tool kits for custom user interfaces have been layered on top of X11. The X Toolkit, distributed by the X Consortium, has been the basis for a number of graphical user interface models such as OSF's Motif, AT&T's Open Look, DEC-Windows, and NextStep. As higher-level graphical user interface (GUI) tools, they provide the capability to program sophisticated and highly intensive graphical interfaces.

NextStep, a notable advance in high-level application development environments, is based on *Display Postscript*[2] and is supported primarily on *NEXT*[3] computers. NextStep has been designed to make the applications developer's task much easier.

---

[2] Postscript is a trademark of the Adobe Corporation.

[3] NEXT is a trademark of NEXT, Inc.

The applications designers continue to have the following responsibilities:

1. Organizing data, functions, tasks, and roles (called the cognitive model).
2. Visually communicating the data and functions in a highly comprehensive manner.
3. Designing efficient navigation paths through the functions and data.
4. Creating an intuitive user interaction sequence and procedures.
5. Presenting an aesthetic and high-quality appearance.
6. Designing a well-defined exception management methodology.

GUIs allow the use of topography, symbols, color, and other static and dynamic graphics to convey facts, concepts, and even emotions. They present information in a systematic and efficient manner. Information-oriented, systematic graphics interfaces help users understand complex information rapidly. They are a highly effective means of communication between the system and the user. What is important to understand is what makes one design better than another.

Design considerations.   Designing a user interface, like any other design effort, requires identifying the main considerations and the design objectives before embarking on the design effort. The following considerations are germane to a successful design:

- The profile of the users. Are the users computer literate or are they users from functional areas far removed from computers?
- Has a clear conceptual model been developed for presenting the data to the user and the user's reaction to this data?
- A profile of applications that will use this user interface.
- What tool kits will be used for the design? It is important to note the capabilities and widgets provided by the component libraries that come with the GUI product.
- What platform constraints must be taken into account? Network traffic considerations and translations from one system architecture to another are important.
- Is visual identity with other products or with a corporate image required? Visual identity with existing products in use may accelerate acceptance.
- Consistency across applications supported by the graphical user interface is very essential for a user-friendly design. The concept of intuitiveness, an integral component of a user-friendly design, requires that similar functions operate in the same manner across applications to avoid potential confusion among users.

These design considerations are an important step for ensuring that the interface meets the expectations and anticipations of the user.

User interface components.   Once the design considerations are fully documented and understood, the exact definitions of the layouts and graphical techniques used for the interface can be determined. These definitions and techniques are used for all applications and provide the level of consistency expected in the user interface. The layout organization and the user interface techniques include the following:

- Layouts: consisting of formats, sizes of windows, three-dimensioned organization if any, and grid-level dimensions.
- Selection of text fonts and typefaces. Selection of features (such as use of kerning if available) and attributes for the text display and any other text-related issues.
- Use of color and three-dimensional effects based on light sourcing techniques; three-dimensional effects can be used very effectively to highlight window areas and clearly demarcate boundaries within and outside windows.
- Effective use of icons and symbols; defining standard functions (such as HELP features) to be constantly visible icons that the user can point to easily.
- Intuitive navigation among windows; users need constant feedback as to which window is current.
- Video animation, both in terms of moving images as well as constantly updated graphs.
- Effective use of sound; different conditions use distinguishable sound cues.
- An overall intuitive sequencing of operations.

The primary role of the designer is to combine these techniques into a user interface that fully addresses the design considerations and needs of the users, as well as the application developers. The interface designer must combine these factors into a graphical user interface that has the following characteristics:

- The GUI is intutively easy to use.
- The interface is very efficient and anticipates potential user actions.
- The GUI is very functional and addresses the needs of the applications supported by the GUI.
- The user interface is uncluttered and visually pleasing.
- The interface is consistent and does not require extensive learning.
- The design helps the user to focus on the important aspects of the application rather than on the user interface itself.

GUIs for distributed applications.   Distributed applications run a distributed set of clients (note that in the X Windows terminology the application is a client and the display station is the server). A GUI provides the user the capability to interact with a number of application clients at the same time.

1.6 OBJECT ORIENTATION

The concept of a paperless office has not really reduced the volume of paper in offices, but it has had an impact on visual electronic representation of text, as well as in the management of data elements consisting of text from long documents, document images, geographic maps, and voice mail. The display capabilities provided by GUI lead one to an obvious conclusion that a contemporary information system must provide storage for all datatypes that can be displayed on a GUI display. In fact, this kind of data should be stored and retrieved in a manner so that at least some of the functions applicable to traditional text field data are also applicable to graphics, voice, cartographic, and other similar data. In a sense, the database management system is being tasked to serve as a multimedia electronic filing cabinet.

Performing this task involves integrating a database used for traditional database applications with a database that can manage image, text, and voice storage for database applications. The structured organization of data in tables and the capability of the database system to interpret each column of data (both characteristics of relational databases) served well for applications involving pure numerical and textual data. Data elements such as free-form text, images, and voice did not fit well into the structure of relational databases.

A new concept was adapted to address these new datatype requirements. Data elements were organized differently under this new concept, with much less structure and greater freedom for creating ad hoc relationships. Advances in object-oriented programming assisted in the development of object-oriented database management systems (called ODMSs or object-oriented databases). While object-oriented databases provided the flexibility required for managing objects, they lacked the tightly managed organization.

Relational database vendors addressed the need for multimedia data objects by creating a new class of datatypes generically called binary large objects (BLOBs). These datatypes can be very large (on the order of gigabytes in some implementations) and are not interpreted by the database.

Object-oriented databases or relational databases (extended with BLOB datatype) address the advanced requirements for multimedia data management. A major part of this text is dedicated toward designing applications for a database with object orientation. In our view, object orientation is essential for a contemporary advanced information system designed to support multimedia data management.

1.7 SUMMARY

We started out this chapter with a brief review of the history of database management systems and the requirements of a contemporary information system. We then defined the salient features of on-line transaction processing and the architecture necessary to support distributed OLTP.

An important aspect of the discussion in this chapter was to highlight the design issues that must be addressed both in the next generation of database management systems and in application design. We looked at the importance of new user interface technologies. These technologies have, in fact, driven home the need to store multimedia data in a database.

We introduced the topic of the object-oriented database. In our view, it is not a characteristic or a requirement of contemporary information systems. Rather, an object-oriented database is an excellent tool for constructing an elegant solution for the advanced information system requirements.

1.8 EXERCISES

1. Explain the characteristics of an on-line transaction processing system.
2. Print out the query execution plan for a query using a database system available to you. Change the query and explain how the query plan changed.
3. Explain location transparency. Explain restrictions on location transparency in the network you have access to. How can it be improved?
4. Describe the query optimization scheme used by the database management system you use currently. How would you change it to make it better?
5. Discuss the pros and cons of setting up network security.
6. Compare the features and functions of X11 desktop environments such as Motif and Open Look with the Apple MacIntosh, Presentation Manager, and Microsoft Windows. What are the common features across these GUIs?

2

Relational Database Systems

2.1 INTRODUCTION

The relational model of data introduced in the 1970s[1] and early 1980s[2] and established via a set of rules introduced by E. F. Codd[3] in 1985 is based on a firm mathematical foundation called relational algebra. The relational model addressed a number of problems in database management. Codd addressed the problem of providing a data model that is independent of implementation. It also provided users with very high level, nonprocedural data definition and data manipulation languages. And, finally, it has been proved that the relational model has been successfully adapted for business problems.

Codd further presented his views and the basis for much of the modern thinking on the subject of the relational database model. He laid down the three objectives for the relational database model.

[1] E. F. Codd, "A Relational Model for Large Shared Data Banks," *Communications of the ACM*, 13, 1970, pp. 377–387. *and*
E. F. Codd, "Extending the Database Relational Model," *ACM Transactions on Database Systems*, 4, 1979, pp. 397–434.

[2] E. F. Codd, "Relational Database: A Practical Foundation for Productivity," *ACM Transactions on Database Systems*, 1981.

[3] E. F. Codd, "Is Your DBMS Really Relational?" *Computer World*, October 14, 1985.

1. Data independence objective
2. Communicability objective
3. Set-processing objective

The *data independence objective* established a clear boundary between the logical and physical aspects of database management. This boundary applies to the database design, data retrieval, and data manipulation.

The *communicability objective* set the guidelines for making the data model structurally simple so that users and programmers could have a common understanding of the data (that is, ad hoc access as well as programmed access) and could, therefore, communicate with one another about the database.

The *set-processing objective* introduced the concept of a high-level language that would enable users to express operations on large segments of information at a time in the form of set-oriented processing of multiple sets of records.

With these three objectives as the primary motivation, a relational data model was established that consists of at least the following three components:

1. A collection of data structure types
2. A collection of operators or rules of inference
3. A collection of general integrity rules

Data structure types are the basic building blocks of the database. Data structures are used to define the static requirements and the format for the data. Commonly supported data structures include CHAR (fixed-length character field), SMALLINT (small integer; 2 bytes), INTEGER (large integer; 4 bytes), DECIMAL, MONEY, FLOAT (floating point), DATE (calendar date), and DATETIME (a moment in time with a precision of a fraction of a second).

Physical structures specify the areas on disk volumes where the space for database *tables* is allocated. Logical structures group one or more actual tables together and assign them to a specific physical structure. (We recommend that readers not familiar with the fundamentals of relational database technology consult a text dedicated to the structure and operation of relational databases.)

Operators or *rules of inference* are used to retrieve and/or update data from any data structures in any desired set combination. The process of combining facts and rules to deduce new facts is referred to as inference. Rules consist of premises and conclusions. We can construct inference trees whose nodes are the clauses used in rules and whose branches are arrows connecting the clauses. Inference trees often provide good intuition about the structure of the rules. We can visualize the process of inference as a traversal along the branches of this tree. Operators are a simpler version of inference where there are no conditions and therefore no branches.

General integrity rules define implicitly or explicitly the set of consistent database states or changes to states (or both). Data integrity is of eminent importance in database management. Some integrity rules are built into the database. Integrity rules built into the system ensure that the data entered in a field is appropriate for that field and that a row that is referenced by a key in another table cannot be deleted. Users can define integrity rules that reflect business rules or standard practices. For example, for a class of workers, overtime is paid only after completing 45 hours of work.

In addition to these components, the operations that can be performed on data within a database were defined in the relational model. These operations are defined in terms of set operations. *Relational algebra* is a method for operating on relations. The authors recommend that readers not fully familiar with the fundamental operations of relational algebra, *selection, projection, product, union, set difference, and join,* consult a standard text describing the fundamental operations of relational database management systems. After providing a brief introduction to these terms, the authors have concentrated on the issues of what makes a database relational as a basis for comparing relational systems with object-oriented systems.

After establishing the components of a relational database more clearly, Codd[4] also established the range of services provided by a relational database management system. These services include the following:

- Data storage, retrieval, and update.
- A user-accessible catalog (also known as the data dictionary) for data descriptions.
- Transaction support to ensure that all or none of a sequence of database changes is reflected in the pertinent database.
- Recovery services in case of a failure (system, media, or program failure).
- Concurrency control services to ensure concurrent transactions behave the same way as if run in a sequential order.
- Authorization services to ensure that all access and manipulation of data be in accordance with specified constraints on users and programs.
- Integration with support for data communications.
- Integrity services to ensure that database states and changes of state conform to specified rules.

With this introduction to the beginnings of the relational model, we will now review some of the basic definitions used in the relational model and then analyze the salient features of the relational model. This analysis is important as a backdrop to the study of the object-oriented database model described in Chapter 3. The two models are compared and the notable features of the relational model that must be carried through to the object-oriented model are also discussed in Chapter 3.

---

[4] E. F. Codd, "Is Your DBMS Really Relational?" *Computer World*, October 14, 1985.

2.2 BASIC DEFINITIONS AND CONCEPTS
OF THE RELATIONAL MODEL

We will define some special terms used for the relational model here. The following terms are used in the discussion of the relational model:

- A *domain* is usually a finite set of values.
- The *Cartesian product* of domains $D_1, \ldots, D_n$ is denoted by $D_1 \times \cdots \times D_n$ and is a set of all possible tuples.
- A *relation* is any subset of the Cartesian product of one or more domains. Note that if a domain is a single table the table is the relation.
- Names associated with columns in a table are called *attributes.*

The relational model consists of three parts that constitute the full definition of a database (and associated applications):

1. Structural part
2. Manipulation part
3. Integrity part

The *structural part* consists of domains, relations of assorted degrees (with tables as their principal conceptual representative), attributes, tuples, candidate keys, and primary keys. Examples of the structural part are entities that describe people or things. For example, the attributes describing a customer, such as name and address, are structural components.

The *manipulative part* consists of the algebraic operators (select, project, product, join, and so on) that transform relations into relations. (*Note:* Relations are transformed into other relations; that is, a selected set of records from a table forms another temporary subtable in memory.)

The *integrity* part consists of two integrity rules: the *entity integrity* and the *referential integrity.* Other database specific constraints may also be needed.

2.3 RELATIONAL ALGEBRA

Relational algebra is based on set theory and provides a methodology for performing set operations on relations. Data is organized in tables consisting of rows (or records). Each row is described in terms of attributes of the entity (or fields of a record). All rows in a table can be accessed by a primary key that uniquely identifies each row (and, consequently, each record). Two entities or tables can also form a relation if they have a common attribute. The fundamental operations introduced here include the following:

1. Selection   4. Join   7. Set difference
2. Projection   5. Union
3. Product   6. Intersection

The fundamentals of set theory, used as the basis for relational algebra, introduced the terms *Cartesian product* and *set difference*. A new term *tuple* was introduced in the original formulation of the relational model by Codd in 1970 to give precise meaning to the concept of a *record*. In practical terms, a *tuple* is the equivalent of a row in a table.

While we will give a brief introduction to the fundamental set operations here, along with an example, we encourage readers to refer to a text dedicated to relational algebra for a more detailed analysis. The understanding of these concepts is important, because relational algebra formulates the basic mathematical foundation of the relational model. Let us now review these six operations.

Selection.   The *select* operator retrieves a subset of rows from a relational table based on values in a column or columns. That is, rows are selected and returned in a result if the values in the designated columns of the tables match the selection criteria specified in the request. Selection criteria are expressed by means of expressions that include comparative operators (such as, equals, greater than, less than, and so on), Boolean operators, literals, names of other columns, and so on. For example, selecting all businesses of type corporation from Table A produces Table B in Figure 2-1:

TABLE A   *(company)*: MASTER LIST OF COMPANIES

CompanyName	CompanyType	Address	City	State
Johnson Sugar Mills	Partnership	120 Maple Street	New Haven	ME
New Boston Trucking	Proprietor	75 Sumner Street	Boston	MA
Business Systems, Inc.	Corporation	100 Silicon Street	Palo Alto	CA
Moscariello Appliances	Proprietor	100 Main Street	Hartford	CT
Smith Hardware	Partnership	36 Broadway	New York	NY
Beverages Unlimited	Corporation	255 Congress Ave	McLean	VA
Software Solutions	Corporation	30 Township Lane	Norristown	PA
Software Solutions	Corporation	150 Main Street	Norristown	PA

TABLE B   *(company)*: TABLE CREATED AFTER SELECTION

CompanyName	CompanyType	Address	City	State
Business Systems, Inc.	Corporation	100 Silicon Street	Palo Alto	CA
Beverages Unlimited	Corporation	255 Congress Ave	McLean	VA
Software Solutions	Corporation	30 Township Lane	Norristown	PA
Software Solutions	Corporation	150 Main Street	Norristown	PA

Figure 2-1.   Example of SELECT operator.

The following SELECT statement produced Table B from Table A in Figure 2-1.

SELECT * FROM company WHERE CompanyType = ''Corporation''

Projection. The *project* operator retrieves a subset of columns from a relational table. The resulting table contains the same number of rows but fewer columns. Any duplicate work rows are also removed. For example, the following statement, when applied to Table A in Figure 2-1,

PROJECT CompanyName, CompanyType, City, State FROM company

produces the table in Figure 2-2.

Product. The *product* operator produces a set of all rows that are a concatenation of a row from one relation (or table) with every row from another table. A product multiplies two tables such that, if one table has M rows and I columns and the other table has N rows and J columns, the product will contain $(M \times N)$ rows and $(I + J)$ columns. This product is called a *Cartesian product*. A Cartesian product is usually an interim step in a *join*.

Join. The *join* operator allows combining several tables according to a specified criteria. Join is not a basic operator but it is described here because it is of critical importance for database operations. The join operator is derived by combining the *product* and *select* operators. The product of the tables being joined is used as the input for the select operator. The select operator uses the join criteria as the select criteria to produce the final result.

Figure 2-3 describes the product and join operators. If we join the table *company* (Table A in Figure 2-1) with table *employee-detail* (Table C in Figure 2-3),

CompanyName	CompanyType	City	State
Johnson Sugar Mills	Partnership	New Haven	ME
New Boston Trucking	Proprietor	Boston	MA
Business Systems, Inc.	Corporation	Palo Alto	CA
Moscariello Appliances	Proprietor	Hartford	CT
Smith Hardware	Partnership	New York	NY
Beverages Unlimited	Corporation	McLean	VA
Software Solutions	Corporation	Norristown	PA

Figure 2-2. Example of PROJECT Operator.

TABLE C (*employee-detail*): COMPANY EMPLOYEE DETAIL

CompanyName	EmployeeCount	TradeUnion
Bluejay Sugar Mills	18	N
New Boston Trucking	32	Y
Business Machines, Inc.	175	N
Moscariello Appliances	10	N
Smith Hardware	12	N
Beverages Unlimited	110	Y
Software Solutions	242	N
Systems Software, Inc.	30	N

TABLE D PRODUCT OF TABLE A OF FIGURE 2-1 AND TABLE C

CompanyName	CompanyType	Address	City	State	EmployeeCount	Trade Union
Johnson Sugar Mills	Partnership	120 Maple Street	New Haven	ME	NULL	NULL
New Boston Trucking	Proprietor	75 Sumner Street	Boston	MA	32	Y
Business Systems, Inc.	Corporation	100 Silicon Street	Palo Alto	CA	NULL	NULL
Moscariello Appliances	Proprietor	100 Main Street	Hartford	CT	10	N
Smith Hardware	Partnership	36 Broadway	New York	NY	12	N
Beverages Unlimited	Corporation	255 Congress Ave	McLean	VA	110	Y
Software Solutions	Corporation	30 Township Lane	Norristown	PA	242	N
Software Solutions	Corporation	150 Main Street	Norristown	PA	NULL	NULL
Bluejay Sugar Mills	NULL	NULL	NULL	NULL	18	N
Business Machines, Inc.	NULL	NULL	NULL	NULL	175	Y
Systems Software, Inc.	NULL	NULL	NULL	NULL	30	N

TABLE E JOIN OF TABLE A OF FIGURE 2-1 AND TABLE C

CompanyName	CompanyType	EmployeeCount
New Boston Trucking	Proprietor	32
Moscariello Appliances	Proprietor	10
Smith Hardware	Partnership	12
Beverages Unlimited	Corporation	110
Software Solutions	Corporation	242

Figure 2-3. Example of a JOIN Operator.

Table D will be the product and Table E the join, where the selection criteria are defined in the following query:

```
SELECT CompanyType, EmployeeCount
FROM company, employee-detail
WHERE company.CompanyName = employee-detail.CompanyName
```

Union.   The *union* operator adds the rows of two tables to produce another table as the result. The union operator is useful only if the tables have the same number of fields with matching attributes within the fields. Any duplicate rows are removed. If the tables have M and N rows, respectively, the resulting table will have $(M + N)$ rows less duplicates.

Intersection.   The *intersection* operator results in a new table that contains only the rows common to two (or more) tables. Only rows for which all column values are equal across the two or more tables are selected. For example, Tables F and G in Figure 2-4 produce a new table, Table H, as the intersection of the two. The intersection of Tables E and F produces Table G, which lists all companies with both current accounts and credit accounts.

Set difference.   The *difference* operator results in rows that appear in one relation but not in another relation (or table). The difference operator applied to Tables E and F above would give a new table listing all companies that have either

TABLE F   COMPANIES WITH CURRENT ACCOUNTS

CompanyName	City	State
Johnson Sugar Mills	New Haven	ME
New Boston Trucking	Boston	MA
Business Systems, Inc.	Palo Alto	CA
Moscariello Appliances	Hartford	CT
Smith Hardware	New York	NY
Beverages Unlimited	McLean	VA
Software Solutions	Norristown	PA
Software Solutions	Norristown	PA

TABLE G   COMPANIES WITH CREDIT ACCOUNTS

CompanyName	City	State
Athena Corporation	Augusta	ME
New Boston Trucking	Boston	MA
Business Systems, Inc.	Palo Alto	CA
Hartford Insurance Corp.	Hartford	CT
Photos Unlimited	New York	NY
Beverages Unlimited	McLean	VA
Software Solutions	Norristown	PA
Software Solutions	Norristown	PA

TABLE H   COMPANIES WITH BOTH CURRENT
AND CREDIT ACCOUNTS

CompanyName	City	State
New Boston Trucking	Boston	MA
Business Systems, Inc.	Palo Alto	CA
Beverages Unlimited	McLean	VA
Software Solutions	Norristown	PA
Software Solutions	Norristown	PA

Figure 2-4. Example of INTERSECT Operator.

a current account or a credit account, but not both types of accounts. In this example, the results of an intersection can be used for producing targeted mailings encouraging the companies to open the type of account they do not currently have.

2.4 FOUNDATION RULES OF THE RELATIONAL MODEL

Not satisfied with the level of adherence to his concepts of the relational database model established in 1981,[5] Codd set out to create a more rigorous definition of the requirements for a relational database in 1985. Codd[6] established a definition of what constitutes a relational database management system. These rules define structural and integrity requirements as well as data manipulation and data independence requirements.

The basic foundation rule, *Rule 0*, is stated as the following:

Rule 0: *For any system that is advertised as, or claimed to be, a relational database management system, that system must be able to manage a database entirely through its relational capabilities.*

There are a number of implications of this rule. This rule implies that the database neither has data structures based on nonrelational concepts nor should have access methods that may subvert the integrity of the relational structure.

In addition, Codd has defined another 12 rules as a test for ensuring the mathematical integrity and authenticity of relational database management systems. Originally established in 1985, these rules were revised to tighten the evaluation criteria. We will first state these 12 rules as presented by Codd[7] in his 1990 book and will then discuss the key areas of significance from a design perspective. Section A-7 of Appendix A of Codd's book contains a table that

---

[5] E. F. Codd, "Relational Database: A Practical Foundation for Productivity," *ACM Transactions on Database Systems,* 1981.

[6] E. F. Codd, "Is Your DBMS Really Relational?" *Computer World,* October 14, 1985.

[7] Courtesy (and with permission) of Dr. Edgar F. Codd.

E. F. Codd, "The Relational Model for Database Management: Version 2"; *Addison-Wesley,* 1990, Appendix A (Section A-7).

specifies the correspondence between the 14 features of the revised relational model (RM-V2). These 12 rules (with the RM-V2 feature cross-references) are as follows:

Rule 1: The information feature   RS-1
The DBMS requires that all database information seen by application programmers (AP) and interactive users at terminals (TU) is cast explicitly in terms of values in relations, and IN NO OTHER WAY in **base relations**. *Exactly one additional way is permitted in* **derived relations**, *namely ordering by values within the relation (sometimes referred to as inessential ordering).*

Rule 2: Guaranteed access   RM-1
Each and every datum (atomic value) stored in a relational database is guaranteed to be logically accessible by resorting to a combination of table name, primary key value, and column name.

Rule 3a: Missing information: representation   RS-13
Throughout the database, the fact that a database value is missing is represented in a uniform and systematic way, independent of the data type of the missing database value. Marks are used for this purpose.

Rule 3b: Missing information: manipulation
The truth tables of Four-valued Logic   RM-10
The DBMS evaluates all truth-valued expressions using the four-valued logic defined by the following truth tables:

P	NOT P
t	f
a	a
i	i
f	t

P OR Q		Q			
		t	a	i	f
	t	t	t	t	t
	a	t	a	a	a
P	i	t	a	i	i
	f	t	a	i	f

P AND Q		Q			
		t	a	i	f
	t	t	a	i	f
	a	a	a	i	f
P	i	i	i	i	f
	f	f	f	f	f

In these tables, t stands for true, f for false, a for **missing and applicable,** *i for* **missing and inapplicable**.

Rule 4: A dynamic on-line catalog   RC-1
The DBMS supports a dynamic catalog based on the Relational Model. The database description is represented (at the logical level) just like ordinary data, so that authorized users can apply the same relational language to its interrogation as they can to the regular data.

Rule 5: Comprehensive relational language   RM-3
Excluding consideration of logical inference, the DBMS supports a relational language RL that has the full power of four-valued, first-order predicate logic[8]. The DBMS is capable of applying this power to all of the following nine or more tasks:

---

[8] A. Church, "Introduction to Mathematical Logic", Princeton University Press, 1958.

"Indirizzi di normalizzazione nell'area delle technologie dell'informazione nella publica administrazione", *Gazetta Ufficiale della Republica Italiana*, Supplemento N. 38, 30 maggio 1990, pp 24–27.

H. Pospesel, "Introduction to Predicate Logic", Prentice-Hall, 1973.

R. R. Stoll, "Sets, Logic, and Axiomatic Theories", 1960.

P. Suppes, "Introduction to Logic", *Van Nostrand*, 1967.

1. *retrieval (database description, regular data, and audit log)*
2. *view definition*
3. *insertion*
4. *update*
5. *deletion*
6. *handling missing information in a uniform way (independent of data type)*
7. *integrity constraints*
8. *authorization constraints*
9. *database definition*

and if the DBMS is claimed to be able to handle distributed data:

10. *distributed database management with distribution independence, including automatic decomposition of commands by the DBMS, automatic recomposition of results by the DBMS, and site-straddling integrity constraints*

Rule 6a: Retrieval using views   RV-4
Neither the DBMS nor its principal relational language RL make any user-visible distinctions between R-tables and views with respect to retrieval operations. Moreover, any query can be used to define a view by simply prefixing the query with a phrase such as CREATE VIEW.

Rule 6b: Manipulation per views   RV-5
Neither the DBMS nor its principal relational language RL makes any user-visible manipulative distinctions between base R-tables and views, except that:

1. *some views cannot accept row insertions, and/or row deletions, and/or updates acting on certain columns, because algorithms VU-1 or some stronger algorithm fails to support such action;*
2. *some views do not have primary keys and therefore will not accept those manipulative operators that require primary keys to exist in their operands.*

The need for revision of the original rule 6 was shown by Buff[9].

Rule 7: High-level insert, update, and delete   RM-4
The relational language RL supports retrieval, insert, update, and delete at a uniformly high, set level—multiple records at a time, including zero records, one, two, etc. without special casing.

Rule 8: Physical data independence   RP-1
The DBMS permits a suitably authorized user to make changes in storage representation, in access method, or in both—for example, for performance reasons. Applications programs and terminal activities remain logically unimpaired whenever such changes are made.

Rule 9: Logical data independence   RP-2
Application programs and terminal activities remain logically unimpaired when information-preserving changes are made to the base R-tables, provided that these changes are of any kind that permit unimpairment according to the algorithm VU-1 or according a strictly stronger algorithm.

Rule 10: Integrity independence   RP-3
Integrity constraints specific to a particular relational database must be definable in the relational data sublanguage RL, and storable in the catalog. Application programs and terminal activities must remain logically unimpaired when changes are made in these integrity consists, provided that such changes theoretically permit unimpairment (where "theoretically" means at a level of abstraction for which all DBMS implementation details are set aside).

---

[9] H. W. Buff, "The View Update Problem is Undecidable", private communication from the Swiss Reinsurance Co., Zurich, Switzerland, August 4, 1986, published in *ACM SIGMOD*, Record 17-4, December 1988 with the title "Why Codd's Rule No. 6 must be Reformulated".

Rule 11: Distribution independence   RP-4

A relational DBMS has a sublanguage RL, which enables application programs and terminal activities to remain logically unimpaired:

1. *when data distribution is first introduced (this may occur because the DBMS originally installed manages non-distributed data only);*
2. *when data is re-deployed, if the DBMS manages distributed data—note that the re-deployment may involve an entirely different decomposition of the totality of data.*

Rule 12: Non-subversion   RI-16

Languages other than RL may be supported by the DBMS for database manipulation (the Relational Model does not prohibit such languages). However, if any of these languages are non-relational (e.g., single-record-at-a-time), there must be a rigorous proof that it is impossible for the integrity constraints expressed in RL and stored in the catalog to be bypassed by using one of these non-relational languages.

Rule 12 expands on Rule 10 to define a requirement that restricts data manipulation by a 3GL (third-generation language) such as the C language. All relational databases complying with this rule provide the capability to embed 4GL (fourth-generation languages such as an SQL) statements for data manipulation in a 3GL program. In other words, an application can be developed in the C language, but the application's database access code will be in the form of embedded 4GL statements. Typically, relational database management systems do not provide the capability of accessing the database directly from a C language routine.

The better and more advanced 4GLs have gone beyond the SQL standard to implement procedural control statements and other 3GL-like capabilities to avoid the need for 3GL programming altogether.

Both rules 10 and 12 also discuss the key issue of integrity constraints. Let us take a closer look at the key design issue of integrity constraints in the following section.

2.4.1 Data Integrity Rules

Consistency of the data within the database is essential for the proper operation and reliable functioning of the database. Consistency is enforced in a database by integrity constraints. Constraints are expressed as assertions that the database states are compelled to comply with. These assertions are also called data integrity rules.

There is a very close and important link between data integrity rules and data manipulation capabilities within the relational model. The integrity rules are concerned with preserving the underlying meaning and integrity of the logical data model during data insertions, updates, and deletions.

Integrity constraints may be classified in a variety of ways using different sets of criteria. In the following we will discuss two different types of classifications.

The first classification is based on criteria distinguishing between *state constraints* and *transition constraints*, which impose restrictions on the possible state transitions of a database. Among state constraints, different subclasses can be defined as *type constraints* and *dependency constraints.*

Type constraints are specified by arguments of relations that belong to specified domains. We will call these constraints *domain integrity rules.* Dependency constraints are built into data dependencies that express structural properties of relations and permit relations to be decomposed without losing certain properties based on structural relationships. We call these dependency constraints *relational integrity rules.*

Transition constraints are generally of two types. Some transition constraints are based on structural properties and are expressed in relational integrity rules. Another class of transition constraints results from constraints defined by the user and control the state transition on updates. We will call these *user-defined integrity constraints.* Starting from a database state that complies with a given set of constraints, consistency of a transaction is achieved when the state arrived at after the transaction has been executed also complies with the constraints.

In the discussion above, we defined three principal classes of integrity rules as follows:

1. Domain integrity rules.
2. Constraints enforced automatically by the relational database management system and requiring no user programming. These include entity constraints and referential integrity.
3. User-defined integrity constraints.

The following discussion presents a brief review of the implications of these three classes of integrity rules. We encourage the reader to study the programming, operation, and impact of integrity rules in a dedicated relational database designer's guide.

Domain integrity rules.   Domain integrity rules govern the allowable values that each attribute within the logical data model can assume. For example, a column defined to be a DATE field must always contain DATE values in each row of the table. Generally, all relational databases provide this sort of integrity constraint capability.

Domain integrity rules ensure a consistent structure of the database. The domain integrity rules go beyond the definition of a single table. A key defined in two tables is subjected to a domain integrity rule that spans the two tables. Other data types subject to domain integrity rules include MONEY, INT, CHAR, and so on.

Some databases allow user-defined datatypes or domains. Some databases also allow rules to be defined that constrain the range of values for a field (or column), for example, "all integers <100". A variant of this is the capability to define default values entered in the field when insertion of NULLs is attempted.

System-defined constraints.   Most advanced relational database management systems provide two categories of automatically enforced rules or constraints. These two categories are *entity integrity* and *relational integrity.*

Entity integrity rules state that no attribute that is a part of the primary key of a relation can be a NULL. This rule ensures the relational property that each row is unique and can be accessed unambiguously. When the primary key for the rows of the table is not unique, all rows in the table cannot be addressed uniquely. If the primary key has duplicates, a query will return multiple rows if the duplicate values meet the query criteria. This can be very troublesome. For example, if the primary key is a nonunique customer account number, a query to update a customer account returns two or more accounts for different customers. Most database systems provide a feature that allows defining an index (for example, the one used as the primary key) to be unique.

Referential integrity ensures that, whenever a relation includes a foreign key that matches a primary key in a referenced relation, every foreign key value must equal the primary key value of some tuple in the relation or be wholly NULL. Explained another way, referential integrity ensures the existence of a reference for any foreign key.

The most common example of how referential integrity is applied is a master-detail relationship. The master record (or table), for example, describes a client account and the detail record (or table) describes the open "buy" and "sell" orders for that client. As long as the detail record (that is, the detail table) has a key that references the client account (in the master table), the master record cannot be deleted. Deleting the master record will leave all the detail records in an inconsistent state. Obviously, the converse is also true; that is, no detail record may be created that references a nonexistent primary key. A relational database management system with good referential integrity implementation will automatically check for such references and will not allow the master record to be deleted if it is referenced in a detail record.

User-defined integrity rules (or constraints).   Most databases provide mechanisms such as *triggers* and *stored procedures* for programming rules specific to the business or the applications. For example, an "open buy order" to purchase stock as a "stop price" is canceled automatically after 30 days if the stock price does not drop to the level of the "stop price." Other rules can set automatic "margin account" limits on classes of clients. Generally, user-defined constraints are applied at update time. In a classical sense, triggers are defined at the field level and are *fired* whenever the field is updated or deleted. Triggers are stored in the database and fire automatically. Triggers can be used to perform user-defined domain checks and integrity constraint checks. Another typical use for triggers is to program business rules.

Some databases also define what they call triggers that are administered at the field, block (or table), or form level. These triggers are not stored in the database; rather, they are a part of the application development front end. These triggers are not enforced by the database and, consequently, are not applicable to application code developed in an embedded 3GL.

Stored procedures are provided by some databases that allow precompiled SQL routines (including queries) to be stored in the database. These stored procedures can be used by application code as well as by triggers defined in the database. This allows stored procedures to be used automatically when triggers are fired or under program control in application code (for example, for aging accounts). Relational update-triggering rules specify the follow-on actions of successfully selecting, updating, inserting, or deleting entities in a base relation or other relations. For example, if a "buy order" or "sell order" is executed, the brokerage commission is automatically added or subtracted from the transaction amount and added to the "corporate sales" and "broker commissions" accounts.

Triggers and stored procedures represent the most significant tools for controlling the flow of complex applications. We will discuss triggers and stored procedures in greater detail in the following sections.

Storage of integrity rules.   Codd recognized the importance of integrity rules in maintaining the consistency of the database. Codd also recognized the potential for violating integrity rules when multiple designers develop an application, unless all designers operate through the same set of rules. Rule 10 requires not only that the 4GL or SQL should be capable of defining integrity rules, but also that the rules should be stored in a catalog (or a data dictionary) and not within the application program (a common practice among some leading databases). Storing rules within a data dictionary as a part of the database itself ensures that rules are applied uniformly and consistently for all applications. Writing a new application does not violate the basic integrity rules. Key business rules can be coded as integrity constraints, and if a change takes place in the business rules, a single point of change updates the integrity rules for all applications.

Not only should the relational database ensure domain entity and relational integrity rules, but it should also automatically enforce user-defined integrity rules set up as rules, defaults, or triggers. Not all relational database systems support this feature. Furthermore, not all relational databases support a centralized data dictionary. This is an important point to note here. This notion will show greater relevance to our discussion when we start analyzing object-oriented database designs.

2.4.2 Triggers and Stored Procedures

In the discussions above, we used the terms *triggers* and *stored procedures* (as in SYBASE) as two common means for establishing user-defined constraints in a database. Other implementations of database systems provide the means for user-defined integrity constraints through *user-defined functions* (UDFs) and *dynamic procedures* (another name for stored procedures). Stored procedures (and

UDFs) allow calling *C* language user routines that perform specific tasks. For example, a stored procedure can call a *C* routine to format the data in a certain manner for external presentation. While both triggers and stored procedures can be used to define constraints, the manner in which they are used and how the database treats them are very different. A clear understanding of their roles is crucial to good database design.

Triggers.   Triggering operations (or triggers) are rules that govern the validity of insert, delete, and update operations. Triggers can affect other entities or attributes within the same entity. Triggers encompass domains and insert/ delete rules, as well as a variety of attribute-related business rules. Following are some examples of triggers:

- A client may not have an outstanding balance exceeding $10,000. This trigger checks updates to the balance resulting from new orders.
- The client account must be credited within five business days after the sale of a security (that is, shares of company stock).
- Odd-lot stock transactions (that is, a volume of shares that is not an even multiple of 100) carry an additional charge for handling.

We described two types of triggers in the example above, *data related* and *time related*. Both types of triggers are automatic functions that change another attribute or entity. A third type of trigger, an application-driven trigger, causes a new operation to be initiated. For example, a trigger set to fire if the aging function shows the account to be 60 days overdue can start an operation that prompts the user to place a credit hold on the account.

A trigger *fires* when the specified condition in the trigger occurs. An action, called an *operation,* is performed when a trigger fires. The operation may perform one or more of the following functions:

1. Return an error condition for the insert, update, or delete statement (and possibly rollback the transaction to ensure consistency).
2. Automatically modify one or more attributes within the entity.
3. Automatically modify one or more attributes in another entity.

An important point to note here is that an operation defined by a trigger is performed automatically when a trigger fires. Furthermore, note that most relational database systems store triggers in the data dictionary and enforce the triggers automatically.

Generally, in relational database systems, operations within the trigger execute in the context of the current transaction. In some relational and, more particularly, some object-oriented databases, triggers may be queued for execution after the current transaction completes. Queued up triggers can be a cause of inconsistencies, such as when orders continue to be processed after the inventory is exhausted while the trigger to flag a hold on orders is queued up. The reader is encouraged to use a real example and think through the effects of, and potential inconsistencies due to, queued up trigger actions.

Stored procedures.   Stored procedures can be described as user-developed routines that are typically stored in the database in a precompiled form. Stored procedures are called by name and are callable by application programs as well as triggers. Stored procedures provide a means of filtering data on the basis of desired business or integrity rules. For example, if an application requires obtaining a particular range of data from one table if a certain condition is TRUE and from another table if the condition is FALSE, the SQL query to achieve this becomes complex. If this operation is extended to a series of similarly complex operations, the coding can become very complex, thereby creating an extreme problem for an optimizer attempting to determine an access plan for the query. Procedural extensions such as IF-THEN-ELSE, WHILE, and BEGIN-END can help in the programming, but the complexities remain. Stored procedures are a solution to this predicament. The more complex the query, the greater is the time required for parsing and optimizing the query. Stored procedures are compiled once, and the query optimization plan need be determined only once. All future use of the stored procedure saves the parsing and optimization time. Furthermore, stored procedures allow writing a library of routines in SQL (or 4GL code) that reduces each complex operation to a routine and storing the routine within the database. These routines may be shared by a number of applications. Any changes to one routine due to a change in business rules or database enhancements uniformly affect all applications that call the procedure. While triggers are applied to every application that accesses the field or the form, stored procedures apply only to applications that call the procedure.

Another notable advantage of stored procedures is the capability to pass parameters in a manner similar to a subroutine call. User-defined return codes and return parameters provide a means of setting the direction for follow-on runtime processing on the basis of the processing actions and results within the stored procedure.

Stored procedures offer a level functionality akin to objects in an object-oriented program. Stored procedures can be used to define the *operations* that can be performed on the database and filter all access to the data (object). The attributes of an object can be represented by rows in a table where the table is the equivalent of an entity or an object. If the data can be manipulated only via the stored procedures, a form of *encapsulation* is achieved. The example in Figure 2-5 illustrates how stored procedures may be used for managing data objects.

It should be noted that there is another significant benefit in using stored procedures. Stored procedures are compiled and stored in the database. When

A relation for *clients* contains the following fields:

cli_name	char(30)
cli_address	char(30)
cli_city	char(15)
cli_state	char(2)
cli_zip	char(9)
cli_acct_no	char(8)
cli_id_nbr	int

The following stored procedures will be defined to manage client objects:

cli_create name, address, city, state, zip, acct_no
        returns cli_id_nbr

cli_get_client_by_name name
        returns cli_name, cli_address, . . . , cli_acct_no, cli_id_nbr
        (Note: wild cards may be used to return multiple rows)

cli_get_client_by_id id_nbr
        returns cli_name, cli_address, . . . , cli_acct_no, cli_id_nbr

cli_update id_nbr, name, address, city, state, zip, acct_no

cli_update_name id_nbr, name
cli_update_address id_nbr, address
–

—and so on,

cli_delete id_nbr

Figure 2-5.   Example of Stored Procedure Usage.

the database server is initialized, the stored procedures are loaded into memory and are available to calling routines. Figure 2-6 illustrates the performance-enhancing feature of stored procedures as used in SYBASE.

The shorter execution path (they are already parsed and precompiled and have a query execution plan set up) and the ready availability in memory, leading to much greater performance, are very evident in Figure 2-6. The stored procedures are always loaded in memory when the database server is operational and

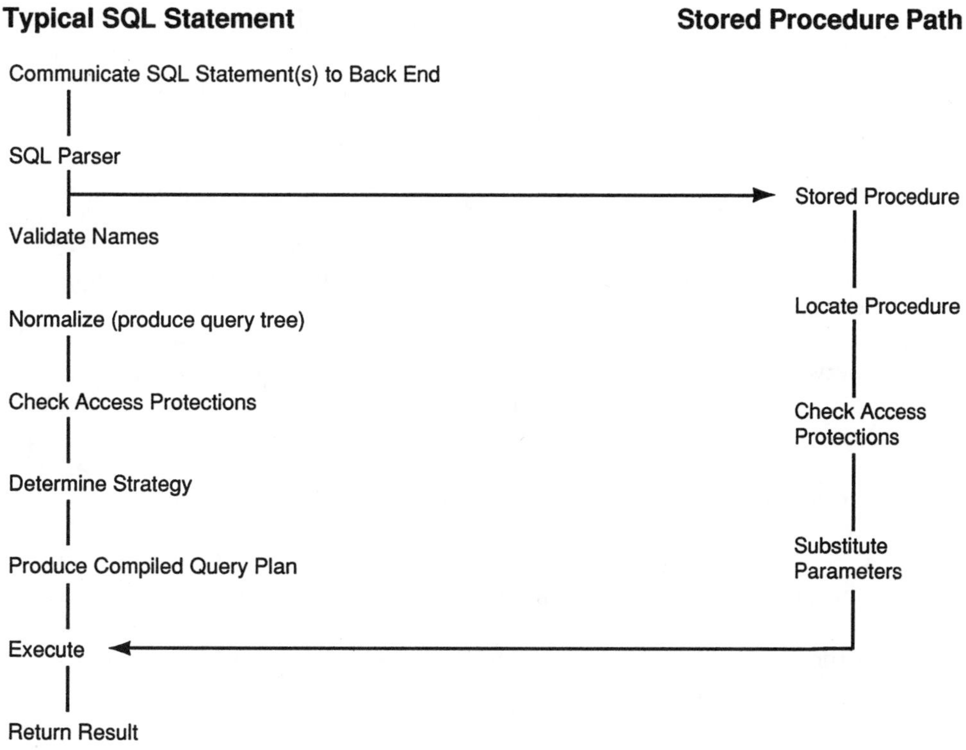

Typical SQL Statement   **Stored Procedure Path**

Communicate SQL Statement(s) to Back End

|

SQL Parser

|——▶ Stored Procedure

Validate Names |

Normalize (produce query tree)   Locate Procedure

| |

Check Access Protections   Check Access
                                                                                   Protections
| |

Determine Strategy |

| Substitute
                                                                            Parameters
Produce Compiled Query Plan

|

Execute ◀———

|

Return Result

Figure 2-6.   Execution Path for Stored Procedures.

are reentrant. Consequently, multiple users can be using the same stored procedures.

Uses and benefits of stored procedures.   Stored procedures can be used to update base tables of views if used carefully. This may be preferable to the more conventional view update (which is generally considered a violation of Codd's rules unless all fields in the participating tables are defined for the update). Stored procedures offer a means of modifying base tables as well as performing the functions of a SELECT on a VIEW.

The most significant benefits of stored procedures to the database designer and application developer are that information-preserving changes to the database schema have no effect on the invocation or execution of the procedure when such changes theoretically permit unimpairment (note rule 9). In simple language, this means that, if changes are made to the database schema that do not damage its structure or cause any information loss, the stored procedures can absorb all changes and the application is not affected. Changes to column domains (that is, range of values acceptable for a column) also do not affect invocation or execution of stored procedures, although they may require recompilation of the stored procedure.

Stored procedures can be called by a 4GL or a 3GL program module used for application development as long as the program module adheres to the calling syntax. The stored procedure is treated like any other database object, is maintained in the database dictionary, and can be shared by as many applications as may wish to use it. Stored procedures may be protected from access and update just like any other object in the database. The stored procedure can be very simple and it can be a part of a complex transaction, or it may be very complex and comprise one or more transactions.

One notable benefit of stored procedures is the significant reduction in network traffic and improved performance in client/server applications. Instead of sending long, complete queries to the database server, a single statement invoking the procedure may be sent.

Stored procedures, typically, have the full 4GL syntax available for programming and have no database-imposed program size restrictions. Stored procedures also allow using procedural constructs, variables, and call parameters.

In summary, stored procedures provide a powerful capability to a programmer. Like all other powerful programming capabilities, stored procedures have to be used carefully and with good advanced planning and design. Where stored procedures become part of a complex transaction, careful thought is required in the handling of rollbacks and recovery from failures.

2.4.3 Joins

Concatenation of rows from one table to the rows from another table (called a *union* if the tables have identical columns or *product* if not) is a very common and frequent operation in any database application. The *join* is the equivalent of selecting every row from the second table for every row from the first table (a Cartesian product) and then selecting the rows from this product based on the *join criterion*. One or more join criteria are defined in the *join predicate*.

There are two basic types of joins, *inner joins* and *outer joins*. Inner joins are also called *natural joins*. *Inner joins* are joins that compare each row in the first table with each row in the second table and select only the rows where the values of certain key fields (called *join fields*) are equal. Any duplicate rows are removed. *Outer joins* are an extended form of join in which the rows in one relation that do not match the rows in the other relation are concatenated, but the rows that do not match are filled with NULLs. The outer joins provide essentially a list of all potential combinations. The differences between inner joins and outer joins are illustrated by the example in Figures 2-7 and 2-8. The tables W (*company*) and X (*balances*) are described in Figure 2-7.

Other types of joins can be created as subsets or variations of inner joins or outer joins by specifying the join criteria to a greater level of detail. Join criteria

TABLE W (*company*)   MASTER LIST OF COMPANIES

CompanyName	Address	City	State
Johnson Sugar Mills	120 Maple Street	New Haven	ME
New Boston Trucking	75 Sumner Street	Boston	MA
Business Systems, Inc.	100 Silicon Street	Palo Alto	CA
Moscariello Appliances	100 Main Street	Hartford	CT
Smith Hardware	36 Broadway	New York	NY
Beverages Unlimited	255 Congress Ave	McLean	VA
Software Solutions	30 Township Lane	Norristown	PA
Software Solutions	150 Main Street	Norristown	PA

TABLE X (*balances*)   TABLE OF ACCOUNT NUMBERS AND BALANCES

CompanyName	Account number	Balance
Johnson Sugar Mills	1001	1234.56
Business Systems, Inc.	1005	513.47
Smith Hardware	1003	51.7

Figure 2-7.   Source Tables for JOIN Operations.

TABLE Y   *INNER JOIN* OF TABLES W AND X

CompanyName	Address	City	State	Account number	Balance
Johnson Sugar Mills	120 Maple Street	New Haven	ME	1001	1234.56
Business Systems, Inc.	100 Silicon Street	Palo Alto	CA	1005	513.47
Smith Hardware	36 Broadway	New York	NY	1003	57.13

TABLE Z   *OUTER JOIN* OF TABLES W AND X

CompanyName	Address	City	State	Account number	Balance
Johnson Sugar Mills	120 Maple Street	New Haven	ME	1001	1234.56
New Boston Trucking	75 Sumner Street	Boston	MA		
Business Systems, Inc.	100 Silicon Street	Palo Alto	CA	1005	513.47
Moscariello Appliances	100 Main Street	Hartford	CT		
Smith Hardware	36 Broadway	New York	NY	1003	57.13
Beverages Unlimited	255 Congress Ave	McLean	VA		
Software Solutions	30 Township Lane	Norristown	PA		
Software Solutions	150 Main Street	Norristown	PA		

Figure 2-8.   Example of Inner and Outer JOINS.

can include comparators such as less than, greater than, all values equal to, and so on. These conditions determine the rows selected from the join product.

Equi-joins, for example, are formed by cancatenating two or more tables when data in one or more pairs of columns are equal. Duplicate columns are not removed. Note that if the duplicate columns are removed this becomes an *inner join*.

We used a simple example of a two-way join, that is, a join based on two relations (tables) only. More complex joins are created by joining three or more relations (remember, this gives rise to a geometric product or Cartesian product). Optimization of a join has a major performance impact. Use of joins, especially for reports, must be very carefully planned. The database design must be denormalized to balance insert, update, and delete performance with join performance. Methods for achieving high performance in joins have been a subject for significant research for relational databases. Any benchmarks performed to compare the performance of the relational databases invariably test the database performance against increasing complexity of joins. Depending on the join method used in the architecture of the relational database product, the sequence of relations specified in the join predicate can have a notable impact on performance. We will review a few common join methods to illustrate some of these concepts.

Join methods.   Two common join methods are called *nested loops* and *merging scans* methods. Originally designed for System R in the 1970s, these two methods have been the basis for many contemporary designs and have been adapted frequently for a number of relational databases. In addition to these methods, contemporary relational database systems use artificial intelligence concepts in combination with other methods.

In the *nested loops join method*, the inner and outer joins are determined. For each tuple in the outer join, the inner join is scanned, and all tuples of the inner join that satisfy the join predicate are selected. The composite tuples formed by the outer-relation-tuple/inner-relation-tuple pairs comprise the result of the join.

The *merging scans join method*, used primarily for equi-joins, scans the outer and inner joins in join column order. This implies that along with columns specified in the ORDER BY and GROUP BY clauses, columns of *equi-joins* also define the scan order. If there are two or more join predicates, one of them is used as the join order predicate and the others are treated as ordinary selection predicates. It should be noted that the more complex logic of the merging scans join method takes advantage of the ordering of join columns to avoid rescanning the entire inner relation for each type of the outer join as in the nested loop method. This is achieved by coordinating the inner and outer scans by reference to the matching join column values and by keeping track of where matching join groups are located. Joins performed on previously sorted columns run much faster.

Multiway joins (that is, joins across three or more relations) are treated as a sequence of two-way joins. The first two relations are joined, and the resulting relation is joined with the next relation in the join sequence. It is not essential to reduce the first join to its finished result before performing the next join. However, the larger the number of relations being joined, the more complex is the join process and, therefore, full reduction as an intermediate step is advisable.

Join order.   We earlier touched on the notion that the join order affects performance even though the Cartesian product (or cardinality) is the same irrespective of the order. This notion is derived from a study of memory management. Joins that retain close to a full Cartesian product in memory use up a lot of the memory workspace, making the selection task more disk intensive. Therefore, the smaller joins, especially those that reduce down to inner joins, should be performed first, and the join order should take into account the size of the result of each successive join to make the most efficient use of available memory.

We also touched on the need for an efficient *query plan*. The *join plan* is an important component of the query plan. The optimal join plan is determined either by building a tree of possible solutions or by using heuristics based on artificial intelligence methods (and with expert system assistance). Most relational database systems allow storing a join plan as a part of the query plan for future use. The decision to select a join plan is made on the basis of a tree describing the operations for each possible plan. The tree describes the join plan in terms of operations required for creating the inner and outer joins and performing the comparision to address the join criteria. In a cost-based optimizer system, the cost of operations is calculated for each potential query plan and the least costly plan is selected. The cost may be based on table size, histograms (frequency analysis) on the join columns, relative size of one table to another, and other relevant criteria. In an expert system (or AI based system), join plans use heuristics (a set of rules of thumb developed from experience and focused tests conducted previously) to determine the recommended query plan.

2.5 DATA INDEPENDENCE

Codd's rule 8 provides for independence between data storage and application programs that access data. According to this rule, if the database storage representation is changed, the application program should not require a change and should continue to provide the same functionality. This rule implies that there is no recoding. A database storage representation change may affect performance. This rule is the primary basis for performance tuning by database administrators.

Database administrators often fine-tune a database and add and drop indexes on the basis of statistical monitoring of functions and data access by the applications. An index improves performance. Creating indexes for the keys that are used most often improves the performance of the overall database system. On the other hand, indexes use up disk space. Consequently, performance has to be weighed against disk usage. Rule 8 ensures that the system adminstrator has the freedom to create and drop indexes and to physically relocate data on disk to optimize system performance.

Performance can be improved by restructuring the database in terms of the physical locations of the tables and index structures. Such a change should not require reprogramming the application. The existing logical index setup should be able to handle the restructuring of the physical storage.

Another kind of data independence is established in Codd's rule 9. This rule states that, when the database structure is altered by combining or splitting tables, the associated application programs should not be logically impacted. The logical data independence applies primarily to views. As long as the components of the view comprise the same set of tables with the same aggregate set of columns, a view should be able to adjust to any changes in the underlying combinations that make up the respective tables.

Codd was looking ahead to the future in establishing rule 11. This rule implies that the location of the data over a network or across multiple systems should be fully transparent to the application. The rule as stated is very simple. However, implementation of a relational database that can achieve total distribution transparency is a subject for significant research and discussion.

From an implementation perspective, rule 11 implies that changes in the underlying storage of the data do not cause existing SQL queries to fail. That is, SQL specifies what data should be retrieved or manipulated; the underlying database determines how to access the data. This does not ensure that, if substantial changes are made to data location, clustering, or indexing, there will be no effect on performance. It is reasonable to assume that performance of exisiting queries can be improved (or it may degrade) if structural changes are made in the database. It may also be reasonable to assume that such major restructuring of the database may require recoding or recompiling of user programs. Creating the illusion of a centralized integrated database when components of the database are actually distributed is a very complex task. This notion has also given way to significant thought along the lines of managing distributed objects. We will discuss this issue in greater detail from a design perspective in Part III.

2.6 INTEGRATED DATA DICTIONARY

Codd's rule 4 requires that the database description be presented at the logical level in the same way as ordinary data accessible to authorized users. A physical and logical description of the relations (colums and tables and the relationship between tables) in the database is also known as the *database dictionary.* A dictionary, typically, includes physical (usually machine readable) and logical (usually user accessible) descriptions of the database tables and their attributes, relationships, and interpretations. It is a compact but rich description. A data dictionary is usually accessible interactively via a metalanguage.

A data dictionary according to Codd's rule 4 must be a part of the database itself. A data dictionary not adhering to this rule may reside separately. A separate data dictionary capability has benefits and disadvantages. The benefits arise from not adhering to the constraints of Codd's rules. These benefits can be stated as follows:

1. Multiple data dictionaries can be maintained, each with a different view of the database and customized for the application it serves.
2. In a distributed access system, local copies of data dictionaries can be maintained for fast access.
3. The database can be customized for a specific application by constraining changes to only the data dictionary used by that application.

While providing this level of flexibility, an independent data dictionary also has some important disadvantages.

1. Changes made in the database may not get propagated to all implementations of data dictionaries for that database. One or more data dictionaries may become unsynchronized with the database.
2. An application can violate integrity rules by bypassing the official data dictionary. Similarly, business rules established in the data dictionary can be bypassed.
3. A separate data dictionary, while violating rule 4, also leads to violation of a number of other rules.

It would be an interesting exercise for the readers to determine which of Codd's rules can potentially be violated by a separate data dictionary and under what circumstances.

The issue of separating or distributing data dictionaries is going to become even more fascinating when we start discussions on distributed systems and object-oriented approaches to database management in Chapter 3 and in Part III.

2.7 TRANSACTION MANAGEMENT

Codd's rule 5 states the requirement for a 4GL to handle transaction management. Relational database systems are designed for multiple users to concurrently access data. The database system provides the facilities for starting a series of queries, updates, and deletions, all treated together in an atomic manner as a transaction. If any of the operations within the transaction fail or if the system fails during the transaction, the transaction is backed out and the database system is returned to a state of full consistency by a process called *recovery*.

The concept of a transaction is key to a successful recovery philosophy. If a complex update fails or if the system crashes during a database operation, the state of the database will probably become inconsistent or confused. The database system must be able to undo partially completed transactions, that is, transactions that did not perform their final update.

This capability is achieved in most contemporary database systems by a feature called a *transaction log* used in conjunction with *before-image* and *after-image journals*. Before-image journals retain a copy of the record before the update, and after-image journals keep a copy of the record after the change. If the transaction is unable to complete, the system can undo the transaction by backing out the transaction. A transaction is backed out by comparing the data record with the image in the journals. A transaction can be undone as long as it has not executed a *commit transaction* (that is, up to the point where a <*commit transaction*> is executed). At this point, the transaction is written out to the database and removed from the journals. In case of failures, the journals are useful in returning the database to a state of full consistency.

Transactions also supply the blueprint to concurrency control. If multiple transactions concurrently read or write the same data, anomalies can occur. A number of different approaches have been applied for addressing transaction management for multiple users. We will investigate the following methods used for managing multiuser access:

1. Locking of records being updated
2. Versioning
3. Use of centralized transaction manager

Locking of records being updated.   Locking is used by most databases to prevent multiple users from updating a record at the same time. Three levels of locking may be employed:

1. Row locking
2. Page locking
3. Table locking

Row-level locking provides the highest granularity and allows locking to be performed on exactly the records being updated. However, row-level locking usually has a significant impact on performance.

Page-level locking is faster; however, all records on the page being locked are inaccessible for updates for the duration of the locking user's transaction.

When the number of locked rows or pages reaches a certain threshold, the database may elevate the locks to a table lock. In this instance, no other users will be allowed to update rows in the table until the lock is released.

Versioning.   A database system may create a new version of a record being updated so that the updating user has access to the new version, while other users are allowed continued read access to the old version. Depending on implementations, various levels of versioning capability are provided by relational database vendors.

Use of centralized transaction manager.   A centralized transaction manager is used in a distributed database environment where a single server manages all transactions. The transaction manager tracks locking and version management functions to ensure consistent operation. This subject has been explored in greater detail in Chapter 10, which also covers other design issues applicable to distributed systems.

2.8 LIMITATIONS OF RECORD-BASED INFORMATION MODELS

Record-based information models, including the relational database model, have proved to be generally efficient and easy to use for a variety of batch applications. They have been used widely for interactive applications even though their limitations have become more and more obvious as business enterprises move toward enterprise-wide interactive information management systems.

Record-based information models are not complete in their ability to represent information required for contemporary information management. They typically describe the structure of the data in the record, but not the behavior of the data or the operations that can be performed on the data. In this section we will discuss the following vital concepts:

1. Basic definition of a record
2. Characteristics of record structures
3. Implementations of record structures
4. Lack of semantic information about relations
5. Limitations of implementations

2.8.1 Defining a Record

A *record* has been defined to be a fixed sequence of field values conforming to a static description usually contained in a catalog (or a data dictionary) or specified as a structure in a program. Each *field* in a record is assigned an identifier (a field name) and is described in terms of *field length,* a *data type,* and its *characteristics,* such as the field is a key field or that it may contain NULLs or not. A field is synonymous with a column in a table of a relational database, and a record is synonymous with a *relation* or a row in a *table.* (*Note:* A table is typically also known as a relation.) In a relational system, a record must have fields that are unique within the table. A relational database provides a very structured form of data storage. Each row in a table contains the same set of fields in the same sequence. The columns of the table represent the fields of a record. Each column contains the same type of information for each row.

In the relational model, a table represents an entity. An entity describes a real-world description, such as a "company" description. All companies that are clients of a stock trading corporation have the same kinds of attributes or fields in a record describing the company. These fields can include the name of the company, its address, a contact person, type of business it is in, its stock portfolio, and so on. The example of stock portfolio immediately brings up the issue that a company may be trading in a number of different stocks, and the stock portfolio may have a number of different entries for different stock types for each company. The concept of maintaining a consistent structure is supported by creating separate *detail* tables for different types of stocks and storing stock portfolio information for all companies in the stock portfolio tables. The stock portfolio tables can have a record for every stock traded by every company.

2.8.2 Characteristics of Record Structures

In the brief description of record structures above, a few characteristics become very obvious.

1. The record structures are consistent.
2. The data and their description are maintained separately.
3. Changing data descriptions is not simple.
4. Behavioral relations are not described.

The concept of a data dictionary, while being a powerful concept, also places a number of restrictions on the ability to change the structure or contents of a record. While the data is in the data tables, the description of the data tables is maintained in catalogs (catalogs are tables used by the system) stored in the system information tables (system information tables are tables maintained by the RDBMS software for that database). Frequently, changing the structure of a table requires dropping all index structures, creating another table, and then copying the information into the restructured table, deleting the old table, and renaming the new table to the name of the old table. While a field can be added fairly easily in most RDBMSs, changing a field data type or deleting a field can be a fairly complex operation.

Another characteristic of the record structure is its inherent inability to address two different types of data for the same record. For example, clients for a stock trading corporation may be individuals, corporations, and mutual fund managers. While they are all classified as clients, they all have different types of stock portfolios and vastly different trading patterns. An adjustment to this behavioral difference is the creation of separate master tables for the three classes of clients. This distribution of information disperses relevant client information to three different classes of records. The impact of this is significant on the programming of such a system. Separate routines are required to address each class, and this class difference is carried through a number of operations coded for the applications. Differences such as the existence of a separate contact person in addition to the client name, salutations, account types, and so on, have to be maintained.

Another important relational characteristic is that some relations are entities and some relations, in reality, are not entities. These relationships, while they are not entities, are still expressed partially in records. For example, an agent at a stock trading corporation has a relationship to the employer. The agent's skills are a little different from the stock broker on the trading floor at the stock exchange. Representation of these skill differences is achieved by creating records defining these skills. A skill, in this relation, is an entity, but the relationships between the skill, the stock broker and the agent, and the employer are not really entities. The concept of *joins* provides a mechanism for maintaining this relationship. This is illustrated in the example in Figure 2-9.

```
Broker
        Name        char(30)
        Emp_id      int
        Phone       char(10)
        Acct_no     int

Skills
        Skill_id    int
        Skill_desc  char(40)

Emp_skills
        Emp_id      int
        Skill_id    int

SELECT Skills.Skill_desc
        FROM Skills s, Broker b, Emp_skills es
        WHERE b.Name = 'Smith'
        AND b.Emp_id = es.Emp_id
        AND es.Skill_id = s.Skill_id
```

Figure 2-9.   Example of Nonentity JOIN.

It should be noted that a *join* provides a dynamic form of relationship based on static relationship information. This transition of a static relation to a dynamic interpretation has a significant potential for misuse. While the relational model has a fairly good grasp on the syntax of a relationship, there is very little, if any, semantic information in the relational model. The semantic information is implied, but it is not defined.

2.8.3 Lack of Semantic Information

As we just noted in the previous section, the semantic structure of relations is implied, but is not stored in a record format. The relation may be defined structurally in one or more tables by defining fields that establish different information about an entity in different records. For example, the semantics of the relation between a contact name at a client corporation is implied in the client information record. However, it is not defined in the table (or record) describing names and telephone numbers of clients.

The limitations of defining semantics within the data structure become even more acute when the data structure defines a database that is physically distributed across a network. Not only are the definitions incomplete, but further limitations are imposed by the location of the data dictionary. The data dictionary can be centralized for all database servers stored with each database server. Alternately, the data dictionary can be stored in client nodes.

2.9 SUMMARY

A detailed review of relational database systems was the primary goal of this chapter. We started out by reviewing the basic definitions and concepts of the relational model consisting of the structural, manipulation, and integrity parts.

Based on set theory, relational algebra is the fundamental mathematical base for relational database management. This mathematical base differentiates the relational model from other database architectures, especially the object-oriented database systems.

We also saw that there are very specific rules enumerated by E. F. Codd for measuring the conformity of a relational database to the basic mathematical foundations. Not all rules are followed by all databases. The analysis of the rules demonstrates the impact of not conforming to the rules. These rules have a significant impact on data integrity, flexibility in maintaining the physical database environment, and presentation of data to the user or to an application. Furthermore, we looked at the pros and cons of managing data dictionaries that do and do not subscribe to these rules.

Finally, we outlined the limitations of record-based database models (such as relational database systems). This part of the discussion is useful for comparing the relational model with the object-oriented model.

2.10 EXERCISES

1. Explain the advantages and disadvantages of the following three methods for maintaining referential integrity in a database:
   a. Hardcoded database enforced integrity.
   b. Programmed triggers stored in the database.
   c. Programmed triggers stored in client applications.

2. Describe the advantages and disadvantages of field domain rules and defaults used in the following manner.
   a. Enforced within the database.
   b. Enforced within client applications.
   c. Enforced both within the database and client applications.

3. What is the advantage of database support for NULL field values?

4. What effect does NULL value support have on updates?

5. The following information needs to be maintained in a database for employees:
   Employee ID
   Name
   Address
   Department
   Social security number
   Salary grade
   Payroll type (exempt or nonexempt)
   Salary (for exempt)
   Wage rate (for nonexempt)
   Hire date
   Assign field names and datatypes to the above items to specify the fields in an employee table.

6. Define a set of domain rules where appropriate for the fields specified in Exercise 5.

7. Assume that there are 1000 employee records (for Exercise 5) and the database uses B-tree indexes. Which field should be indexed to provide the best performance for looking up individual employee records? What datatype should this field have?

8. How would you change the results of Exercise 7 if the database had only 50 records?

9. What kind of index would be best if the search were made by employee name in Exercise 7?

10. Assume there is a Department table that defines the set of departments to which an employee may belong. Write pseudocode for a *delete* trigger for the Department table that will enforce referential integrity between the two tables.

11. Define a set of stored procedures that would provide a complete set of services for retrieving and manipulating employee records.

12. Assume the following view on the Employee and Department tables is defined in the database:

```
create view emp_dept as
      select employee.emp_name, department.dept_name
      from employee, department
      where employee.dept_id = department.dept_id
```

Give an example of an update view statement that would not be permissible in a relational database.

13. Describe a method whereby a database may be fully backed up while active operations are being performed on the data without losing any transactions or data changes. What role does a transaction log play in database recovery?

14. Describe a mechanism for performing transactions across multiple distributed databases.

3

Object-Oriented Database Management

3.1 INTRODUCTION

Programming is a highly repetitive activity involving frequent use of common patterns. However, there is considerable variation in the manner in which these patterns manifest themselves. The complexities of using and combining these patterns have remained a major challenge in the attempts to develop reusable code. Maintaining effective libraries of reusable code in a manner accessible to a large number of developers is a daunting task. Besides just the problems of organizing large numbers of code modules are some major technical problems, such as defining levels of modules that all developers can agree on.

Simple approaches like subroutine libraries of reusable code and reusable designs of basic modules have met with some level of success in specific development environments. Nonetheless, the limitations of the subroutine library approach stand out clearly when one considers the case of overlapping code, naming conflicts, time to compile the code, and the subtle variations required for handling different types of data entities.

The variations in data entities that frequently require slight reprogramming of the code modules can be addressed by packaging data with the code. A packaging like this combines the modified code module with the type of data and stores them together.

If we view the code as performing some action, then the package is a combination of data and an action that can be performed on the data. This combination is an *object*. The real concern here is not the set of functions required for the application, but rather what information is being manipulated and what potential manipulations are meaningful to it. In other words, the goal is to manipulate objects in a manner dictated by the external interface of the object. This is a very basic definition of object-oriented programming.

Special extensions have been built around the C language, and there are other custom object-oriented languages such as *Eiffel* and *Smalltalk*. Object-oriented programming support (OOPS) has found its utility in other areas, such as specialized user interface designs, relational database management systems, and object-oriented database management systems.

Object-based systems, user interfaces built around objects, and relational database systems capable of storing and retrieving objects have become the prevailing technologies for integrated information systems. An object-oriented database (called, in short, object database) encapsulates data in code that *comprehends* the database system's data structure and provides services based on this knowledge of the structure. Object databases support abstract data types and are not restricted to records. The code to implement services may or may not be stored in the database itself. This code is activated when the object is accessed. As a result, object databases support operations more complex than the typical relational SQL commands such as SELECT, JOIN, and UNION because the data can be manipulated depending on the context in which it is being used. The concept of objects in this classical sense reduces the level of linkage maintained in a relational model.

The concepts of *relations* in the relational model are based on relational algebra. The mathematical foundations and Codd's rules for *normalization* based on these mathematical foundations ensure that information in a database is kept uncorrupted. These rules impose a structure on relations within the database and limit the flexibility of the relational model. A significant argument can be made in favor of maintaining databases restricted within the confines of these rules as the output from a database is used for crucial corporate decisions, and the accuracy and integrity of the data are very important.

So why the level of interest in object databases? The answer to this question is found in the nature of the application and the relative flexibility that an object database provides. Object-oriented databases are an excellent choice for data structures that are not handled easily by the relational model. Freedom from primary keys and field values for accessing data items is applicable to a variety of graphics-based applications where data is not organized by numeric fields. The classical relational model is incapable of handling data such as voice or binary graphics screens. Such data can be stored by the database but not interpreted and, consequently, not indexed. Interpretation of data has to be programmed separately. An object-oriented data model addresses this problem by including the code to interpret the data within the object.

Another major issue is the data distribution requirements for an enterprise-wide information system. The relational model addresses this need by using the *client/server* model. Programming in the client/server relational database model involves two parts. On the server the tables that comprise the database are defined. Depending on the DBMS in use, constraints on the data may also be defined, such as defaults, rules, and triggers. On the client side, application code is developed using a 4GL forms development tool and/or a custom 3GL program using a language such as C. Some DBMSs provide a programming language for implementing procedures that are stored as a part of the database. This offers significant performance improvements by allowing queries to be precompiled and reducing the amount of data that has to be passed in a network in the form of complex queries. It also provides for uniform, centralized control of the data. The client/server model addresses the primary needs for distribution of data, but leaves a number of issues for maintaining consistency of distributed data unanswered.

Another disadvantage of current DBMS implementations is the need to develop an application in two or three different languages: the database query language (SQL), procedural extensions to SQL such as those required for stored procedures, and a user interface and processing language such as a 4GL specific to the DBMS, or a 3GL such as C, or both. In an object-oriented database system, on the other hand, it makes a great deal of sense to provide a single object-oriented language for defining both the data and the user interface. Object-oriented languages are by definition designed to allow the definition of data objects and the operations that can be performed on them. The development of applications with common look and feel is also facilitated by an object-oriented approach wherein common user interface tools such as menus and push-buttons can be implemented as objects in a sharable library.

In early relational database systems the only operations that could be performed at the database level were the definition of the tables and indexes and system administration functions such as the size and location of the database on disk. In some systems these operations are not even implemented in SQL; special tools must be used to perform them. Some newer systems have provided extensions to SQL that allow complex queries to be precompiled and stored in the database. However, being extensions to SQL, a nonprocedural language, there are some limits to the usefulness of these languages in defining complex processing on database objects.

What is needed in an object-oriented database system is a new integrated approach to defining objects and the operations that are performed on them. An object-oriented language is ideally suited to this.

All code for the application from data definition to user interface would be developed in the same object-oriented language. Common database concepts such as tables (sets of objects), indexes, and location of data can be implemented through supplied class libraries or through simple extensions to the language. All modules of the application associated with database objects would be loaded into the database server. The user interface and processing modules would run on the client workstation and communicate with the database modules via RPC calls. Again, a supplied class library would provide the mechanisms for establishing connections to the data server. Alternatively, the locations of each module, whether local or remote, could be defined in an application start-up or configuration file, with the compiler or loader providing transparent connections to remote classes.

A good object-oriented design can address a variety of problems faced in the design and operation of a complex information system. Designing an object-oriented system, nonetheless, presents some interesting challenges that must be understood well and surmounted at the early stages of the design. Chief among these challenges is maintaining a well-defined organization and hierarchy of objects.

The very nature of object databases and the flexibility in accessing the data, however, make truly large object databases unwieldy due to the multitude of objects. The authors believe that the evolution of database design will lead to the consolidation of the best features of relational databases with the level of flexibility provided by object databases. This has been achieved, albeit to a limited extent, in relational databases by extending the relational data model to include an abstract datatype capable of handling digitized voice and image data. Further extensions of the concept on noninterpreted fields in the database will provide object database-like features to the abstract datatypes, while retaining the benefits of the mathematical foundations of the relational model.

Truly object-oriented database systems are not very prevalent at the present time. A number of relational database systems have introduced "object" support, but what they call objects has very little in common with what a true object-oriented database would provide. Nevertheless, these are positive developments and much use can be made of these new features.

The two most common features provided are support for binary large objects (BLOBs) and procedural extensions to SQL. BLOBs are a new datatype that allow a very large block of binary data to be stored as a column in a table. In practice, the data for columns of this type are usually stored in a separate segment of the database, with a pointer stored in the table's data segment. BLOBs can be used to store large data objects such as spreadsheets, video images, or bitmaps (pix maps). Interpretation of the contents of these objects is left strictly up to the application. Most relational databases use extensions to the programming environments to address these new datatypes. The nontabular structure of data stored in BLOBs may require significant programming control to manipulate data. Many relational databases already support procedural extensions to standard SQL for program flow control.

Procedural extensions to SQL allow complex queries, data processing, and data integrity constraints to be compiled and stored in the database. Features such as control of flow statements, local variables, and error handling are typically provided. One advantage of stored procedures is a significant increase in performance for on-line transaction processing systems. Another is flexibility in defining data integrity constraints. However, one aspect most useful from an objected-oriented programming viewpoint is the ability to provide a level of abstraction, above SQL, for data access in an application. That is, an application can be developed such that all database access occurs through stored procedures. The application need not have any knowledge of the underlying database implementation. The concept of keeping the database implementation completely in the server fits very nicely with our concepts for programing in an object-oriented database system.

A number of concepts have been presented so far in this chapter. In the following sections, we present, in detail, the basics of object-oriented programming and architectural constructs of object-oriented databases. We also examine the true definition of object-oriented databases. Follow-on discussion analyzes the uses for object-oriented databases, addresses the issue of why there is so much interest in object management, and evaluates specific benefits gained by equipping a database system with the capability to manage objects. We will also perform a detailed comparison between the relational model and the object-oriented database model.

3.2 DEFINITION OF OBJECTS

The definition of objects and of object-oriented programming is not bounded to a clear-cut definition. A number of interpretations exist. Before starting the detailed discussion of our interpretation of object-oriented database management, it is important to clearly define what we mean when we refer to an *object*. In this section we provide the definition of objects as being distinct from the context of relational database management systems. This definition differentiates between the use of object definitions for identifying data storage by itself and the use of object definitions in classifying and accessing stored data. While objects in a relational database are defined by data storage alone, objects in an object-oriented database are defined by *attributes* (data elements) as well as *methods* (operations) that manipulate the data.

In its simplest form, object-oriented programming is a way of structuring software so that data and the relationships between pieces of information and code for processing the data are combined. Data, relationships, and the functions that process them are collectively called *objects*. Hence, objects are manipulated as a unit in which the code cannot be separated from the data or the relationships.

Objects are similar to records of a database in that, when a new object is made, disk space is allocated to store its *attributes* (fields or variables), and the attributes can be manipulated as data elements of fields of a record. Objects are different from records in that an object has a list of *methods* (analogous to a routine in conventional programming) which manipulate the attributes of the object. Methods are special functions associated with the object and ensure that data is processed correctly for the defined environments. Once *methods* are defined for an *object*, applications that manipulate objects do not need to know how methods work or what the attributes mean.

An existing *object class* can be used to create similar new object classes; the old object class is used as a template. The new object *class* is said to have *inherited* the features of the object class from which it was created. An example of an object is an "account" in a general ledger system. Subclasses of accounts can be derived from the general class "account." The subclasses start with the same properties that characterized the "account" class. For each specific type of account, the inherited properties can now be modified.

Before going deeper into definitions and the functioning of object-oriented programming methodologies, let us determine the key characterizations of object orientation. We shall look at four fundamental characterizations: *data encapsulation* (also called *abstract data types*), *inheritance*, *object identity*, and *methods*.

3.3 REVIEW OF KEY OBJECT-ORIENTED PROGRAMMING CONCEPTS

Before we can attempt to understand the operation and structure of object-oriented databases, it is essential to understand the basic concepts of object-oriented programming. These concepts address the fundamental issues of defining, creating, and manipulating objects. In this section we review the key concepts of abstract datatypes and classes, inheritance, and object redefinitions. A firm understanding of the theory behind object-oriented programming is essential for attaining a good grasp on the design of object-oriented databases.

3.3.1 Abstract Data Types

An unambiguous description of a data structure can be achieved by completely defining the implementation of the data structure. The description of the data structure not only defines the properties of the data structure, but also defines the physical implementation of the data structure. This may make the data structure unique and generally not reusable. The data structure can become *overspecified* for reusability. A data structure must exhibit some generality for it to be reusable.

How do we achieve reusability and still maintain a complete and unambiguous description? Let us analyze this question further. If we change the model for our description from *implementation* of the data structure to *services* provided by the data structure, we can define a very complete set of features and functions of the data structure without a description of the implementation. Through this process, we achieve a level of abstraction that allows reusing the data structure in all cases that require exactly the same set of services. This model of a data structure definition that describes only the services offered to the outside world represents an *abstract data type*. An implementation of an abstract data type is called an *instance*. An instance of an abstract data type is known by the *object class* and exists as an instance of the object class, generally known as *object*.

In the abstract data type model of a data structure, a data structure minds its own internal manipulations and accesses other data structures strictly on the basis of their exported methods (advertised functions). These exported methods are called *operators* (we use *operations* and *functions* interchangeably for operators). Based on the discussion above, abstract data types define sets of similar objects with an associated collection of operators. It should be noted that operators are the equivalent of methods (or functions) being executed with a given set of parameters.

In conventional programming, programs can be viewed as collections of procedures or subroutines that pass parameters to procedures they call. The called procedures manipulate the parameters and perform a function and/or return a value. In object-oriented programming, the equivalent view is one of a collection of objects that communicate with each other through procedures (called *messages* in object-oriented programming terminology). Messages allow an object to invoke a method in another object. Messages are used for communications between objects, while methods generally act on the attributes of an object. We encourage readers interested in object-oriented programming to refer to a good text[1] devoted to object-oriented programming for a detailed study.

Some key properties are required for defining the type and operation of abstract data types. These include:

1. Type
2. Functions
3. Preconditions.
4. Rules or axioms

Type.   An abstract data type defines a collection of similar objects with a similar set of services. The *type* defines the objects to be of a certain type. Association of the object with a type connotes a set of functions or services defined for that type. For example, an object can be defined to be of the type "account." The definition of an object in a program is a *class* definition. Whereas *type* defines an abstract data type to have a certain set of properties, a *class* is an implementation of that abstract data type supporting that set of properties. (Note that a class definition provides the means of programming the properties of an object; only the object exists at runtime).

More simply stated, an object can be identified to be of a certain type (and therefore embraces a set of properties associated with that type) until it is associated with a class. As a member of a type, a set of properties is associated with the

---

[1] Betrand Meyer, *Object Oriented Software Construction*, Prentice-Hall, Englewood Cliffs, N.J. 1988.

object. As a member of a class, the object is implemented to embrace those properties.

Functions. Functions define a list of services provided by the instance of that abstract data type. A function is specified in terms of the abstract (nonimplementation related) description of the operations. In general, some or all of these functions (or services) will be provided by the operations (or methods) implemented within the object.

Preconditions. Preconditions modify the relationship between functions and operations. Preconditions restrict the applicability of every function to every instance of the abstract data types. Some instances may support a function partially. To clearly establish this fact, preconditions are attached to the abstract data type. Preconditions may be viewed as modifying features (restrictions or constraints) programmed within each specific instance (or object) of the abstract data type. For example, for an abstract data type of "Broker," the preconditions for an instance of "AccountBroker" may be different from preconditions for "FloorBroker" due to the differences in the job functions of the account broker and the floor broker and the handling of commissions for each.

Rules or axioms. Rules or axioms add semantic properties to the descriptions of functions. They express the constraints on the scope of the properties based on the internal environment of the instance of the abstract data type. In other words, while functions describe a generalized set of services, for each function (or service) rules can be defined that limit or constrain the scope of the function to a more specific function. For example, the abstract data type "Broker" may have defined a general function for calculating commissions; the "AccountBroker" may set up specific rules on the terms of payment of commissions.

Programming abstract data types. As mentioned in the introduction to this chapter, language extensions have been provided for the C language. The extended language called $C++$ (and a variety of other custom-developed, object-oriented programming languages) provides language constructs to facilitate the definition and manipulation of abstract data types.

The key language construct in $C++$ for handling abstract data types is the *class* definition as shown in the example in Figure 3-1. A class definition is similar to a *struct* declaration in C. However, in addition to allowing the fields to be defined, it also allows the declaration of all functions or methods that may manipulate objects of its type. For example, the code example in Figure 3-1 defines a simple "account" class.

Note that the label "private" indicates that users of this object are not allowed to directly access the elements defined in that section (in this case, the account number, name, and balance). Rather, access must be through the methods (or attributes) defined in the "public" section.

```
class account {

private:
        short        account_number;
        char         account_type;
        char         account_name[20];
        double       balance;

public:

        Account(short account_number, char account_type,
                    const char account_name);
        ~Account();
        double GetBalance();
        char GetAccountType();
        const char *GetAccountName();
        void Debit(double amount);
        void Credit(double amount);

};
```

Figure 3-1.   Example of C++ Construct for Abstract Data Type of Definition.

3.3.2 Constraints

Correctness in software is achieved by ensuring that the software will always comply with the conditions established in the specifications. The discrepancy between anticipated results and achieved results is reduced by constraining the software from actions that violate the conditions. A simple means to address this is to include all conditions in the code. That is, an expression defining the condition is included in an executable routine. Such an expression is called an *assertion* or a *constraint*. An assertion or a constraint can be looked on as a property of some value of a program entity. While both assertions and constraints have been used to define this concept, we will use the term *constraint* in the following discussion.

Constraints allow semantic specification of a method (or a routine). A routine that implements a function from an abstract data type performs a useful *task*. The action defined by this task must be expressed precisely for correct results. The action, in effect, sets conditions that precisely define the functioning of the task. These conditions are constraints.

One would expect preconditions and postconditions on methods to also be a form of constraints. Indeed preconditions and postconditions are forms of constraints. Constraints can be applied to the two main characteristics of objects: the object attributes and object methods (the routines or operations). Constraints applied to object attributes define all allowable values for object attributes on entry to a method (precondition) and on exit from the method (postcondition). Constraints applied to object methods determine the code execution path (branching in the code based on values of attributes) within the method. Constraints are essential to control the semantics of the object definition and, therefore, constraints reflect the semantics of the abstract data types. Let us explore this notion further by analyzing the programming implications of constraints.

Programming implications of constraints.   Let us now look at the significance of preconditions and postconditions. Preconditions can be used to set up the norms for the calling methods (or routines). Preconditions define the conditions under which a call to the called method is legitimate. Obviously, if the precondition is satisfied, there is implicit assurance that there is no further need to check the conditions in the body of the routine and that the called method will produce the expected results. The concept of preconditions can significantly reduce the complexity of programmed checks for conditions. More importantly, it sets the norm for future enhancements.

A postcondition, on the other hand, can be used to define the conditions that must be ensured by the routine on return. A postcondition binds the class and guarantees that certain results with known properties will be obtained after the call. This again helps in standardizing the call interface for programmers associated with a project.

Constraints on objects and object attributes are applied through access and update routines that manipulate instances of the abstract data type for the object class. The access and update routines are typically incorporated in the definition of the object class and are associated with either the instance of the object class or with particular variables of the instance (also called *instance variables*). Constraints allow the programmer to code program checks on the values of the variables and branch on predetermined conditions. For example, a value can be checked against the new value and updated only if the new value is higher than the old value. An example of this is a variable that tracks the highest price for the day for a particular stock in a trade management application.

We will summarize here by restating that constraints help in writing software that is correct and in documenting specific requirements in the code. The constraints make debugging easier for the following reasons:

- Constraints facilitate testing the correctness of a class implementation.
- If the class implementation can be tested in isolation and is determined to work correctly, then the bugs can be narrowed down to the code that uses objects of the class.

- Constraints also help in making objects reusable through redefinition, thereby making the overall code execution path simpler. We will discuss the issue of reusability in greater detail in the next section.

3.3.3 Classes

We defined a *class* to be an implementation of an abstract data type (or a type of object). A class can be defined by using a language construct that combines the type definition (of an abstract data type) and delineates its structure with the operations performed by the abstract data type. A number of objects may be derived from a class definition. The collection of objects represented (instantiated) by a class are called *instances* of that class. We used the example of "Broker" earlier as a type definition of an abstract data type. The abstract data type for "Brokers" also includes the operations performed on the object. The class is "Brokers" and it represents instances that are defined as brokers such as "AccountBroker," "FloorBroker," and so on.

It is important to note that a class definition is an abstraction. While an object exists as a distinct runtime entity, a class is a programmed definition of a collection of objects. This implies that objects that still have existence at runtime belong to a class from which they are derived. Programming the concept of a class into the application makes it easier to make global changes to a set of objects. While objects are dynamic and change at runtime, classes are static; classes define properties common to a set of runtime objects.

Before investigating the programmability of class definitions, let us review what constitutes a class definition. A definition must include at least the following information that differentiates one group of objects from another group:

1. The name of the class (for identification)
2. A representation of the contents or structure of the class objects
3. The external operations that manipulate the contents of the objects
4. Internal implementation of the external operations defined in item 3

As we have discussed, objects are characterized by data, called attributes similar to fields in tables, and *methods* (routines that perform some operations on the data). Since a class is a definition of a collection of objects, a class also has dual characteristics similar to the objects derived from it. A class of objects is characterized by attributes that have a particular set of common data. A class is also characterized by a common set of methods (or functions) that modify these data attributes in some manner.

Let us now determine how this concept of classes is applied to a real application. Going back to our example of "Accounts," we defined a class of accounts. For this example, let us say that the operations on an account involve debiting and crediting it. Operations such as processing invoices, making payments, calculating interest, and aging accounts involve information and semantics that must be defined in related classes such as "customer," "interest rates," and "aging schedules"; or they involve operations on two or more account objects at the same time, for example, debiting one account and crediting another. (For our example, we will only address a simple transaction.)

Programming of classes.   We have talked about inheriting attributes and operations of a class. The programming mechanism used for defining (and inheriting) the attributes is a structure in the C or C++ language (or any other suitable object-oriented programming language). A simple class definition is described in Figure 3-2.

The *class* describes the structure of a set of objects. Each object in a class is called an instance of that class. The attributes of a class, also called instance variables, translate into variables or fields in an object (for example, fields in a table). The operations performed to manipulate these attributes translate into methods.

For example, the internal representation of an account consists of the following attributes:

- Name
- Number
- Type
- Balance

For objects in the class "account" just defined, the external operations for manipulating an "account object" are as follows:

- Creating an account object
- Destroying (or deleting) an account object
- Debiting an account
- Crediting an account
- Getting the account balance
- Getting (or reading) other account attributes such as account type, account name, account number, and so on

The example in Figure 3-2 shows how the class "account" is coded. This example includes the attributes as well as methods.

All instances of the class "account" will have the same set of variables. The instances of the class "account" can be created and used by manipulating the instances through the methods associated with the class. Objects that call for such manipulations are generally called *clients* or *instantiating clients*.

It may be worth reiterating here that an important means of using a class is creating a *subclass* that inherits the properties of the parent class (also called

```
enum AccountType {
      AT_UNDEFINED,                  // Undefined Account Type
      AT_CLIENT_MARGIN,              // Client Margin Account
      AT_CLIENT_PORTFOLIO,           // Client Portfolio Account
      AT_CLIENT_MM,                  // Client Money Market Account
};

class Account {
private:
      short           acct_number;
      AccountType     acct_type;
      char            *acct_name;
      double          acct_balance;

public:
      Account(short p_acct_number, AccountType p_acct_type, const char
            *p_acct_name, double p_acct_balance);
       ~Account();

      // Methods for reading Account attributes
      short GetAccountNumber();
      AccountType GetAccountType();
      const char * GetName();
      double GetBalance();

      // Methods for updating account balances (all other attributes
      // are static once an account object is created)
      Debit(double p_amount);
      Credit(double p_amount);

};

Account::Account(short p_acct_number, AccountType p_acct_type, const char
                *p_acct_name, double p_acct_balance)
{
      acct_number = p_acct_number;
      acct_type = p_acct_type;
      acct_name = new char[strlen(p_acct_name)+1];
      strcpy(acct_name, p_acct_name);
      acct_balance = p_acct_balance;
}
```

Figure 3-2.   A Class Definition.

```
Account:: ˜Account()
{
        delete acct_name;
}


short Account::GetAccountNumber()
{
        return acct_number;
}


AccountType Account::GetAccountType()
{
        return acct_type;
}


const char * Account::GetName()
{
        return acct_name;
}


double Account:: GetBalance()
{
        return acct_balance;
}


Account::Debit(double p_amount)
{
        acct_balance += p_amount
}


Account::Credit(double p_amount)
{
        acct_balance −= p_amount
}
```

Figure 3-2.   *(continued)*

superclass). Attributes of objects in a class (instance variables) are also inherited. The inherited attributes may be different from the new attributes.

Messages.   We have frequently mentioned class methods as being functions that manipulate attribute values. It is worthwhile at this point to understand how methods are invoked. For this we will introduce another term used commonly in object-oriented programming, *messages*. Like *methods,* the term *messages* has been derived from SMALLTALK and has become common parlance in object-oriented programming with a specific meaning. While a method is a routine that manipulates attributes of an object, a message is a communication that invokes a method. The invocation of a method involves calling (and executing) the code that implements the method and binding the parameters of the call to the arguments of the call invocation.

Messages are sent to target objects. A message is sent with the name of the method, called the *selector* of the message, and one or more arguments that undergo binding with the actual arguments of the method. If this appears very similar to a subroutine call in conventional programming, it really is so. The primary difference is that the subroutine in object-oriented programming is a part of the object, a method.

The discussion above was a brief introduction to the concept and usage of classes. In the following sections, we will study how classes are used from a programming perspective.

3.3.4 Inheritance

Reusability of software has long been a significant issue. But rarely does one find that exactly the same routine fully addresses multiple phases of development (or software releases). Typically, the routine is imitated, refined to adapt to new requirements, and given a new name. All too frequently, the name is not changed, an occurrence that can cause real maintenance problems. Conventional programming environments have not adequately addressed this need. In object-oriented programming, on the other hand, this is a notable concern.

The concept of classes is the basic building block for reusable software. Classes provide a good modular decomposition technique for the application. For reusability, repetition and variation are essential. *Inheritance* provides the means for building new classes on top of an existing, less extensive hierarchy of classes instead of redesigning the class of objects in totality. The new class inherits both characteristics of the parent class: object attributes (as defined by instance variables) and the methods (or operations). This provides for not only inheriting the data representation of the object but also the operations that can be performed on the data within the object.

The operations defined for the class provide a set of services to the other objects. Inheritance allows creating a new class of objects that feature the same set of services. The new objects can be enhanced to provide new additional services not available in the parent. Existing services can be overloaded to adapt to new requirements (note that *overloading* is a feature whereby a class may have different methods sharing the same function name, but with different parameter declarations; the appropriate method is selected at runtime based on the argument datatype). Rather than developing the new class of objects from scratch, this process allows building on top of existing classes.

A significant benefit of inheritance is the ability to adjust objects to new requirements. The parent class is left in place to address current requirements while new requirements are addressed by the new class, both operating at the same time. Note that the changes to the inherited class have no impact on the parent class. The clients using the parent class remain undisturbed.

Inheritance can also be applied in the case where a number of related objects share a common set of attributes and services. A primary class may be defined that implements all the common properties, and a set of subclasses may be defined that implements the attributes and services unique to each type of object. As a simple example, consider a class of type "vehicle." All vehicles have attributes such as size, weight, color, miles per gallon, and so on. Subclasses may be defined for different vehicle types such as "land_vehicles," "water_vehicles," and "air_vehicles." These classes would each inherit the properties common to all vehicles. In addition, they would define additional properties relevant only to the specific vehicle type in the subclass. A class hierarchy of this nature is depicted in Figure 3-3.

Using classes.　　The determination that a class contains all the features required of the class is not a simple one. Very often, features change slightly or a new feature is added that would slightly modify the class. The decision and planning behind the definition of each class should be based on a conscious determination that the class as it stands already provides a coherent set of services to its potential users (or callers, otherwise called clients). If it turns out later that the class is indeed inadequate in addressing all needs and there is no way of updating the class definition without affecting at least some of its clients, then a new class has to be created. But rather than starting from scratch on defining a class, we can use the principles of inheritance (as described in the previous section and illustrated in Figure 3-3) and redefinition to create a new class by reusing parts of the old class.

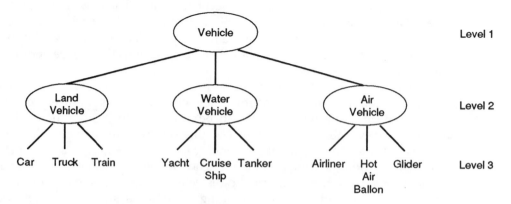

Figure 3-3.　Class Hierarchy due to Inheritance.

Using inherited methods.   Methods or operations define the services that can be provided by a class. A class is typically inherited for the specific purpose of defining a new class. A method defined for a certain class is inherited by its subclass. The inherited methods are now a part of the group of functions that can manipulate the set of instance variables of the subclass.

Typically, inheritance is used to create a subclass in which *structural* and *behavioral* changes have to be made. Structural changes change the instance variables and behavioral changes change the methods (or operations). In other words, structural changes change the structure of the object and behavioral changes change the services provided by the object.

Metaclasses.   The concept of a *metaclass* was originally defined for Small-talk and is a basic part of the SmallTalk terminology. We will therefore start with the SmallTalk view of the definition of a metaclass and then explain the more common principles for using metaclasses.

SmallTalk treats classes also as objects. A class is viewed as an instance of a higher-level class called a *metaclass*. A metaclass by itself is not different from a class except that it has instances that are also classes. Each class is a unique instance of its metaclass. This principle allows creating multiple levels of classes. It should be noted that the metaclass hierarchy is very similar to the class inheritance hierarchy.

We discussed earlier in this chapter the notion of objects being entities that exist at runtime and that classes, being different in concept, really do not have an existence at runtime. SmallTalk, however, allows class definitions to exist at runtime as objects. A class hierarchy in a system like this can encompass all aspects of the design of an application program.

Figure 3-4 describes the concept of a multilevel class hierarchy. In this figure, the root metaclass is called *object*. The instances of the metaclass object are

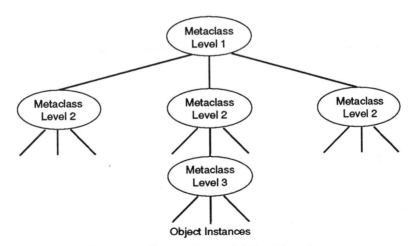

Figure 3-4.   Generic Class and Object Hierarchy.

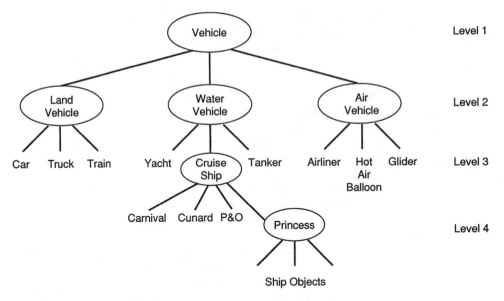

Figure 3-5.   Example of Class and Object Hierarchy.

the classes at the next lower level. The lowest level of the class hierarchy leads to the objects that are instances of the lowest-level class that comprises the objects.

If we replace the generic class and object names in Figure 3-4, we get the hierarchy illustrated in Figure 3-5. In this figure, the object's classes such as

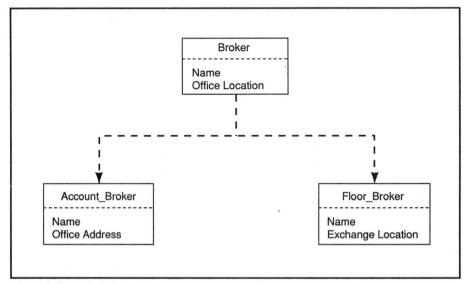

Client Hierarchy for Brokers

Figure 3-6.   Example of Class and Object Hierarchy.

"car", "truck", and "train" are at the lowest level. Each instance of a "car" is the lowest-level object in the "vehicle" hierarchy.

Figure 3-6 describes the class hierarchy for brokers. Figure 3-8 illustrates the coding for methods for object class *AccountBroker*. Note that one key difference between the AccountBroker and the FloorBroker objects is the office location versus the exchange location.

The example in Figures 3-7 through 3-9 describes how metaclasses are coded for inheritance and how the inherited properties are changed. In this example, the class "Broker" is inherited by the classes "AccountBroker" and "FloorBroker."

Figure 3-9 describes the methods for the object class *FloorBroker*. The difference in the methods has been kept very simple to point out advantages of object-oriented programming. The definitions for the *AccountBroker* and the *FloorBroker* are inherited from the class *BROKER* and then modified to make the required changes that distinguish the two subclasses.

3.3.5 Multiple Inheritance

We have seen the advantages of inheritance. In single inheritance, a subclass inherits the structural and behavioral properties of its parent class (sometimes called *superclass* or *metaclass*). Multiple inheritance allows combining the properties of several existing classes into a subclass. Manipulations performed on the subclass address the variables defined for all parent classes. For example, in Figure 3-3 we defined classes of vehicles by transportation method, such as, "land_vehicles," "water_vehicles," and "air_vehicles." We can also define classes of vehicles by the means they are powered, such as, "steam_turbines," "nuclear_reactor," "jet_propulsion," and "gasoline_engine." The properties of a car are derived from the classes "land_vehicles" and "gasoline_engine." A subclass "car" can be created by inheriting from both class "land_vehicles" and class "gasoline_engine." Figure 3-10 illustrates this example of multiple inheritance.

In the example just reviewed, the class "car" inherited properties from both classes it was derived from. In this kind of inheritance, both parents contribute toward the definition of a class "car" and add attributes and methods in comparable measure. Another use for multiple inheritance is to combine properties of two classes, primarily for convenience in handling the consolidated class so derived. In this case, one class may have the attributes and the other the methods; that is, the contribution of the parents is complementary and, in a sense, directly related.

A subclass created through multiple inheritance can undergo three types of redefinition. These three types are the following:

1. Static redefinition of variables and operations
2. Dynamic binding
3. Deferred classes

```
struct CommissionPlan
{
        SecurityType sec_type;
        Client * client;
        int num_shares;
        double percentage;
};

class Broker {
        String last_name;
        String first_name;
        String middle_name;
        String phone_number;
        int employee_id;
        Vec(CommissionPlan) commission_plan_list;
        Account * commission_acct;

public:
        void SetName(String p_last_name, String p_first_name, String
                        p_middle_name);
        void SetPhoneNumber(String p_phone_number);
        void SetEmployeeId(int p_employee_id);
        Money UpdateCommissionAccount(Security * p_security, int num_shares,
                                        Money p_price, DateTime
                                        p_trade_date);
        void AddCommissionPlan(CommissionPlan * p_plan);
        void RemoveCommissionPlan(CommissionPlan * p_plan);
};

void Broker::SetName(String p_last_name, String p_first_name, String
                        p_middle_name)
{

        last_name = p_last_name;
        first_name = p_first_name;
        middle_name = p_middle_name;
}

void Broker::SetPhoneNumber(String p_phone_number)
{

        phone_number = p_phone_number;
}

void Broker::SetEmployeeId(int p_employee_id)
{
```

Figure 3-7. Definition and Methods of Object *class BROKER.*

```
            employee_id = p_employee_id;
}


Money Broker::UpdateCommissionAccount(Security * p_security, Client *
                                p_client, int num_shares, Money
                                p_price, DateTime p_trade_date)
{
      // Brokers can receive commissions based on the type of security traded,
      // the client who requested the trade, and on the number of shares traded.
      // The commission_plan_list is searched first for a match on the specific
      // client.
      // If not found, then the list is searched for the security type. For simplicity
      // in the example, we will assume that the same commission rate will apply
      // regardless of the number of shares traded.

      CommissionPlan * cp;
      Money commission_amount;

      for (cp = commission_plan_list.First(); cp; cp = cp—>Next()){
            if (cp—>client = = p_client){
                  commission_amount = num_shares * p_price *
                                    cp—>percentage;
                  commission_account—>Credit(commission_amount);
                  return commission_amount;
            }
      }

      for (cp = commission_plan_list.First(); cp; cp = cp—>Next()){
            if cp—>sec_type = = p_security—>type){
                  commission_amount = num_shares * p_price *
                                    cp—>percentage;
                  commission_account—>Credit(commission_amount);
               return commission_amount;
            }
      }
}

void Broker::AddCommissionPlan(CommissionPlan * p_plan)
{
      commission_plan_list += p_plan;
}

void Broker::RemoveCommissionPlan(CommissionPlan * p_plan)
{
      commission_plan_list -= p_plan;
}
```

Figure 3-7. *(continued)*

AccountBroker Object

```
class AccountBroker : public Broker {
     String office;
     Vec(Client) client_list;

public:
     AccountBroker(String p_last_name, String p_first_name, String
                   p_middle_name, String p_phone_number, int
                   p_employee_id, String p_office);
     ~AccountBroker( );
     void SetOffice(String p_office);
     void AddClient(Client * p_client);
     void RemoveClient(Client * p_client);
     static void GetAccountBrokerByName(String p_last_name,
                                        Vec(AccountBroker) & broker_list);
};

AccountBroker::AccountBroker(String p_last_name, String p_first_name, String
                            p_middle_name, String p_phone_number, int
                            p_employee_id, String p_office)
{
     last_name = p_last_name;
     first_name = p_first_name;
     middle_name = p_middle_name;
     employee_id = p_employee_id;
     office = p_office;

     commission_acct = new Account(AT_BROKER_COMMISSION, 0.0, 0.0);
}

AccountBroker::~AccountBroker( )
{
     for (CommissionPlan * cp = commission_plan_list.First( ); cp;
        cp = commission_plan_list.Next( ))
        delete cp;
}

void AccountBroker::SetOffice(String p_office)
{
     office = p_office;
}

void AccountBroker::AddClient(Client * p_client)
{
```

Figure 3-8. Methods for Object *class AccountBroker*.

```
      for (Client * c = client_list.First( ); c; c = client_list.Next( ))
          if (c == p_client) return;

      client_list += p_client;
}

void AccountBroker::RemoveClient(Client * p_client)
{
      for (Client * c = client_list.First( ); c; c = client_list.Next( ))
          if (c == p_client) {
              client_list -= c;
              break;
          }

static void AccountBroker::GetAccountBrokerByName(String p_last_name,
                                                  Vec(AccountBroker) &
                                                  broker_list)
{
      for AccountBroker * b in AccountBroker suchthat
          last_name = p_last_name
          broker_list += b;
}
```

Figure 3-8. *(continued)*

```
FloorBroker Object

class FloorBroker : public Broker {
      String exchange_name;

public:
      FloorBroker (String p_last_name, String p_first_name, String
                  p_middle_name, String p_phone_number, int p_employee_id,
                  String p_exchange);
      ~FloorBroker( );
      void SetExchange(String p_exchange);
      static void GetFloorBrokerByName(String p_last_name, Vec(FloorBroker) &
                                       broker_list);
};

FloorBroker::FloorBroker(String p_last_name, String p_first_name, String
                         p_middle_name, String p_phone_number, int
                         p_employee_id, String p_exchange)
{
```

Figure 3-9. Methods for Object *class FloorBroker*.

```
            last_name = p_last_name;
            first_name = p_first_name;
            middle_name = p_middle_name;
            phone_number = p_phone_number;
            employee_id = p_employee_id;
            exchange_name = p_exchange;
            commission_acct = new Account(AT_BROKER_COMMISSION, 0.0, 0.0);
}

FloorBroker::~FloorBroker( )
{
      for (CommissionPlan * cp = commission_plan_list.First( ); cp;
          cp = commission_plan_list.Next( ))
          delete cp;
}

void FloorBroker::SetExchange(String p_exchange)
{
      exchange_name = p_exchange;
}

static void FloorBroker::GetFloorBrokerByName(String p_last_name,
                                        Vec(FloorBroker) & broker_list)
{
      for FloorBroker * b in FloorBroker suchthat last_name = p_last_name
          broker_list += b;
}
```

Figure 3-9. (*continued*)

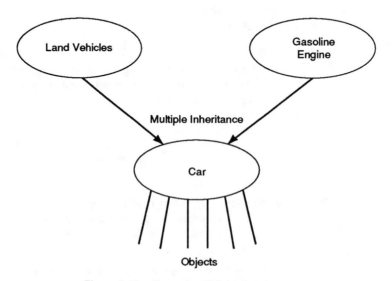

Figure 3-10. Example of Multiple Inheritance.

As we noted earlier in the section on inheritance, redefinition itself can create some level of complexities. Dynamic binding and deferred classes have the potential of adding significant new levels of complexity. One major potential for problems is due to conflicts, especially in the case of deferred actions (both dynamic binding and deferred methods). A name clash is a very common example of a conflict. Other types of conflicts are more complex. Very careful designing is required to successfully use multiple inheritance.

Uses for multiple inheritance.   We used a quick example of a car to illustrate the concept of multiple inheritance. There are a number of significant practical uses for multiple inheritance. We will list just a few of the interesting uses for multiple inheritance:

1. Creation of a subclass that has properties common to the parents; this is a very common use for practical business applications.
2. Creating a library of routines defined as methods in "utility" classes. These basic methods can be used by a number of classes through multiple inheritance. A class that needs to use them is created through multiple inheritance from its functional parent as well as the "utility" classes. These methods can be redefined to serve the specific functions for the new class. This is analogous to the use of subroutine libraries in conventional programming.
3. Creation of *persistent objects,* that is, objects that are retained in memory or disk for long durations. A special subclass can be created for all objects that need to be stored for long durations in files or in memory. The primary operations supported by this subclass are *store* and *retrieve.*

3.3.6 Dynamic Object Redefinitions

Inheritance facilitates re-creating object classes with identical properties. But the primary objective is to create an object class with similar, but not identical, attributes and methods. The structure and behavior of an inherited object class is changed by redefining it or by changing its behavior dynamically. In the discussion in this section, we will review the following means for changing the structure and behavior of inherited objects:

1. Redefinition
2. Dynamic binding
3. Polymorphism
4. Deferred classes

Redefinition.   Use of dynamic binding has some pitfalls associated with it. Chief among them is the potential for redefinition of an object that may result in a change in the semantics of the routine. *Redefinition* is frequently used to redefine the features inherited by a child class from its parent class. The redefinition is intended to achieve a different implementation from the inherited object. The redefined version of a method (or routine) has arguments that match those of the original in number and (usually in type, but not necessarily in value or semantics. The redefined method may operate differently from the original. Managed properly, this is the equivalent of creating a new version for the method. If not properly managed, redefinition with dynamic binding can produce binding errors or strange unexpected results. The impact of redefinition in dynamic binding is controlled by defining preconditions and postconditions for the routine. Preconditions limit the scope of the input parameters, and postconditions limit the range of output parameters, thereby limiting what the object will accept as valid input and what the object will return to the caller. The preconditions and postconditions carry through the redefinition and, if properly defined, prevent potential dynamic binding errors.

Dynamic binding.   Multiple versions can create an interesting side effect. The variables cannot be predefined for binding because the version of the corresponding method that should be used is not known beforehand. Any versions available can be selected dynamically at runtime. The capability to bind the variables dynamically at runtime after selecting the method is called *dynamic binding* (or *late binding*). This is indeed a very potent capability in object-oriented programming. Dynamic binding implies that the dynamic form of the object at runtime determines which version of the method (or operation) is applied. In effect, the methods (operations) are being adjusted dynamically for the state of the object. Note that with normal binding (also called *static binding*) the methods are allocated at compile time.

For dynamic binding, the parent class defines a method as *virtual.* Defining a method as virtual implies that derived classes have the option of redefining methods (that is, provide their own implementation or version of the method). Invocation of that method at runtime will result in the dynamic allocation of the method appropriate to that object.

Dynamic binding provides a number of general benefits. The following lists the key benefits of dynamic binding:

1. Objects at the subclass level perform different functions even though they are invoked by the same message. In other words, the program can be set up in a generalized manner and the differences in the handling of data are achieved through dynamic binding.
2. Programming is made easier because generalized program flow and messages (object-to-object communications) follow a generalized design. The subtle differences in the operation of similar objects are achieved through dynamic binding.

3. Applications can be designed in an identical manner for geographically distributed facilities of the enterprise and can be customized for local differences using dynamic binding. The local differences are achieved through multiple versions of the methods.

Polymorphism.   Polymorphism is an ability that allows an entity to take different profiles. It is the property that allows an object to dynamically change, at runtime, the class and instance of that class it is referring to. Since different classes of objects can interpret a message in their own manner and apply the variables according to the methods stored within the objects of that class, the same message is interpreted in different ways by different classes of objects.

The notion of polymorphism is a very powerful capability for programming. It is complementary to dynamic binding and presents a potential for layering of programs where uniformity can be maintained at a higher level even though lower-level processing may be significantly different. Inheritance, redefinition, and dynamic binding play an important role in the use of polymorphism in object-oriented programming for achieving a high level of programming flexibility and functionality.

Deferred classes.   Typically, when a class is inherited, the methods undergo redefinition when a subclass is created. Some programming languages provide the concept of *deferred classes* to facilitate forced redefinition. We have already discussed the use of *dynamic binding*, which allows the programmer to specify dynamic binding for variables at runtime, after selecting the method.

Dynamic binding does not address the case where the method needs to change to provide a service of the same name and general type but adapted to the dynamic requirements based on the object selected at runtime. The solution to this problem is provided by *deferred classes*. A deferred class contains a *deferred method*. A deferred method makes it incumbent on the subclass, after inheritance, to provide its own implementation of the deferred method. The method as defined in the parent class is effective only as long as it is not deferred.

Let us review an example (see Figure 3-11) of the pseudocode describing how a deferred method is set up.

Benefits of redefinition for prototyping.   In conventional programming, rapid prototyping is achieved by creating stubs for subroutine calls that have not been coded. This allows checking the high-level logic of a program or a function. The stub is replaced by different versions of code to see the effect of changes from one version to another. The concepts of inheritance, especially dynamic binding and deferred classes, yield the same benefits for rapid prototyping. The higher-level classes are created as deferred classes. A variety of different actions can then be integrated and checked by recoding the methods or operations in the lower-level classes. This scheme of prototyping allows testing out a number of approaches at the lower level while keeping the overall design very consistent

```
class drawable {

protected:                                    (Note: this allows subclass access)
        short       center_x;
        short       center_y;
        int         size;

public:
        virtual     ˉdrawable() = 0;
        virtual     draw() = 0;
        virtual     erase() = 0;
};

class circle : public drawable {

public:
        circle(short x, short y, short diameter) : (x, y, diameter) {}
        ˉcircle();
        void draw();
        void erase;
};

circle::draw()
{
        Point       P;
        P.x = x;
        P.y = y;
        win_draw_circle (P, size/Z);
}

circle::erase()
{
        Point       P;
        P.x = x;
        P.y = y;
        win_erase_circle (P, size/Z);
}

circle::ˉcircle()
{
        erase();
}
```

Figure 3-11. Example of Deferred Methods.

throughout the prototyping process. In fact, this allows prototyping a number of different outcomes at the lower level with the same higher-level design. In this scheme, the deferred modules can indeed start out as stubs and are added once the high-level design is clearly established. This approach is akin to the top-down programming approach.

It may be worth pointing out here that, unlike the traditional concepts of either *top-down* or *bottom-up* programming styles, object-oriented programming is a little of both. The top-down component represents the class hierarchy and the bottom-up component represents the lowest-level object definitions. The two components meet in the happy middle ground of binding available objects to required classes through intermediate objects and classes.

3.3.7 Object Identity

The property of an object that distinguishes it from all other objects is called *object identity*. In object-oriented systems, this property of an object is independent of content, type, and addressability. Object identity is the only property of an object maintained across structural and behavioral modifications of an object. That is, the identity of the object is maintained even when an object undergoes *redefinition* (note that no new object is created when either the structure or behavior is changed for an object that already exists).

Another way to look at it is that an object's identity is analogous to a *handle* that distinguishes one object from another. The identity of the object remains permanently associated with that object despite structural and state changes. Every object created in an object-oriented system is assigned an object identity. If the object is designed as a persistent object, the identity is maintained through the life of the object, even if the object is stored on disk.

The ability to uniquely identify each object is essential for managing persistent objects. It is also essential for maintaining relationships among objects. Object identity allows distinguishing between objects of the same class that may have very subtle differences.

Identification method.   There are potentially many ways to distinguish objects from one another. At the very highest level, they are distinguished by the class of objects. While in memory, they can be distinguished by storage address, usually maintained in most languages as a variable name. A variable name is a temporary means of identification. The same variable name may be assigned to a different object at a different time frame. Similarly, the location of an object also distinguishes one object from another. For example, two objects with identical variable names at two separate network nodes are really different objects. An address-based or variable-name-based identification is implemented in most programming languages through *pointers* to variables. The pointer addresses are assigned at runtime. Until the program is loaded, the pointers remain as relative addresses. Binding an object to a variable and, consequently, to an address provides a temporary means of identification.

For a truly distributed network, persistent objects residing in servers at various locations require a permanent means of identification that is unique across the networks. This identification must be maintained within the object and must not be changed irrespective of potential bindings that the object may undergo. We will define a rule for unique object identification as follows:

> **Rule:** *An object must have an identifier that is unique in a time dimension (that is, it does not change with time) as well as with location (that is, its identity does not change with its location in a network) such that it cannot be modified by any programmed action.*

The unique identifier of an object may be an attribute of the object that is unique for each instance of an object in a particular class. Alternatively, an object may be assigned a name attribute (for example, a combination of a class identifier and the instance number of the object) that uniquely identifies the object. Let us review the implications of unique identification of a persistent object in a network.

When an object is created, its object identifier must be unique across all hosts (or database servers) in the network. Probably, 32 bits will not be sufficient for an efficient general-purpose algorithm. The algorithm must also take into account the potential for methods to be stored on a network host different from the network host for attributes. To be unique in a distributed environment, it should probably contain some component of the host name or address (such as its internet address) or a server ID where the object was first created. (This component is only used to guarantee uniqueness, since an object may move from one server to another; it will have no other relevance.)

Another component of the object identifier may be a class identifier. (Note that this issue of assigning class identifiers in object-oriented databases is similar to the issue of assigning identifiers to metaclasses as objects in SmallTalk). Using a class identifier as part of an object identifier could be useful, but it may not be necessary to guarantee uniqueness. Furthermore, if class identifiers must also be unique and if they use the same algorithm for assignment, this could lead to infinite recursion. It may be better in a real system to reference an object by two identifiers, the class identifier and the object identifier.

We have specified that an object identifier must include as a component the host or server identifier. It must also contain a component that is unique within that host. It could use a counter that is incremented for each object that is created. The counter, of course, must be a persistent object in the database. It could also use date and time of day (a 32-bit value). This could be useful for other reasons as well. However, date and time of day may not be adequate to ensure uniqueness; two servers may coincidently assign the same date and time. If a single server process across the entire network is assigning identifiers, these conflicts can be overcome. Further granularity, if necessary, can be achieved by using fractions of seconds in the time of day.

This discussion indicates that a network-unique identifier has a number of components, including the host name, class identifier, object ID, creation date and time, and so on. This composite identifier is, in a sense, the equivalent of a *handle* and can be used as such in programming.

Object identification of database systems.   Relational database management systems use record identifiers (unique keys derived from one or more attributes of an entity) to distinguish among records. The record identifier is a unique label for every row in a relation. Common examples of such record identifiers include account numbers, names of individuals or businesses, social security numbers, and so on. Names of individuals or businesses may be used in combination with addresses and social security numbers to overcome the potential of two people having an identical name.

While similar identifiers can be used for objects in a database, this approach has the potential of violating our basic rule for uniquely identifying objects. Any field in a database table is subject to being modified as long as it is accessible to users. Most relational databases also provide the capability for using a system-generated autoincrement number as a unique key that a user cannot alter. Uniqueness can also be maintained by hiding the identifier from the user and never reusing the same identifier. While this approach works well in a relational environment where the keys in two tables must be identical for a join, this may lead to problems in an object-oriented system because instances of the two classes equivalent to the two tables must have unique identifiers. The equivalent functionality can be achieved in an object-oriented database by using identical attributes in the join criteria. Arbitrary joins of this type are not inherently supported in object-oriented databases. It will be an interesting exercise for the reader to explore this further to determine how joins can be achieved in an object-oriented database environment.

Identities of copied and merged objects.   Some key questions remain for managing objects that may be copied and modified and for objects that may be identical but have different identities. While the two notions are very clear and straightforward in relational databases, the object-oriented environment presents some challenges due to the nature of encapsulation of an object.

When a row is copied, it is identical to the original row until an attribute is modified. In fact, copying is used just for that purpose so that additional data entry is avoided. Copying an object is a little different in that the very act of copying requires that the new object have a unique identifier. This implies that the objects may be identical with respect to all their attributes, but are still different because of a unique identifier. Typically, after copying an object its attributes or methods are modified in a manner very similar to a relational record.

In a typical relational database, duplicate rows are essentially ignored. However, duplicate objects have unique object identifiers and the duplicate cannot be ignored. If a message is sent to either of the objects, theoretically, either of the objects will perform the same function. This may change, however, if dynamic binding is applied. It is not trivial to compare objects automatically in a system, especially a large system, to determine if there are duplicate objects. Care should be taken during design to ensure that no duplicate objects are created. If duplicate objects must be created, it may be desirable to store identical copies of objects in different sets or as components of different parent objects. Otherwise, for normal inheritance functions, care should be taken that any copy operation is followed by changing the object attributes or methods to ensure that duplicate objects are avoided.

Versioning.   Objects may have one or more versions. Multiple versions are created to address the need for slight dissimilarities in the services provided by these objects and, consequently, in the operations and methods. Such a need may arise if the software architecture is highly decentralized and the same functions are performed in a somewhat dissimilar manner at different locations. In typical conventional programming this is taken care of by dividing the function among a number of routines that fragment the knowledge about the operation, thereby adapting to the variety of requirements. For example, data transfers via a stack of communications protocols are split across back-end and front-end modules of software. A change in the back end common to all protocols (even if it is prompted by a change in one of the front-end protocols) may affect the operation of all other protocols unless specifically excluded. This problem is solved in object-oriented programming by defining a number of versions for the methods to address the diverse processing requirements for a particular object. Alternatively, a unique object can be derived for each unique version of an operation.

Tracking multiple versions may become unmanageable. An approach to resolving this problem is to rebind the new version of the object with a new class library.

Object identity in networks.   We touched on earlier the issue of maintaining a unique object identity across networks. Objects in general, and persistent objects in particular, must be identified uniquely across the entire network. This is crucial for maintaining database integrity and ensuring that proper transaction management can take place. A unique identity across the network ensures that the object can be accessed no matter where it is currently in use (and therefore, potentially, in memory). Unique identification of objects is also very important for maintaining different versions of objects created as a result of distributed transactions in progress.

Objects *replicated* in different hosts for achieving high performance must be addressable via the unique identifier. Replicated objects must be updated in a synchronized manner. Objects may be duplicated and updated locally on a temporary basis for transactions.

Once again, it is essential that the unique identifier of an object in a distributed environment not be subject to modification by the user by virtue of relocation of the object from one node to another in the network. Especially in systems that maintain historical data through various versions of updates to the attributes, identity becomes the only means of distinguishing between the objects. Strong support of object identity is essential for temporal data models, because a single retrieval may involve multiple historical versions of a single object. Such support requires the database system to provide a continuous and consistent notion of identity throughout the life of each object, independent of any descriptive data or structure that is user modifiable. This identity is the common thread that ties together these historical versions of an object.

3.4 OBJECT ORIENTATION FOR DATABASE SYSTEMS

In this chapter we have reviewed object-oriented programming and the object model in some detail. It is time to collect our thoughts and analyze how these notions of object management apply to the realm of object-oriented databases. There is no clearly established definition of object-oriented databases. Rather than leave it as an open issue, we will define our perspective of an object-oriented database and use this perspective as a working model throughout the design exercise in Part III. Our basic model consists of the following rules or requirements for an object-oriented database:

Rule 1: *The following basic properties of object-oriented systems are adhered to by the object-oriented database.*
- *Object-based modular structure*
- *Data abstraction*
- *Dynamic binding*
- *Automatic memory management*
- *Classes and deferred classes*
- *Inheritance*
- *Repeated and multiple inheritance*

Rule 2: *The object-oriented database provides support for persistent objects, atomic transactions, concurrency control, and rollback recovery.*

Rule 3: *The object-oriented database provides support for complex object storage, indexing of objects for fast update and retrieval, and grouping of objects by classes.*

Rule 4: *A high-level object-oriented programming language is provided for ad hoc query and update as well as for developing object-oriented application programs.*

The rules enumerated above form the basis of a minimal object-oriented database management system. The rules are embodied in a number of features visible externally to the application developer and the user. In the following section we will discuss these features in detail.

3.4.1 Object Paradigm for Database Management Systems

As we saw in Chapter 2, database management systems consist of two major components: the access mechanism and the storage mechanism. The access mechanism determines the essential features of the programming language. The storage mechanism defines how data is stored and, specifically, how relations are specified.

Object orientation in a database can be implemented either in the access mechanism or the storage mechanism, or in both. Object orientation in the access mechanism is achieved by providing an object-oriented programming language as the front end that may actually connect to a relational back end. The normal properties of classes, inheritance, and constraints are programmed and maintained in the front end. Similarly, the application developer must also maintain the association of the *methods* with the corresponding data objects in the back end. Obviously, the programming task becomes quite complex. The primary benefit is that the real advantages of object-oriented systems can be derived from such a system. A common implementation of such a system is the use of C++ language as the programming front end. Some implementations have gone beyond this to facilitate object-level programming in a higher-level, custom-designed programming language.

As we noted earlier in this chapter, the basic difference between object-oriented programming and traditional (or conventional) programming methods is that object-oriented programming calls for data and functions to be encapsulated into *reusable objects*. Remember that objects are themselves instances of a "class," which is basically a template for creating objects. One notable advantage of this *object-class* approach is that whenever a programmer changes a function or adds a new function to a particular class, all the subclasses and all the objects represented by these classes will inherit the same capabilities. This is a very considerable benefit because a third of the programming time, for information systems, is spent in making changes emanating from changes in user requirements. Object-oriented programming provides long-term benefits, particularly in the reduction of software maintenance costs.

It is important to note that if the database storage mechanism is object oriented it stands to reason that the programming environment is also object oriented. Otherwise, manipulation of objects can become very complex to program in a traditional nonobject-oriented environment. True object-oriented databases, in our definition, implement object orientation in both the access mechanism and the storage mechanism. They create the actual class and object data structure.

In our view, a true object-oriented database is based on the *object* paradigm. The object paradigm is a natural way of organizing data. It offers an integrated data model for both structural data components and general-purpose manipulation routines associated with these data components. The object paradigm allows users (and programmers) to structure, retrieve, and update data in terms of the context of the application. Having defined true object-oriented databases, we can summarize by stating the following rule as our measure of a true object-oriented database management system:

> **Rule:** *A true object-oriented database management system is based on the object paradigm, and both the access mechanism and the storage mechanism are object oriented.*

According to this definition, the characteristics of object management described in Section 3.2 are all applicable to object-oriented database management. Let us analyze these concepts as they apply to object-oriented database management. The following lists the features that an object-oriented database must have to be effective:

1. Encapsulation
2. Classes
3. Multiple inheritance
4. Capability to define sets
5. Persistence of objects
6. Versions of objects
7. Object-oriented programming

3.4.2 Features of Object-oriented Databases

A real object-oriented database must provide the capabilities to create and maintain persistent and versioned objects. These features are in addition to the basic properties of objects, such as encapsulation, classes, and multiple inheritance. We will, in the following discussion, describe how each of these features molds the functionality of an object-oriented database.

Encapsulation.   *Abstract data typing* (described in detail in Section 3.3.1) or *encapsulation* permits a class of data structures representing object instances to be specified by the *services* available on the data structures (that is, operations that can be performed on them) and the formal *properties* of the services (features). This implies that an abstract data type is a class of data structures whose internal implementation is hidden from the outside world. The outside world sees only an external view consisting of available services and properties of these services. In an object database, encapsulation facilitates creation of objects (via abstract data-type definitions) that have the operations to preprocess the object attributes in a format expected by external programs. For example, if the attribute consists of image or voice data that must be preprocessed, the outside world sees the data only after the preprocessing. Handling of complex data in this manner ensures completeness and precision in handling and nonambiguity to the external interfaces. The external interfaces get the data in precisely the form they expect it. The internal implementation can be modified without affecting the external definition.

Encapsulation is an essential feature for the database of an enterprise-wide system where storage and presentation of data may differ significantly across storage locations and the display facilities. Encapsulation allows specification of data structures such that the same data can be presented in a different manner to different users by performing required transformations internally to convert to advertised external interfaces (part of exported services for the data structure).

Data structures that have the same properties are members of the same class. Let us take a closer look at why *class* definitions are so important in an object-oriented database.

Classes.   An important concept in object-oriented programming is that of *class* (described in Section 3.3.3). Class definitions provide the programming mechanism for implementing data encapsulation, inheritance, and multiple inheritance. Using classes makes it easier to define a set of objects with common properties. Refer to Section 3.3.3 for examples of how classes are defined and used.

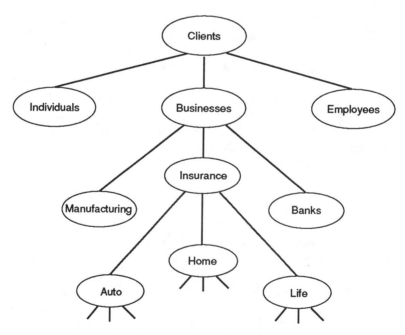

Figure 3-12.   Example of Class Hierarchy for Accounts.

The examples in Section 3.3.3 describe how classes and subclasses can be set up for a hierarchical view of vehicles. Similarly, a hierarchical view can be set up for clients consisting of the levels described in Figure 3-12. This practical use of classes demonstrates the importance of class definitions in an object-oriented database.

A review of classes of objects automatically brings into perspective the features of inheritance of objects. Two other important properties of objects used in databases are *persistence* and *versioning*.

Multiple inheritance.   Aside from the features already described in Section 3.3.5, *multiple inheritance* has additional importance in a database. In an object-oriented database, it is possible to design all objects as inheriting attributes of a generic *persistent database object* (we will call it a base object). These attributes may include the following:

- Object ID
- Class ID
- Owner/creator
- Creation date
- Modification date
- UID of last user to modify object
- Permanent object location (DB server in charge of object)
- Lock status
- Use in current transaction
- Version

The capability of multiple inheritance is required to allow objects to inherit properties from their class in addition to the base object.

Object set definition and object clusters.   In relational databases, all records of a given type can be thought of as members of a set of objects known as a table. A table is a real runtime entity in a relational system, just as records are. In an object-oriented database, the class definition shares some of the properties of a relational database table in that it defines the structural characteristics of the objects. But a class is, in general, not regarded as a runtime entity. Object-oriented databases require additional constructs to provide the characteristics of set processing in a manner somewhat similar to the set-processing characteristics of relational databases.

Sets are useful in object-oriented databases both as a means of grouping objects for application manipulation and grouping objects for storage. Objects sets for storage are typically referred to as *object clusters*. A given database may cluster and store together all objects of a given class (and/or its derived classes). However, in a fully distributed database, objects of a given class may move from one server to another quite frequently. In this situation, each server may maintain just a subset of all objects of the class. It may be useful for an application to be able to refer to and manipulate specific subsets of objects. A good object-oriented database should provide the capability to create named sets of objects. Such sets of objects may either be implemented as a group of actual objects that are stored and distributed together or as dynamic arrays of object IDs that reference the objects that may or may not exist on the same server (that is, act as an object group name server).

The object-oriented database programming language $O++$[2] includes set-oriented features for retrieving objects from the database in a manner similar to relational query languages. There is an extension to the *for* statement that allows a set of objects to be retrieved based on specifications of certain attributes. For example, given the class

```
class person {
        char name[30];
        int age;
};
```

to find and print the names of all persons older than age 30, the following code could be used:

```
for p in person
    if (p -> age > 30)
        puts(p -> name);
```

In the $O++$ environment, all objects of a given type are grouped within a cluster with the same name as the class. Thus all *person* objects belong to the *person* cluster. *Subclusters* may be formed so that subsets of the person objects may be grouped together.

The set-processing features of the object-oriented database programming language should allow optimizations on retrievals to be performed within the data server, not unlike that provided in relational databases.

Persistent objects.   Database objects persist either in memory or on disk beyond the lifetime of the program that creates them and are usually stored on disk in an organized manner for future use. In a relational database, all records are persistent because they are retained on disk in the form of database tables. In an object-oriented database with a fully integrated object-oriented programming

---

[2] R. Agrawal and N. H. Gehani, "ODE (Object Databases and Environment): The Language and the Data Model," AT&T Bell Laboratories Technical Memorandum, Murray Hill, N.J., 1989.

R. Agrawal and N. Gehani, "Rationale for the Design of Persistence and Query Processing Facilities in the Database Programming Language O++," *2nd International Workshop on Database Programming Languages,* Oregon Coast, June 1989.

environment, objects may be either temporary (process based) or permanent (database server or disk based). The methods defined for an object class may operate on either type. Objects can also become persistent due to inherited attributes and methods of a class (for example, base class), which defines the object to be a part of database storage. Persistence of objects can occur due to their relationship with other persistent objects and due to methods within the objects that, under certain circumstances, may change their definition to make them persistent objects.

Versioning.   Many database applications, such as computer-aided design, use multiple versions of the same object. Object versions are also important in databases such as accounting and financial applications that maintain historical information. For example, versions can be used to store previous year financial information. In addition to maintaining a history of changes, version management is also very useful for managing concurrent access to objects. Generally used for transaction management, a new version of the object is created for each update transaction in progress. The unmodified object remains available for nonupdate queries. Sequencing of updates and version management at the application level must be determined by the application developer if multiple updates are allowed to progress in parallel. The updates can be applied to the object in the same sequence in which versions were created so that the changes are not really lost. In other words, the changes are applied as if the transactions took place sequentially rather than concurrently.

Object-oriented programming.   Object-oriented programming is a way of structuring software so that data, relationships between data components, and code to manipulate the data components are combined into single entities known as *objects*. Thinking in terms of objects makes it easier to organize and maintain large programs.

Object-oriented programming makes use of the characteristics of encapsulation, classes, inheritance, persistency, and versioning noted in the section above. For example, the ability of object-oriented programming to encapsulate (or hide) all but the most necessary information about each object means that programmers do not need to know or modify an object's internal implementation scheme while maintaining a system. In fact, in a large development team, programmers can use objects effectively without the need to know the internal implementation of an object. As is obvious, once designed, objects can be reused by many applications. Newer applications can build on older applications by inheriting objects and customizing inherited objects for the needs of the new application.

Reusability of code has been touched on a number of times. There are some basic programming requirements to ensure reusability. For objects to be reusable, autonomous classes must provide the only structuring mechanism for the system. We noted earlier in this chapter that a class is an implementation of an abstract data type, and an object is an instance of a class. Classes can have *client* or *inheritance* relationships. In a client relationship, one class uses the services of another class.

As compared to conventional programming that is driven by what a system *does*, object-oriented programming is driven by what the system *does it to*. Consequently, object-oriented programming is driven by data structures that describe the objects. Since objects also include *methods*, these data structures must also manage the functions used in conventional programming. In conventional programming, functions drive the program. In object-oriented programming, while functions no longer define the system or program structure or drive the program, functions (or methods) still play a critical role in that they are essential to the complete definition of the class. Figure 3-13 illustrates the use of data structures and functions for defining a class.

It is obvious that if object-oriented programming is so different from conventional programming, prototyping an object-oriented system will be very different also. Conventional programming is characterized by analysis, prototyping, design, implementation, and testing. An object-oriented design is characterized by a much greater user-level input in the early phases for designing

```
class account {

private:
        short       account_number;
        char        account_type;
        char        account_name[20];
        double      balance;

public:

        Account(short account_number, char account_type,
                const char account_name);
        ~Account();
        double GetBalance();
        char GetAccountType();
        const char *GetAccountName();
        void Debit(double amount);
        void Credit(double amount);

};
```

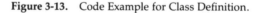

Figure 3-13. Code Example for Class Definition.

the objects. Consequently, the data definition and prototyping stages of an object-oriented design are considerably more intense. The classes must be defined very clearly to reflect the business operations accurately. The more complex the object classes, the more intense is the prototyping phase. Object classes that are very broad in definition, with many subclasses and innumerable relationships, will make the prototyping and design phases very strenuous. The designer must address a number of different levels of abstraction in a large system.

Object-oriented programming requires an extended compiler such as C++, as well as an object-oriented programming environment. A language such as C++ is the equivalent of a 3GL (third-generation language) such as the C language. While C++ is very useful for object-oriented programming, 4GLs (fourth-generation languages) dedicated to object-oriented database management systems are appearing in increasing numbers and with greater sophistication.

It is important that object-oriented programming languages be able to support *polymorphism* (the ability of objects from different classes to respond in their own appropriate manner to a single common message). It is the combination of inheritance, encapsulation, and polymorphism that brings object-oriented programming its true superiority as a programming discipline. When properly implemented, object-oriented programming results in class libraries that are more generic and reusable than typical subroutine libraries created within conventional programming languages. Furthermore, due to encapsulation, they are easier to debug and maintain.

In addition to extensions to the C language and its extension to the C++ language, a number of other dedicated object-oriented programming languages such as O++ and programming environments such as *SmallTalk*, *Objectworks*, and *QuickPascal* are in use.

It is imperative to point out here that, while object-oriented programming has considerable advantages, it is very different from conventional programming and demands much greater attention and analysis in the early stages of design. Object-oriented 4GLs associated with an object-oriented database and supported by a rich object-oriented development environment make the task of programming an object-oriented system easier. Nonetheless, there are no shortcuts to analysis and design.

In this section, we looked at some basic features of an object-oriented database management system. It should be recognized that the features described above are the minimum necessary for a database to qualify as an object-oriented database. There are some features that are commonly available in relational databases that would significantly enhance the capability of object-oriented relational databases and would also remove some of the major concerns relative to database integrity and consistency of an object-oriented database.

The following section presents a hybrid approach that benefits from the better features of object-oriented and relational database management systems. We believe that this hybrid approach removes the limitations of flexibility in a relational database and database integrity in an object-oriented database.

3.5 RELATIONAL EXTENSIONS TO OBJECT-ORIENTED DATABASE SYSTEMS

As we have noted in the previous sections, relational databases have a different set of strengths from object-oriented databases. More interestingly, some of the key strengths of relational databases are weaknesses in object-oriented databases. Adding some of these specialized features of relational databases to object-oriented databases provides an answer that potentially combines the best of both worlds. In this section we will analyze the design of a true object-oriented relational database system by analyzing how some of the salient features of relational databases are applied to the object-oriented databases.

The features of true object-oriented databases were discussed in the previous section. Close scrutiny of these features reveals a few major deficiencies in object-oriented databases as compared to relational databases. These features are essentially the features derived from the rigorous mathematical foundation of the relational model, as well as the ability to apply constraints uniformly on a class of objects. The following lists the features considered to be the major strength of relational databases.

1. Automatically enforced relational integrity
2. User-defined constraints
3. Business rules

Adding these features, typical to relational databases, in object-oriented databases provides the benefits of the developments in relational databases in a true object-oriented environment. The hybrid so created overcomes the limitations of object-oriented databases as well as relational databases. This may indeed pave the way for the evolving generation of database systems. Let us evaluate the implications of the factors noted above.

Automatically enforced integrity. In the relational world, as we saw in Section 2.4.1, there are three types of system-defined integrity, as noted in the following, that can be enforced automatically by the system:

1. *Domain integrity:* Domain integrity governs the allowable values that each attribute within the logical data model can assume. This check includes a datatype check as well as a data range check.
2. *Entity integrity:* No attribute that is a part of a primary key of a relation can be a NULL. This implies that not only is an object identified uniquely by its object identifier, but also that it has a unique relation and a unique reason for existence. In other words, the object can be referenced unambiguously by one of its attributes.

3. *Referential integrity:* This type of integrity constraint implies that an object (the equivalent of a row in a table) cannot be deleted if its primary key is referenced by a foreign key in another object.

A good relational database not only stores these integrity checks within the database, but also applies them automatically whenever the value of the attribute is updated or deleted.

Note that the important point here is that in a relational database the database stores these checks and applies them automatically and uniformly to all applications. No application can bypass them. A good object-oriented database implementation would also handle integrity checks in a similar manner. The structural flexibility of object-oriented databases makes this all but impossible. Let us analyze the differences between the enforcement of constraints and integrity checks.

Preconditions and postconditions allow setting up rules for domain integrity and entity integrity in object-oriented databases. However, they are applied at the object class level and can be changed easily by redefinition of the objects or rebinding of objects to another class library.

Object-oriented databases do not accommodate the concept of a foreign key. An object identifier is the primary key for an object. Consequently, referential integrity checks have to be programmed into the methods that update or delete objects.

User-defined constraints.   Developers use constraints in a relational database to ensure database consistency and proper handling of updates of data for interrelated actions. Constraints are applied to updates to ensure that only legal updates are allowed. Like integrity constraints, *triggers* monitor the database for occurrences of certain conditions programmed in the trigger. They perform user-programmed actions on occurrence of the conditions during updates and deletions. For example, if the account is 60 days past due or the balance has reached a predetermined level, the trigger can be set to turn off further charges against the account. Triggers may force operations involving other tables in the database.

In an object-oriented database, *preconditions* and *postconditions* are two types of potential constraints that can be used as triggers. Precondition constraints are checked at the calling function to ensure proper conditions for calling. Postconditions are checked on return to ensure a proper return. Object-oriented databases, due to their inherent flexibility, generally do not provide the rigid integrity constraints built into the better relational databases. However, careful programming can provide the same level of protection in an object-oriented database as in a relational database. For example, methods in other objects can be invoked if a particular condition is met. Once again, while it is feasible to set up constraints, there is no mechanism to ensure automatic uniform application of constraints.

Ideally, the capability to define triggers should be built into the object-oriented database and should be applicable with very simple programming actions. Objects can be *ordinary* (exist only for a short duration), *persistent*, or *versioned*. At least two classes of triggers are required to address this variety of object types. *Once-only* triggers fire once and are automatically turned off. *Perpetual* triggers fire every time the predetermined conditions are met. Perpetual triggers are used, typically, for persistent objects (the dominating class in database management systems). Once-only triggers are very useful for managing versioned objects. Once-only triggers can be set to an *inactive* status while a new version of the object is being created. The trigger is then set to fire once to initialize the newly created object.

Business rules.   Business rules require checking for every action that updates or deletes any objects in the database to ensure that incorrect actions are not performed inadvertently. Triggers, stored procedures, or user-defined functions are used in relational databases for programming business rules. An example of a business rule may be that a finance charge is applied to any account more than 15 days past due.

Object-oriented databases, properly implemented, allow the use of pre- and postconditions, constraints, and methods. These three means are generally sufficient to handle the requirements for business rules. A key problem that needs to be addressed is that, when objects inherit the attributes and methods of a class, there should be a means of preventing redefinition for attributes and methods that define a business rule. Uncontrolled redefinition would allow each developer to change the very nature of the business rule. If restrictions can be placed on redefinition of attributes and methods during class definition, it may become easier to control the integrity of the business rule through various levels of inheritance.

3.6 OBJECT ORIENTATION IN RELATIONAL DATABASES

In the previous section we discussed adding features of relational databases to object-oriented databases. But one can say that it is like putting the cart before the horse. The relational databases established themselves in commercial information systems much before object-oriented databases, and considerable amounts of data already exist in commercial establishments using relational database systems as their flagship databases. Consequently, there is a need and a practical trend toward adding object-oriented features to existing relational database management systems.

The approaches to augmenting relational databases consist of enhancing both the storage mechanisms and the access mechanisms. There are basically three common approaches to enhancing relational databases:

1. Binary datatype
2. User-defined functions
3. Object-oriented programming front ends

Binary datatypes.   A relational database with binary datatypes allows objects of any arbitrary type to be stored in the database. The most common use of this facility is to store data that cannot otherwise be represented in the database, for example, video images, audio, bitmaps, or even raw spreadsheet data. Typically, data of this kind are numerous and do not fit easily with the more standard CHAR or VARCHAR datatypes. Binary datatypes typically allow up to 2 gigabytes or more to be stored as a column in a table.

From an object-oriented standpoint, binary datatypes provide the ability to store raw class data in a database without requiring that the individual attributes of the class be defined. With an object-oriented front-end programming language, it would be quite easy to define a base database object class that all classes would inherit, which could provide basic operations for storing and retrieving objects from the database, thus providing a persistent object capability.

There would need to be a capability of defining keys for object retrieval. These would, typically, be stored as additional columns in the database table along with the binary object data. The number and type of these keys would, of course, vary with the application, which would determine whether all object classes could be stored in the same table or whether a separate table for each class would be better. The size and number of objects in each class would also be factors in this determination. (Note that indexes would most likely have to be created on the key columns.)

User-defined functions (or stored procedures).   Stored procedures are a SYBASE implementation of user-defined functions (UDFs). Stored procedures (and UDFs in general), usually written in SQL and a procedural language similar to C (programmed as an extension of SQL), can be precompiled and stored in a database. These functions can be executed via a remote procedure call (RPC) at runtime, and they provide significant performance benefits over standard dynamic SQL requests.

Stored procedures approach the object-orientation problem from a functional perspective, just as the *binary datatype* capability approaches it from a structural perspective. Whereas binary datatypes allow object data to be stored in an uninterpreted (binary) form in the database, with external functions (such as related fields in the table) providing class functionality, stored procedures allow data stored in tables and columns to be manipulated by functions stored with the database. Although there is not a strict relationship or binding between the data and particular functions as there would be in a true object-oriented database, stored procedures can help in abstracting the actual structure of the data from the application programmer.

Object-oriented programming front ends. The crux of this approach is to provide either a C++ like programming language as an embedded 3GL capability and a development environment that emulates object management, or to provide a custom 4GL with the capability to link data objects with functions in a manner similar to encapsulation of methods within objects. The binary datatype provides a mechanism for storing methods in the database alongside the data elements.

Why we use these extensions. The driving force behind the development of features such as binary datatypes, stored procedures, and object-oriented development front ends has been the need to include binary images such as parts descriptions for computer-aided design, bit-mapped images for document management, and voice mail segments within the confines of the database. Binary datatypes allow storage of images, free-form text, and voice data that can be manipulated by user-defined functions. Binary datatypes, stored procedures, and object-oriented front ends have generated significant new interest in relational databases for the following reasons:

- They provide a start in the direction of object-oriented design and implementation and related potential benefits without the loss of relational integrity.
- Some flexibility of object-oriented systems is derived without a loss of relational integrity and performance.
- These developments have breathed a new life into relational databases. They allow relational databases to be used for applications that classical relational database structures were not designed to handle. The relational integrity is lost only for the data within the binary datatype. However, access to such data is still governed by the relational integrity rules.

3.7 USES FOR OBJECT-ORIENTED DATABASES

Object-oriented databases are optimally suited for data structures that are not handled easily by the relational model. For example, in a manufacturing application, a bill of materials list consists of parts as well as subassemblies. The bill of materials may itself represent a subassembly that is used in a higher-level subassembly. Treating each component and the subassembly as an object makes it easier to manage data items at a variety of levels.

Current object-oriented databases have been targeted for users who have to store complex databases in a centralized distributed repository. Products such as the GEMSTONE Object Oriented Database are targeted for CIM, CASE, and document management applications that require huge volumes of complicated data. The client/server architecture is as appealing for object-oriented databases as it is for purely relational databases.

Geographical information systems (GIS) do not typically rely on numerical data values for organizing their information. Encapsulating graphical information and attribute data about the graphical information within an object makes it significantly easier to manage GIS applications.

An extension of desktop publishing, enterprise-wide electronic publishing is another good example where object-oriented databases may provide notable benefits. Enterprise-wide electronic publishing includes networked computer systems and a procedural environment in which a number of people contribute to the creation of a document. Enterprise-wide electronic publishing allows users to write copy, import graphics, images, and other information from other systems and applications as objects, and combine these into complex higher-level objects. The versioning capabilities of object-oriented systems provide the means for easily tracking revisions, and dynamic binding helps address the issues of display technologies for a variety of workstations.

However, the greatest use of object-orientation technology will be in the area of common business applications. In conventional programming and even in contemporary object-oriented programming, application developers must write their own code to load objects from disk and construct object environments and manipulate these in a limited amount of memory. Once an object has been used, the special environment created for that object is lost. True object-oriented programming techniques and tools make it easy to develop applications to handle objects. The objects along with their environment-creation functions are stored on disk, and they are brought automatically into their correct environments in memory when needed. This provides a uniform object management and automatic storage and retrieval capability even for very large applications.

Let us look at a few examples to understand these concepts:

• In an accounting system, adding new accounts is easy in an object-oriented database system. The existing class or constructor of objects provides the templates for creating new accounts. For example, an account for a vendor is created using a class descriptor (or constructor). The same class descriptor can be used as the base for creating an account for another vendor. All vendor accounts are derived from the same object class. The new account for each vendor can be modified to change the inherited properties to the set of properties required for the new account.

• In a transportation system, adding new kinds of vehicles is easy. The code to select a vehicle examines cost per ton per mile, ability to reach the origin (for load pickup), time for pickup, cargo limits, speed and time to reach destination, fuel required, and so on. The data structures and the methods are defined for a class "vehicle"; the scheduling program can handle objects such as "truck" and "train"; it can also handle objects such as "airplane" and "ship" without change, as long as the new object classes can function within the methods provided in the class "vehicle" to handle the variety of potential options. The scheduling program does not even have to know that a new class of vehicle has been put in operation. If the new types of vehicles do require special handling, a new class can be inherited from the class "vehicle" and redefined as needed.

• Computer-aided design systems use large databases for parts. For most designs, very often existing parts are used or the basic part is copied and then modified to create a new one. The new parts typically undergo the same processing as the old parts. For example, a new bolt is created by changing the diameter or the pitch of the old bolt. Object-oriented databases provided a significant benefit to the designers of CAD/CAM systems because new parts inherit features of old parts, and new products or subassemblies inherit parts from the old ones. Designers need only define the attributes of new parts that differ from those of the old ones, thereby saving significant design effort.

We did not mention text retrieval (or hypertext) searches in the examples above. The importance of text-retrieval technologies is appreciated when one looks at the ratio of text versus data in an average office. The predominant ratio of text versus data is almost 10 to 1 in terms of storage requirements in the office filing systems. Yet the real emphasis has always been on automating data retrieval. Perhaps, limitations of retrieval technologies and hardware costs were a deterrent and did not make text retrieval an attractive alternative to manual retrieval methods. Improving hardware form factors and emerging text-retrieval technologies are injecting an increased interest in text retrieval. Good hypertext systems merge full-featured text-retrieval systems with mainstream database management. They provide a definitive interface between full-featured data repositories in both realms. Object-oriented systems are expected to play a major role as a repository of choice for the database component of hypertext technologies. Object-oriented databases provide the freedom to adapt a database for storing text objects and manipulating text objects, a function that could not really be performed by a relational database.

3.8 SUMMARY

This chapter started out with the fundamentals of object-oriented programming and extended those concepts to object-oriented database management systems. A study of the basic concepts of object-oriented programming is essential for understanding the modeling and design discussions of Part III.

The important concepts reviewed in this chapter include abstract data types, classes, inheritance, and multiple inheritance. We also discussed how classes are used in programming and how inheritance helps in creating similar subclasses. Redefinition provides the flexibility for creating new classes that have some attributes and methods different from the class they are derived from. Classes can also be changed dynamically by using dynamic binding and deferred class definitions.

We also defined some rules for object-oriented databases. While not as extensive as Codd's rules for relational database management systems, these rules forge a basic model for object-oriented databases. These rules form the minimal requirements for object-oriented databases. Most importantly, a true object-oriented database is based on the object paradigm, and both the access mechanism and storage mechanism are object oriented.

An important discussion presented potential extensions to object-oriented database systems that add notable features of relational database systems to object-oriented systems. We also looked at the efforts to enhance relational database systems with features leading to object management.

3.9 EXERCISES

1. Design an object that could be used to represent a security (such as stock or bond) in a security trading management system. List the attributes of the object and the set of services provided for manipulating objects of this type.

2. Extend the design of the security object to include subclasses for different types of securities, such as stocks, bonds and options. List the common attributes and services (provided by the parent class) and several different attributes and services unique to each subclass.

3. Pick one of the objects from Exercise 2 and list the constraints for each attribute for which constraints would be appropriate.

4. For the object in Exercise 3, describe the preconditions upon entry for each method and the postconditions upon exit from the methods. (Recall that pre- and postconditions are constraints on the attributes affected by a method; the constraints must be valid upon entry or exit.)

5. Design a scheme for assigning unique object identifiers in a distributed object environment. Such an environment would consist of multiple object servers wherein objects may be created. Describe each component of the object identifiers, including the number of databits for each.

6. All objects in an object-oriented database would share a common set of attributes such as class and object identifiers, update functions, and access control information. These common attributes could be inherited from a single base object class. Define such a base class, describing at least 15 attributes, and list and describe the methods for manipulating the base objects and their attributes.

7. In an object-oriented database, any object may be defined to contain a reference to another object by including the object identifier as one of its attributes. Discuss an approach that an object-oriented database or an application may take to maintain referential integrity when a referenced object is destroyed or when an attempt is made to destroy the object.

8. Discuss the uses of joins in an object-oriented database in contrast to the uses of joins in a relational database.

CONTEMPORARY INFORMATION SYSTEMS DESIGN METHODOLOGY

The relational as well as the object models have excluded the semantics of the database. This implies that the effect insertions, deletions, and updates have on the database is understood independently, and possibly differently, by the designer and the user of the information system. Their subjective view of what the information in the database means drives their actions. This makes database consistency a subjective notion that can easily be violated.

It is important to record sematic information about a database to ensure consistent usage of the database. The well-known methodologies such as normalization and entity relationship diagrams do not show semantic relationships. Some depiction methodologies presented in this chapter have attempted to address this issue. Unfortunately, no established methodology in use is ideal, hence the wide variety of methodologies in use. These database design representation methodologies provide the means for depicting varying levels of semantic information. They have not succeeded in gaining wide acceptance due to the special graphical symbology (arcs, circles, loops, and so on) that were traditionally not provided by programmer tool sets. Advanced CASE systems have attempted to address the problem.

Most of these methodologies, designed primarily for the designer, form the basis for conceptual data models; however, they do not provide any design information to the user and the user remains at liberty to violate consistency rules. Most developers program the information using stored procedures or user-defined functions to achieve application-wide consistency.

What is lacking is an effective means of depicting semantic information in a design document as well as within the database itself using diagramming techniques that are easily achieved by standard programming tools such as text editors. The depiction methodology should be adaptable to an interactive graphical development environment, such as a graphical user-interface-based application-building utility.

In Chapter 4, we will discuss a number of database design depiction methodologies that represent knowledge about a database. We will also present our own adaptation of existing techniques such as entity relationship diagrams, semantic analysis, and frames. We call this methodology *Frame-Object Analysis*. Frame-Object Analysis diagrams are designed to be adaptable to a CASE tool. The CASE tool can create the database and substantial components of the application from the Frame-Object Analysis diagrams.

Chapter 5, another major component of the design methodology, is devoted to explaining the sequence of events for analyzing requirements, classifying objects, and developing a detailed model for an object-oriented database.

Chapter 6 completes our discussion of design methodology by addressing the overall project management perspective. This chapter addresses the issues of interacting with users, prototyping systems, and other analysis aspects of the design methodology.

4

Information Engineering Survey of Depiction Techniques

The following steps are involved in clearly understanding the requirements of the application:

1. Interviewing potential users to gain a better insight regarding their understanding of what the system will do.
2. Collecting available information on current operation of the specific activity being automated or redesigned.
3. Analyzing documented requirements statements. Establishing data entities and their relations.
4. Explaining the relations between the data entities to the users to ensure that the information is correct and complete.
5. Drawing a network topology map and the requirements for interacting with other systems.

Large corporations have a wide variety of information sources, such as different departments, divisions, and field offices. The timely dissemination of information to the appropriate recipients is crucial for efficient and competitive operation of the enterprise. Good information engineering discipline is necessary for achieving the twin goals of the developers gaining a good understanding of the requirements and the users gaining a good understanding of the design.

4.1 INFORMATION ENGINEERING METHODOLOGY

Successful implementation of relational database systems requires the application of sound analytical techniques to ensure data integrity and reliable operation. Relational database systems are particularly sensitive to good design and organization of data. The database design should provide flexibility for creative application development and should be laid out to perform efficiently. A good design should take into consideration current as well as future requirements to minimize database redesign as the needs of the business change.

The goal of the database design endeavor is good object identification, clear enumeration of object uniqueness constraints, and a detailed analysis of relational integrity constraints. The processes associated with the day to day operation of business require careful attention to ensure that the fully developed application meets the criteria set by the users.

The design methodology should aim for synergy between the user (the functional expert) and the developer. In situations where the user is new to relational database design, information engineering methodologies that can simply and successfully depict the design graphically become an important component of the overall project. The graphic depiction of data in a symbolic model of the database provides a powerful visual tool for a review and detailed critique of the design. At this level, selection of the relational database is not an issue. The design at this level should be independent of the relational database.

The design methodology should maximize user participation in the creation of customized application software. Such a design methodology ensures consistent and easy to use interfaces, optimal response time, and high levels of functionality. Prototyping the application using the tools provided by the selected database is an important component of this methodology. Prototyping ensures useful feedback from the user and the functional experts during a very early stage of application development. At this stage, it is feasible to make required design changes and user interface changes without substantial additional cost.

4.1.1 Structured Analysis for Information Systems

Database schema design is only one stage in the process of information systems development. It is important that the database schema be based on specifications of the user's current and anticipated needs. The data needs specified during the analysis stage should dictate the data structures and relationships among these structures in the database schema.

The structured analysis methodology is well known and broadly in use. Structured analysis identifies the following:

1. Functions or activities to be handled by the system
2. External entities that interact with the system

3. Logical data stores
4. Data flow among all the above

Structured analysis takes a top-down approach, identifying major functions first and presenting a top-level data-flow diagram. Then every function is decomposed into subfunctions or activities, and flow of data between these functions and activities is identified, leading to a more detailed data-flow diagram. Further levels of detail may be required to adequately describe an information system.

While structured analysis is concerned primarily with the processes of collecting, identifying, and classifying information, the following methodologies pertain to depicting information systems designs:

1. Normalization
2. Entity Relationship modeling
3. Data-flow diagrams
4. Information Analysis
5. Semantic networks
6. Frame analysis
7. Frame-Object Analysis

Some of these methodologies are currently used for depicting expert systems. They are presented here because contemporary information systems feature knowledge-based back-ends that require this level of expert systems depiction capability.

4.1.2 Data Dictionary and Data Modeling

A database consists of a number of data objects, also called data entities. These objects have attributes that define the properties of the data objects. While a data entity is a logical representation of an object, a table or a record is a physical representation of an object. The attributes of that object are represented by fields or columns in a table that defines the properties of the object. An entity may be a person, place, thing, or concept. The characteristics of these entities may be an address or a description stored within the table. The characteristics or attributes of a data entity called "office," for example, may consist of attributes "street address," "city," "state," and "zip code." These attributes may, instead, be included in a larger entity called 'customer.'

The data dictionary stores the logical relationships among objects as well as relationships between an object and its attributes. The data dictionary maintains relationships in a physical database among tables, as well as between a table and its columns. The relationships identified include keys (indexes) for accessing information within a table, common keys between two tables that connect related information, and integrity constraints that prevent a row from being deleted if a dependent row exists in another table. For example, if a row exists corresponding to a 'customer' in a 'detail' table, the row in the 'customer' table cannot be deleted.

The dictionary documents indexes on one or more columns for fast access to rows in a table. The data dictionary also maintains access and security parameters to ensure that only authorized users can access data.

4.1.3 Structured Analysis Tools

A data-flow diagram consists of a graphical representation of data storage areas (data stores) and flow of data (data flows) between these data stores. The contents of the data stores, the data elements emanating from them or entering them, and the processing of these elements in the data-flow areas are analyzed to perform the database schema design. The following components define an information system:

- A list of data elements entering a data store or emanating from a data store. (These data elements only need to be stored in that data store.)
- A relation created among the elements of this data store.
- Comparison of a data element emanating from one data store with its format and value as it enters the next data store. (This defines the processing required for it.)
- The dependencies among all data elements.

At this point the data has been collected and one of the following approaches can be used for building a data model. The data models frequently use the concept of an object. In this context, an object may be viewed as a data element, that is, one of the components of a data store. An object, typically, is represented in the physical data base by a table.

4.2 NORMALIZATION

Relations in a relational database are always normalized, in the sense that they are defined over simple domains that contain atomic values only. Examples of atomic values are *city*, *product name*, and *location* in Figures 4-1 through 4-3. Normalization theory takes this basic concept much further by allowing database designers to recognize cases that may still possess some undesirable properties, such as one field (or data component) being duplicated or being inclusive of another field (or data component), and converting such cases to more desirable forms.

Normalization theory is built around the concept of *normal forms*. A relation is said to be in a particular normal form if it satisfies a certain specified set (or level) of constraints. For example, a relation is said to be in *first normal form* (abbreviated 1NF) if and only if it satisfies the constraint that it contains atomic values only. Codd[1] originally defined first, second, and third normal forms (abbreviated as 1NF, 2NF, and 3NF).

As we just observed, the *first normal form* (1NF) defines all relations that contain atomic values. Therefore, every potential relation is included in 1NF. Figure 4-1 describes a 1NF relationship by including *all* unique attributes (or fields) required for a simple application. We will use the example of a distributor that has suppliers who provide products for distribution to various customers. The data elements necessary to track each shipment include the following:

*Customer ID	*Supplier ID
Customer Name	Supplier Name
Customer Address	*Product ID
City	Product Name
State	Packaging Code
Zip	Package Description

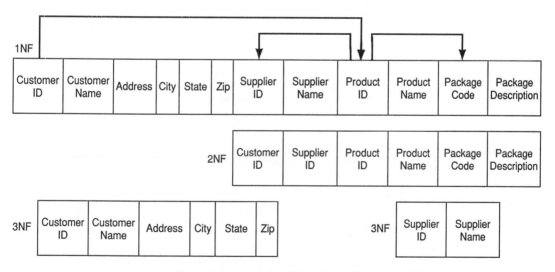

Figure 4-1.   Example of Data Normalization to 3NF.

---

[1] E. F. Codd, "Normalized Data Base Structure: A Brief Tutorial," *Proceedings of ACM SIGFIDET Workshop on Data Description, Access and Control*, 1971;

    E. F. Codd, "Further Normalization of the Data Base Relational Model," *Database Systems*, Courant Computer Science Symposia Series, Vol. 6, Prentice Hall, Englewood Cliffs, N.J., 1972.

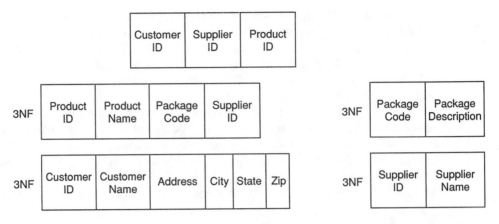

Customer ID	Supplier ID	Product ID

3NF

Product ID	Product Name	Package Code	Supplier ID

3NF

Package Code	Package Description

3NF

Customer ID	Customer Name	Address	City	State	Zip

3NF

Supplier ID	Supplier Name

Figure 4-2.   Normalized Database for Example of Figure 4-1.

In this set of data elements, we can define three keys (marked by asterisks). Since all other fields depend on these key fields, this relation meets the criteria for 1NF.

We further define a relation to be in *second normal form* (2NF) if and only if it satisfies all 1NF conditions for atomic values, and every nonkey attribute is dependent on all elements of the primary key. This distinction of a nonkey attribute's dependence is very significant. It implies that the fields of a table in 2NF are all related to the primary key and describe the entity pointed to by the

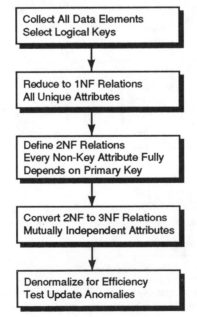

Collect All Data Elements
Select Logical Keys

Reduce to 1NF Relations
All Unique Attributes

Define 2NF Relations
Every Non-Key Attribute Fully
Depends on Primary Key

Convert 2NF to 3NF Relations
Mutually Independent Attributes

Denormalize for Efficiency
Test Update Anomalies

Figure 4-3.   Normalization Steps.

key in some manner. Let us illustrate this through the example. In our example, we find that the same product can be sold to multiple customers. A product is actually dependent only on a supplier and not on a customer. To meet the 2NF criteria, we must separate customers to a separate table as shown in Figure 4-1. The tables will then be as follows:

Customer	Supplier	Product
Customer ID	Supplier ID	Customer ID
Customer Name	Supplier Name	Supplier ID
Address		Product ID
City		Product Name
State		Package Code
Zip		Package Description

Interestingly, the tables *Customer* and *Supplier* actually meet the requirements for a 3NF relation.

A relation is said to be in the *third normal form* (3NF) if and only if, for all times, each type (or row in a relational table) consists of a primary key value that identifies some entity, together with mutually independent attribute values (or columns) that describe that entity in some way. Continuing with our example, we find that a product may be packaged differently depending on the different packaging styles used by the supplier. To meet the 3NF criteria, we must separate Packaging Description into a separate table. The following lists the fully normalized tables:

Shipment	Customer	Supplier	Product	Packaging
Customer ID	Customer ID	Supplier ID	Product ID	Package Code
Supplier ID	Customer Name	Supplier Name	Product Name	Package Description
Product ID	Address		Package Code	
	City		Supplier ID	
	State			
	Zip			

The tables normalized to 3NF are shown in Figure 4-2.

Other normalizations are defined as Boyce and Codd (B&C) normal form, fourth normal form (4NF), and fifth normal form (5NF), which further reduces the inadequacies of the normalization process.

You will note that if the information is retained in 1NF form the size of the data tables becomes very large because we need additional rows for every permutation of the customer, supplier, product, and packaging. For each permutation, the fields such as customer name, address, and city combined with the fields describing the product and supplier are repeated. When the fields are assigned to five tables, each table contains unique information in addition to the keys, and the permutations are performed on much smaller record sizes. This significantly reduces record size and number of rows that have to be maintained in each table.

We performed a number of steps to normalize the database. The normalization technique described above, and illustrated in Figure 4-3, is used extensively due to its simplicity and ease of diagramming relations. The final step in Figure 4-3 is labeled "Denormalize . . .". A fully normalized database (that is, with all tables in 3NF) has a large number of tables and requires frequent look-ups between tables. The trade-off between performance and storage is a significant consideration for database design, often leading to a design that falls somewhere between the 1NF and 3NF forms.

Denormalization.   One major problem with full normalization to the 3NF form is a proliferation of tables. In a very large and complex database, not only does a proliferation of tables make the database unmanageable, but also a lot of functions, especially reports, require a large number of joins. Simply converting each entity into a table does not necessarily lead to a good database design. A query that requires a *join* of three or more tables executes much slower than a query that requires a single join, that is, a join of two tables. This implies that full normalization is not the final answer in database design. Some of the tables that resulted from full normalization must be recombined to improve performance. The number of potential joins reduces due to the recombination. The term *denormalization* denotes recombining tables to a state that is less than full normalization. One major issue to be kept in mind when denormalizing is its impact on update integrity. Consequently, denormalization cannot be taken lightly.

It is important to determine the objectives for the denormalization process before denormalization is attempted. These objectives should include:

- Determining what tables are joined and what functions are affected by this join. This is a function road map in relation to tables.
- The frequency with which these functions are used. This determines the weighting factor; heavily used functions carry a heavy weighting factor.
- A trade-off ratio in terms of performance, that is, a factor consisting of a product of the number of joins for a function and function use. Tables used by functions above a predetermined (or a computed) threshold become candidated for denormalization.

A good approach for developing these objectives is to create a matrix of all functions against the tables. The next step is to separate the functions selected as potential candidates for performance optimizations. Once the candidate tables for denormalization have been selected, the following steps need to be performed.

- Composite tables are created by combining the tables selected as candidates for denormalization.
- All functions affected by these new composite tables are evaluated to determine the impact.
- Any update anomalies are determined, and denormalization is backed off where update anomalies present a problem.

When data from both entities (combined as a result of denormalization) is accessed together, there is usually no problem in combining them. However, if entities accessed separately by some functions, updates can be a problem. Another point to note is that denormalized tables frequently have multiple keys and potentially two or more indexes.

In summary, it is worth noting that denormalization, unlike normalization, is not an exact science. It requires detailed analysis and a judgment on the trade-offs of performance against a problem-free database. Compared to a fully normalized database, a denormalized database may show inelegant links. Nonetheless, denormalization is a practical necessity. And the smaller number of tables in a denormalized database makes it easier to grasp the substance of the database.

4.3 ENTITY RELATIONSHIP DIAGRAMS

Entity Relationship (ER) modeling is a widely recognized and commonly used technique for depicting objects or data entities. The basic premise underlying the use of an ER data model for relational databases is that the database, if properly designed, can actually be a static model of the enterprise business itself. The database of an enterprise contains relevant information concerning entities and relationships in which an enterprise is involved. The data model drives the development of the physical database. The ER data model technique lends itself to modeling just about any kind of a database, whether for a business application or a manufacturing application.

ER data models are easier to read than relational diagrams like Information Analysis described in section 4.5 because the relationships are at a higher level, are explicit and spatial, and depict one-to-one, one-to-many, and many-to-many relationships. ER data models prepared in concert with process models such as data-flow diagrams produce a comprehensive description of the design of an application. The process model defines the processes (that may represent the dynamics of the business enterprise) and the input and output data for each data entity.

The term *entity* is used in database systems to mean any distinguishable object that needs to be represented in the database. Entities are classified into different entity sets, for example, *customers*, *products*, and *locations* are all entities

Figure 4-4. Examples of Entities.

in the following example. This example describes sales presentations for customers set up in different locations for different products. Figure 4-4 illustrates how entities are depicted.

The role of an entity in a relationship is the function that it performs in that relationship. While an entity is a *thing* or *object* that can be distinctly identified, a *relationship* is an association among entities. For example, "EMPLOYEE-PLANT" is a relationship between a *person* entity and *place of work* entity.

An attribute is defined as a function or information about an entity that characterizes the entity in some manner. For example, the entity EMPLOYEE may have an attribute "Title." When this attribute is assigned a value "Manager," the entity EMPLOYEE is characterized by the role of the person.

It should be noted that relationships can also have entities. For example, an EMPLOYEE can be related to a *Plant* if the value for the entity EMPLOYEE is "Inspector." INSPECTOR may itself be an entity that describes the characteristics of various classes of inspectors such as "Electrical," "Safety," "Quality," and so on.

Conceptual model.   How information associated with entities and relationships can be organized is an important concern for the development of an information system. Commonly called a conceptual model, this organization is the base for the design of an information system.

ER data models can be prepared at different levels within an overall project. A conceptual ER model can depict the overall business and the relationship between the divisions within the business enterprise. At a logical level, an ER data model depicts entities that correspond to tables in the data base and the attributes (or fields) of the data entities.

The logical ER model presented here is based on the concepts presented by Peter Pin-Shan Chen in 1975.[2] Chen's model as presented consists of four levels

---

[2] Peter Pin-Shan Chen, "The Entity Relationship Model—Toward a Unified View of Data," presented at the International Conference on Very Large Data Bases, Framingham, Massachusetts, September 22–24, 1975. Permission by ACM, © 1976.

of logical views as follows:

Level 1: Information concerning entities and relationships
Level 2: Information structure
Level 3: Access-path-independent data structures
Level 4: Access-path-dependent data structures

At level 1, an *entity* is considered to be a distinctly identifiable *thing* (such as a COMPANY or ACCOUNT) an *action*, and so on. A *relationship* is an association among entities. For example, a COMPANY has an ACCOUNT. We are primarily concerned here with the aspects of this relationship that can be depicted in an ER diagram and stored in the database. We look on these entities and relationships as conceptual objects. In the example of Figure 4-2, CUSTOMER, SUPPLIER, PRODUCT, and PACKAGING are entities at level 1.

At level 2, the information structure defines the representation (of attributes) of conceptual objects. In Figure 4-1 we presented some entities after normalization. These entities have attribute sets associated with them. The PRODUCT entity has "Product Name" and "Product ID" as attributes. The "Product ID" attribute is a key attribute that relates it to the SHIPMENT entity.

At level 3, the access-path-independent data structures are defined. Entities that can be uniquely identified by their own attributes are access path independent. All entities used in the system must ultimately be identifiable directly or indirectly by a uniquely self-identifiable entity. A CUSTOMER is a uniquely identifiable entity in the example of Figure 4-2.

At level 4, the access-path-dependent data structures are defined. This includes entities that cannot be uniquely identified by their own attributes. A relationship must be used to identify them. For example, the entity PACKAGE DESCRIPTION in Figure 4-1 cannot be uniquely identified by its own attributes. It needs the relation to "Product Name" and/or "Supplier ID" for identification. The same supplier can present multiple package types to the same customer. Knowing the "supplier" and "product name" is essential for unique identification. This method of identification of entities can be applied recursively until entities that can be uniquely identified by their own attributes are reached.

Types of relationships.   We noted above that some relationships are due to unique identification. We will call these *existence relationships*. Other relationships are due to a function, for example, a "stockbroker" has a "client." This is a *functional relationship*. The third kind of relationship is due to an action or an event. For example, a "stockbroker" sells "stock" for a client. We will call these *event relationships*.

Associations or relationships define the roles between entities and link different entities together. A relationship has a direction that indicates how two entities are associated. A direction is pointed out by an arrow that defines a *from/to* relationship. For example, a COMPANY has an ACCOUNT.

It is not necessary that a company have only one account. A company can have many accounts. The *one-to-many* ratio between the company and its accounts is called the *cardinality ratio*. The cardinality ratio defines the expected number of related occurrences of the second entity. The cardinality ratio is expressed in one of the following forms:

1. One-to-one or Zero-to-one
2. One-to-many
3. Many-to-one
4. Many-to-many

The *one-to-one* (also expressed as $1:1$) and *one-to-many* ($1:n$) cardinality is very clear. It is important to understand the difference between a *one-to-one* (or *one-to-many*) and *zero-to-one* (or *zero-to-many*). A one-to-one relationship implies that every instance of the first entity has a corresponding instance of the second entity. A zero-to-one relationship, on the other hand, implies that every instance of the first entity may or may not have a corresponding instance of the second entity. Some versions of ER diagramming methodologies use dotted lines for arrows to depict a *may-or-may-not* relationship. Other versions of ER diagrams show only a $1:n$ relationship and do not recognize a $0:n$ relationship.

ER diagramming conventions.   The simplicity of the ER diagrams has caused many add ons to the basic diagramming technique. The basic diagramming technique consists of the following components:

1. Rectangles represent entities. The identifier for the entity is used as the label for the rectangle. The same identifier is also used as the identifier for the table.
2. Arrows represent the direction of the relationship.
3. A diamond is used to describe a relationship. (A relationship is alternately described as "$<$ relationship.").
4. The cardinality ratio labels are noted at the head and tail of the arrow.

For example, Figure 4-6 shows a basic entity relation. Some ER diagramming techniques further decompose the ER diagram to show the attributes of each entity as circles labeled with the attribute identifier. The links shown in Figure 4-6 are an example of the relationships.

These links are described by the use of arrows. While different conventions are in use, Figure 4-5 describes the most common set used.

A line or an arrow connects two entities. A number of entities can be connected by arrows to represent a complete set of relationships for a project. Figure 4-6 describes an application where each entity is resolved into a table. Each table is normalized to 3NF for this relationship diagram to be useful.

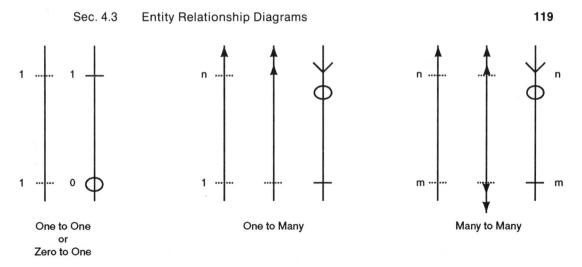

Figure 4-5. Drawing Conventions for Entity Relationship Diagrams.

In Figure 4-6, the entities are described for the example of Figure 4-2. This example shows a *one-to-many* relationship between a COMPANY and a SUPPLIER. Similarly, there is a one-to-many relationship between a SUPPLIER and PRODUCT; that is, a supplier may stock many products. A PRODUCT has a one-to-many relationship with *package,* implying that products may be presented in many packaging styles. There is no direct relationship between a SUPPLIER and a PACKAGE; there are neither any implications relating specific suppliers to specific packages nor are there any restrictions on suppliers carrying different packaging styles. Similar ER diagrams can be created for any business application. For example, relationships between sales and inventory or sales and accounts receivable can be displayed in an ER diagram.

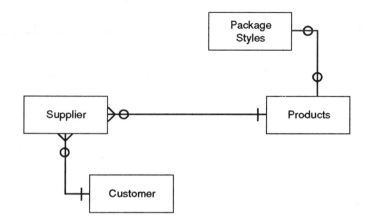

Figure 4-6. Entity Relationship Diagram for an Application.

ER diagrams not only help in understanding the logical relationships among operating entities within a business enterprise, but also provide useful documentation for database designs that can be called on for business reviews as organizational needs change. ER diagrams can be used to create new organizational relationships or change existing organizational relationships.

Data integrity issues.   Constraints on entities and relationships ensure data integrity. Constraints are necessary for both *allowed value types* for an entity as well as *attributes* of an entity.

4.3.1 Strengths and Weaknesses of ER Diagrams

The strengths of the ER model lie in its ability to depict associations between real-world concepts in a very simple and comprehensible pictorial representation. Traditional data modeling languages tend to inhibit the creativeness of the designer during the design phases because they are implementation driven. ER modeling is data driven.

The ER model pictorially describes the structural relationship between the entities. It presents an easily achieved diagramming methodology to build a good conceptual model to correctly model structural relationships among real-world data objects. The design can concentrate on the analysis of the relationships rather than detailed mechanics of representing them. A complex diagramming technique is likely to be a deterrent for updates, and a design depicted by means of a complex diagramming technique is frequently not updated when the program is modified. On the other hand, due to their inherent simplicity, ER diagrams lend themselves to frequent updates as relationships change.

The very simplicity of ER diagrams that provides its major strengths is also the cause of its major weaknesses. A major weakness of ER diagrams is the static nature of information management. That is, ER diagrams depict the relationship in a static mode. ER diagrams by themselves are not sufficient to define an information system. Data-Flow diagrams (DFDs) are necessary to complement information provided in ER diagrams. In combination with DFDs, ER diagrams provide a wealth of information about a database design. The ER diagrams provide the structural realtionships between the entities, and the DFDs provide the behavioral relationships decribing the data flow. Let us now study the data-flow diagrams in the next section.

4.4 DATA-FLOW DIAGRAMS

Structured system analysis and design require well-defined statements of inputs to the system, outputs from the system, data structures within the system, and processing logic that the system has to implement. A disciplined top-down approach to the implementation helps in addressing the requirements for major functions and in resolving potential major problems at an early stage. Depicting this information in a graphical format that users can understand easily ensures that the design meets the requirements. The graphics depiction can be a multi-level depiction. Large, complex systems are decomposed into smaller, more manageable tasks that the users can comprehend and evaluate. From the diagrams, users can determine if the inputs to the system reflect the real business model, the outputs from the system are appropriate, that the data structures represent the information as it is currently stored (or should be stored), and that the processing logic takes into account all business rules and practices.

Data-Flow diagrams (DFD) are used for structured systems analysis. While an ER diagram presents the view of a system from a functional perspective, a high-level DFD presents a system overview depicting its overall purpose and its interaction with external objects. A DFD provides a general picture of data transformation in the system. Decomposition techniques are used to divide the system into individual processes. The decomposition technique is carried down to as many levels as necessary to fully define the system.

Every process in a DFD transforms incoming data and passes its output data to another process or a data store. The transformation of data is identified by a control flow tag. Any primitive process that is not decomposed further is tagged with a control specification. A completed DFD is particularly useful in identifying the functions of a system and the ensuing data transformation.

The basic symbols of data-flow diagrams are called *transforms*. Transforms are represented by round-edged rectangles in the Gane & Sarson model and by circles in the Yourdon/DeMarco model. Each transform identifies a function that transforms data. The transforms are connected by labeled arrows that represent the inputs to and outputs from the transform. Transforms may have multiple inputs and outputs. Other symbols used in DFDs include *source, destination* (note that source and destination are also known as *externals*), *processes, data flows,* and *data stores.* Figure 4-7 depicts the pictorial representation of these symbols for Gane & Sarson and Yourdon/DeMarco models.

Before evaluating examples of data-flow diagrams, it is necessary to clearly understand the basic building blocks. The building blocks are essentially the same for the two methodologies. The following describes the building blocks:

Sources: Data streams come from a source (and go to a destination). A source is depicted as a rectangle (or a set of rectangles arranged as a deck of cards). In our example, the "License Application" is a source. It is an external input to the system.

Destination: Data streams go to a destination (usually from a transform). A destination is also depicted by rectangles in the same manner as a source. The "License" is a destination in our example. It is the printed output that goes to a license (hence it is an external).

Process (or Transform):   A process performs some function on the data that transforms the data in some manner. A process is depicted by round-edged

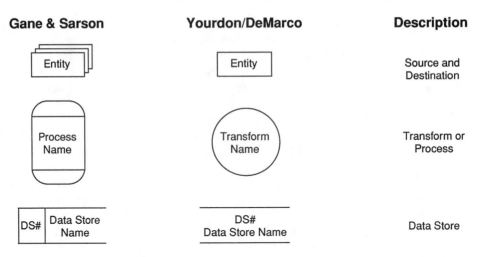

Figure 4-7. Symbols for Data-flow Diagrams.

rectangles (Gane & Sarson) and a transform is depicted by a circle (Yourdon/DeMarco). A process represents some kind of action. For example, "Create License Record" performs the function of creating a new database record. Similarly, "Enter Payment" adds a payment to the database.

Data Flows: Data flows are depicted by labeled lines with arrowheads indicating the direction of the data flow and the labels describing this data that is flowing.

Data Stores: Data stores are represented by partial rectangles. A data store represents a database for that particular transaction.

There are two commonly used depiction methodologies for DFDs. These are known as Gane & Sarson diagrams and Yourdon/DeMarco diagrams. There is little difference between the two in terms of the information detail or perspective of the information presented. For a variety of reasons, the Gane & Sarson model has become the more commonly used model. The primary difference lies in presentation styles. Let us study the two DFD methodologies.

While other methodologies are in use, in addition to the two presented here, these two are the most widely used. Readers may find it worthwhile to explore other DFD methodologies for comparison with these two.

4.4.1 Gane & Sarson Diagrams

The Gane & Sarson methodology is credited to Chris Gane and Trish Sarson. It is described first, not due to a chronological order, but because it is the more established of the two methodologies.

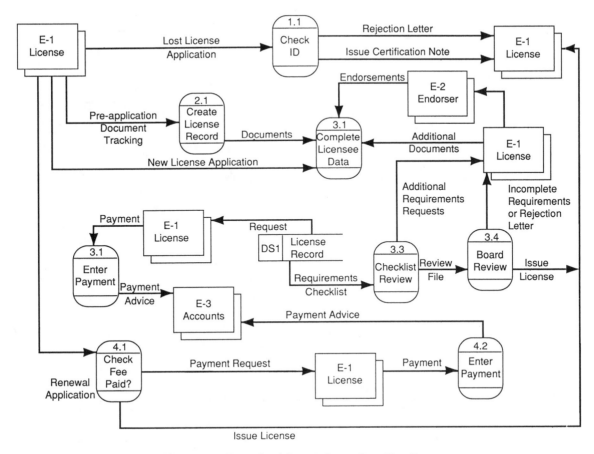

Figure 4-8.   Example of Gane & Sarson Data Flow Diagram.

Figure 4-8 illustrates the use of a data-flow diagram for describing a professional licensing process using the Gane & Sarson depiction methodology. You will notice that the Gane & Sarson depiction methodology provides more clearly distinguishable visual differences among different components as compared to the Yourdon/DeMarco DFD methodology.

4.4.2 Yourdon/DeMarco Diagrams

Figure 4-9 describes the Yourdon/DeMarco methodology for depicting the example described in Figure 4-8. Both DFD methodologies are used widely in CASE tools for database modeling. The Yourdon/DeMarco methodology is easier to use with CASE as well as non-CASE tools due to the simple drawing components. Most of these components are available as extensions to text editors or word processors.

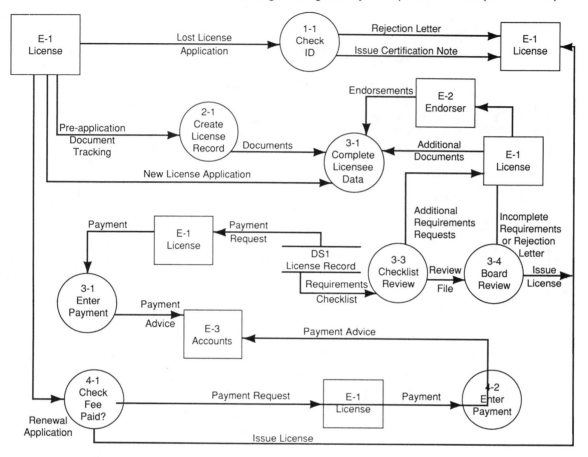

Figure 4-9. Example of Yourdon/DeMarco Data Flow Diagram.

4.4.3 Strengths and Limitations of DFDs

A physical system is defined by a physical data-flow diagram. A logical system is defined by a logical data-flow diagram. Both physical and logical data-flow diagrams are essential for building an information system. The physical data-flow diagram represents the physical entities such as personnel, paper forms, reports, and the facilities used by the information system. A logical data-flow diagram describes the conceptual framework for authorizations, approval stages, and status at various stages. The data-flow diagram is a tool that analysts can use to define both the current system and the proposed logical system. The users can analyze the diagrams to improve efficiency and streamline operations. The two diagrams together present the complete operating picture for the analyst. This operating picture is used for programming the application. The potential separation between the physical and logical depiction of the same process is a major strength of the data-flow diagram methodology.

A second strength is the ability to capture the overview of a system and then decompose each process within it. For each such process, a physical and logical data-flow diagram can be created. This procedure can be carried down to the lowest level.

Limitations of data-flow diagrams.   Data-flow diagrams provide an excellent means of analyzing the data flows and processes within an information system. They are very useful for examining and optimizing the logical processes within an organization. Nonetheless, some limitations remain, as described in the following:

1. When multiple inputs enter a transform or the transform has multiple outputs, the DFD does not tell us if these inputs and outputs are required in any particular sequence. In addition, the DFD does not tell us if there is a required or an implied sequence in which the inputs must be received or the outputs produced.
2. Data-flow diagrams provide very little information on the data entities. Data entities are used primarily as a part of a transaction, and each data entity participating in a transaction is considered part of the database. However, there is no information on the structure or logical relations within the database.

Use with ER diagrams.   Used in conjunction with Entity Relationship diagrams, data-flow diagrams play a very useful role. Data-flow diagrams and Entity Relationship diagrams are very complementary to one another. While ER diagrams define the relations within the database and the logical organization of the database, data-flow diagrams define the processes using these entities in the database. Together, these two methodologies provide a fairly complete definition of a system.

4.5 INFORMATION ANALYSIS

Information analysis (IA) was developed as a methodology for depicting relations between objects by G. M. Nijssen of the University of Brussels. Based on the concepts of natural language, this methodology produces a data model that clearly, accurately, and unambiguously presents the design of the information system to the user and guides the implementation of the system. Verheijen and Van Bekkum's[3] review of the methodology in 1982 provided a more detailed perspective on its applicability to database design.

---

[3] G. M. Verheijen and J. Van Bekkum, "NIAM: An Information Analysis Method," in *Information Design Methodologies: A Comparative Review*, T. W. Olle, H. G. Sol, and A. A. Verryn-Stuart (eds.), North Holland, Amsterdam, 1982, pp. 537–590.

The concepts of IA are based on objects. The objects are classified and identified for an accurate description and depiction of data. Natural language constructs are then developed to depict the relations between objects. The information collected is then converted to diagrams that follow very specific data and relation representation guidelines.

4.5.1 Classification and Identification of Objects

An object is classified by an English language description that uniquely identifies an attribute of the object. For example, companies may be classified by the *class name* customer. In an accounts receivable system the class name *customer* may include all companies that receive an invoice. We noted that each object within a class must be uniquely identified. In our example, a customer is uniquely identified by a customer number. A customer number is a unique number for each customer and is known as the *object identifier class name* (or *object name*). The object identifier class name is the naming convention used for representing objects.

Facts about objects or entities are represented as binary relationships called sentences. Every flow of information can be expressed in the form of a binary sentence. A *binary sentence* is an elementary sentence that defines the elements of a relationship. Let us, in the following section, analyze the structure of a sentence.

4.5.2 Sentence Structure, Vocabulary, and Classification

A sentence can have nouns, verbs, prepositions, and determiners (such as *a, the, an*). In addition, a sentence can have noun phrases, verb phrases, and prepositional phrases. Sentences in IA do not have pronouns, adjectives, or adverbs. Let us look at an example of how a binary sentence is constructed. The following binary sentence has two objects: the *customer* and the *car*.

The customer	: object class
with customer-number	: object identifier class name
of ABC123456	: object identifier
leases	: verb
a car	: object class
with car-id	: object identifier class name
of HF12345SE6789	: object identifier

The two objects in this example are related by the verb *leases*. Complex information can be broken down to binary sentences. Nested sentences make it possible to define a complex hierarchy of actions. A binary sentence can itself be used as an object in a higher-level nested binary sentence.

Binary sentences can be used to define the following three classes of dependencies:

1. *One-to-one:* The occurrence of one object class uniquely determines the occurrence of another object class, and vice versa.
2. *One-to-many:* An occurrence of one object class determines one or more occurrences of the other object class, but *not* vice versa.
3. *Many-to-many:* An occurrence of one object class can be related to many occurrences of another object class, and vice versa.

Using these relationships and the binary sentence structure, any information system can be reduced down to its lowest-level structures. The information flows can be converted into binary and nested binary sentences and then presented as diagrams. A collection of examples of current operations such as reports, forms, and descriptions of operating processes is analyzed and described using the IA methodology. A full information structure diagram is created. This information structure diagram describes the schema of normalized record types by applying a grouping algorithm. The grouping is based on the binary relationships in the structure diagrams and builds up record types by grouping together relations that have the object class that determines the relationship.

4.5.3 Sentence Diagrams

The binary sentences can be represented in diagrams. A number of symbols are used to represent objects classes, object identifiers, and relations. Let us study these symbols in detail.

The object class symbol.   An object class is represented by a circle. The name of the object class is written inside the circle. Figure 4-10 shows an object class symbol for the object class customer.

The relation symbol.   A relation is represented as a rectangle with two parts, where each part touches an object class symbol. Figure 4-11 shows the graphical representation of a binary sentence. It depicts the relation between two object classes. The name of the relation is written above the rectangle and the verb in the relation is written in one of the two parts of the rectangle. The inverse relation is written as a verb in the other part of the rectangle.

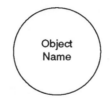

Object
Name

Figure 4-10.   Object Class Symbol.

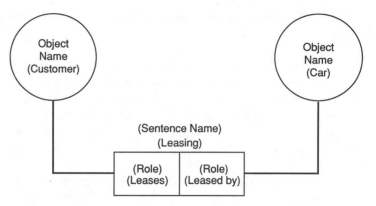

Figure 4-11.   Graphical Representation of a Binary Sentence

4.5.4 Relation and Constraint Representation

Data constraints are important in deciding how the actual relations will be stored in the information system. Two types of constraints must be shown on a sentence diagram: uniqueness constraints and set constraints.

Uniqueness constraints include the one-to-one and one-to-many (or many-to-one) relationships where one object is unique in its relationship with other objects. Many-to-many relationships are a special case of uniqueness constraints where no object is unique in its relationship with other objects. All these cases are called uniqueness constraints because they define the uniqueness (or lack of uniqueness) of an object.

Set constraints define object constraints between two or more elements of the same object class in different relations. Very often, these constraints are expressed as rules. Another case of set constraints is one where every element in the subset appears in the primary set.

4.5.5 Building a Database Design from Sentence Diagrams

Information Analysis is most valuable to the system analyst when the information system database is first designed or is being enhanced. A number of steps are required for collecting information, categorizing objects, and drawing the diagrams. The diagrams are then examined to determine the existence of the following dependencies:

1. If an object class has a one-to-many dependency, then a new record type is defined. The object class at the one side of the relationship becomes the key for accessing the object class at the many side of the relationship.

2. If this object class has identical one-to-many dependencies with other object classes, those other object classes become fields of the same table (unless normalization requires keeping them separate).

3. If the object classes have a one-to-one relationship, they are treated as a one-to-many relationship for both in turn. The relation as viewed from one is a $1:n$ dependency.

4. If the object classes have a many-to-many relationship, both object classes become key fields, and their individual roles are defined by other relationships.

The application of these general rules results in an object structure that is fully normalized. The object classes are given table and field names. While it is possible to convert an IA sentence diagram into a normalized data base schema, the IA method by itself is not sufficient to design a database schema for an information system under development. A data-flow definition is required in addition because IA diagrams do not articulate that level of detail. The IA diagrams are designed to show relationships in a static manner. A combination of structured analysis/data-flow diagrams with information analysis is essential for fully defining an information system.

4.6 SEMANTIC NETWORKS

A *semantic network* is a graphical representation of a relationship between two objects. It is a labeled directed graph where both nodes and edges may be labeled. The labels of nodes are typically used for reference purposes only and are usually mnemonic names. Designed originally for representing predicate calculus for logic programming, the semantic network concept can be easily extended to represent relational database designs. A semantic network gives a simple structured picture of a body of facts. The basic building block of a semantic network is a structure describing a relation (or a *predicate*) as shown in Figure 4-12.

The object representations in semantic networks are called *nodes*. There are four types of nodes: *concepts, events, characteristics,* and *value nodes*.

Concepts are the essential constants or parameters of the information systems and they specify physical or abstract objects.

Events are used to represent actions that occur and are represented on the basis of a case-grammar model. The representation consists of an event node and other nodes that specify who plays the roles associated with the event.

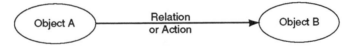

Figure 4-12. BiModal Semantic Network.

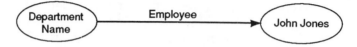

Figure 4-13.   Example of BiModal Semantic Network.

Characteristics are used to represent states or to modify concepts, events, or other characteristics. TRUE and FALSE are examples of characteristics.

Value nodes represent values of characteristics such as names, amounts, addresses, and so on. For example, "john brown," "$50.00," and "100 main street" are all values of characteristics.

A network is created by combining a number of nodes. The nodes are labeled with object names. For example, a structure for an *employee* may look as shown in Figure 4-13. A simple network of only two nodes as shown in Figure 4-13 is called a bimodal semantic network.

In Figure 4-13, "John Jones" is an employee of the "Department Name". A more complex network is achieved by connecting a number of nodes that are related. Typically, such a combination represents a major component of the information system. We will call this a *frame* for now. A combination of nodes may appear as in Figure 4-14.

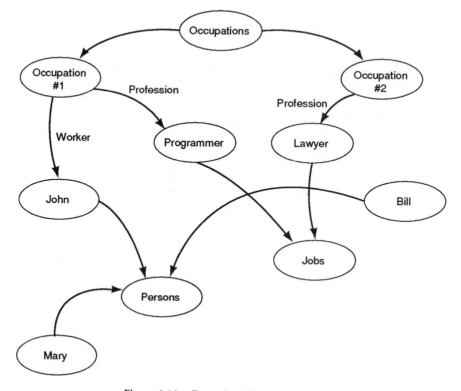

Figure 4-14.   Example of Semantic Network.

It should be noted that this network displays a number of different types of relationships that do not necessarily follow a logical decomposition of the business information system. To deal with this situation, the relationship can be expressed at a higher level to describe the complexity of the semantic network, as in Figure 4-15. Each node in this network can now be decomposed further to its own network at the next level down. Each of these lower-level networks can also be viewed as *frames.*

In this top-level frame we present the relationships between the four object classes. Each object class can be decomposed to the next level. For example, *Jobs* can be decomposed to "Teacher," "Doctor," "Lawyer," and so on. Similarly, *Professions* can be decomposed to "Legal," "Medical," "Engineering," and so on.

Let us now look at some terms that define the properties of a semantic network. Semantic networks feature *form modifiers* to define the following conditions within a network.

1. Conjunction
2. Disjunction
3. Negation
4. Implication

Conjunctions are represented by the multiple areas emanating from a single node. Enclosures can be used to represent semantic network implications. For example,

(Mary, Programmer)

is an enclosure. These features are used primarily in defining formulae described in examples that follow.

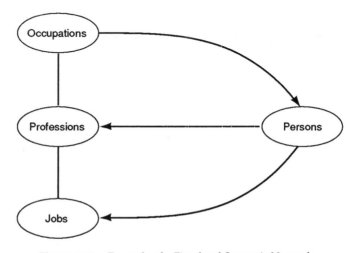

Figure 4-15.   Example of a First-level Semantic Network.

A *disjunction* is the equivalent of the use of parentheses to set off two relationships. For example,

[Worker (Department, Name) WSS# (Name, Numbers)]

is used to identify a person by department as well as by social security number. It is called a disjunction because two separate relations are defined within an enclosure.

A *negation* is defined by using a period (.) to imply the *not* condition, as in the following:

worker. (Mary, Programmer)

Here "Mary" is a worker in an occupation and is not a programmer in a profession. Figure 4-16 presents a graphical depiction of an example of *negation*. The inclusion of "profession" and "worker" within the ellipse implies that the relations must be read jointly as a negation.

An *implication* is a dual relationship; one relationship implies the other. For example, a relationship that "John" is a programmer implies that "John" has an address because, by implication, any person with the occupation of a programmer has an address. This may be represented as in Figure 4-17, which shows the impliction that workers in the programming profession have an address as the location. This implication is defined as follows:

[Worker(John, Programmer) → Location(John, Address)]

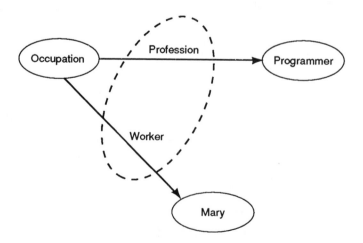

Figure 4-16.   Example of a Negation.

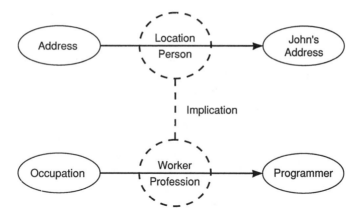

Figure 4-17.   Example of an Implication.

4.6.1 Uses for Information Analysis and Semantic Networks

Both Information Analysis and semantic networks are complex depiction methodologies not easily understood by end users. Furthermore, they are not easy to portray with ordinary programming and development tools such as text editors and word processors. And not many CASE tools support these two technologies. These limitations have combined to restrict the use of these techniques to highly scientific endeavors. They have not found much acceptance for commercial information processing design.

Nonetheless, the techniques in themselves have notable benefits. The notions presented by these techniques can be adapted to other techniques and methodologies. Some of the notions that characterize semantic networks, in particular, are eminently useful for other methodologies. In fact, the concepts of semantic networks can be used to extend the basis of Information Analysis relationships. Moreover, we have presented our own methodology in Section 4.9 that uses some key concepts of semantic networks.

Three overriding factors are essential for the success of any depiction methodology:

1. The ready availability of easy to use tools that analysts can use to depict the information system.
2. The ability of the technique to depict all important aspects of the information system, such as inputs, logical data entity relations, processes, and outputs.
3. The ability for an end user to intuitively understand the depiction taxonomy (symbols and their interpretation) without any training. A methodology

that is complex and requires end users to be trained is less likely to be reviewed.

Interestingly, none of the techniques noted above (and currently in use) fully satisfies all three criteria. Entity relationship diagrams are not sufficient for describing an information system; they do not depict processes within the system. Data-flow diagrams, on the other hand, depict processes, but not logical data entity relations. Information analysis and semantic networks do both, but are neither easy to draw (due to a general lack of drawing capabilities in usual programming tools) nor easy to understand for end users.

We believe that there are other depiction techniques in use in the world of artificial intelligence and expert systems development that are eminently applicable to information systems development. The primary technique is frame diagrams. We have expanded on the frame diagram technique to include some notions of semantic networks to define relations between *objects*. We call this new technique *Frame-Object Analysis diagram* methodology.

Let us first review frame diagrams before analyzing our new methodology of Frame-Object Analysis diagrams.

4.7 FRAME DIAGRAMS

We introduced the concept of *frames* in the previous section. We defined a frame as an element in the logical decomposition of an information system.

Frames are used to collect information components (that we will call objects for this discussion) that define an aspect or an area of an application. The representation of these objects can also include the relationship between these objects.

A database can be described using the concept of frames. Each object in the frame defines a component of the database that may be resolved into a single field, a group of fields, or even a table. The database description is further enhanced by descriptions of relationships between the objects.

The following examples of the uses of frames will make the concepts a little clearer.

Examples of frames.   Frames are applicable to a wide variety of problems. In the simplest form illustrated in Figure 4-18, frames represent a collection of information objects or other frames. The example in Figure 4-18 depicts a collection of frames describing the possible locations of a ship.

This example collects all of the possible locations (from a database perspective) that a ship can be at. The objects displayed in Figure 4-18 describe these locations. Each object has instances (or rows in a table) that define the location of a specific ship.

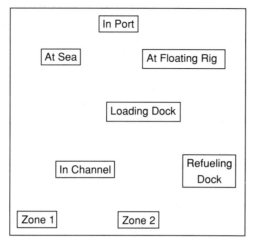

Figure 4-18.   Location Frames.

The frame "In Port" can be decomposed further to depict other information objects for the ship while it is in port. The frame would depict its activities while in port, such as unloading, disembarking passengers, refueling, loading, and boarding passengers.

Alternately, an "activities" frame can be defined to show all activities, including activities while the ship is at sea. The "activities" frame can be further decomposed to describe each activity. Figure 4-19 describes a *frame* for activities for ships.

The activities frame shows all activities, but provides no relationship or activity sequencing information. It gives no clue if refueling is performed before or after unloading, or if the ship can be unloaded while it is en route. This lack of information is a significant gap in the specification of an information system. The sequence of events is critical for a business information system. For example, in a business information system, aging accounts requires a clearly defined sequence of operations. It becomes obvious that frames require enhancement to define the relationship between information objects.

The frame described in Figure 4-19 can be made more meaningful by building an activities relationship within the frame as in Figure 4-20.

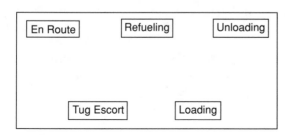

Figure 4-19.   Activities Frame.

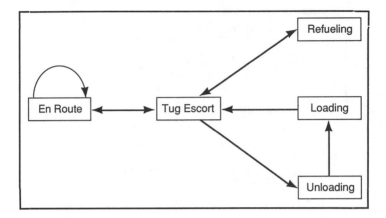

Figure 4-20.   Frame for Sequence of Activities.

4.8 FRAME-OBJECT ANALYSIS DIAGRAMS

We introduced the concepts of *frames, information analysis,* and *semantic networks* in earlier sections as methodologies for depicting a database design. All these methodologies have been used for information systems design documentation. However, a new breed of information systems based on knowledge engineering and object-oriented programming techniques (or object extensions to relational database management systems) calls for advanced information system design depiction methodologies.

The authors believe that as the technologies advance a more flexible and capable depiction technology is required. *Frame–Object Analysis diagramming methodology* proposed here combines the features of object definitions of information analysis, relation depiction of semantic networks, and the structured/ layered concepts of frames. This methodology is presented here to provoke some thoughts and start a debate that may lead to standardizing depiction methodologies for the next generation of object-oriented database management systems.

4.8.1 Objects

As we saw earlier in Chapter 3, objects contain structural as well as behavioral properties. In our concept of Frame-Object Analysis, an object is a basic entity. An object may be viewed as the end result of a full decomposition of data and methods (or operations) to a level where further decomposition does not add useful information to the knowledge base. Encapsulation at this level makes it easier to understand the external properties of objects and to manipulate them. This lowest-level object is our basic building block.

In object-oriented programming, objects have two kinds of relationships: *structural* (describing attributes) and *behavioral* (describing operations). Objects

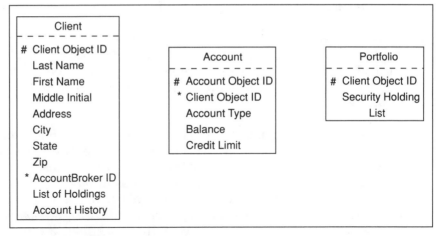

Client Account Objects

Figure 4-21.   Representation of Object Attributes.

are a part of a class definition and have common properties as described in Figure 4-21. Note that this is primarily a *structural* relationship, and Figure 4-21 describes only the attributes of object classes.

A frame can be used to show the relationship between object classes, as illustrated in Figure 4-22. Note that we have used a condensed form of objects to fit a larger number of entities within the frame.

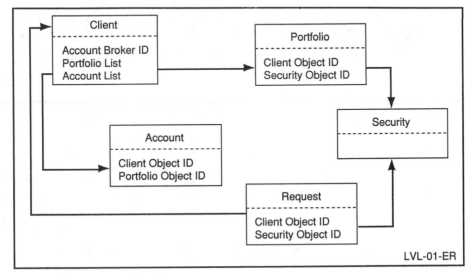

Entity Relationships for Client Account

Figure 4-22.   Objects and Relationships in Frame-Object Analysis Diagram.

4.8.2 Structural Relationship

A class of objects has a number of instances of objects that have similar properties. This similarity gives rise to an object class that has a subclass (*metaclass* in
SmallTalk terminology). We can represent an object subclass as shown in Figure
4-23. Note that dashed lines are used to distinguish metaclasses from class
hierarchies.

Depicting metaclasses.   In Figure 4-23, we have a frame that we call the
Subclasses of *Class Account* frame. This frame consists of two levels of subclasses.
At the higher level are the subclasses *Client_Account, Agency_Commis-
sions_Account,* and *Broker_Account.* The subclass *Client_Account* is decomposed
further to *Business_Account* and *Individual Account.* Similarly, the subclass *Broker
Account* is decomposed to *StockBroker_Account* and *Trader_Account.* When a client
buys or sells securities (such as stocks), the broker gets a commission that is
deducted out of the client account, and the agency account is also credited with a
commission. We have not shown the details of other accounts to keep our
discussion simple. The frame in Figure 4-23 not only represents a class of objects
but also subclasses of an object. This approach gives us a capability to represent
complex structural relationships for object subclasses.

Depicting aggregation.   Object classes may include other object classes
(*aggregation*). This is a "contained in" relationship between object classes. Note
that this is different from the concept of metaclasses. Figure 4-24 illustrates a class
hierarchy based on aggregation. A *Client_Account* object class may have a number
of *Portfolios.* A client may be serviced by a number of brokers. An object class
hierarchy provides a convenient mechanism for setting up this relationship.

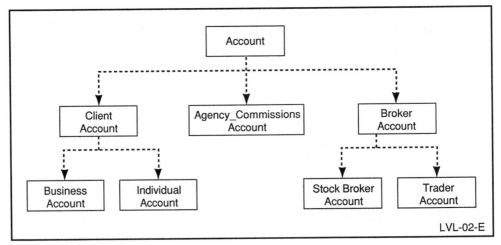

Sub-Classes of Class Account

Figure 4-23.   Structural Relationship in Frame-Object Analysis Diagram.

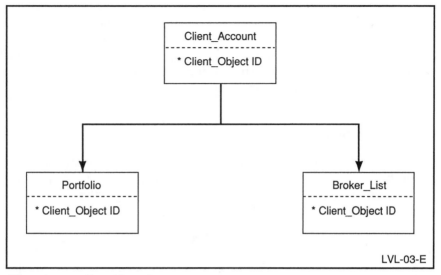

Client_Account Class Hierarchy

Figure 4-24.   Depicting Class Hierarchy in Frame-Object Analysis Diagram.

Class relationships.   Interestingly, frames can be used to show object class relationships using the same conventions as ER diagrams as in Figure 4-25. In our view, the Frame-Object Analysis methodology should not be restrictive and should support methodologies that are widely used for contemporary modeling. The key to using frames is to depict ER diagrams for each level of structural decomposition.

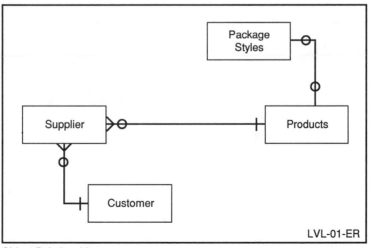

Object Relationships

Figure 4-25.   Behavioral Relationship in Frame-Object Analysis Diagram.

The Frame-Object methodology facilitates depicting object classes at a composite level for an overview of the system or at the decomposed levels as the designers progress through the details of the system requirements. As more information becomes available about object subclasses, the relationships can be depicted at lower levels. The concepts of frames and decomposition facilitate setting up a graphical design environment in a CASE (computer-aided software engineering) tool.

4.8.3 Behavioral Relationship

Objects interact with other objects via messages. Messages represent a request to perform a certain function that defines an action and, consequently, a behavior. A frame in a behavioral perspective depicts a function (or an operation). For example, we have an object relationship depicted in Figure 4-26.

Depicting processes. A process is a sequence of events that take place for a major function in the application. For example, reconciliation of accounts at the end of a month is a process. Similarly, the sequence of events that takes place when securities (stocks) are sold is a part of a process. Processes show the normal flow of operations in a business.

Figure 4-26 shows a frame called *Trade Operations* for security trading. Obviously, we have oversimplified the frame to clearly portray the relationship. Within this frame, we have the events *Create Client Order, Create Request, Create Trade Order,* and so on. These events, shown as objects, represent methods (or operations) and attributes encapsulated within objects that participate in a stock sale. When stock is sold, it starts a sequence of events depicted by the frame. We have deliberately ignored details of transactions to illustrate more clearly an important behavioral relationship.

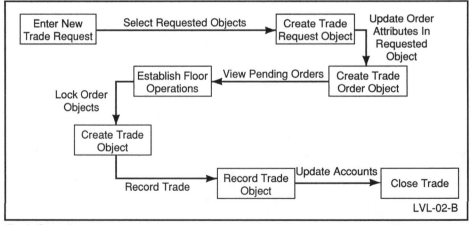

Trade Operations

Figure 4-26. Behavioral Relationship in Frame-Object Analysis Diagram.

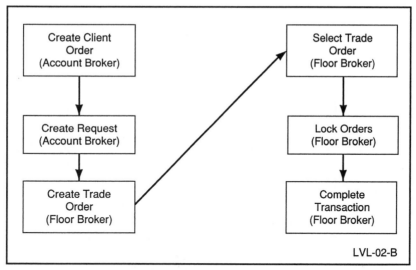

Sequence of Operations for Security Trading

Figure 4-27.   Example of Behavioral Relationship.

Depicting behavioral relationships.   A frame, in a behavioral perspective, represents functional parts of an application. For example, we have illustrated an object relationship in Figure 4-27.

We can decompose the *Create_Request* object class further to depict all operations related to managing *Request* objects. A request object is used by the stockbroker to request a trader to perform a specific trade. The next-level decomposition of the *Create_Request* object gives us the frame in Figure 4-27.

We can continue with the decomposition of the rest of the objects in Figure 4-28. This method can be extended to all processes in a target application. We will leave it as an exercise for the reader to determine further levels of decomposition for both the structural and behavioral frames and objects of Figure 4-28.

4.8.4 Developing System Documentation

It would be useful to review here the utility that the Frame-Object methodology provides to the designer or developer of an information system. The following lists some uses for Frame-Object Analysis diagrams presented in the discussion of the methodology:

STRUCTURAL

1. Structural view of all object classes in frames, that is, the attributes of all objects.
2. Condensed view of object classes showing relationships between objects.

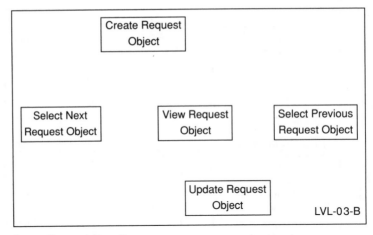

Create Request Functions

Figure 4-28.   Example of Decomposing Behavioral Relationship.

3. Depicting object metaclasses.
4. Depicting object class hierarchies based on aggregation relationships.
5. Showing ER diagrams in a more structured and multilevel manner.

BEHAVIORAL

6. Showing major processes that are a part of the information system.
7. Depicting functions at a high level.
8. Decomposing functions to show the detailed operations that constitute a major function.

An information system consists of structural as well as behavioral properties. Good analysis and design for an information system require that both structural and behavioral properties be modeled to a level of detail sufficient for accurately defining each entity and each process within the system.

It should be noted that the use of Frame-Object Analysis methodology does not negate the use of ER diagrams or even data-flow diagrams. In our view, the structural (or data) components of objects equate to tables in a relational database or object classes in an object-oriented database. Unlike the process of normalization, which treats the lowest-level data as its center of attention, the Frame-Object Analysis approaches the problem top down as well as from the level of objects. The normalization of data and detailed definition of data are performed after the overall application design is clearly defined.

The behavioral diagrams can be used to drive detailed data-flow diagrams and process diagrams for a more focused analysis of operations at all levels. We believe that, given this approach, Frame-Object Analysis is not only a thorough methodology for object-oriented database applications, but is equally adept at analyzing relational-database-based information systems.

4.9 SUMMARY

This chapter introduced an important component of a design methodology, the diagramming technique used to model an information system. A number of methodologies in current use were presented in this chapter.

It is important to understand the underlying theme behind these methodologies. Normalization approaches the issue from adhering to the mathematical foundations of relational databases. ER diagrams on the other hand depict relationships between entities at a high level and are useful for an overview of the information system. These methodologies depict primarily the structural relationships between data entities.

Data-flow diagrams, Information Analysis, and semantic analysis approach the issue from a processing perspective and show the data flows and/or operations. These methodologies depict primarily the behavioral relationships.

The Frame-Object Analysis methodology has borrowed from these other methodologies and combined them with frames to present an integrated methodology that shows structural and behavioral relationships at multiple levels. We believe that this methodology is more readily adaptable to the next generation of application builders.

4.10 EXERCISES

1. Expand the data elements depicted in Figure 4-21 to show AccountBroker objects also. Show the process of normalization for all data elements. Does the organization of object classes meet this definition of normalization?

2. Explain under what circumstances you would denormalize a database. What potential problems can be expected? What is the performance impact? Use a practical example and program it to confirm your analysis.

3. What are the benefits of ER diagrams? What are the limitations? Can ER diagrams be used for object-oriented database designs?

4. Are data-flow diagrams sufficient to fully define an information system? Explain. How would you use the combination of ER diagrams and DFD diagrams?

5. Explain the advantages and disadvantages of Information Analysis. Use the information provided in Figure 4-26 and build an Information Analysis diagram for it.

6. Use the information in Figure 4-26 and develop a semantic network to depict the relationships.

7. How much information about the structural components of the entities can be attained from the Information Analysis and semantic network diagrams in Exercises 5 and 6? Is it sufficient to describe the information system for future maintenance? How would you improve on it?

8. Determine further levels of decomposition for both the structural and behavioral frames and objects of Figure 4-28.

9. Describe what information should be included in system documentation for an information system. How would you use Frame-Object Analysis diagrams to meet these requirements?

5

Systems Design Methodology for Object-oriented Systems

We reviewed the key design issues for object-oriented systems in Chapter 3. In Chapter 4, we reviewed a number of techniques for depicting and analyzing information systems design. A question we have not addressed as yet is the kind of design methodology required for designing object-oriented database systems. The methodology consists not only of the methodology for depicting the database, but also the deeper issues of designing the objects that determine the functionality of an application. We will employ the object-oriented programming concepts discussed in Chapter 3 for developing the system design methodology presented in this chapter.

We introduced a new information systems design diagramming methodology in Chapter 4, which we called *Frame-Object Analysis diagrams*. As you may have concluded by now, we plan to use this methodology in our approach to systems design for object-oriented information systems design. We will also use the Frame-Object diagramming methodology introduced in Section 4.9 to depict an object-oriented design.

Obviously, system designs for information systems should be independent of the methodology. This is true in theory, but not entirely so in practice. The depiction methodology has a measurable impact on the depth and accuracy of the design. In that measure, the methodology is extremely important for a rigorous and successful design. An obvious question here is whether this methodology applies to relational database systems, or object-oriented database systems, or both. Let us first analyze what it is that is being designed and determine the similarities and differences between relational and object-oriented design concepts from a design methodology perspective. With this analysis as an important backdrop, we will present an approach to designing an object-oriented system.

5.1 ADVANCED INFORMATION SYSTEMS DESIGN

For any advanced information systems design, it is essential to follow an advanced methodology that has the capability to graphically depict the detailed functional decomposition of the systems and show clear and well-defined data relationships. As we have seen, in a relational database, while a fully normalized system is sound from a database update perspective, it is not good from a performance perspective. A relational database must, however, be fully normalized to determine the potential for update anomalies. Tables within a fully normalized database can then be analyzed and combined to improve performance. It should be noted that denormalization is a task that cannot be taken lightly. More so, denormalization cannot be achieved successfully if the information system is not fully defined and clearly depicted in a fully normalized manner. A good information systems design depiction methodology is as applicable to a relational system as it is to an object system. An object-oriented database system requires a level of analysis much deeper than a relational system to achieve an application system that is sound and has a high level of performance.

Before the actual design of the objects in the database can be performed, a detailed analysis of existing forms and procedures, business rules, applications, and expectations is necessary. Based on this analysis, the information elements required in the database and the functions supported by the application can be determined. The elements generate the definitions of the attributes of the objects. The functions determine the services that need to be supported.

The proper design of objects requires a clear definition of all object *attributes* and *services* that are required to manage the information and perform the required functions. Once the attributes and services are defined, the power of *object classification* and *object inheritance* can be applied for determining the classes of objects that have similar attributes and provide similar services. Inheritance provides the capability for rapid design as well as reusability of objects within a class hierarchy. The attributes of the objects and services provided by the objects are organized around the requirements of the information system, and they are made to conform to the class definitions. These object definitions are then encapsulated to form the basic building blocks for the information system. These basic building blocks are reusable for other functions and applications required of the information systems.

Properly designed objects go a long way in ensuring that business rules are not bypassed and that data integrity is not compromised as a result of changes to the information system, enhancement to the information system, and, more importantly, the distribution of the information system across dispersed geographic locations.

5.2 DESIGN METHODOLOGY: OBJECT ORIENTED VERSUS RELATIONAL

Most relational systems designs are based on the notion of entities and relations between entities. The entities store knowledge (or attributes) about the structure (and content) of the information represented by the entity. The entities do not store any information about the manner in which this information is utilized. There is no information describing the functions that are based on this information. Moreover, there is no information about the external presentation of this information beyond the basic datatyping. The relations between entities are the only additional information describing the entities. This information is generally referred to as *structural* information about the data elements.

A basic difference in object-oriented systems is that object-oriented systems are based on the notion of objects, that is, on the basis of an entity and associated operations encapsulated within the object. The object consists of attributes and methods. The object attributes are similar to the attributes stored within entities in a relational database and describe the *structural* aspects of the object. The methods describe operations that may be performed to manipulate the attributes before they are presented to the calling object. The methods can be designed to perform a variety of tasks. For example, methods can be designed to check the value of an attribute and perform conditional actions, methods can convert the attribute to a form appropriate for a specific external presentation requirement, and so on. Objects that include methods can be designed to perform some of the functions directly related to the values of attributes or to changes in the values of the attributes. Known as services, these methods define the *behavioral* aspects of the object.

The key point to note here is that objects in an object-oriented database carry significantly greater information than a relational database entity and are, consequently, more complicated. Designing an object-oriented database requires a coordination of the structural and behavioral features of the information system. One can conclude that the approach to designing an object-oriented database must be much more rigorous than designing a relational database system. Hence, it is important that the methodology for designing object-oriented systems be studied in great detail. We recommend that readers follow through the design of a simple application while reading through Section 5.3 to achieve a much better hands-on appreciation of the design methodology.

5.3 OBJECT-ORIENTED DESIGN METHODOLOGY

Designing an object-oriented system involves a number of steps. For each step a number of actitvities have to be performed to collect the required information about the enterprise, to classify this information, to determine the range and classes of operations that have to be performed, and to document the results of a detailed analysis in a highly organized and visually comprehensible manner. The following lists the major steps in this process:

1. Analysis of the information system requirements using object-oriented techniques.
2. Identifying the lowest-level objects and their attributes; note that these are the building blocks for the design.
3. Identifying classification and assembly structures.
4. Defining attributes in detail for each object to conform to the classification.
5. Defining connections between objects.
6. Defining services provided by each object.
7. Incorporating object-oriented design in a frame-object diagram.

The methodology is important to ensure that the objects are defined correctly and rigorously. A good design requires the object classification to be performed to produce the most efficient structure of class hierarchy. Similarly, messages between objects have to be clearly defined so that pre- and postconditions can be set up to address the range of supported messages. The following sections address the steps noted above (except the last one) in a methodical manner. Step 7 on object-oriented design is explained in Chapters 8 and 9.

5.3.1 Information System Analysis for Object Design

The key to any successful design is knowledge and insight about the enterprise and the requirements for the information system. The information must be collected, clearly depicted, and then analyzed. There are a number of dimensions for a detailed and complete analysis. Detailed analysis requires not only understanding functions and associated data structures at higher levels, but also an understanding of a process for achieving sufficiently detailed functional decomposition of the tasks. Once the tasks have been decomposed, the data flow across relevant combinations of tasks must be determined. Frame-Object Analysis diagrams (introduced in Section 4.9) can be very beneficial in this process.

Task decomposition.   The Frame-Object diagrams provide a means of describing the high-level tasks in a top-level frame. The tasks are then decomposed, one frame for each high-level task, as illustrated in Figures 5-1 and 5-2. A frame describing the decomposition at the lower level provides significantly more detail about the task. It presents a hierarchical view of the tasks at two levels.

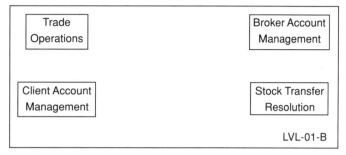

Stock Trading

Figure 5-1.   Example of High-level Task Frame.

Figure 5-2 describes the decomposition of one of the tasks described in Figure 5-1. As you will notice in Figure 5-2, the decomposed task produces another set of lower-level tasks. These tasks can be decomposed further into a lower-level set of tasks.

The task frames provide a behavioral perspective of the information system. To complete the behavioral picture, we need to also determine the services required for or provided by each task. These services can also be documented in a frame, as illustrated in Figure 5-3.

For each task, a set of services can be described that is necessary for supporting the task. These services in turn define the methods (or operations) required within each object that must provide these services. This illustrates how tasks are transformed into methods that must be encapsulated within an object.

Organizing data.   In general, entities as used in a relational model are similar to objects (the structural components in objects) in an object-oriented design. Entities consist of things or items or states. Customers, transactions, and account information are examples of entities. Customer names, addresses, and

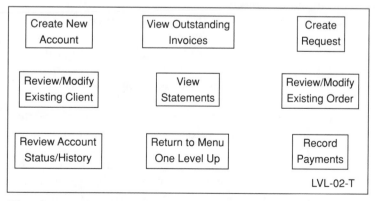

Client Account Management

Figure 5-2.   Example of Decomposing a High-level Task.

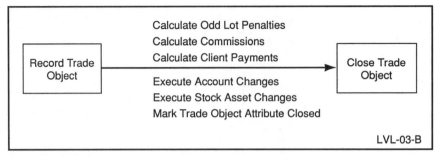

Create Trade Order

Figure 5-3.   Example of a Services Frame for a Task.

account balances are examples of fields within entities (or attributes of the entities). In an object-oriented design, objects can be used to describe customers, transactions, and account information. The fields within entities, such as customer names and addresses, can be defined as attributes within objects. In this sense, the design of the structural components of objects requires the same information as entities in a relational database. The major difference arises when one considers the behavioral components of objects.

Task frames can be used to define tasks and the entities that participate in performing that task. At the top level, the tasks are defined by the main menu for the application. These tasks can be decomposed in lower-level frames, and entities required for each frame are determined. These entities and their attributes are further defined as lower-level task frames are examined and compared with the information available within the enterprise. The entities and their attributes required for each level of the task frames are determined. With the definitions of entities and their attributes established by tasks (or functions), we are in a position to define objects.

The field-level details of the entities (attributes) just defined are the attributes for the objects. It is essential to develop a clear understanding of the composition of the entities and to analyze the logical combination of entities based on how they are used. This step is the equivalent of full normalization and planned denormalization to achieve performance.

Encapsulation criteria.   How the entities and related operations (translated from functions defined in the frames) are combined is a question with no easy answers. Detailed analysis is necessary to determine the optimum combinations of data and operations. Before such analysis can be performed, the criteria must be established on which the encapsulation process is based. The criteria will consist of issues such as performance of complex functions, ease of programming, and flexibility of future enhancements. The relative trade-offs must be determined and the guidelines for encapsulation should be established on the basis of a detailed analysis of these trade-offs.

5.3.2 Establishing Objects

The information collected in the previous section is examined in detail to establish the basic (or the lowest-level) objects and the functions at all levels. For each level of functions, a hierarchy of potential objects is established until the lowest level using the basic objects is reached. The basic objects are fine-tuned until all higher-level requirements can be adequately addressed by the basic objects. The basic objects are the primary building blocks for the application. The composition of objects at higher levels is determined significantly by the classification process that establishes the class hierarchy. It is possible that two or more frames are combined horizontally or vertically to define a class of objects.

Object naming conventions.   Successful design requires well-defined naming conventions so that the name of an object has a close bearing to the contents of the object. This makes it easier for other developers to understand the programming logic. In a team effort, clearly established naming conventions help in removing potential duplication as well as confusion regarding the function of the objects. In other words, establishing sound naming conventions for objects is as important as establishing sound naming conventions for tables in a relational database. All objects are named and given a unique object identity. Note that the object name is not necessarily the same as the object identity (quite possibly the object-oriented database in use may automatically assign object identity tags). The International Standards Organization (ISO) has also produced a standard for conventions for assigning object identifiers.

The naming conventions should go beyond object names and should also address the naming of attributes within objects and operations within objects. A recommended practice is to include a part of the object name (for example, the first three characters) for naming the attributes and operations. This makes it easier to determine the association of the attributes and operations while programming. This is especially useful when the programming is performed as a team effort.

Refining basic objects.   The objects created at the lowest level are further analyzed to ensure that only the required attributes are included in each object. Duplicity of attributes across objects must be reduced to a minimum because duplicity introduces the potential for update anomalies, especially if the operations are also very similar. Additional objects may have to be created to reduce the impact of duplicity of attributes. Note that this step, again, is the equivalent of what is recognized as normalization in a relational database. A unique complication in an object-oriented database is that the objects at a higher level may also have attributes that are unique and nonderivative (that is, are not derived from other attributes). These objects must also be clearly analyzed at this stage. The detailed analysis of all other objects must wait until the object classification is complete.

In addition to attributes, objects contain operations that define the services that the object is capable of performing. As in the case of redundant attributes, operations supporting services that are not required or are redundant can be removed. Unlike attributes, there may be duplicate operations or very similar operations in more than one object that are necessary due to the class definitions. Operations may appear similar, but may be associated with very different attributes within different objects. For example, an update operation will be needed with most of the objects, but the code associated with the update action could be significantly different.

We have mentioned normalization a few times in the discussion above. Normalization is a major effort in relational databases. Normalization helps remove duplicate field definitions. Full normalization implies that the only fields duplicated in more than one table are foreign keys (usually the index fields). However, real-world information systems require some denormalization to reduce joins and achieve acceptable performance. The designer of an object-oriented system is inherently less concerned about duplication of data because the objects are treated differently from tables in a relational database. Nonetheless, it is important to determine which objects have common attributes and services. This information is extremely useful in maintaining integrity of objects when the common attributes are updated. It also helps in avoiding very complex updates involving a large number of objects in a single update.

Completion of this phase of the analysis results in the creation of the lowest-level object layer and a generalized structure of object class hierarchy.

5.3.3 Indentifying Classification and Object Assembly Structures

The design up to this stage addressed the objects at the lowest level only (except for objects with nonderived attributes). The classification phase of the analysis and design is concerned with identifying the component parts of all objects and determining how they are assembled into functioning objects. The problem space addressed by the object (that is, the services the object is required to provide) is mapped to the components (both structural and behavioral). Additional complexity, in the form of attributes and methods, is added to the object model if needed to address all specific requirements.

Another design function concerned with adding a level of complexity is based on the notions of *classification* and *inheritance*. Commonality of attributes and operations must be established for classification. Inheritance plays a major role in creating objects that demostrate a high level of commonality in attributes and operations. All objects are examined for *generalization* and *specialization* features. Objects that have notable commonality and that share common attributes and operations (that is, have very similar methods) are grouped under a single class of objects. The notion of generalization introduces the potential for defining a class of objects with the same general properties.

The notion of specialization extends the notion of generalization by inferring the potential for *inheritance* of an object of that class (which has the same general properties). The object inherits the common properties of the class, which are customized to meet the specialized requirements of that object. The class becomes a template from which the instances of objects within the class can be created. The objects so created inherit the common attributes and methods. They are then modified by adding attributes and methods to support the specific data and services supported by those objects. Some attributes and operations may be dropped or modified for the object instances.

Multiple inheritance.   There may be some objects that have a level of commonality with more than one class of objects. In other words, these objects have properties that must be inherited from two or more classes of objects. A good example of this is a checking account that operates in a manner very similar to a revolving charge account. The hybrid account must inherit the properties of a class that defines revolving charge accounts as well as a class that defines checking accounts. Of course, the hybrid account can be created as an independent class without using inheritance. But then a major strength of object-oriented programming leading to *reusability*, called *multiple inheritance*, is not being applied.

The concept of designing object classes from higher-level object classes is quite essential for large and complex information systems. The objects created at the lowest level may indeed have inherited properties from two or more higher-level objects. A careful analysis of the function hierarchy diagrams helps in developing the class hierarchy diagrams. The class hierarchy diagrams clearly establish which objects need to address multiple inheritance issues.

The completion of this phase produces a detailed set of structure diagrams describing the structural and behavioral properties of the information system. These structure diagrams are very important in understanding the overall design of the application.

5.3.4 Defining Attributes

Having established the overall hierarchy of objects and Frame-Object Analysis diagrams describing object as well as function hierarchies, we can turn inward to defining objects in greater detail. Up to this point, we have defined the attributes in very general terms to facilitate classification. During this phase we will become very specific in the definitions of the attributes. Attributes can be descriptive in nature or they can be abstract in nature. The attributes must be analyzed down to the atomic level. In a manner similar to objects, attributes should also be classified and the notions of generalization and specialization applied to them. Note that attributes can be unique and nonderived, or they can be derived as the result of an operation on another attribute and retained within the object. A detailed description of all attributes so developed is very similar in concept to the database schema developed for conventional database design. We will call it the *object attribute schema.*

Attribute identification.   Every attribute in every object in the object attribute schema must be named. This name becomes the attribute identifier. The naming convention established in Section 5.3.2 must also guide the naming of the attributes. There is a general tendency to associate names to attributes that describe the nature of data contained in them. Nonetheless, from a programming perspective, it is important that the attribute can be easily related to the object that it is a part of.

Typically, in a relational database design the designer assigns primary keys, embedded keys, foreign keys, and pointers at this stage. While there is a strong temptation to do that, it is not necessary in an object database to define *pointers* (the equivalent of keys in objects) at this stage. Indeed, it may be preferable to delay the definition of keys to the next stage, that is, the stage where all the object interrelationships and interobject messages are defined.

Attribute details.   Each attribute has a number of characteristics associated with it. The following characteristics form the basic set of attribute properties that must be defined as a part of the object attribute schema:

1. *Required:* Is the attribute value REQUIRED? That is, can the object be created or updated without it?
2. *Duplicates:* Will there be repeating values (duplicates) for this attribute? That is, may object instances of this class have identical values for this attribute?
3. *NULLs:* Will NULL values be allowed as values for this attribute?
4. *Range definition:* Are any rules being defined for limiting the range of values that are acceptable for this attribute?
5. *Datatype:* Datatype and units of measure for this value if it is numeric value.
6. *Precision:* What kind of precision is needed for storing a numeric value?
7. *Internally Derived:* Is it derived from any other attribute in this object?
8. *Externally Derived:* Is it derived from an attribute in another object?

On completion of this phase we now have, in addition to our structural Frame-Object diagrams, a detailed object attribute schema. The attributes are organized and are ready to be mapped into a tabular form (or a matrix) that defines the object, the object classifications, and the relationship with other objects (similar to the relational model). The *pointers* (or keys) within each object are also defined as a part of defining the relationship between objects. Note that, unlike relational database tables where the primary key is used to establish a relationship, in the object-oriented database system the object identifier is used to establish relationships. An attribute equivalent to a primary key is not required. Pointers, therefore, are equivalent to foreign keys in relational database tables. Correlation tables should be developed that include a number of objects linked via foreign pointers. Interestingly, the concepts of normalization can also be applied to objects to ensure that the lowest-level objects are uniquely identified by their primary pointer.

On completion of these tasks, we have an object-oriented database schema. We can proceed with the next phase that defines the interrelationships among objects.

5.3.5 Defining Inter-Object Relationships

The goal of this phase of the design is to model real-world interactions between objects. One object can manipulate or interact with another object in one of two ways. In the first type of interaction, an object can execute a method that performs an action directly on an object. The following are examples of an action of this type:

- An object contains another object (or a pointer to another object) as one of its attributes. It can manipulate this object during any of its operations.
- An operation may create instances of any object either for temporary use or to add to a global dataset; for example, persistent log objects may be created to record certain operations.

Note that interactions between objects of this type can be a result of structural (an attribute) or behavioral (an operation) components within an object.

The second form of interaction between objects is realized through a *message* communicated from one object to another. The message specifies the nature of the interaction. The nature of the interaction may be one of the following types:

- An object (or an attribute from an object) is passed as an input parameter to an operation. The operation may retrieve information or include any of that object's methods.
- Flow of data (attribute data or variable) as a result of satisfying a postcondition from one object to another that influences the execution of the operation.
- The message requests the second object to initiate an operation defined as a method within the object.
- The flow of data as well as a request to initiate an operation. The data is interpreted by the second object on the basis of the action specified in the message. A return parameter may also be specified in the message.

Two major tasks are involved in designing and depicting messages connecting objects. The first is to define the format for all messages. A common format is fundamental for good consistency and uniform programming for all objects and all messages. The second major task is to define the connections themselves in detail. As you may have surmised, the semantic analysis depiction within Frame-Object Analysis is pertinent for describing the connections. This method of depiction allows attaching descriptive labels to lines connecting objects that express the nature of the connections.

Defining message formats.   As we just stated, defining uniform message formats is extremely important. The message format must, at the very minimum, include the following:

1. Object pointer
2. Message name
3. Message type
4. Input parameters
5. Output parameters

The *object pointer* points to the object that this message is directed to. Every message must be identified by *name* to allow invocation of the message. The *type* of the message defines the set of input and ouput parameters that must be included in the message. Messages can be of *direct invocation* type or they can be *IPC messages*. Generally, every message has input parameters. However, the type of message determines if there are any return parameters.

If a message is of type *direct invocation* (that is, it remains within a single process), then the output parameters could be addresses in which to return data. For *IPC messages,* output parameters can be used to specify if there is an expected return message or parameters. More commonly, no output parameters would be included in the first message, and a separate definition would be provided for any return message. When one gets down to the real nuts and bolts of IPC mechanisms, the messages need to be self-describing; that is, each parameter would be specified, such as, *type, length,* and *data.*

Defining object connections.   Before object connections can be established, it is necessary to determine which objects interact with one another. This interaction can be within a class or can be across class hierarchies. The connections will therefore occur both in the *structural* as well as *behavioral* frames. Data flows can be depicted as *instance connections* in structural frames. Actions that initiate operations, *message connections,* may be depicted on the behavioral frames. The first part of the analysis consists of identifying the flows and actions that link the objects. We have defined the objects in the last four sections. Note that we have already performed task decomposition in Section 5.3.1. Armed with the definition of objects and the task decompositions, we are in a position to develop both the structural and the behavioral frames that define the complete

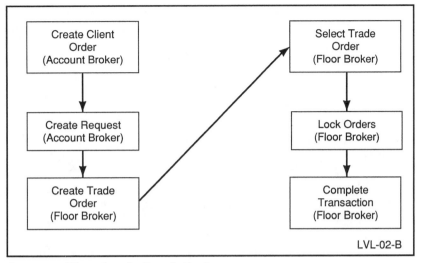

Sequence of Operations for Security Trading

Figure 5-4.   Example of Object Instance Connection Lines.

application system in a simple form. We can now add the complexity derived from the messages and the exact nature of object interactions.

The first step is to connect objects by *instance connection* lines as shown in Figure 5-4. The instance connection lines at this stage give no clue as to the nature of the instance connection. Arrowheads are used with the instance connection lines to denote the direction of the message, that is, the sender and the receiver for the message. The use of instance connection lines with arrowheads is depicted in Figure 5-5.

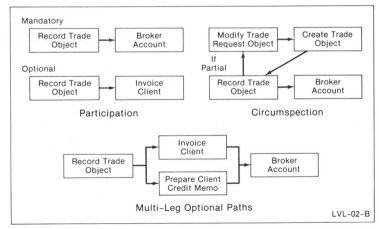

Trade Operations

Figure 5-5.   Types of Object Instance Connections.

To further enhance the definition of connections, we must analyze *multiplicity*, *participation*, and special cases such as multileg operations and many-to-many relations. *Multiplicity* is defined as the potential number of object connections from one object to another. For example, an object may send messages to two other objects and receive a message from one object. This particular object has a multiplicity of 3 because it interacts with exactly three objects in this frame. A more complex level of multiplicity is achieved by analyzing each frame where this object is used and adding up unique connections to determine the total multiplicity for this object. This information is very useful, especially when the object needs modification. The level of multiplicity is a good indicator of the potential complexity. Not only is it a good indicator of complexity, but a multiplicity matrix (or table) identifying the objects that each object interacts with helps in ensuring that, when an object is changed, the impact of that change on all other objects can be predicted and managed properly. This ensures that the affected objects can also be analyzed systematically to determine if they need to be changed in turn.

Participation determines if the type of linkage is tight or loose. In object terms, it means if it is *optional* or *mandatory*. When the object linkage is optional, that is, if the connection is loose, the data modifications and operations in the first object may or may not affect the second object. For example, the "sale of stock" may or may not affect a specific "client account" where the client has separate accounts for different stock portfolios. However, the "sale of stock" always affects the "agent commissions" account. Figure 5-5 provides examples to illustrate the concepts of the different types of object instance connections. Usage of these concepts is illustrated in Figure 5-6, which lists the major tasks that must be performed for executing a client order for a stock trade and illustrates how instance connections are depicted. Note that the dashed lines indicate an optional linkage; that is, one of those four actions may be selected.

There are other special cases of instance connections that must be determined and illustrated in the frame diagrams. These include circumsections, multileg optional paths, and many-to-many connections.

A *circumsection* is a case where a change in an object affects other objects, which in turn affect the original object. A change of this nature is rather complex. The simplest case of circumsection is when a change in one attribute within an object changes other attributes within the same object.

Multileg optional paths define a more complex relationship than a direct link between two objects. The change in one object may affect the second object via the direct instance connection as well as indirectly through a multileg instance connection (that is, the change cascades through a number of intermediate objects). These connections are somewhat difficult to visualize. If not properly accounted for, these connections also cause more complex and hard to pinpoint side effects in the operation of the information system.

Many-to-many links describe the situation where a number of objects are linked in a number of different ways. In other words, unlike the simple one-to-one direct links (where there is only one way in which one object can affect

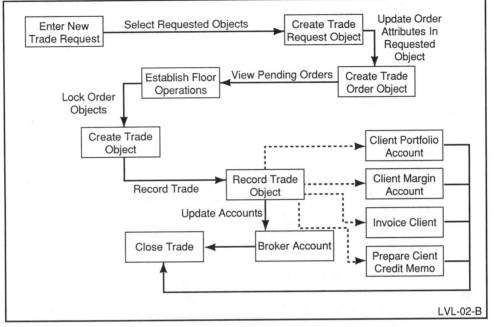

Trade Operations

Figure 5-6.   Example of Object Instance Connections.

another object), in the presence of many-to-many links a change in one object affects another object in many different ways depending on the operations. All the potential links must be analyzed to determine what conditions cause the link to start functioning, what operations are performed in each case, and how many of these links can be functioning simultaneously.

Note that *message connections* are direct links. Message connections specify links that describe actions and initiate an operation in the target object. For example, message connections are used for each leg of a multileg optional path or a many-to-many link. Before the complex links can be defined, the message connections must be defined as the initial step in outlining the functions being performed by these objects and the operations required for each object. The message connections are further refined after a detailed analysis and design of the object services, as described in the next section.

5.3.6 Defining Object Services and Operations

As we mentioned in Section 5.3.1, each task is decomposed down to the level of services and operations provided by each object in the system. Every object in the information system has a specific role and, consequently, provides a specific set of services and operations. Objects combine and through their links of services and operations perform a higher-level application function. It is necessary to depict this relationship clearly to ensure that all application functions are properly addressed.

The methods (operations) encapsulated within the object define the services provided by the object. These can be very basic database services, such as CREATE, UPDATE, SELECT, DESTROY (or even "read and update specific attribute"), and so on. Or the services can be fairly complex, for example, decomposing the information within a file and displaying it. The object services definition describes the services available as functions within the object as well as the services available to outside entities. These outside entities are other objects (or operations encapsulated within other objects). An outside entity can also be a processing routine at a higher level. Not only is it necessary to define the interobject service requirements, but it is also necessary to determine the service requirements of all external entities such as user programs. Figure 5-7 illustrates how object services are depicted in a frame.

Some services not clearly defined as parts of functions address special states, such as unexpected conditions, errors, or abnormal processing. These services must also be defined. Some of these services are coded in the pre- and postconditions within the object.

Another set of services not clearly defined by functional requirements is object life histories. These include issues of persistence, object life within memory, programmed transformations of objects, versioning, and so on. Further analysis is necessary to uncover all these issues and to design the objects with these issues in mind.

At this stage, we have completed frame diagrams for the behavioral component of the information system. These diagrams depict the detailed service layers within the information system.

5.4 ADVANCED OBJECT-ORIENTED DESIGN

The previous two sections described the approach to an object-oriented database design. The key to ensuring a manageable design is controlling the complexity of the object relationships, encapsulating system-state and finite-state behaviors, and selecting the appropriate design methodologies and tools.

You will recall that object classification and inheritance (especially, multiple inheritance) are very powerful concepts in the design of object-oriented systems. The key to depicting the design in a clear and comprehensive design notation methodology is extremely important for designing a complex enterprise-wide system. Furthermore, unlike relational database systems, where the prototype can be developed without fully designing the internal functions of the systems, object-oriented systems required additional up-front effort in establishing object designs that include all internal functions. Object-oriented systems require much greater design effort in the initial stages than a relational database system. The design developed for an object-oriented system must be as close to the final as

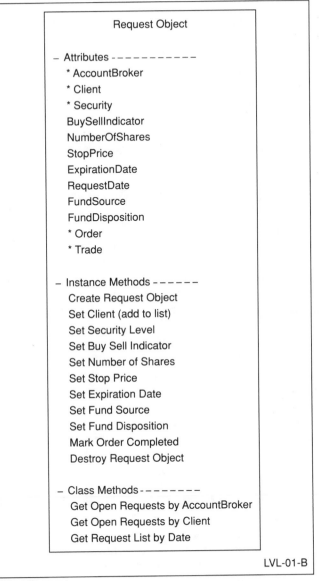

Object Request

Figure 5-7. Example of Object Services Frame.

possible. While relational database systems do provide the luxury of postponing the complex aspects of the design to later stages of development (and consequently making potential changes easier), changes to initial designs in object-oriented systems can be expensive. Changes can affect the attributes and methods in a large number of objects, the links between objects that have changed must be adjusted; and the message connections must be reestablished.

Following a rigorous design methodology is much more important for an object-oriented database design than it is for a relational database design. A well-designed and well-documented object-oriented system produces good results due to the isolation of attributes and methods provided by encapsulation. Changes to objects can be made more easily, and the external impact of the change can be minimized. It is important that all changes made to the design after deployment of the application be fully documented also. If the design document is not kept up to date, there is always the potential that changes will be made without evaluation of their full impact on the system. Fully documented designs make it considerably easier to determine the impact of the changes under consideration.

The analysis of an advanced information system spans a number of domains. These domains include distributed systems, major financial systems, and embedded sytems for real-time operations, all using the database as the active information repository. Each domain has its own special set of requirements in areas of volume of data, distribution of data, real-time performance, overall code size, operational flexibility, reliability, and so on. The relative merits of the design must be measured for each of the areas important to the domain and, if necessary, optimized further.

The major issue for distributed environments is the dilemma of *replicated* versus *duplicated* objects. In our definition, *replicated* means that all the object components within a particular subset are resident in multiple locations. The objects are replicated at each location and are updated dynamically as needed. A replicated object is treated as a single object instance with copies on two or more servers, each referenced by the same object identifier. The location of objects is important for accessing the object from both performance as well as data integrity considerations. Replicated objects require mechanisms to ensure that identical objects at all servers remain synchronized. In our definition, *duplicated* means that objects are duplicated on a temporary basis only while they are in use, and one server is considered the owner. This scheme is a little bit easier insofar as maintaining the updates to objects.

For real-time systems the location of data, object persistence in memory, and response times of the system are very important. Location of data has a direct effect on performance and overall responsiveness of the system. Maintaining a large number of objects and automatic management of object persistence in memory also have a notable effect on performance. Real-time systems may need to respond to time-driven inputs; that is, if the system does not respond in time, information can be lost. Management of objects in memory becomes crucial to such applications.

5.5 KEY FEATURES OF ODBMSs

A number of available databases have been designed for object managment. Some key differences from RDBMSs noticeable in these ODBMSs are in the areas of designers' and programmers' interfaces. Most ODBMSs provide a graphical *schema generator, database browser,* and *source-level debugger.* These three utilities provide a comprehensive graphical development environment. The graphical input from the user is converted to C++ (or some other) object-oriented code.

A further capability provided by the *schema generator* is that when users design the schema graphically they can also create the inheritance relationships instead of writing them separately in textual form. This approach allows developers to easily view the underlying data models and helps them eliminate database creation errors.

Most of the ODBMSs automatically provide an architecture that supports networked client/server usage and can be accessed from workstations as well as PCs. They also provide the capability for distributed database management, which allows for distributing objects. Generally, mapping an RDBMS-based application to an ODBMS-based application is not too complex a task, and a range of utilities is provided for such mapping. (Programmers do not have to recode to an object-oriented paradigm.)

Typically, the ODBMS uses the same interface for both transient as well as persistent data; data characteristics are declared when data is allocated in memory by the application program. The developers do not have to (although they can if they wish to) declare data to belong to a persistent class or type.

A good ODBMS must be a full object-oriented database system that is designed to support large-scale object databases. It should reflect the object paradigm with *object encapsulation* and *inheritance* of both data and functions (or methods). It should provide the capability to define persistent, shared objects that can address both single and multiple inheritance. Unlike relational databases, object-oriented database structures should resemble C++ or some other object-oriented language program structures for data in memory (that is, the equivalent of class instances or objects), thereby minimizing discontinuities between programming and database operations and structures.

Most ODBMSs also provide prebuilt libraries of predefined classes and predefined methods for data definition, access, and manipulation.

The key to a successful large-scale database for multiuser operation is its capability for shared access to persistent objects. The capability for concurrent operation with multiuser access has a significant performance impact on large and complex multiuser operations.

Polymorphism is another important feature for a full object-oriented database. Polymorphism is the ability of objects from different classes to respond in their own appropriate manner to a single common message. It is the combination of inheritance, encapsulation, and polymorphism that confers on ODBMS-based object-oriented programming its true power.

5.6 SUMMARY

This is the second chapter in the object-oriented design series. Chapter 3 addressed the basic concepts of object-oriented programming and how these concepts are applied to object-oriented databases. In this chapter we concerned ouselves primarily with the methodology for designing objects. The object design base developed in these two chapters is used as the base for the development of the Transaction and Object Models in Chapters 8 and the object design in Chapter 9.

This chapter also explored the use of Frame-Object Analysis diagrams for designing objects. Frame-Object Analysis diagrams help in consolidating objects as well as operations in logical groups. They also help in clearly depicting the results of decomposing tasks down to the lowest-level objects.

The object design methodology consists of analyzing the information system requirements and identifying the lowest-level objects and their attributes. The objects are then classified and the object assembly structures are identified. The attributes are fine-tuned to conform to the classification. The connections between objects are established, and the services provided by each object are determined. An integral step of the design process is to document the design using the Frame-Object Analysis diagramming methodology.

5.7 EXERCISES

1. Discuss the notable differences in the design methodologies applied to relational database systems as compared to object-oriented database systems.
2. Explain the concept of task decomposition. Describe an application function in your environment and show the decomposed task components for that function.
3. Explain the concept of encapsulation. How is encapsulation applied in the design of objects?
4. Create a top-level behavioral frame and at least one second-level behavioral frame for the application.
5. Using the lower-level behavioral frame, derive a set of low-level objects that can be used to build up that piece of the application. Specify the important attributes of these objects.
6. Determine whether generalization and specialization may be applied to these objects to derive an inheritance hierarchy. Describe the general attri-

butes and services provided by the parent object and the additional attributes and services provided by the child objects.

7. Think up a simple application (or an application you have recently worked on) and apply the object-oriented design methodology described in this chapter. The design should include the steps noted in Exercises 4 and 5.

8. Select two objects and describe each attribute in detail, according to the properties listed in Section 5.3.4.

9. Determine the relationships and interactions between the objects in the application. Draw a frame depicting the connections between a set of objects and the action associated with each connection.

10. Define the set of operations (methods) for each of the derived application objects. The object interconnections defined in Exercise 9 will provide input to this process, as well as an examination of the user interaction with each object.

6

Effective Project Design Management

A successful project is achieved by ensuring effective project management at each stage of development. A professionally developed information system leading to user satisfaction entails careful adherence to a formal systems development life cycle. A formal design life cycle, essential for creating large systems, follows specific phases or steps. The life cycle should include steps to lessen some of the problems inherent in developing a complex system, such as insufficient or incorrect information, lack of user and functional expert involvement, designers working with different sets of information, mismatches between designs of different components, coordination of a large development team, clear definition of requirements, and availability of a well-documented functional specification. Careful planning is essential for the success of a project. The planning effort must take into account the following factors:

- The nature and complexity of the project.
- The size and organization of the development team.
- Functional knowledge of the target application, for example, the functional knowledge of securities trading for designing a securities trading management system.
- Involvement of the end users and functional experts during the development stage.

- Setting up work breakdown structures so that all parties have a clear understanding of their roles.
- Estimating resources and planning a schedule for the design, implementation, and testing phases.
- Specifying the design and the development methodology.
- Setting expectations and specifying the norms for evaluating progress and resolving issues.
- Following a methodology for building in and measuring quality.

A major activity in any software development, and even more so in information systems with large, complex custom designs, is the analysis associated with understanding and documenting current processes and the specification of software requirements. Communication between end users and the designers is a critical component of any successful design effort. The designers and end users must be able to communicate in a language that both can understand. Hence, the importance of a graphical design depiction methodology and available tools for presenting the design in a clear and succinct manner is paramount.

The requirements definition and follow-on information system design must follow clearly defined and documented steps. Some key activities necessary for designing a large and complex distributed information system include the following:

1. Feasibility survey
2. A study of the current system
3. Evaluation of the requirements
4. Construction of a prototype
5. Completion of systems design

We will combine the first three topics under the general category of *requirements analysis.* This chapter describes these topics and the critical stages in application development projects, how the project is planned, and the follow-through needed to achieve a project within budget and on schedule.

6.1 REQUIREMENTS ANALYSIS

Analysis of user requirements is very important for developing any information system, large or small. The users must have the opportunity to mold the system according to their convenience. Besides the concept of ownership, the functional knowledge embodied in the user is essential for developing an information system that performs its intended task. A number of factors are critical for meaningful evaluation of the user requirements, as follows:

1. Evaluation of the current processes and procedures.
2. Users' perspectives on the objectives for the information system, especially if the processes and procedures need to be changed for the new system.
3. Availability of functional experts to assist in defining the requirements (and assist in the design phase) of complex processes.
4. User familiarity with information systems and the training required to effectively communicate the features of the design that may affect the requirements analysis, that is, features that were not planned or that do not exist in the current system but that are feasible in the new design (potentially due to advanced technology).

It is important that the results of this analysis be documented in a manner that the functional experts and the end users participating in this effort can understand. We described the Frame-Object Analysis diagrams in Section 4.9 for this very purpose. Such diagramming techniques provide a graphical description that is easy to comprehend and requires very little training on the part of the user to understand the design.

Feasibility Survey: A feasibility survey is carried out to determine the need for a new information system and whether it makes sense to develop one from scratch or to adapt an existing system. The survey helps determine if designing and developing an advanced custom information system will benefit the business.

The survey should also include a cost-benefit analysis to allow management to assess the merits of developing a new system. The survey helps make a *go–no go* decision. Feasibility surveys may need to be performed during various phases of the project as advanced product development stages allow more accurate cost estimates. The scope of the project can change after arriving at any of the milestones, thereby affecting the cost-benefit analysis.

6.2 KNOWLEDGE ENGINEERING AND USE OF FUNCTIONAL EXPERTS

Knowledge engineering is a term used frequently for the development of expert systems. In its simplest form, knowledge engineering implies the ability to convert the knowledge (based on years of experience and functional expertise) of an expert into programmable designs. Analyzing the requirements for an information system and designing it are somewhat akin to knowledge engineering. The functional expert is a storehouse of information such as the following:

1. The life cycle of each process, that is, the stages of processing for a particular task or function.
2. Crucial relationships between different functions and special sequences of operations that must be followed.

3. General and specific business rules that must be applied to different processes.

4. Handling of abnormal conditions as well as situations not obvious to the designers.

5. Boundary relationships with other tasks, processes, and functions.

6. Any problems noted with the current processes.

7. Problems that must be avoided with the new system, especially those that the users have noted already.

The functional expert works very closely with the designers. The team effort produces a synergistic effect as the designers impart their knowledge of applicable system features to the functional experts and the functional experts impart their knowledge of the operational requirements to the designers. As both parties gain further knowledge of the other areas, they can combine their knowledge to produce a better and more robust design with enhanced utility and greater efficiency.

Study the Current Information System: A study of the current system and procedures is essential to determine the basic flow of information, the paper forms in use, and the expected reports. Users normally like an enhanced system, not necessarily a different system. The information system should adapt to the requirements of the users and should require no relearning to the extent feasible. The new system should include features that mimic the real-world entities and activities that the users are used to. Hence, it should duplicate the current process with the following exceptions.

1. Where significant benefits are derived from the use of new techniques and new technologies such that changes to the current system are justified.

2. Different, but more efficient, automated communications among groups and departments within the enterprise.

3. Implementation of a distributed database that integrates a number of functions.

Even if the new information system is designed to be significantly different, a detailed study of the current system is very useful. The study of the current system should include the following:

1. Functional decomposition

2. Data-flow modeling (behavior model)

3. Data-structure modeling

4. Determination of objects

While structured analysis methodologies can be used for requirements analysis, we recommend the use of object-oriented analysis for all kinds of systems. We suggest that you refer to Chapter 5 for a detailed description of object-oriented analysis and design. You will notice that the design phase is independent from the development phase. Performing the design in an object-oriented methodology does not imply that an object-oriented database must be used for implementation. The object-oriented design techniques are very useful for determining the requirements and documenting the structural as well as behavioral models of the system.

Evaluate Results of Study: In this phase, the options arrived at after studying the current information system are assessed. It has to be decided how much of the system should be made automatic and how much should require user interaction.

At this stage the designer can decide how the system will work. Flow charts can be created for each potential programming solution. The Frame-Object Analysis diagrams can now be evaluated from the perspectives of technical, operational, and economic feasibility. For each alternative, practical feasibility of the solution has to be determined. Another important test for each alternative solution is the operational perspective; that is, will the model of the information system design satisfy the users and meet their needs? How will it change their work environment and will it create new procedural problems?

The economic perspective is important and, as a part of an economic evaluation, the development and support costs are determined. The design effort consists of two phases: prototyping and designing a solution. The primary intention of prototyping is to emulate the application by developing the look and feel components such as screen forms, field definitions, function keys, help screens, and reports. The complete solution is designed (not coded) during the prototyping phase as a parallel effort and is then documented. Consequently, we will discuss prototyping first and then we will discuss how a complete solution is designed.

6.3 PROTOTYPING

Prototyping of information systems is a methodology that can increase the quality of a developed information system while reducing the resource requirements and development time. The concept of prototyping is antithetical to the rigid, third-generation systems development methodologies that were designed to follow a highly predictable development path. Because prototyping is based on characteristics inherent to the human nature, the process is more natural for information systems that are designed for heavy human interaction. Humans work by a process of conceptualizing, exploring, and then refining their ideas. Consequently, prototyping can be used to enhance the quality of systems development by employing techniques natural to human behavior.

The prototyping process allows the user to assess the look and feel as well as ease of use issues before the application is developed. This section discusses how you can use the prototyping process effectively and create design documentation as a result of this process.

Prototyping allows you to use iterative techniques to develop higher-quality systems faster with significantly increased user satisfaction. Users are involved in requirements definition analysis and design in a manner that gives them the feeling of ownership of the final system.

We noted earlier in Section 6.1 that you must fully understand the business problem before you can competently program a solution. As you learn the current system, you are likely to uncover other problems and opportunities for improvement not noticed by the functional expert or the users. A business model is very useful in measuring the significance of each issue that you uncover. In fact, a business function model is useful for prototyping because it gives you a clear perspective on the goals and objectives of the enterprise.

Clearly documented structural and behavioral models help you in designing the database menus, screen forms, and reports. More importantly, you can use them to convey the logic of your design to the user and the functional expert. The design of the prototype is based on these models. As each function and screen form is approved during the prototyping process, it is documented in the design specifications.

As more and more screens and functions are prototyped, the users or even you may realize that the earlier approved screen form or sequence of operations needs to be changed. As long as all information has been documented, changes can be made to the structural as well as behavioral models and the design specifications. Maintaining these documents current ensures that at the stage where the prototype is complete the design specification is also nearly complete. The solution you have designed is well understood by the users and, consequently, the users are willing to sign off on it for implementation.

For successful prototyping, the following factors are very important:

1. A good business function model.
2. A well-defined conceptual (structural) data model that a user can comprehend easily.
3. A descriptive conceptual behavioral model that clearly defines the functions and processes within the enterprise.
4. Managing changing requirements and maintaining design documents.
5. Prototyping and maintaining a consistent user interface.

Prototyping has been used successfully for developing relational database applications. Contemporary prototyping methodology is fairly straightforward in relational systems designed with independent structural and behavioral constructs. Prototyping object-oriented systems is an entirely different approach. Let us review the key differences.

6.3.1 Prototyping Object-Oriented Systems

At the outset, it is obvious that there is a close link between structural and behavioral properties in object-oriented programming. This link makes the prototyping process considerably more complicated. Issues contributing to this complication include the following:

1. Defining requirements to a level necessary to build basic objects.
2. Developing the screen objects to ensure a consistent user interface throughout all applications within the information systems.
3. Developing other objects to prototype all major functions and the relationship among the functions of the applications.

Defining requirements.   In a purely relational design, the structural components are independent of the behavioral components. This makes prototyping relatively easy because the structural model can be created in virtual isolation from the behavioral mode. The screen forms and the entire user interface can be designed and prototyped without defining a detailed behavioral model. Only the high-level functions are necessary for the prototyping effort. The detailed functions and processes are determined during or after the prototyping phase.

This is not so in object-oriented design. The design requirements have to be defined for the behavioral model at all levels, right down to the services and operations provided by the lowest-level objects. These lowest-level objects are the basic building blocks of the system. To some extent the concept of *stubs* can be used in implementing prototypes. That is, it is not necessary to implement every object. The lower-level objects and some functional layers above them can be emulated by stubs. The stubs are not true objects that would be used in the final system. The stubs would be replaced by true objects. During the prototyping phase, the stubs can be used to emulate different functions and design alternatives.

This approach to prototyping has the benefit of reducing the extent of coding necessary for implementing the prototype. Nonetheless, the analysis for defining objects at each level is essential; that is, it is essential to perform the tasks of classification of objects, creating inheritance hierarchies, and defining attributes and services (as defined in Chapter 5).

Developing screen objects.   The primary focus of a prototyping effort is to determine the high-level sequence of operations and completely define the user interface, including all screen forms, function keys, help screens, context sensitive help screens, and so on. In conventional design and programming, the windows, use of function keys, help capabilities, and the like, are designed as either independent dedicated routines or as callable reentrant routines.

In object-oriented programming, each window is treated as an object and each widget (for example, *push-button, switch,* and *menu selection window*) within a window is treated as an object. Actually, prototyping the user interface in an object-oriented environment could require less coding than a conventional environment insofar as the user interface is concerned. Each window, widget, and so on, may be separate objects, but they are all instances of identical classes. In the prototype, a single class or a set of classes may be designed that incorporates all the look and feel attributes for the system. If the users request a change to the user interface, that change need only be made in a single class or a parent class to affect the presentation of all application windows.

Prototyping the application.   Prototyping the application requires developing all screens and user interface objects. Screens are themselves objects. But so are the subwindows, function keys, icons, menus, and other display attributes. Each window, widget, icon, menu, and so on, is created as separate objects, but as instances of the same class. The complete look and feel of the application is embodied within a class of objects.

6.4 DESIGNING APPLICATION SOLUTIONS

The application solution (that is, the design of the application) must take into account all aspects of the enterprise and the applications: users, sources of information, uses and dissemination of information, distribution of data, and so on. The solution includes network topology, establishing the DBMS requirements, selecting a DBMS and the hardware platform, defining the forms and reports, and documenting all these aspects of the solution. This section provides a detailed discussion of these issues and presents a continuation of the application design methodology started in the earlier sections.

A key aspect of designing a good solution is fully understanding the business problem and recognizing the strengths and weaknesses of the current system. The users of the current system are a major source of information, and detailed discussions with the users, especially during the prototyping phase, can potentially uncover problems in the existing system. More importantly, the users may present future plans that could lead to interesting design opportunities for crafting a more advanced system. The users are also an excellent source of information. This may have an impact on the database aspects and the type of networking required.

An important goal of the requirements analysis and prototyping phases is to determine what the users and their management expect from the new system. It is important to understand what they think the system will do, what kind of data distribution is likely, and what kind of performance they are expecting.

A number of potential solutions may address the requirements and expectations. Each solution should be evaluated from the perspective of technical, operational, and economic feasibility. Once it is determined that a solution meets all goals and requirements, the model must be tested against the operational requirements to determine if it will meet the users' needs. Furthermore, it needs to be determined how this solution will change the way they work and if there is a noticeable impact on their work environment, especially if there is potential for it to create new problems.

The selected solution is documented in a formal design specification. The formal documentation gives you, the designer, the opportunity to conduct a multiparty review of the design and receive some excellent feedback on its shortcomings and potential problems.

There are four major components required for an advanced database design, as follows:

1. User interface objects design
2. Data objects design (the structural component of the database)
3. Design of all behavioral components
4. Business rules design

The user interface and behavioral components are all determined as a natural part of the prototyping activity. We have described database design at some length in Chapter 5. For now, we will concentrate on business rules programming.

6.5 BUSINESS RULES PROGRAMMING

Business rules programming is a topic we have touched on but not described in any detail. The following describes some examples of business rules:

- On all sales of over $50,000 the commission rate for the agent is 60% of the standard commission rate.
- On all sales of over $1,000,000 the commission rate is 30% of the standard commission rate.
- The commission is not entered into the agent's account until the funds are collected.

Business rules are, in a sense, rules of thumb or written rules used by the enterprise for conducting its business uniformly in an orderly manner. Business rules are essential for the enterprise to ensure correct and reliable operation of the business.

Business rules define some of the behavioral components of the system. They are a part of the processing of data and are typically coded in the *methods* within objects. For example, an "interest" object has methods for calculation of interest. The methods would have been coded with business rules for interest calculation.

Business rules are compiled from a number of different sources, including the following:

1. Evaluation of the current system.
2. Discussions with users during the analysis stage as well as during the prototyping stage. These are exceptionally useful for understanding business rules.
3. Discussions with functional experts to specifically determine business rules.

Clear documentation of business rules and which objects each rule is associated with ensures that the application of the rules is perceived clearly and is well understood by the user before the coding of the rules. It is especially important to note all exceptions to the rules, that is, processing that should normally follow the application of a business but, for some reason, does not. For example, some high-volume clients may have special commission rates in the example we used earlier to illustrate business rules. In these cases, the standard rule does not apply. The exception overrides the rule.

Designing the database.   The design of the database is a very critical element in the application design process. The level of normalization and the joins needed for data display and report output can have a significant performance impact. The design of the business rules can affect the correctness of the application. This section surveyed the issues that need to be taken into account for designing the database. A real database design is presented later in Chapter 9 as a continuation of the application design started in the previous sections.

6.6 TESTING AN ADVANCED INFORMATION SYSTEM

While testing is really out of the purview of advanced information systems design, we bring this topic up here because testing has become a critical phase of a complex advance information system development. The success or failure of the information system will depend on the quality of testing. A thorough, well-designed approach to testing is essential.

Effective use of advanced testing techniques, procedures, and tools requires a well thought out design of the test process. This design should start at the same time the information system design is in progress. The following key testing aspects are important for this approach to work well.

1. Objects are designed in a manner such that each object or predefined set or sequence of objects can be tested independently. This forms the lowest level of unit testing.

2. The knowledge of *how* the system works and *what* it does is utilized to design tests that check a particular path through the system from start to finish. The path may define a complete process or a function.

3. All business rules must be tested independently. Therefore, the design of the rules should be such that testing is possible in this manner.

4. All exception conditions must be tested.

An object-oriented environment can reduce the complexity of testing to a large extent. Well-designed objects have a very clear interface and set of behaviors. As each object class is fully tested and debugged, the level of confidence in the system increases as any potential errors are isolated within the users of tested objects.

6.7 EFFECTIVE USE OF CASE TOOLS

As we can see, there is a very close link between design and testing. This link is even closer if a CASE tool is used for the design of the information system. The design documented in the CASE tool also provides a test matrix. An initial design consisting largely of the user interface (forms, data entry fields, function key layout, and so on) is created for prototyping. The necessary application design detail is added later to the design document created during the prototyping stage. A good design and clear and comprehensive documentation are the primary goals for using a CASE tool.

In addition to the goals just mentioned, CASE tools are used to address a number of other goals and objectives. We can summarize the principal goals and objectives of CASE tools as follows:

1. Improving the accuracy, performance, and reliability of the software product being developed.

2. Following a well-defined methodology that is uniformly applied by all developers involved in a project.

3. Providing clear communications between project manager and the developers associated with the project, as well as among the developers.

4. Providing comprehensive documentation of the project as well as the software design trade-off decisions.

5. Facilitating product upgrades.

A number of CASE tools have been developed for building applications developed on top of relational databases. Some CASE tools also support object-oriented databases. CASE tools are designed for application generation and maintenance. CASE tools generally have the capability to generate SQL code for database applications.

Typically, CASE tools consist of analysis tools, a data dictionary, and a code generator. The analysis tool is known as *UPPER CASE* and the data dictionary is called the *LOWER CASE*. A good CASE tool is independent of the underlying database; that is, the data dictionary is built independent of the underlying database. This helps in designing an application that can use any database or if necessary a combination of database systems. Figure 6-1 describes a typical hierarchy of layers within a CASE tool.

The following lists some of the available CASE tools:

1. TOP*CASE for use with the ORACLE RDBMS, developed by Contecno Corporation, a Dutch software company
2. Development Environment by Interactive Development Environments
3. Cadre Technologies' Teamwork
4. Knowledgeware, Inc., CASE tools
5. AD/Cycle (Application Development CASE tool) by IBM
6. COHESION CASE Environment by Digital Equipment Corporation

CASE technology is an evolving technology that must change as the underlying database architectures change. While a generalized architecture has emerged for CASE tools and standardization is in progress to provide common interfaces (and protocols) between layers, the CASE products will continue to undergo substantial redesign. The UPPER CASE and LOWER CASE components are the primary design interfaces for the developer. These two levels define the

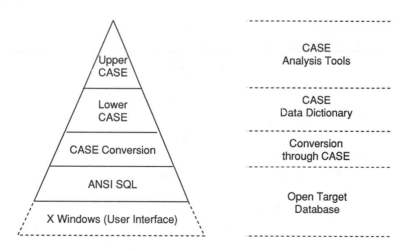

Figure 6-1.   CASE Hierarchy.

tasks that the developer can perform. The following sections analyze and discuss various aspects of the CASE tool architecture.

6.7.1 Why an Integrated CASE Tool?

The success of any development project depends to a large extent on the tools used for the development process. This is not only true but is crucial for very large projects where a number of programming groups are involved in development. Quality can be introduced early to the development cycle by ensuring clear communications with and among the project team and documenting not only the design but all other relevant project information at every step of development. A common tool set and consistent methodology go a long way in achieving this. Assembling an effective computer-aided software engineering (CASE) environment can go a long way in achieving the goals of quality software development on schedule.

The major components of a useful CASE tool should include, at the very minimum, the following utilities:

1. Graphical editor (with built-in support for common diagramming methodologies)
2. Design checking program
3. Shared document repository

A comprehensive CASE development environment consists of a number of additional components that form the basis of an effective tool set. The following lists some of the key additional components that are typical of a comprehensive CASE development environment:

1. Shared requirement definition and software specification utility
2. Other technical documentation tools
3. Flow-charting and other diagramming utilities (usually a component of a graphical editor)
4. Automatic code generation utility
5. Static and runtime error checkers
6. Incremental compilers and linkers
7. Source-level debugger
8. Graphical data and source code browsers

Together, these components assist in standardizing design and project documentation, especially the diagramming methods. Standardized documentation templates ensure that functional and design specifications follow recognizable and manageable outlines.

The CASE tool should provide a pictorial (or windowed) environment where code modules generated by a code-generation component can be viewed and linked into an integrated program. The tool should provide appropriate documentation linking code modules to flow-charting and design diagrams. The document provided by a CASE tool is very useful for future reengineering (or enhancements to the system).

We can summarize by saying that a good CASE tool, consisting of a large complement of utilities, assists in performing the following tasks:

- Create annotated data-flow and other design diagrams.
- Develop and document functional specifications.
- Generate code modules from flow charts (and other means such as pseudocode).
- Combine code modules into an integrated program.
- Generate documentation of the design based on the design diagrams.
- Locate useful existing code modules in the shared repository.
- Minimize *build* time through network distribution of compiles and links across LAN and WAN.
- Create annotated code hierarchy and procedure structure charts.
- Develop a data dictionary with descriptions of all data elements.

As you will notice, what we have described here are the UPPER CASE and LOWER CASE components. These components form an effective development environment. An effective integrated development environment obviously needs the underlying support of a documentation tool and a shared repository. Figure 6-2 describes the overall architecture of an integrated CASE environment.

A repository is a critical component that can determine how successful the development environment will be. Let us analyze that in greater detail.

6.7.2 Portable and Distributed Repositories

An operational repository for a CASE environment was first released by Digital Equipment Corporation as a part of the CDD/Plus CASE product. Figure 6-3

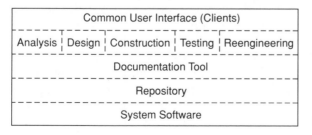

Figure 6-2. CASE Architecture.

```
┌─────────────────────────────────────────────────┐
│                    Clients                        │
│          (Graphical Integrated Toolset)           │
├─────────────┬─────────┬───────────┬──────────────┤
│ Development │  Code   │Active-Data│  Program     │
│ Workbench   │Generator│ Dictionary│ Development  │
│             │         │           │  Utilities   │
├─────────────┴─────────┴───────────┴──────────────┤
│               Repository Server                   │
├─────────┬───────────┬───────────┬────────────────┤
│ Naming  │  Version  │  Object   │    Data        │
│Standards│Management │Extensions │ Management     │
│         │Access Control│        │                │
└─────────┴───────────┴───────────┴────────────────┘
              │
        ┌─────────────────────┐
        │ Portable Repository │
        └─────────────────────┘
```

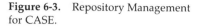

Figure 6-3. Repository Management for CASE.

illustrates how a repository fits in with the concept of an integrated CASE environment.

A repository is the storage for the CASE tool data. It is the mechanism through which tools share data and communicate information. An important function provided by a repository is version management. A centralized control of versioning in this manner ensures that all users get the core versions. Another major function is naming standards for data objects and operations (or identifiers in code). Naming standards help simplify traceability and comprehension of the role of the object.

6.7.3 CASE Tool Integration

An integrated CASE tool environment requires integration of at least two levels: *control integration* and *data integration.* Control integration implies that all tools follow the same control procedures and that development processes or work flow can be managed in a predetermined manner. Data integration means that the tools can share data among themselves and with the outside world.

In a single CASE, that is, where the components (or tools) of the integrated CASE environment are from a single vendor, the integration is relatively simple. The data, typically, reside in a single database (or, if distributed, use a common server interface), and the integration is relatively seamless. Another advantage is that uniform development practices and standards can be enforced more easily.

In an environment that integrates tool sets from multiple vendors, the general issues include integration of control interfaces and of repository databases. CASE tool standards become very important for achieving seamless integration when multivendor environments are involved. This situation becomes even more complex when multiple databases are used. A means of addressing this is to define a level of object granularity that a repository server can manage effectively.

6.7.4 Distributed CASE

A multivendor CASE environment leads to the concern that the different CASE tools may be on different systems. In other words, the development environment is a *distributed* CASE environment. CASE tools will be used on workstations, departmental development systems, and shared servers. Not only is there potential for multivendor CASE tools in use *horizontally*, but also *vertically*. The UPPER and LOWER CASE may reside on a workstation while the repository may be distributed among a number of departmental development computers. A truly open distributed CASE tool based on well-defined standards is necessary. The CASE environment should be extensible and must provide flexibility in policy control attributes and organization of program and project management facilities.

It is essential for distributed CASE that the database used for the repository provide a clear understanding of the data structures, details of data items and their attributes, relationships between data items, and the rules for maintaining consistency for all data maintained in that database.

6.7.5 CASE Standards

Any widely used technology begs standardization for effective and economical usage. Whether the field is electronics, data transfer, or software development, standardization ensures portability and a wider distribution of knowledge that can be applied uniformly.

For CASE to become a widely used technology for software development, standardization is essential. As we have seen earlier, standardization is required for control as well as data integration.

The first major effort in that direction was launched in 1987. The CASE '87 conference provided the forum for an exchange of ideas and set an initial foundation for goals for the advancement of CASE technology. A number of issues were identified for interaction between CASE components. A follow-on conference, CASE '88 further enhanced the awareness of CASE. The present and future directions of CASE were explored, and working groups reviewed, among other topics, the current state, research areas, future research requirements, and requirements for standardization. There has since then been a growing interest in the need for a standard. A number of efforts, even though fragmented, have been in operation since then. IEEE and ANSI committees are spearheading the standardization effort. A common standard is neither a reality nor an expectation. While a common reference model of underlying concepts is critical and has been generally accepted, it is clear that multiple standards are a reality for CASE since no single standard can satisfy the diverse requirements. A well-structured collection of compatible standards appears to be a better compromise. This would allow an exchange of information between CASE tools. CASE '89 made further headway in this direction, followed by CASE '90. An annual CASE conference has been a regular feature.

As a technology that will remain in evolution for a number of years, standardization will promote the aim of better CASE integration (both horizontally and vertically) and a common development interface for the user.

Major new entrants in the standardization picture are the concept of object-oriented software development for object-oriented databases at one end and the use of object-oriented repositories at the other. Object-oriented databases present both new challenges and opportunities. As a technology, itself in evolution, it presents the opportunity for better coordination of standardization activity.

6.8 SUMMARY

The primary thrust of this chapter was to develop a systematic methodology for managing the modeling and design phase of a project. It started out by explaining the importance of understanding and analyzing the requirements of users and determining the feasibility of meeting specific requirements. The users have functional experts and the success of any project depends on making the most effective use of the knowledge base possessed by the experts.

The communication between the developers and the users is extremely important throughout the project. Prototyping is an excellent means of improving this communication. It helps the developers in understanding the users' perspective and in ensuring that the users will be comfortable with the look and feel of the application.

The design of the application, understanding of the business rules, and designing programmed checks for ensuring business rules are important steps. The design must take into account alternative solutions and select one that best meets the requirements. We completed this part of the chapter by discussing issues related to testing of the application.

A major part of the chapter is devoted to a discussion of CASE tools. We presented a generalized description of a CASE tool and the advantages and disadvantages of an integrated CASE tool. We also touched on the architecture of repositories and their potential use for distributed CASE tools.

6.9 EXERCISES

1. Consider the working environment around you and select an application that would be of use to a number of people that you work with. Consider the knowledge base that these people possess and explain how you would go about learning the functional knowledge from these people to develop the application.

2. Did you use an interview approach? If so, how useful was this approach? Is a group interview more effective or are individual interviews more effective? Explain your findings.

3. Did you prototype the application? Did the users participate in enhancing the prototype to their satisfaction? Explain the differences in the user participation level and enthusiasm between interviews and prototyping.

4. Did you explain any alternative solutions to users? Did they show an interest and were they forthcoming in making a selection? How did the importance of technical reasons compare with the importance of business reasons? How did their current operations affect their decision making?

5. Can you build test cases for testing the application on the basis of real data from day to day operations? Can the test data be enhanced to cover all exception situations? Is it better to use this test data or is it better to create test data from scratch?

6. If you have access to a CASE tool, describe its data dictionary and repository features.

7. How much effort did you spend on the design using the CASE tool? How does this compare with the effort without a CASE tool? Compare the results (printed output) provided by the CASE tool with what you produced otherwise.

8. What are the advantages and disadvantages of CASE tools? What kinds of improvements in their design would remove these disadvantages?

III

ADVANCED INFORMATION SYSTEMS DESIGN

Programs developed in COBOL require substantial resources to upgrade as the business requirements change. Hard-coded data formats make database changes complex and expensive.

Relational Database Management Systems (RDBMSs) and associated fourth-generation languages (4GLs) have been designed to address these key issues. RDBMSs organize data in table format, thereby making it easy to manipulate the data and to change the organization of the database. 4GLs and application development tools provided with the major RDBMSs such as SYBASE, INGRES, and INFORMIX require substantially smaller effort and provide a highly cost effective development environment.

Figure III-1 describes the typical application life cycle and the impact of introducing a database management system to that life cycle. The life cycle is affected in all three areas: porting applications, adding new features, and adding new resources to an existing network of systems.

Shortened time frames to develop and modify applications allow the applications to be adjusted to the changing business needs. Changes in business objectives and requirements are reflected more easily and in a timely manner in the applications. The RDBMSs provide the tools to modify the underlying data structures quickly and easily. Smaller code (almost by a factor of 10 to 20 times) makes it easy to adapt the code rapidly to modifications in the database.

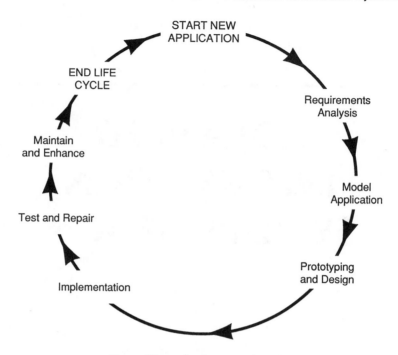

Figure III-1.   Application Life cycle.

Emerging technologies, especially the concepts of object-oriented programming, are changing the nature of the relational database management systems. In this part, we will first study the basic foundations of the relational model for database management systems. Using that as a backdrop, we will explore new data modeling and designing technologies based on object-oriented systems that are likely to affect the evolution of database management systems and present current thinking (in some cases authors' ideas) on future DBMS directions. An important aspect of our presentation is the use of an example based on a financial application. While we have made this application very realistic, we should point out that we have taken some liberties with true accounting and stock trading principles to make points and to create the appropriate design problem. Let us first study the scope of the application that we are using in our design exercise.

THE INTERNATIONAL TRADING CORPORATION

The International Trading Corporation (we will call it ITC) is a multinational stock and bond trading corporation with worldwide headquarters in New York City. It has major regional headquarters in Chicago, Frankfurt, and Tokyo. It also maintains business offices in Boston, Houston, and Los Angeles in the United States, in London and Paris in Europe, and in Hong Kong, Taiwan, and Singapore in the Far East. These business offices tie into the regional headquarters.

The International Trading Corporation deals primarily in stocks, bonds, and futures options as the primary financial instruments. Trading is performed on all major stock exchanges, and ITC uses its own agents on the trading floors, who have access to the computers at the business office. All trades performed during the day are matched by the clearinghouses at the stock exchanges and are electronically reported to the business office at night. The report also includes all unmatched trades (that is, trades recorded but that actually did not take place, usually due to improper tracking and recording at the trading floor).

The business offices also maintain current prices on all stocks, bonds, and options. The prices are fed electronically as they change. However, only the opening price, daily high, daily low, and the current price are maintained for reporting to clients. The same information is maintained for the previous day. ITC also maintains separate price history information in a distributed manner for two years for all stocks, bonds, and options that were traded through its offices. This allows adjusters to look up any prices in question when clients raise doubts about their accounts. Due to the multinational nature of some of their clients, they frequently get questions about a trade in New York from an office in Europe or the Far East. This requires worldwide access to the price history information.

The ITC clients consist of a mix of business and individual investors. Margin accounts are maintained for all clients. Usually clients are handled by a single broker. The commissions are split between ITC, the stock broker, and the pit broker (the broker on the stock trading floor). The commission structure is fully programmable for each broker by an authorized system administrator. In addition, a bonus structure is set by the size of the trade.

The Trading Management system (we will call it the TMS) includes the following application functions:

1. Broker and client account management
2. Securities pricing management
3. Securities trading functions
4. Foreign exchange rate history
5. Reference information
6. System administration functions

It is assumed here that the price information is available on regular ticker and can be recorded from that. However, for our purposes, we will use the price out of the daily trade information tape generated by each exchange for the price history file. The company trades an estimated 10 million shares a day spread over 5000 transactions of sizes ranging from 100-share blocks to 1 million-share blocks. Trades originating in Europe or in the Far East may actually be carried out in New York. On-line database information is required in the office where the trade originated, the regional headquarters, and the world headquarters in New York. All offices are networked.

While the overall system can be made much more comprehensive, we will limit the functionality of our system to improve comprehension of the design process. We will further make assumptions as and when needed for our imaginary corporation (these assumptions may not be fully realistic, but will assist us in understanding the design process).

We will use the International Trading Corporation as our case study for the data modeling and design discussion in the chapters in this part of the book.

7

Advanced Design for Data Dictionary

The relational model is based on a mathematical foundation developed and described by E. F. Codd in his original papers published in 1969 and 1970 while he worked at IBM. Further work on the R data management system and follow-up articles and books by Codd and C. J. Date further defined and enhanced the model. The role and importance of a centralized data dictionary are clearly evident from the descriptions of these models.

Consequently, we have mentioned data dictionary in a number of places in this book. As we saw in Chapter 2, the data dictionary is a very critical component in enforcing the rigorous mathematical discipline in a relational database. In this chapter, we will analyze the data dictionary components of the relational model in some detail to evaluate the variety of architectures, the impact of each architecture on the issue of relational integrity, and the management of integrity in a distributed environment.

While the importance and the function of a data dictionary are fairly well understood for relational databases, its role in an object-oriented database system is in a stage of discussion and evolution. The relative flexibility of object-oriented databases and the diverse nature of information stored in objects make data dictionaries a significantly more complex issue for an object-oriented database. In this chapter, we will present some of the key issues and design considerations for data dictionaries for object-oriented database systems. The shape that specific implementations take will depend on how these issues and design considerations are addressed and the goals and objectives of the object-oriented database.

Before we start a discussion on data dictionaries, let us first clearly elucidate what constitutes a data dictionary and what really belongs in a data dictionary. This will help in a clearer understanding of the rest of the discussion.

7.1 DATA DICTIONARY

A *data dictionary* is a manual or automatic repository, usually managed by the database, containing information about applications, databases, logical data models and constituent objects, users and user access authorizations, and any other information useful for defining the organization and use of data within the database.

All entity, relationship, and attribute names are generally composed of English words (or whatever the selected language for the user interface, be it French or German, for example). The organization of entities, relationships, and attributes into tables, columns, column attributes, and keys is information crucial for creating, populating, and accessing a relational database. This information is stored in a data dictionary.

A full logical data model consists of not only a diagram but also of descriptive specifications. The descriptive specifications are stored in a data dictionary. These specifications may include simple business rules that are checked before every insertion or update into the database. For example, commissions can be posted to an agent's account only after the funds from the sale of the stock or purchase of stock have been collected. A more interesting example of a business rule is one designed to prevent an illogical operation. For example, when a client requests the sale of stock on a stop order (that is, sell at a certain price within n days if the stock reaches that price), the stop date must be some days (usually 30) in the future. The stop date is always in the future with reference to the start date of the stock order. If, for example, a 30-day stop order is to sell 5000 shares at $30 per share for stock trading at $27, the START_DATE is recorded as the current date and the END_DATE is recorded as 30 days in the future. The user may inadvertently type the wrong date, thereby making the END_DATE earlier than the START_DATE. If such an order is accepted by the system, depending on the manner of date comparisons, the stock will not trade at all or (in the extreme case) will have no effective END_DATE. A proper design of the database should reject insertion of this order containing illogical dates.

In this same example, referential integrity is violated if the user is allowed to close the customer account while the stop order is in effect. Note that as we have used it here, *relational integrity* includes *referential integrity* and *data validation rules.* The stop order will execute even though the customer no longer has an account. Properly enforced referential integrity maintains the master-detail link to prevent closing the master account while any detail records exist.

Integrity rules, as noted above, are specifications that preserve the integrity of the data model by controlling which values the attributes may assume. Business rules must apply to all operations that affect the attributes governed by a business rule. In other words, the rule is enforced centrally irrespective of the application.

A complex logical data model for an advanced information system incorporates numerous rules about the *integrity* as well as the *structure* of information used within the enterprise. Some of the structure rules are based on the business rules of the enterprise. For example, a business rule may be set up such that the commission for a stock purchase is posted to an agent's (account broker) account only after the transaction is settled with the customer and the customer has paid for the purchase. This ensures that the agent has an interest in following up the trade with the customer. Other business rules may be used to better manage the business of the enterprise.

A number of different types of rules combine to fully define a business system. These include the following:

1. Domain integrity rules
2. System-defined constraints
3. Business rules and triggering operations

These rules and triggering operations are defined in greater detail in Chapter 2. They are summarized here for a quick review.

Domain integrity rules govern the types and ranges of values that attributes may assume. For example, a column defined to be CURRENCY (or MONEY) can contain only currency values. Some databases allow users to define their own datatypes. The domain integrity rules are applied in these cases also.

System-defined constraints consists of entity integrity and relational integrity constraints. Entity integrity ensures uniqueness of all records by requiring that no attribute that is a part of a primary key can be a NULL value. Referential integrity ensures that, whenever a relation includes a foreign key that matches a primary key in a referenced relation, every foreign key value must equal the primary key value of some tuple in the relation or be wholly NULL.

User-defined constraints and triggering operations govern the general effect of inserts, updates, or delete operations on other entities or attributes. Implemented through triggers (and sometimes through stored procedures), these constraints and triggering operations ensure that programming rules specific to the business or the application can be implemented.

7.2 CONCEPTUAL DATABASE SCHEMA DEFINITION

In 1977, the ANSI/X3/SPARC Committee of the American National Standards Institute developed a set of requirements for databases. The requirements, specified in terms of a three-part framework for organizing data, included the following levels of database schemas:

1. Internal schema
2. External schema
3. Conceptual schema

The *internal schema* describes the storage structures within the database and the retrieval strategies for accessing and retrieving data from the database. This consists of multiple occurrences of *internal records* (an ANSI/SPARC term equivalent to a row in a table). The internal schema views the data space as being a contiguous logical space. The physical implementation of pages and physical records per page are defined one level below the internal schema level. The internal schema is commonly referred to as the database schema.

The *external schema* is the view of the database that is visible to the users. The external schema defines the manner in which the data organization is presented to the user. The external schema may be different from the internal schema depending on the application and the programming interface used to access the data. A single database can support a large number of applications. Each application may have its own view of the database that is concerned only with the data items required for that application. Consequently, a number of external schemas can be supported by a single internal schema.

The *conceptual schema* provides the mapping between the internal schema and the external schema. Also known as the *conceptual business model* or the *integrated model*, the conceptual schema is almost always the most important component of the business modeling and design activity. As an integrated description of the business's data, the conceptual schema is, effectively, a consolidation of multiple logical data models. The conceptual schema helps to ensure consistency of multiple logical data models defined to support a variety of user groups and different functions and areas of the business. The conceptual schema also helps in designing a shared database supporting a number of user applications.

The conceptual view of the database is a somewhat abstract representation of the physical data and the way that data is stored. The conceptual schema maps the internal schema to this abstract view of the data. The conceptual schema describes the information content and the structure of the database. The issues of storage structures and retrieval strategies are described in the internal schema and are not considered a part of the conceptual schema. Consequently, the conceptual schema is independent of the underlying database software. The conceptual schema remains unchanged even when the internal schema is changed to adapt to new database software. The development of the conceptual schema must, obviously, precede the definition and implementation of logical and physical databases. In other words, a conceptual database schema is a structural and (partially) behavioral abstraction of the real world that focuses on the elements of the information that are relevant to the users or applications using the database.

The basic building block of a conceptual schema is the logical data model for a particular function. At the very least, the logical data model must include the primary and the foreign keys, since they identify the entities and their relationships. The conceptual schema is created by merging two or more data models. This process is continued by extending the conceptual schema by successively merging each new data model with the integrated user view. Occasionally, there may be conflicts when a new data model is added to the integrated conceptual schema. The data model or the conceptual schema may need to be changed in that case. Obviously, a conflict implies that one of the logical data models does not represent the business function correctly. Note that, because the conceptual database schema is a combination of all logical data models, any particular logical data model can be derived from it.

It is important to note and record the following when combining logical data models into a conceptual schema:

1. Naming differences, that is, if names used in the logical data models are changed in the conceptual schema.
2. A matrix of operations performed on the conceptual schema to obtain a specific logical data model. The matrix consists of operations such as selects, projects, joins, or aggregations of entities.
3. Additional constraints applied by a particular logical data model to domains or triggering operations defined within the conceptual schema.
4. Resolution of any conflicts between data models.

7.2.1 Representation of Schemas

A conceptual schema can be described in many forms. For example, it is possible to use ER diagrams along with data-flow diagrams or, alternatively, a semantic data model where the key object types, events, and constraints can be identified and modeled. For advanced object-oriented work, we proposed the Frame-Object Analysis diagrams in Chapter 4. We recommend using the Frame-Object Analysis diagrams, and we have provided an example in Chapter 8 on the specific use of Frame-Object diagrams. Once the Frame-Object Analysis diagrams have been completed, the conceptual schema is realized by translating the data attributes, operations, and constraints into data definitions, procedures, and constraints of a relational (or an object oriented) model.

You should note that the narrative descriptions have also been used to describe the conceptual schemas. However, converting narratives to useful constructs is more complex and, therefore, not a highly advisable methodology. The graphical route is the most productive.

A conceptual schema consists of descriptions of the various record types and of the ways in which these record types are related. A subschema may be defined to represent a logical subset of the schema. A subschema describes the record types and relations for the subset.

Most commercial database products provide a data definition language (DDL) to catalog relations (tables) and attributes in a database. The catalogs so created are also tables (or relations) within the database. These tables (which store the data dictionary) consist of the following information:

1. Definition of tables, columns, and datatype attributes for each column.
2. Information about primary and foreign keys relating different tables. (Note that foreign keys are used to maintain master-detail relationships between records.)
3. Definition of physical schema concepts, including data locations and utilization of disk volumes.
4. Definition of views, including information on what tables and columns are included in the view.
5. List of authorized users and their levels of authorization (that is, access restrictions on certain functions).
6. Domain information as well as business rules information.

The last item here, even though we have included it in this list, is not without controversy. Some leading implementations of relational databases do not provide storage of domain information and business rules within database catalogs. Both *domains* and *business rules* govern integrity (correctness and consistency) of data values. Additionally, item 2 (relationship of primary and foreign keys) governs the master-detail concept of *referential integrity*.

An additional business rule type is called a *triggering operation*. Triggering operations are rules that govern the effects of insert, delete, update, and (less frequently) retrieval operations on other entities or on other attributes within the same entity.

7.3 DATA-DICTIONARY-ENFORCED INTEGRITY ISSUES

We have defined in Chapter 2 and Section 7.1 four mechanisms that help in maintaining the integrity of a database:

- Primary and foreign key relationships
- Domains (acceptable values for an attribute or field)
- Business rules
- Triggering operations

Not all commercial database products support the same level of functionality for maintaining integrity. The key concerns for handling integrity issues are as follows:

1. Does the database product provide the language constructs for storing each of these four types of information within the data dictionary? If the database

product does not provide these constructs, the developers must program these in every application.

2. Are these constructs stored centrally in a data dictionary or are they distributed in data entry forms as a part of the application?

3. If stored centrally in a data dictionary, are they enforced automatically (usually the case)?

4. Are they applied stringently to the extent of preventing a user from performing a function that would allow the user to damage the integrity of the database (for example, updating an improperly defined view involving multiple tables or deleting a master record while detail records exist)?

The automatic enforcement of integrity constraints takes on a significant new dimension in a distributed database. We will address this issue further in the section on advanced data dictionary design for distributed databases.

7.3.1 Role of a Data Dictionary

A data dictionary is a critical component for a distributed database, providing location transparency for the user/developer in viewing data dispersed around the network. When the user asks to see what data are available, the appropriate information on tables and fields from each local and remote database must be somehow captured, consolidated, and presented to the user in a format consistent with what the user is accustomed to seeing.

Ensuring consistency of data and preventing updates and deletions of fields or data that may cause data inconsistency require special attention in the design of the database and the associated application. The mechanism referred to as *referential integrity* attempts to ensure that tables retain consistency according to the rules set up for the database. For example, a master record for a customer cannot be deleted until all detail records (for example, invoices) have been posted and archived. Said another way, *referential integrity* is the ability of the database to define intertable constraints within the database. Data entered, modified, or deleted in a table cannot circumvent these constraints. In addition, there are validation rules for data entered in specific fields. Some RDBMSs provide very methodical consistency checks automatically. Others allow the developer to program the checks in the data dictionary. Still others leave it all to the programmer to build in the application. Typically, consistency information is stored in the data dictionary.

7.4 DEFICIENCIES OF RDBMS DATA DICTIONARIES

The primary deficiency of RDBMS data dictionaries as presently structured is that they do not allow the operations that are allowed on objects to be defined and stored in the database. Stored procedures provide a loose mechanism for defining such operations; permissions can be set up on objects such that access is allowed only through the stored procedures. Unfortunately, this is a rather ad hoc approach that can be bypassed by an unwary developer. In an object-oriented database, however, these operations would be defined in the data dictionary, as well as any hierarchical relationships among the object classes. This dual approach ensures that no developer bypasses the data dictionary constraints.

Relational databases can be significantly enhanced by adapting a methodology for defining some key operations (at the very least, those defined in stored procedures or user-defined functions) in the data dictionary and executing them automatically in a manner similar to database enforced triggers. An enhancement of this nature will bring relational databases much closer to object-oriented databases.

7.4.1 Storing Objects in a Relational Database

As noted above and in Chapter 3, relational databases provide limited support for storing objects as we have defined them here (that is, with objects containing both structural and behavioral attributes). In fact, the question arises, of whether the integrity of a relational database would be impaired if it could store the structural and behavioral components of a data object. The answer to this question is not trivial.

We have seen some initial attempts at extending relational databases to support some key datatypes necessary for the very basic object storage. To what extent these basic attempts can be extended remains to be seen. It does appear that we will see object-oriented databases enhanced to support better integrity management and relational databases enhanced to support better encapsulation.

7.5 DATABASE INTEGRITY FOR DISTRIBUTED DATABASES

Integrity management is fairly complex in a dedicated environment. In a distributed environment, it becomes quite complicated. The data dictionary design has to be such that it can enforce integrity across all servers where objects are located. Let us first examine the issue of relational integrity in a distributed relational system. We will then extend the concepts to object-oriented systems.

In a database, maintaining relational integrity becomes critical as more and more users and developers gain access to the database. Most RDBMSs require the developer to include integrity constraints at the application level. This puts the burden on the developer to ensure that all potential risks to integrity are addressed.

Another approach to relational integrity is to include the rules in the database itself. Both referential integrity and data validation rules are stored centrally in the data dictionary. Built-in validation rules and procedures provide two advantages: no application can be built that circumvents these rules, and the rules can be programmed once and stored centrally. This not only improves programmer productivity, but it also makes maintaining rules much easier. This approach is critical in a distributed environment and eminently sensible for databases in general.

Triggers and stored procedures provide a means of defining and coding additional referential integrity constraints. For example, if an application updates a value that appears in two or more relations, the value must be updated wherever it exists. If the relations become complex or multilevel, the database management system is unable to set up the constraints automatically. Triggers can access other records and relations to provide operations such as collateral inserts and cascading deletes. Arbitrarily complex conditions can be defined in stored procedures. Triggers can also be used to modify or erase otherwise not updatable records resulting from multirelation views. Possible update anomalies are avoided by having triggers that specify appropriate actions for each constituent relation.

A relational data base must be designed to deliver high performance for a large number of users by maximizing data access for multiple, concurrent users. Efficient integrity and concurrency control mechanisms are required to permit multiuser access to a single, shared database without jeopardizing data integrity. A variety of schemes have been employed to manage data integrity in shared environments. These include: row, page and table level locking and version management.

Row-level version management is an interesting mechanism for concurrency control. At the start of a transaction, a unique number is assigned to the transaction. A copy of every row accessed for that transaction is identified with that transaction number and is saved until the completion of the transaction. Changes made by that transaction do not affect other queries in progress, thereby always presenting a consistent result to users, until the transaction is completed. If a number of independent transactions access the same records, versions for each transaction are retained separately until the transactions complete. As each transaction completes, the action is taken for updating that row. It should be noticed that there is no need for row-level locks under the version management scheme. By executing queries without locks, users get more work done at the same time. High concurrency means no waiting, and no waiting translates into higher performance. Conversely, while this scheme solves the problem of presenting consistent results to the users, this scheme by itself does not guard against two conflicting updates in progress at the same time under different transactions. Conflict resolution is handled by locking mechanisms.

The issues noted above address database integrity for a distributed database access environment consisting of only one database server. The database dictionary is uniquely contained in the single database server. In a network with multiple database servers, the management of a data dictionary becomes significantly more complex. Level of integrity control, proper synchronization of updates, and overall performance are key factors affected by whether the data dictionary is maintained centrally in one server or distributed across servers. We will examine these issues further in Chapter 10.

7.6 DATA DICTIONARY FOR AN OBJECT-ORIENTED DATABASE

We have just discussed some complexities of maintaining integrity and concurrency control in a distributed environment. We have addressed concurrency control at some length in Chapter 10 and will restrict ourselves here primarily to integrity issues. An object-oriented database presents some interesting alternatives for managing integrity.

All integrity checks can be defined as a class of objects called *Integrity Check*. These objects are a part of a distributed data dictionary and are stored according to usage requirements. These objects do not automatically enforce any integrity checks.

The capability of defining operations encapsulated within objects allows one to ensure that every object has a method programmed to trigger when an attribute within the object is updated or deleted. This method forces a message to the appropriate *Integrity_Check* data dictionary object instance. Rather than the data dictionary enforcing compliance, the burden for compliance is imposed on an object class that includes the data item. Any derived classes and all instances of these classes must include the methods that enforce an integrity check. Three major impacts of this approach are as follows:

- The data dictionary can be simplified. It consists of objects that define the integrity constraints, but does not require operations to enforce integrity checks automatically.
- A data object is forced to locate the appropriate *integrity_check* object to check integrity constraints. This allows integrity control objects stored as a part of the data dictionary to be distributed around the network (and maintain multiple copies if necessary from a performance perspective).
- Changes in class definitions can be made without affecting the integrity checks.

The reader may find it interesting to follow through on this design concept and come up with the pros and cons, as well as the viability of this concept for a large information system.

7.6.1 Contents of an Object Data Dictionary

An object-oriented data dictionary needs a number of components for viable operation. The following are the key components:

- Class definitions
  - Attributes (structural properties)
  - Methods (behavioral properties)
      User callable methods
      Triggers
- Class hierarchy
- Attribute domain rules
  (In a relational database, domain rules may be defined that specify the allowable values for a field. In an object-oriented database, these rules can take the form of simple class definitions, that is, they can be another user-defined datatype with constraints.)
- Business rules
  - Post-conditions with capability to trigger methods
- Object access authorizations
  - Permissions for attribute as well as method access
- Indexes
  - Attributes used for rapid searches
- Server definitions (and locations)
  - Dynamic list of servers currently in operation
  - Location of the name-server object on each server that defines its contents

We have presented very briefly the key components of a data dictionary that form the basis for a viable data dictionary for a distributed object-oriented database. This is a subject for much discussion and we encourage the reader to perform further research in this area to better understand the operation of large, distributed object-oriented databases.

7.7 SUMMARY

The data dictionary in relational databases (and the equivalent object dictionary in object-oriented databases) is the most important component of the database system. It describes the structure of the database, the layout of the data elements, and their relationships.

In this chapter, we once again reviewed the critical issue of database-enforced integrity checks. We also discussed the limitations of the data dictionary in a relational database system, especially the lack of information about operations (and functions).

An important component of this chapter is the review of the requirements for data dictionaries for object-oriented databases. Database integrity for distributed objects is an important subject for detailed study. The architecture and design of object dictionaries will play a major role in the reliability and precision of an object-oriented database system.

7.8 EXERCISES

1. Describe the data dictionary for a database system that you have access to. Is this a relational database?

2. What information can be added to it to make it more useful? How would you rate some of the leading database products for their implementations of the database dictionary?

3. How do (or should) data dictionaries (or object dictionaries) for object-oriented database systems differ from data dictionaries for relational database systems?

4. What other information items would you add to those listed in Section 7.6.1? Explain why.

5. Are the items listed in Section 7.6.1 sufficient for a distributed object dictionary? If not, how would you enhance it?

8

Advanced Data Modeling

8.1 INTRODUCTION

A detailed understanding of the requirements of the business is essential for developing applications that meet the needs of the business and the users. Elucidation of these requirements and the resulting design in a clear, comprehensible, and concise manner is essential for ensuring good communications between the developers and the users. A number of design techniques have been employed for developing applications in relational database management systems to address the issues of understanding and documenting the requirements as well as the design. A common theme that runs across all approaches is one of a consistent system design methodology. Most design methodologies consist of two steps: modeling the application and designing the database as well as the operations needed to support the functions.

A model is an abstraction of the information objects and the functions. A model verifies that the design based on the model will meet the requirements. When a model is presented in a pictorial manner without complex and confusing detail, it improves the comprehensibility of the design. It allows the users to more readily assimilate the overall design of the entities and their relationships within the information system.

Modeling is, unfortunately, an overused term, and its implications must be understood clearly. Models are built for a variety of designs and for a variety of engineering disciplines. The interpretation of the term model can vary depending on whether the model is for a bridge architecture, a nuclear plant, software architecture, or a chemical process. To ensure that there is no confusion regarding our representation of a model and its utility, we will define in detail our view of modeling not only a database but also the functions of an application. But first let us establish the difference between modeling and system design.

In our view, a rigorous system design methodology should produce three major documentation components:

1. Information System Model
2. Object Model
3. System Design

We define the *Information System Model* to consist of the models of functions and data elements that present the user-level perspective, that is, what the user sees from a perspective of functions and the data elements entered, displayed, and reported for each function. This includes all user-level transactions and information objects entered by the user and that the user can manipulate. The Information System Model presents a description of the information system in a pictorial and intelligible manner.

An *Object Model* consists of the models that define the detailed structural and behavioral components of each object in the system. These objects may or may not be visible to the user. The objects are designed strictly from a perspective of an optimum design for the required operations and attributes and do not take into consideration any aspects of the database. As an abstraction, the model must remain independent of the database management system. You should note that the development of this model is a part of the system design effort. While the components of the Object Model may be of no real interest to the users of the application, the designers of the application need this model along with the Information System Model to design the application.

A *system design* should consist of the internal data structures, flow of data, abstract operations, and rules for combining abstract operations into higher-order abstract operations. For an object-oriented database, this means that all object attributes are defined in terms of the low-level datatypes supported by the database, and the attributes and operations are defined in terms of database objects. Links between database objects are also defined. Layouts of all menus, user forms, and reports are also designed and documented.

While a number of modeling techniques have been presented and used, we have based our approach on a model presented by Brodie and Ridjanovic[1] that

---

[1] Michael L. Brodie and Dzenan Ridjanovic, "On the Design and Specification of Database Transactions," *On Conceptual Modelling:* Perspectives from Artificial Intelligence, Databases, and Programming Languages, Brodie, M. L., Mylopoulos, J., and Schmidt, J. W. (Eds.), Springer-Verlag, New York, 1984.

appears to be well suited for object-oriented design. This model presents an analysis on the basis of the *structural* and *behavioral* properties of database transactions. The concepts for modeling, developed in this chapter, are based on the concepts of properties of transactions presented by Brodie and Ridjanovic.

Structural properties include states and static properties, such as entities and the relationships between the entities. *Behavioral* properties refer to state transitions and operations and the relationships between operations. We have adapted these concepts of the Brodie and Ridjanovic model to the *Frame-Object Analysis* diagramming methodology.

The Frame-Object Analysis diagrams allow modeling the structural as well as the behavioral properties of a database application. Both the structural and the behavioral properties are analyzed, and data object and function hierarchies are developed. These multiple-level abstractions provide for a complete decomposition of the structural and behavioral properties to the lowest-level objects. In this chapter, we will present a detailed, step by step advanced data modeling methodology directed primarily toward complex, distributed, enterprise-wide applications. We will follow this with the methodology for design in the next chapter. The conceptual data model so developed can be used to build either a relational database application or an object-oriented database application. The methodology is, nonetheless, directed toward advanced object-oriented design. But first let us see how these steps fit into the overall system design life cycle.

8.2 SYSTEM DESIGN METHODOLOGY

As we saw in Chapter 6, a good strategic partnership between the developer and the user is integral to successful management of a project for implementing a customized information system. For developing such a relationship, the operating philosophy should be to nurture this partnership with the users through constant contact, open communications, and a constructive exchange of ideas, recommendations, and viewpoints. Clearly, for such a relationship to succeed, both parties must commit resources and make the necessary effort to render the exchanges rewarding.

The activities that lead to the development of the various strategies, data models, and design documents are a part of a methodology. The methodology defines the sequence of orderly steps that must be followed for a successful design outcome. We call this the *System Design Methodology*. An effective system design methodology consists of the following three critical components:

1. Well-articulated objectives
2. Clearly planned process
3. Expected results

A phased methodology followed by the developers ensures a close working relationship and a technical rapport between the developers and the users. While a phased development methodology is followed by many developers, the key factor that distinguishes the successful developer is the integration of the concepts of contemporary life-cycle development in the design phase of a tried and true project management methodology. Whereas a typical organization uses stacks of paper called specifications (consisting of user screen forms, report formats, internal calculation descriptions, and so on) to communicate with the user, an advanced designer uses the concept of pictorial descriptions and prototyping, a "what you see is what you get" approach to application development.

Users cannot relate to stacks of paper, and the written specification does not give them a true picture of the finished product. The use of prototyping (development of the actual screen forms and report formats) during the design stage provides an interactive (contemporary) means for the user to look at the menus, screens, report formats, sequence of functions, and keystrokes required to perform these functions. The benefits of the functional knowledge of the users become immediately available to the programmer as the two sit in front of a screen and page through the prototype. A visual look at the fields and their locations becomes a good basis for discussing the processing and calculations required. Detailed application design specifications (describing the Information System Model, the Object Model, and the system design) are written based on the feedback and processing information provided by the users.

It is important that the user be able to comprehend the design specification. Prototyping gives them a good perspective on the user interface, inputs, and outputs. The models in the design specification give them a clear perspective of the data flow and relationships between entities. When the users understand the specification fully and are willing to freeze it and sign off on it, the application design process is complete. Further designing is required only at the detailed design level for specific calculations and processing algorithms.

Carefully limiting changes to the design from this stage onward provides an approach that avoids surprises and results in a good clean design. The code developed during the prototyping process is enhanced with the calculation and processing components during the coding phase.

A successful phased approach to advanced custom information systems design consists of the following steps in the development process:

1. Developing the project plan (project organization and management, goals, and so on)
2. Technology assessment
3. Developing the business information model
4. Architectural and technology feasibility recommendations
5. Modeling the database and the application
6. Designing the information system

Steps 2 through 5 are the components of the system design methodology concerned with data modeling. We will therefore concentrate only on these four topics in this chapter. We will follow up with step 6 in the next chapter.

8.3 FUNDAMENTAL DESIGN ISSUES

A number of design issues must be considered for an information system. The information system must address the diverse business needs of the enterprise. The architecture and design should cater to these diverse requirements and ensure that the installed system will adequately address all requirements. It is essential for good communication between the designers and the users that there be clear and detailed documentation. The expected level and extent of the required documentation describing the objectives, features, and operating environment of the new applications must be established.

Most corporations have existing Business Models that describe what business the corporation is in and how it conducts its business. A Business Model is indispensable for determination of the corporation's business needs and is an essential input to the Business Information Model.

The Business Information Model describes the information objects that the business collects and stores and details how these information objects are used. The Business Model and the Business Information Model provide critical information for the conceptual data model, porting strategies for existing data, architectural recommendations, lists of applications that must be developed, and so on. All these issues have an impact on the design and must be properly documented.

A design approach must be developed, evaluated against the requirements, and documented. Multiple approaches may need to be modeled and evaluated against the requirements. For this reason a detailed architectural and design study is extremely important.

8.3.1 Key Deliverables

The key deliverables assimilated from the business modeling and system architecture development endeavor are as follows:

1. Business Information Model
2. Architectural Recommendation and Technology Feasibility report
3. Information System Model
4. Object Model

The documents produced for these deliverables become the major guidelines for the database and the application design. The documents should have a level of clarity and detail sufficient for the programmers/analysts to code from.

We defined the *system design methodology* in the previous section. It is important that the system design methodology follow a very clearly defined process leading to well-articulated objectives. The system design methodology is an integral component of the project life cycle and is managed as one of its components.

As in any other engineering discipline, the system design methodology is based on a number of key concepts and a methical approach. A methodical approach implies following through the design process in a structured manner. A similar methodical approach is possible and, indeed, necessary for information systems. The first major step is *Technology Assessment.* Technology Assessment provides key input for the Business Information Model and Technology feasibility determination.

The *Business Information Model* and the *Technology Feasibility Report* provide the initial input for modeling the information system and for system design. Let us review this process in detail, starting with technology assessment and the development of the Business Information Model. Note that an Architectural Recommendation or Technology Feasibility Report is the outcome of Technology Assessment and the Business Information Model.

8.4 BUSINESS INFORMATION MODEL

A detailed analysis of information needs, existing technologies, corporate objectives, and distributed management issues is essential for developing a Business Information Model. The analytical process necessary for developing a Business Information Model is called *Technology Assessment.* Let us first review what we really mean by technology assessment.

8.4.1 Technology Assessment

Technology Assessment is an important step in the process of understanding the operation, benefits, and shortcomings of the current architecture and then using this as the base for understanding and modeling the future architectural requirements. Key steps involved in technology assessment include the following:

1. Determining requirements from the business model.
2. Developing detailed architectural and requirements analysis of the current system.
3. Analyzing volume and traffic in the current system and the bottlenecks associated with it.
4. Extrapolating volume and traffic to projected future growth requirements.
5. Performing detailed evaluation of current architectures in terms of capacity, extensibility and growth, standardization of operating systems and networking protocols, and maintenance.

6. Designing and modifying the architecture to meet current and future growth requirements and addressing the other goals of standardization and maintenance.

7. Addressing the need for more effective user interfaces, including graphical user interfaces such as X-Windows.

8. Evaluating database systems such as SYBASE, INGRES, GEMSTONE, and INTERBASE to determine which database system (whether relational or object oriented) best addresses the specific requirements architecturally as well as from an application perspective.

9. Developing the Business Information Model.

10. Developing the Architectural Recommendation and Technology Feasibility Report (which defines the implementation and porting strategy).

The technology assessment phase involves, as we see from the above, a detailed study of current and future architectural requirements and the business model to determine key business requirements. Technology assessment requires a heavy interaction with the management, key users, and functional experts. The focus is on determining the operations as they currently exist, the shortcomings and strengths of the current operating environment, projected requirements, and expectations.

8.4.2 Components of a Business Information Model

The business information model, that is, the manner in which the business maintains its information and performs its tasks, is a critical component for designing applications that meet real user requirements. A number of factors contribute to success in developing a business information model that truly reflects the information requirements of the business and is adaptable as business needs change. User applications requirements can be derived from the business information model.

The following is a list of the key factors for developing the business information model:

1. CASE tools should be used for depicting the business information model. The CASE tools impose a methodology that is rigorous and leads to good design practices.

2. The managers must sponsor the design effort for the business information model to meet their current requirements and not the past requirements that any previous applications in use were based on.

3. The applications should address the current and projected business plans and objectives.

4. The business information model should be flexible enough to adjust to changing business needs.

5. The applications should be designed for use by the real end users.

6. A clear understanding of the role of the applications in achieving business objectives should be developed.

7. The design of the location and uses of information should be driven by the end users and not just be imposed on them. If the end users are a part of the design process, they exhibit a much higher acceptance of the system.

Careful attention to these success factors ensures that the application helps achieve the business goals and does not work at cross purposes to achieving success. Folding back the user aspirations and their application needs into the business information model ensures that the business information model can adapt to their current and future data-flow requirements.

The Business Information Model is documented both in narrative as well as diagrammatical form. In Section 8.3 we said that the Business Information Model describes the information objects that the business collects and stores and details how these information objects are used. This information, while general in nature, provides the perpectives that help determine the range of specific applications that manipulate the information objects. Development of the Business Information Model is the first major step in the modeling process.

8.4.3 Development Strategy for Business Information Model

A correct and well thought out development strategy is important for the elucidation of a precise Business Information Model, a good robust design, and reliable implementation of the application. The following are critical factors for an implementation strategy:

1. Modeling the business using CASE tools and documenting the model very rigorously. Alternatively, other diagramming techniques must be used that provide capabilities equivalent to a CASE tool.

2. Defining roles and responsibilities for designers and functional experts to achieve a high level of synergy.

3. Listing both short- and long-term objectives by priority to have a clear picture of the direction for the design.

4. Assessing the current system against these objectives to determine shortfalls in meeting the objectives.

5. Developing a roadmap (process and schedule) for the conversion process from the current system to the new system.

Another important aspect of this phase is the strategy used for business information modeling. A good modeling technique ensures that all user issues are accounted for. A business information modeling exercise consists of a number of key steps, including the following:

1. Interviewing key users and functional experts.
2. Developing a function hierarchy of the business functions and decomposing the information system into a set of applications.
3. Determining the information objects required for each application described in step 2.
4. Developing the topological layout of users and the applications required for each user. Users are then combined in groups by location and application.
5. Performing volume and traffic analysis between groups of users.
6. Analyzing performance issues.

The Business Information Model becomes a critical document for current and future management of information needs for the corporation. It should be maintained as a living document that is kept current so that applications can be enhanced as the model is updated in response to changes in business needs.

8.5 ARCHITECTURAL RECOMMENDATION AND TECHNOLOGY FEASIBILITY

The information collected in the technology assessment phase and in the development of the Business Information Model is analyzed and, on the basis of this analysis, an *Architectural Recommendation and Technology Feasibility Report* is prepared. This report defines the following:

1. Location of database servers and the distribution of the database components (that is, the layout of the LANs and WANs).
2. The hardware components for each server and the location of each hardware component.
3. The nature of user terminals and workstations, locations of these, and potential access to each database server.
4. Growth plans for each hardware component, the database servers, and user terminals and workstations.
5. Sequenced implementation plan for the entire network of servers and clients.
6. Evaluation of databases to determine which best addresses the requirements.

The architectural recommendation and technology feasibility report defines the proposed architecture, especially as it relates to the networked components of the system. It defines the major sources of information, where primary information stores should be located on the basis of usage patterns and how information will be accessed and used across the network. Most importantly, the hardware platforms and the target database system are determined.

Porting strategy.   The determination of the database, the number of applications, and the location of the primary stores set the stage for determining and documenting the *porting strategy*. A port of data becomes an issue when there is a significant amount of data already in electronic media storage. For example, the data may be stored in a database on a mainframe. In many cases the applications may have been written originally in COBOL. While the data by itself is extremely useful, it is not necessarily structured in a form required for the new system. One should anticipate that the existing application is probably old enough so that it does not fully reflect current needs, usually the reason for a major upgrade. A complete porting strategy must be developed that determines the steps necessary for a successful port of the data. Some critical issues that must be addressed include the following:

1. The format of the data that must be used for transporting it to the new system. A flat ASCII file (that is, one with no keys or index structures, and therefore usually with fixed-length records) is a very common means of porting data.
2. The port media must be determined. The port media can be a magnetic tape using an industry-standard storage format (such as ANSI labeled tapes), a communications line, or a network.
3. The data objects that can be retrieved must be determined. On completion of the database design, the mapping between these and the new objects is established.
4. The distribution of the data objects among the new primary data servers must also be established so that the appropriate data files can be created.

Step 3 of the porting strategy must wait for the full database design before it can be completed. The porting strategy is also an integral part of the Architectural Recommendation and Feasibility Report documentation set, but it is not of much value after the port is complete and the older system is disassembled. Until that time, however, it serves as the guide for routine data transfer between the two systems.

You will note that, up to this point, we have been discussing mostly surface issues and have not really addressed the modeling and design of data objects and functions. With the three documents, the Business Model, the Business Information Model, and the Architectural Recommendation and Technology Feasibility Report, we have the base information necessary for modeling and designing the information system.

8.6 MODELING AN INFORMATION SYSTEM

We discussed the three major deliverables produced during a rigorous modeling and design exercise as follows:

1. Information System Model
2. Object Model
3. System Design

In this section we will develop the detailed theory and definitions of these models. We will also show examples of how these models are used in practice. But first let us compare our structure to the standard modeling terminology used for relational databases.

The relational database world has imposed a somewhat precise definition on the term *conceptual data model*. A conceptual data model describes an integrated view of all data employed within the business in graphical terms, as well as in the form of a database schema (conceptual schema). It includes the external schema, the conceptual schema, and the internal schema. You may recall that we described this in detail in Section 7.2. Our portrayal of models is very different from the conventional conceptual data model.

In our view, the Information System Model and the Object Model replace the traditional conceptual data model. The Information System Model consists of the Entity Model and the Transaction Model. The Object Model consists of the Structural Model and the Behavioral Model. Figure 8-1 describes the hierarchy of models.

This may be a good time to review the list of models that are essential for a good system design methodology. The following is a brief description of each model:

- *Business Model:* describes what business the corporation is in and how it conducts its business. It describes the corporation's business needs.

- *Business Information Model:* describes the information objects that the business collects, uses, and stores. It details how the information objects are stored.

- *Information System Model:* in our approach to modeling, the Information System Model replaces parts of the conceptual data model and consists of the Entity Model and the Transaction model.

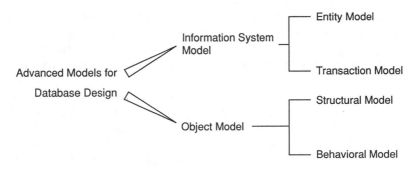

Figure 8-1.   Advanced Models for Modeling Information Systems.

- *Entity Model:* describes the entities, individual attributes, and logical groupings of attributes as seen by the user. It also describes the logical relationships between entities.
- *Transaction Model:* describes the interactions among application objects from the user's point of view. It describes the user-level operations (such as insert, query, update, and delete) in terms of the behavioral relationships among each application object.
- *Object Model:* while there are other definitions for the term Object Model, in our view it describes the structure and the behavior of objects that are constituents of an application. The Object Model consists of the Structural model and the Behavioral model.
- *Structural Model:* describes the structural properties of objects from a static perspective. These properties include the logical elements of the objects required for the application.
- *Behavioral Model:* describes the behavioral abstractions, that is, the set of rules for combining abstract operations into higher-level abstract operations.

It is necessary to point out here that the Business Model, the Business Information Model, and the Information System Model (and its component models listed above) are visible to the user. The Object Model and its component models are visible to the designer only and are, therefore, a bridge to the system design.

The techniques of the Frame-Object Analysis diagramming methodology as demonstrated in the next two sections provide a working backdrop for a design exercise that the reader may be involved in. The basic techniques are applicable to all kinds of modeling and design. This chapter emphasizes their utility for modeling and designing information systems.

8.7 INFORMATION SYSTEM MODEL

The traditional relational database modeling is based on the *conceptual data model* and the *data-flow model*. In the traditional definition, the conceptual data model is primarily concerned with the data entities and the structure of the data relationships. The data-flow model defines the functions and the flow of data from one entity to another. Both models are ncessary to properly describe an information system. The structure as well as the functions must be specified.

An advanced model, called the *Information System Model*, can be developed that consists of two parts: an *Entity Model* describing the abstract data structures (or entities) and attributes of each application object, and a *Transaction Model* describing the interactions among the application objects from the users' point of view. The Information System Model defines both the entities and the transactions at a level visible to the users of the applications.

The Frame-Object Analysis diagramming techniques are very applicable for depicting the Entity Model and the Transaction Model. We will present some examples of these later in this discussion.

Figure 8-2 describes the Entity Model and the Transaction Model components of the Information System Model.

Figure 8-3 describes the *Object Model*. The Object Model consists of a structural component, called the *Structural Model,* describing the attributes and a behavioral component, called the *Behavioral Model,* listing and describing the operations (or the functions provided by the methods).

We said earlier in this chapter that the Object Model is the bridge between modeling and design. We will briefly review our definition of system design to clarify the distinctions between the modeling of objects and the design of objects. Figure 8-4 describes the principal design activity for the structural attributes and behavioral operations of application objects as they would apply to real database objects.

Note that in Figures 8-2, 8-3, and 8-4 the left side is the structural side and the right side is the behavioral side. In other words, the models and the design run in parallel for the data object structures and the functions of the applications. The models at the upper two levels (Figures 8-2 and 8-3) are used by the designers for modeling the user perspective and defining the underlying objects. The models and the design also describe the hierarchical relationships between object classes. For example, the Transaction Model describes each user-level operation of the application (such as queries, updates, and reports) in terms of the behavioral relationships among each application object. Decomposition of the two models, the Transaction Model and the Behavioral Model, leads to the design of

Entity Model (as seen by user)	Transaction Model (as seen by user)
* External view of entities (but these entities may or may not map directly to data objects). * Individual attributes as seen by the user (but the user may have no perception of their link to physical entities). * Logical groupings of attributes (such as address, city, state, zip). * Logical relationships among groups of entities. * Output results of manipulating attributes as seen by the user (such as in reports).	* A set of menu hierarchies that defines user visible functions. * Data input forms that may cause certain operations to be performed. * Data outputs (such as screen displays of data and printed reports). * May include other user-initiated functions such as backup and archival. * Description of the nature of access to lower-level transactions (that is, to operations within objects).

Figure 8-2.   Components of the Information System Model.

Structural Model	Behavioral Model

* Description of the underlying objects.
* Listing of the attributes of each under-
  lying object.
* Relationships among objects including
  links, hierarchy, and inclusion within
  other objects.
* Descriptions of classes and inheritance.
	* Representation of every function defined
	  in the transaction model.
	* Descriptions of higher-level operations
	  that invoke the low-level operations of
	  one or more objects for performing a
	  complex task (possibly recursively).
	* Descriptions of low-level operations that
	  can be performed on each object type.
	* Descriptions of functions at the Transac-
	  tion Model level that may directly invoke
	  a low-level operation at the lower-level
	  objects.

Figure 8-3.   Components of the Object Model.

the behavioral parts of the database objects, the layout of menus, forms, and reports, and the messages between objects. System design bridges the gap between the Object Model and the code.

A *database schema* in a relational database is well understood as the list of tables and fields with descriptions of characteristics for each field. A database schema in an object environment is a detailed object creation list that defines the attributes and operations of objects.

While the methodologies for developing the models are described in this chapter, the methodology for performing the design tasks represented by Figure 8-4 is described in Chapter 9. Note that this approach is also used in the security management application design example of Chapters 15 and 16.

Design of Structural Part of Objects	Design of Behavioral Part of Objects

* Descriptions of object attributes in terms
  of low-level datatypes.
* Definition of data objects by combining
  attributes and operations into real data-
  base objects. (This sets up the objects
  for object creation.)
* Detailed definition and relationships
  among classes.
	* Definition of each operation and its input
	  and output parameters.
	* Denotation of what functions and opera-
	  tions are called by other functions and
	  operations.
	* Representation of all messages between
	  objects.

Figure 8-4.   Design of Object-Oriented Database.

8.7.1 The Entity Model

The Entity Model, as described in Figure 8-2, consists of the following component descriptions:

1. View of entities
2. Attributes, individually as seen by the user
3. Logical grouping of entities and attributes using Frame-Object Analysis diagrams
4. Logical relationships among entities using Frame-Object Analysis diagramming conventions
5. Expected output results such as reports and on-line queries

We will use the example of the Trading Management System (TMS) for the International Trading Corporation (ITC) introduced in the introduction to Part III. The methodology developed in this chapter is used in Chapters 15 and 16 to illustrate a more detailed design example for the Trading Management System. The reader may find it worthwhile to read the introduction to Part V as well as Chapter 15 for better familiarity with our imaginary International Trading Corporation.

View of entities.   The view of entities here is the same as used in the Entity Relationship diagrams. Entities depict real-life objects such as customers, brokers, people, documents, and so on. The first task is to determine the entities that participate in some form in the overall functioning of the information system. The information system must be able to store information describing every entity, even if it is temporary, that participates in the functioning of the system.

Collecting all functions and entities and depicting them graphically within frames as shown in Figures 8-5 and 8-6 places the entire information system in perspective much as an Entity Relationship diagram does. The overview of all entities in this manner helps in isolating the higher-level entities from the lower-level entities and also assists in grouping the entities required for each function. This overall entity frame is very useful throughout the design process. Obviously, it is dynamic in a sense that the diagram is updated as new entities are determined during the modeling process. Figure 8-5 illustrates the use of the basic functions frame for the TMS application for ITC. Note that for simplicity and for better illustrating the methodology, we have deliberately not attempted to make it exhaustive.

As we noted in the previous paragraph, we are really interested in entities that are used for specific component applications within the overall enterprise-wide information system. We therefore create new frames that show the entities for the trading management application as shown in Figure 8-6. Note that the trading management system shares links into other application areas, such as portfolio accounting, pricing, and general ledger. A full-blown financial informa-

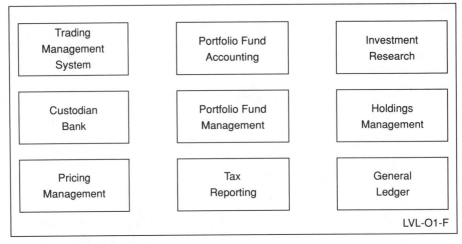

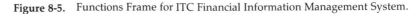

Functions for ITC: Enterprise Level

Figure 8-5.   Functions Frame for ITC Financial Information Management System.

tion management system is, obviously, quite complicated. We will instead take a very simplistic view of the system for our example and focus on the Trading Management System only. This will help the readers concentrate on the modeling and design methodology rather than the complexities of financial management.

Every entity in the frame is a real-world entity that has an existence in the system and is therefore stored in the database, even if it is for a short duration. An

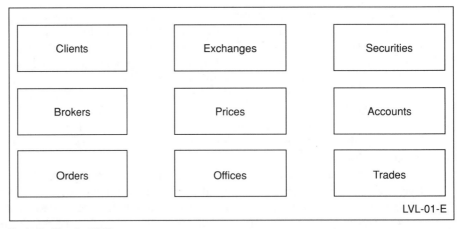

Basic Entities for TMS

Figure 8-6.   Entity Frame with Basic Building Blocks for TMS.

entity is characterized by a number of attributes that collectively describe the content and function of the entity.

Attributes.   An attribute describes a specific characteristic of an entity. For example, *Last Name* is an attribute of an entity called *Customer*. Similarly, *Address*, *City*, *State*, and *Zip* are attributes describing the location of a customer. Attributes such as "the number of securities in a trade" can be determined individually or for an entity such as *Order*. Usually, the attributes are determined individually based on the current information objects used for the application. The information objects may be derived from an existing information system or from the current process (or procedures) used by the enterprise. For example, a stock trading company manages trading of stocks. Consequently, it must manage client accounts, securities, trade orders, and so on. A review of these information objects reveals a list of attributes associated with each of these information objects. Frequently, paper forms used within the organization are a good source for listing all information attributes needed for the application. Some attributes are inherently associated with entities. The association for other attributes may not be clear simply from the perspective of their use in a paper form associated with a manual system.

Logical grouping of entities and attributes.   A logical grouping of entities occurs when a number of entities have similar characteristics. For example, a customer may have a number of accounts for trading purposes. All accounts have some common characteristics and can be grouped together as *Account* entities. Similarly, a number of attributes may describe the characteristics of one entity.

Once the attributes have been collected, they can be organized around entities. An entity that ends up with no attributes is suspect and may not be necessary. Alternatively, requirements related to that entity may have been overlooked and a revised study of the current as well as planned processes and information objects is necessary. The frames developed linking attributes to entities must be complete such that all attributes are associated with entities (there are no spare attributes left over) and all entities have attributes.

Figure 8-7 describes the use of frames to show attributes for one or more entities. We will follow the convention that the name of the entity is always the top text line within the entity box. An entity can be represented in a condensed form by simply a name in a box. An entity can be expanded further to show the attributes by separating the attributes from the name by a *dashed* (or dotted) line. Note that the attributes that are candidates for establishing a relationship with attributes in other entities, called *link attributes*, are indicated by an asterisk. The primary key is indicated by a #.

An entity can also be condensed to show only the name and the link attributes for a frame describing the relationships among entities. A condensed view of an entity describing only the links (called *link view*) is useful for illustrat-

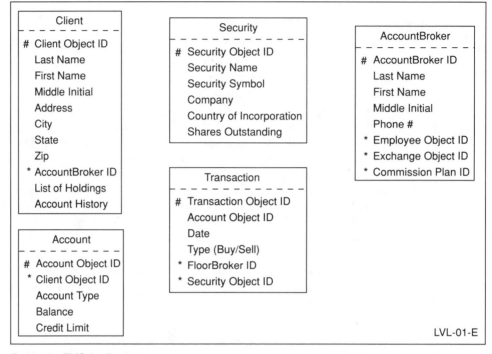

Entities for TMS Application

Figure 8-7. Description of Entities for TMS Application.

ing the relationships among entities. The smaller size of entity boxes allows a larger number of entities to be depicted within the frame.

Logical relationships among entities.   Figure 8-8 illustrates the use of the link view for depicting entity relationships. You will note that we have followed conventions very similar to ER diagrams to realize a level of simplicity while diagramming complex applications.

The level at which the entity is used depends on the level of other entities. If all other entities are at the highest level, a generalized relationship among entities can be established. This relationship can be fine-tuned incrementally by dropping to the next level of decomposition of each entity represented within the frame.

Entity hierarchies.   Another concept adapted from the ER diagramming methodology to the frame-object analysis diagramming methodology is the concept of multilevel entity descriptions. For example, the entity *Brokers* is decomposed to the next level of entities visible to the user (see Figure 8-9). While *Brokers* is a generalized class of entities, *AccountBroker* and *FloorBroker* are specific entities.

Similarly, the entity *Security* can be decomposed to entities such as *Stocks*, *Bonds*, *Options*, and *Warrants*. The entity *Bonds* can be further decomposed to

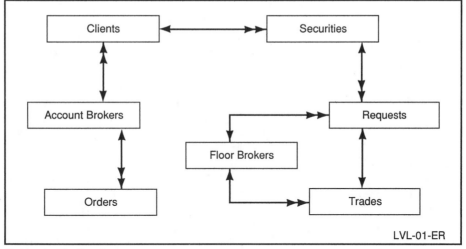

Entities for Trading System

Figure 8-8. Entity Relationships in an Entity Frame.

entities such as *Null Coupon Bonds, Fixed Interest Bonds, Variable Interest Bonds, Convertible Bonds,* and so on (see Figure 8-10). This indicates three levels of entity decomposition. Frames can also be used to show the decomposition of entities, as in Figure 8-10.

The attributes for the decomposed entities change according to their function as illustrated in Figure 8-10. Note that the basic object class can be defined to be *Security*. The attributes for the object class *Security* are defined and the subclasses are inherited from it and redefined.

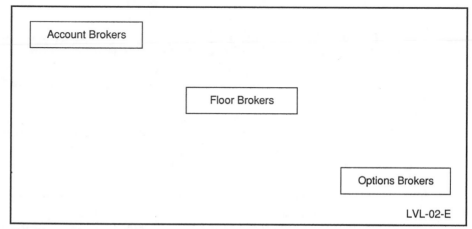

Sub-Classes for Class Brokers

Figure 8-9. Decomposition of Entity *Brokers.*

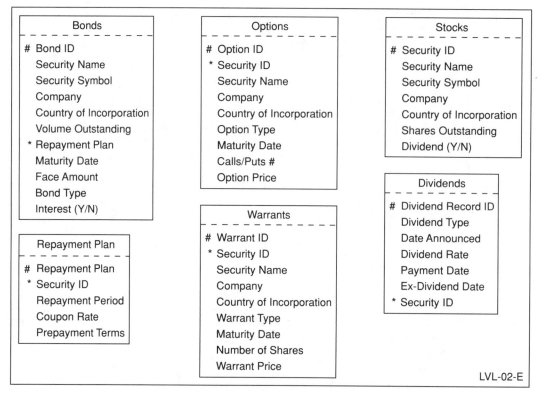

Security Entities

Figure 8-10. Second-level Decomposition of Entity *Security.*

A similar decomposition can be performed for some of the other entities, such as *Clients, Requests,* and so on. The reader may find it worthwhile to develop the other frames by decomposing other entities to more specific levels to assist in the study of the design and coding examples presented in Section 16.3.

Generally, it will not be practical to fit all entities in one frame. The entities can be depicted in multiple frames for clarity and to ensure that there is enough room to describe all attributes.

Expected output results.   The most important output of an information system is processed information, such as reports and on-line queries. An information system designed without careful thought to reports is almost definitely not serving its users well. The nature and extent of reports and their potential impact on the design must be determined early on. An important component of this effort at this stage is determining if additional entities (temporary or permanent) are required for creating complex reports. Hence the importance for modeling the outputs from the system. Figure 8-11 illustrates the high-level model for outputs. This frame is used to define intermediate entities.

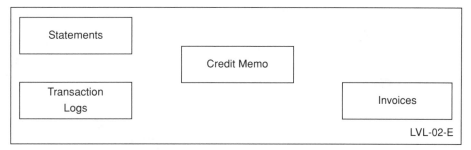

Entities for Output Data Elements

Figure 8-11. Representing Output Entities in Frames.

We have now determined the entities from a user's perspective, that is, entities as visible to the user. But what the user sees is not necessarily what the information system stores. The information system must be designed for the most effective combination of functionality, flexibility, and performance. Hence, it is as important to study the transactions (or functions) that must take place as it is to study the information objects for designing the database objects.

8.7.2 Transaction Model

The Transaction Model describes the interactions among the application objects from a user's point of view. Note that the key here is a user's perspective. Behavior abstractions are concerned with operation at the object level. The Transaction Model describes each user-level operation of the application in terms of operational hierarchies and user-visible functions at each level of the hierarchy. The first step in this process is to collect a list of all functions that must be performed by the information system. This list can then be manipulated to classify functions in a hierarchical manner.

Listing and decomposing functions.   The step of listing all user-visible functions is generally straightforward. It consists of watching the day to day operations and adding to these the planned enhancements for the system. The functions can be grouped in two ways: by the major application function (such as accounting and client information) and by the user performing the function (such as account broker and office clerk). For example, we can list the *broker* functions for the TMS application as follows:

Account Brokers: The account brokers interface with the client and place buy and sell orders with the exchange floor brokers on behalf of clients. The account broker performs the following functions:

- Create/delete client accounts
- Accept client buy/sell requests
- Create orders

- Receive notification of trades (resulting from orders)
- Get list of client requests
- Get list of current orders
- Get list of stop orders
- Get value of client holdings
- Get client account history
- Receive money from client for securities purchases
- Send money to client from sale of securities (actually, money may be to/ from a cash account, with security purchases/sales from/to the same account)

Floor Brokers: The floor broker operates on the trading floor of the exchange and actually carries out the sale or purchase of stock by monitoring the pending stock order list and the current price of each stock listed for a buy or sell on the pending order list. The floor broker is responsible for recording a trade when it takes place. The floor broker performs the following functions:

- Get list of current orders
- Get list of stop orders
- Get notification of trades that would satisfy stop orders
- Create trade

This approach is useful because people in an organization understand and can clearly articulate their own job functions. Very few people understand all job functions and the full impact of interrelationships between what they and their co-workers do. If we carry this approach of functional breakdown through to all categories of system users, we will have a complete list of all user-visible functions for the enterprise.

Depicting menu hierarchies in frames.   The next step in the process would be to organize these user-level tasks into functional breakdowns such as *Client Management* and *Security Trading Functions*. The user-visible functions (by user category) are scanned and collected together into new groups representing user functions. The highest-level funtional groups form the top-level menu. These functions are represented in a frame as shown in Figure 8-12.

Note that the entry at the lower-right corner of the frame identifies it to be a level 1 transaction frame. A similar entry is used in all frames to identify them. Also note that the name of the frame (describing its primary function as well as for identification of the frame) is tagged to the lower-left corner. This frame is called Top-level Menu. The objects within this frame portray the elements of the top-level menu. A corresponding top-level menu would appear as shown in Figure 8-13.

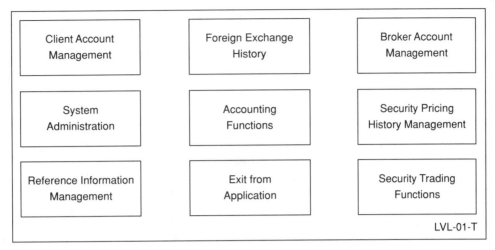

Top-level Menu

Figure 8-12.   Top-level Transaction Frame.

Typically, menu hierarchies are set by the nature of functions at the lower levels. Each function described in the top-level frame must be decomposed to the lower levels until we get to the basic transactions such as *QUERY, INSERT, UPDATE,* and *DELETE.* For example, in the TMS application, functions at the user level are decomposed into constituent transactions. Each transaction represents a task such as "recording commissions for a trade" or "aging an account."

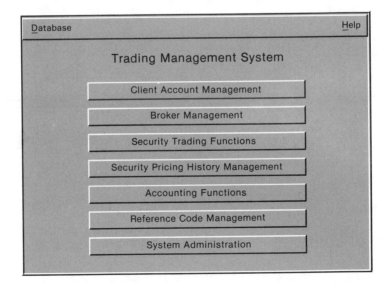

Figure 8-13.   Top-level Menu for the TMS Application.

In the example of "recording commissions for a trade," the user-level function is a "trade" (that is, sale or purchase of a security). At the lowest user-visible level, a transaction consists of all operations (such as creation, update and viewing of basic application objects) connected with the calculation and posting of commissions to the broker accounts. The Transaction Model describes the behavioral abstractions pertaining to all objects used for the calculation and posting of commissions.

Relating user-initiated functions.   The first function in the application is *Client Account Management*. This menu item actually describes a number of functions. We call functions at this level and lower levels *transactions* (we use the term interchangeably with functions except for the lowest-level, user-visible transactions). Functions and transactions can operate in a hierarchical manner or in a horizontal manner; that is, a transaction in client management calls a transaction in accounting. Furthermore, functions or transactions can operate sequentially or a function can call another function or transaction and gain control back on completion of that transaction. The first kind of relationship is depicted in a frame by including all lower-level functions required to perform a higher-level function. Obviously, some lower-level functions will be shared by some higher-level functions. It is important to define the conventions that differentiate between the following three types of relationships between functions:

1. Sequential functions
2. Hierarchical functions
3. Functions calling other functions

Depicting user-visible transactions.   The conventions noted above are used in combination with the Frame-Object Analysis diagramming methodology to describe all user activated transactions, as well as all resulting user-visible transactions. The relationships between transactions are also defined. Typically, a process (for example, a trading sequence) is defined in this manner. Figure 8-14 describes the conventions for depicting the two types of relationships.

Note that the double arrows represent a hierarchical relationship. *Create Portfolio List* and *Create Broker List* are subfunctions of creating a new account. This is a one-way relationship. It may be necessary to complete all sub-functions before the function itself is complete. The relationship between *Create Client Account* and *Enter New Trade Request* depicts a mandatory sequence (or a *sequential* relationship). A customer account must exist before a trade request can be accepted. Note that this also is a one-way relationship but of a different nature than a hierarchical relationship. *Record Trade Object* conditionally calls the functions *Update Client Portfolio Account*, *Update Client Margin Account*, *Invoice Client* and *Prepare Client CreditMemo* depending on the nature of a trade. This illustrates how a conditional function call is depicted.

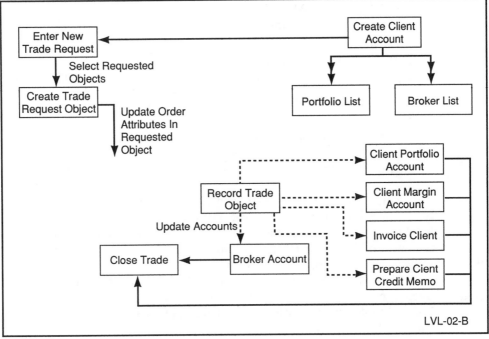

Function Relationships

Figure 8-14. Depiction of Function Calls.

All user-visible transactions are depicted through hierarchical frames lead-ing to the functions described in the top-level menu. In other words, the frames describing user-visible transactions define the complete menu structure for the application. Whether these menus are vertical menus, pulldown menus, pop-up menus, buttons or function key operations depends on user preferences and is determined during prototyping.

Let us use a brief example here to show what goes into a Transaction Model. We will use the first menu item *Client Account Management*. We can start by listing typical client actions:

Client Actions: Client actions are the functions that are performed (usu-ally by an account broker) on behalf of a client. The following lists a useful subset of client functions:

- Buy shares in security at current price, at specified price
- Sell shares in security at current price, at specified price
- Get current value of holdings

- Create account request
- Delete account request
- Create/update portfolios
- Add primary broker and update broker list
- Record payments for purchased securities
- Receive money from sale of securities
- Get account history
- Get security information and current price

The frame for *Client Account Management* functions is described by Figure 8-15.

This frame can be decomposed to one more level for the functions that can be defined at the next lower level. For example, Figure 8-16 illustrates the next-level frame (level 3 frame) for the *Create, Review or Modify Account* function. You will notice that all functions listed in Figure 8-16 will become function key selections (rather then menu items).

Note that the functions noted in Figure 8-16 do not need to be further decomposed. This frame depicts the lowest level of functions visible to the user. We will build objects with encapsulated methods that perform the functions at the next lower level.

From this example, it becomes obvious that a frame is very useful to show a collection of related objects. A frame can be used further to show attributes and methods within an object. As a final step in the transaction model, we can develop the screen forms for the client account management function. Figures 8-17A through 8-17C describe sample screen forms for this function. Note that the pull down menus (top line of the screen) and push buttons (last line of the screen) describe the lowest-level menu items for this function.

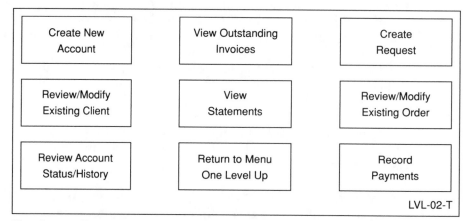

Client Account Management

Figure 8-15. Client Account Management Frame.

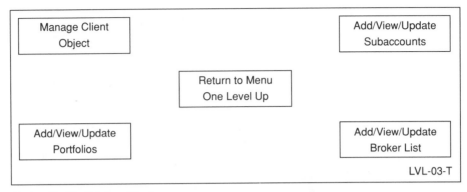

Review/Modify Existing Client

Figure 8-16.   Create, Review, or Modify Account Frame.

The Portfolio List column displays a list of all portfolios being managed for this client. The Portfolio Detail columns describe the details (a list of securities and the number of shares) for a portfolio currently highlighted by the cursor in the Portfolio List column.

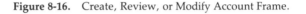

Figure 8-17A: Client Account Screen Form.

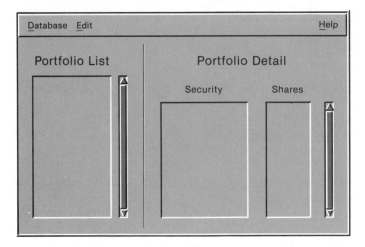

Figure 8-17B: Client Portfolio Form Window.

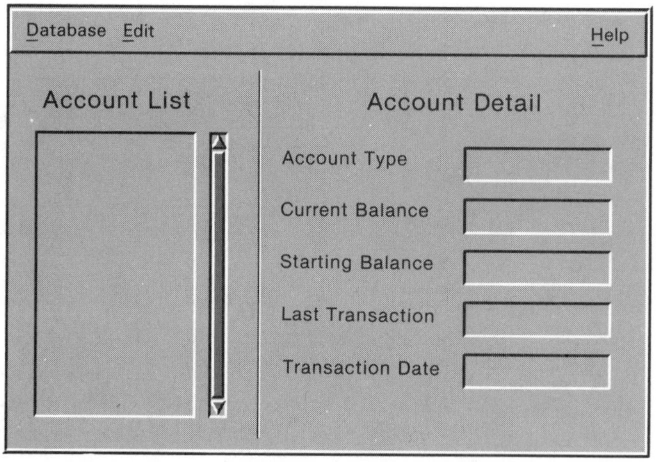

Figure 8-17C: Client Subaccounts Form Window.

The subaccounts window functions in a manner similar to the portfolio window. The subaccounts list is displayed in the left column and the current selection is highlighted by the cursor. The right column displays the details about the highlighted account.

The methodology adopted above for the *Client Account Management* function can be extended to all other functions to develop the complete Transaction Model for the information system. Chapter 16 demonstrates some of these extensions.

8.8 OBJECT MODEL

Most database design techniques concentrate on the *structural* properties of the database transactions. Even though these design techniques appear to have some focus on *behavioral* properties, they do not really describe them very well. A good database and application design requires the definition of both structural and behavioral properties. Good database design tools should provide the capability to include both types of properties in the data model.

An important consideration for any model is its comprehensibility. A high level of detail clutters up a model and makes it less comprehensible. A model is intended to provide a higher-level view of the system. The design addresses the in-depth issues. The model can be made more intelligible by applying two principles while developing the model: *abstraction* and *localization.*

The *principle of abstraction,* based on the integration of structure and behavior by means of data abstraction through abstract data types, states that a detail is suppressed in order to emphasize a more appropriate detail. The *principle of localization* states that each property of the data model (or an application object) is modeled independently (localized), and that the complete design is produced by combining these localized properties.

Modeling an advanced database.   With the completion of the Entity Model and the Transaction Model, we are ready to apply the properties of objects to structural and behavioral abstractions. Grouped together, these abstractions model the database and the applications. We further apply the principles of *set management* used so effectively for relational database management to the model. The following major items are required for developing the structural and behavioral models:

1. Description of major structural objects
2. Variables or components of these objects
3. All atomic operations based on *transaction abstractions* that can be performed for each major object

An *atomic operation* is a behavioral property of an object that causes a state change of at least one variable of the object. A transaction (used here in its generic form where a single query is also a transaction) is a combination of these atomic operations that links a sequence of state changes through logically related objects. A complex transaction is created by combining a number of simple transactions that are executed atomically. A complex transaction must, in itself, also be viewed as an atomic operation in that it is either executed in its entirety or not at all. The manner in which these transactions (or even state changes) are combined, whether sequentially or in parallel, can also be modeled to develop the complete sequence for a function within the application.

The behavioral and structural properties of an object constitute an abstraction that completely defines the semantics of the object. An abstraction offers a selective view of the properties of an object (by potentially eliminating confusing real-world diversions). It allows concentrating on aspects of an object that are important for determining the nature of the properties of the object being examined. Both structural and behavioral properties involve relationships between objects. Indeed, the Object Model is a network of relations among object classes. These relations are characterized by three forms of abstractions that are primarily structural in nature: *association, aggregation,* and *generalization.* The hierarchy of the objects within the conceptual model defines the structure. The control abstractions, *sequence, choice* (or *decision*), and *repetition,* provide behavioral relationships that represent actions. The hierarchy of actions defines the behavior.

At the transaction level, a behavior model involves identification, design, and specification of transactions. A transaction alters one or more objects. The *scope* of the transaction includes all objects accessed within the transaction. Each object is accessed on the basis of an action defined within the transaction. This combination of actions provides the *behavioral* view of a transaction, while the constraints and derivation rules applied within the transaction provide the *structural* view. All preconditions, action invocations, postconditions, and exception-handling rules must be defined for each transaction.

These steps provide the basic building blocks for the development of the structural model and the behavioral model. The behavioral model further requires a top-down decomposition of all functions performed by the application. Remember that a similar decomposition was performed for the Transaction Model and can be used as input here.

The design of multi-level frames describing a complex database application is a nontrivial task. Once the object data and the function hierarchy for the application have been determined, the task of integrating all this information into a cohesive structural and behavioral model must be performed. We will start with the Structural Model and describe the theory behind classifications. We will then use an example to show the methodology for modeling both the Structural Model and the Behavioral Model.

8.8.1 Structural Model

The Structural Model is concerned primarily with classification and hierarchy. Given the four properties of objects used for object management (abstract data types, inheritance, object identity, and methods as described in Chapter 3), we will now look at how these object properties are used in advanced database modeling represented by the Structural and Behavioral models. Since we are using the concepts of semantic networks in our Frame-Object Analysis methodology, the *extended semantic hierarchy*[2] data abstraction model for relating objects is very applicable here. This model defines four forms of abstractions: classification, aggregation, generalization, and association.

Classification is simple to understand because it defines an *object class* in which each object has precisely the same properties. An object is an instance of the object class if it has precisely the same set of properties as defined for that class. Typically, an object class described in the database schema would be represented by an object in the database. For example, class of objects called *AccountBrokers* has a number of instances describing individual brokers.

Association, aggregation, and *generalization* relate objects. Let us analyze these relationships further.

Aggregation.   Aggregation forms a relationship between objects that describes a higher-level aggregate object. In this relationship, objects that represent parts of a whole are associated with an object representing the whole. While association represents a simple relationship, an aggregation represents a very specific "part of" relationship. For example, a *Client_Account* can be represented as an object. A *Client_Account* may have a number of *Portfolios*. Each *Portfolio* is also an object. The *Portfolios* are aggregated to the *Client* in this relationship.

Aggregation has some other special properties. Aggregation provides a tight coupling that can be passed along to multiple levels. For example, *Portfolios* consist of a number of *Securities. Securities* have as attributes PRICES, CURRENCY, EXCHANGES, and so on. This implies that since, PRICES, CURRENCY, and EXCHANGES are a part of *Securities,* they are also a part of *Portfolios.* And *Portfolios* are a part of *Client_Account.* This relationship can get to be very confusing. Aggregation does not imply that every *Portfolio* is a part of an *Account.* Nor does it imply that every *Security* is a part of a *Portfolio.* Rather, it defines a hierarchical relationship that implies that some *Portfolios* are a part of a *Client_Account* and some *Securities* are a part of a *Portfolio.* Note that in true aggregation, unlike a simple association, the relationship cannot be reversed. That is, *Portfolios* cannot become part of a *Security* and *Securities* cannot become part of a PRICE.

By now, it is probably apparent that aggregation provides a technique for organizing hierarchical classes. We can depict aggregation within a frame as illustrated in Figure 8-18. Note that this figure implies that a *Client_Account* can have multiple *Portfolios* and a *Portfolio* can have multiple *Securities.*

Another property worth noting is that a higher-level aggregated object may contain different classes of lower-level objects. For example, as illustrated in Figure 8-19, a *Client_Account* has *Portfolios* and *Broker_Lists* as lower-level objects. In our Frame-Object Analysis methodology, aggregation of these objects and their relationships are described in a *frame.*

---

[2] Smith, J. M., and Smith D. C. P. "Database Abstractions: Aggregations and Generalizations", *ACM Transactions on Database Systems,* 2, 1977, pp. 105–133.

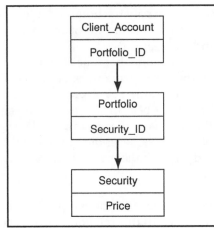

Client_Account Aggregation

Figure 8-18. Frame Depicting Aggregation Relationships.

Generalization. Generalization is an abstraction where the relationship between the category of objects is considered a higher-level generic object. For example, *Account* is a generalization for the collection of account objects. *Account* is called a *superclass* and *Account* objects such as *Mutual_Fund_Account* and *Portfolio_Account* are called *subclasses*. As we discussed in Chapters 3 and 5, the properties of the superclass are inherited by the subclass. Similarly, *Bonds, Warrants, Options,* and *Stocks* are subclasses of *Securities*.

Note that generalization is different from association and aggregation. While aggregation relates objects in a hierarchical manner by class, generalization relates objects that are instances of different classes where the classes have similar (and potentially inherited) properties. Recognize that superclass and subclass refer to properties of a single object. Another approach to differentiating between

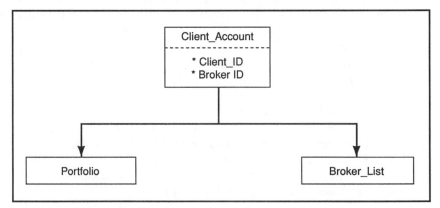

Client_Account Generalization

Figure 8-19. Frame Depicting Multi-Level Aggregation Relationships.

aggregation and generalization is to look at the aggregation tree as being composed of object instances that are all a part of a composite object, while a generalization tree is composed of all classes that describe an object.

Example of a Structural Model.   In the Trading Management System (TMS) application, the structural properties account for only a subset of the properties of the overall application set for ITC. These properties are viewed in a static form that does not depict changes to these properties. In the case of the Trading Management application, these properties include the logical elements of the security management objects, such as securities, trades, customers, and brokers. We had listed these logical elements in the Entity Model. The top-level frame in the Entity Model, Figure 8-6, describes the entities. The objects in the Structural Model are derived from the entities in the Entity Model. Figure 8-20 illustrates the structural properties of the Trading Management System using the Frame-Object Analysis diagrams. Note that this is the top-level structural frame, as indicated by the legend in the lower-right corner of the frame.

Each entity described in a top-level structural frame represents a basic object class. Some of these object classes can be decomposed further, as shown in Figure 8-21. This, in fact, demonstrates the class hierarchy for the object class *Brokers*. Multiple levels of class hierarchy can be depicted in a similar manner using multilevel frames.

Each object of the lowest level of the object class hierarchy may then be described in terms of its component structural attributes. We listed the attributes for the entity called *AccountBroker* in Figure 8-7. Further analysis provides the attributes of the entity *FloorBroker*. These attributes are also the attributes for the object classes *AccountBroker* and *FloorBroker*. We have listed these attributes side by side in Figure 8-22. The attributes are very similar except for one, the *OfficeLocation* or *Exchange*. Note that Options Brokers may also use a slightly different attribute, such as an options exchange. The concept of *generalization* implies that we can combine the *AccountBroker*, *FloorBroker*, and *OptionsBroker* object classes in a superclass called *Broker*.

Note that, as derivatives of the same object class, the structural attributes for *AccountBroker* and *FloorBroker* object classes are very similar. The definition of the

Basic Objects for TMS

Figure 8-20.   Structural Frame for the Trading Management System.

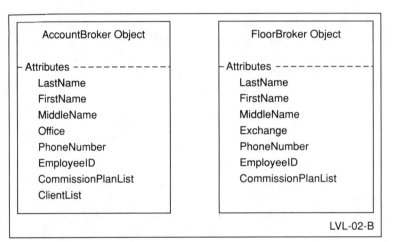

```
┌─────────────────────────────────────────────────────┐
│  ┌──────────────────┐                                │
│  │ Account Brokers  │                                │
│  └──────────────────┘                                │
│                    ┌──────────────────┐              │
│                    │  Floor Brokers   │              │
│                    └──────────────────┘              │
│                                ┌──────────────────┐  │
│                                │ Options Brokers  │  │
│                                └──────────────────┘  │
│                                         LVL-02-S     │
└─────────────────────────────────────────────────────┘
```

Class Hierarchy for BROKERS

Figure 8-21. Decomposition of Object Class *Brokers*.

```
┌─────────────────────────────────────────────────────────────────┐
│  ┌──────────────────────────┐    ┌──────────────────────────┐    │
│  │   AccountBroker Object    │    │   FloorBroker Object     │    │
│  │                           │    │                          │    │
│  │ ─ Attributes ──────────── │    │ ─ Attributes ─────────── │    │
│  │     LastName              │    │     LastName             │    │
│  │     FirstName             │    │     FirstName            │    │
│  │     MiddleName            │    │     MiddleName           │    │
│  │     Office                │    │     Exchange             │    │
│  │     PhoneNumber           │    │     PhoneNumber          │    │
│  │     EmployeeID            │    │     EmployeeID           │    │
│  │     CommissionPlanList    │    │     CommissionPlanList   │    │
│  │     ClientList            │    │                          │    │
│  │                           │    │                 LVL-02-B │    │
│  └──────────────────────────┘    └──────────────────────────┘    │
└─────────────────────────────────────────────────────────────────┘
```

Objects AccountBroker and FloorBroker

Figure 8-22. Structural Attributes for Object classes *AccountBroker* and *FloorBroker*.

```
┌───────────────────────────────┐
│        Broker Object          │
│                               │
│ ─ Attributes ──────────────   │
│     LastName                  │
│     FirstName                 │
│     MiddleName                │
│     PhoneNumber               │
│     EmployeeID                │
│     CommissionPlanList        │
│     CommissionAccount         │
│     ClientList                │
│                               │
│                    LVL-01-S   │
└───────────────────────────────┘
```

Object Broker

Figure 8-23. Structural Attributes for Object class *Broker*.

234

object class *Broker* is important because the subclasses *AccountBroker, FloorBroker,* and *OptionsBroker* are created by inheriting from the object class *Broker* and redefining the attributes that are different. Accordingly, some methods related to this attribute, as well as methods that perform the operations that differentiate the different classes of brokers, will be different. Classification based on methods will be addressed in the next section (Behavioral Model). Figure 8-23 lists the attributes of the object class *Broker*.

We discussed in the beginning of this section the use of the principles of *abstraction* and *localization* to make the model more intelligible. These principles help in achieving data abstraction. Data abstraction is achieved in a model by creating a set of rules for composing higher-level data objects from their constituent data objects. These rules define how the lower-level data objects are combined to form a higher-level data object.

For example, consider the *AccountBroker* object class shown in Figure 8-22. It incorporates commission plan information that could be represented as a separate object. The commission plan specifies the circumstances under which commissions are credited to a broker. A broker can have more than one commission plan. A separate object class for *CommissionPlan* by broker type would appear as in Figure 8-24. The commission plan can be defined instead for each individual broker by changing the BROKER_TYPE attribute to BROKER OBJECT ID.

Alternatively, we can "denormalize" the *AccountBroker* and *CommissionPlan* object classes to incorporate these attributes directly in the attribute list for the *AccountBroker*, as illustrated in Figure 8-25. This would be the case if every broker has a single, potentially unique commission plan.

Analysis of the pros and cons of each approach is required to determine which is correct from the point of view of attributes required and functions (or

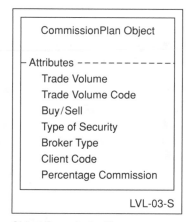

CommissionPlan Object
⊢ Attributes ⎯ ⎯ ⎯ ⎯ ⎯ ⎯ ⎯ ⎯ ⎯ ⊣
Trade Volume
Trade Volume Code
Buy/Sell
Type of Security
Broker Type
Client Code
Percentage Commission
LVL-03-S

Object CommissionPlan

AccountBroker Object
⊢ Attributes ⎯ ⎯ ⎯ ⎯ ⎯ ⎯ ⎯ ⎯ ⎯ ⎯ ⎯ ⎯ ⎯ ⊣
Name (Last, First, Middle)
Phone #
Employee ID
Office Location
Commission Account
Commission Rate—Block Sale
Commission Rate—Individual Sale
Commission Rate—Special Accounts
LVL-02-S

Object AccountBroker

Figure 8-24. Structural Attributes for Object Class *CommissionPlan*.

Figure 8-25. Structural Attributes for Denormalized Object Class *AccountBroker*.

operations) necessary for the application. A separate *CommissionPlan* object allows us to define a commission plan once for each broker type and reference it in each broker object, while in the denormalized version the commission plan information details have to be entered for each individual broker. A more interesting case is where we define a *CommissionPlanList* as an attribute in the *AccountBroker* object. This allows us to attach a number of different types of commission plans (where each commission plan type is represented by a *CommissionPlan* object) to each individual broker.

An important factor in determining the organization of the object classes is the nature of *localization* of changes to commission plans. If changes are global, that is, they affect all brokers in the same manner, the BROKER_TYPE attribute provides a sufficient level of localization. If however, changes are individualistic, that is, each broker has a specialized commission plan, then the rules of localization require that the *CommissionPlan* object have an attribute such as BROKEROB-JECTID.

Our model has so far contained only structural information about objects. Behavioral properties that go with the verbs, such as *create, update,* and *delete,* are needed for the model to be complete. In the more traditional modeling schemes, such as Entity Relationship (ER) diagrams and data-flow diagrams (DFD), the ER diagrams define the structural properties and the DFDs define the behavioral properties. Some behavioral properties are also implied by the structure of the ER diagrams. The separation of the data flows and the data structure and the lack of a clear integration of the structural and behavioral properties make it not only more difficult to develop the design specification, but also make it more incomprehensible for the reader attempting to understand the model. Hence the combination of the Structural and Behavioral models under the common umbrella of an Object Model.

8.8.2 Behavioral Model

The Behavioral Model is the second component of the Object Model. The Behavioral Model consists of the following main components:

- Description of every function at the lowest menu level. These functions invoke methods in objects.
- Descriptions of the methods of the base-level objects.
- Descriptions of higher-level operations that invoke the low-level operations of one or more objects for performing a complex task (possibly recursively). This describes the hierarchy of objects in terms of the methods within the objects.

While the Structural Model uses the data abstractions in the form of aggregation, generalization, and association, the behavioral model uses *control abstractions* in the form of *sequence, choice,* or *decision* and *repetition.* These three control abstractions combined with the *transaction abstractions* of *insert, query, update,* and *join* (or equivalent operations on objects) provide the basis for defining all operations or functions of an application.

A *sequence* is defined as a collection of objects that perform operations in a sequential order. A method in each object of the set calls a method in the next object in a predefined sequence. Figure 8-26 demonstrates the three kinds of control abstractions. A *choice* or *decision* is applied when the next object in a sequence is determined on the basis of a calculated value or the value of an attribute. A *repetition* occurs when a class method is applied to all object instances in a class. For example, a report listing all clients with outstanding balances requires executing a method for checking the *AccountBalance* attribute of a client account object repetitively until all client account objects have been checked.

Behavior abstractions can be achieved in a manner similar to the structural abstractions. By using the structural abstractions, and forms of control and procedural abstractions in the modeling methodology, composite abstract operations can be created. The behavioral abstractions define the set of rules for combining abstract operations into higher-level abstract operations. Object-oriented programming provides the capability to treat these abstract operations also as parts of objects that can be modeled alongside the data (in the Structural Model). In other words, both data and operations are treated as parts of objects that can be combined in an object model and depicted by boxes within frames.

The *behavioral* Frame-Object Analysis diagrams describe the functions of the application system (that is, how the system behaves). The top-level frame of the Transaction Model (described in Figure 8-27) therefore describes the highest-level functions for the TMS application. To demonstrate the modeling process, we will

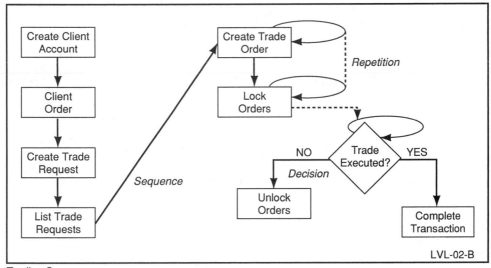

Trading Sequence

Figure 8-26.   Frame Depicting Aggregation Relationships.

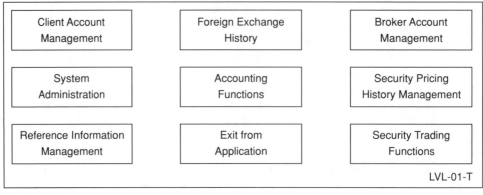

Top-level Menu

Figure 8-27.   Top-level Menu for TMS Application.

determine the methods that directly support the lowest-level menu functions for *Security Trading Functions*. The basic analysis necessary to determine the frames at this level consists primarily of determining the lowest-level menu function for each operational group of functions.

All information systems have processes that are followed from start to finish. For example, the *trading process* consists of the account broker taking the request from the customer and creating an order and the floor broker creating a request for a trade and completing the paperwork on completion of a trade. Similarly, there are other processes such as creating a new client account, creating a new broker account, and performing month-end accounting functions. All of these processes must be analyzed in detail to develop the behavioral model. Frames can be used to describe process flows. These frames help in determining the operations needed at each stage of the process.

Process flows.   The frame described in Figure 8-27 shows all the functions at the highest level of the application. To determine a process flow, we will be cutting through these functions using the concepts of control abstractions, primarily *sequence*. The frame in Figure 8-28 shows the sequence of trading functions. This new frame presents the most powerful feature of the Frame-Object Analysis methodology, the ability to show structural and behavioral objects and the relationships among them. This shows how a frame can be used to describe a process. Use of this capability is crucial for data-flow analysis. Figure 8-28 actually shows the complete sequence of operations from the creation of a client order until the trade is completed. All major intermediary steps are described in the frame. The entity performing the function is shown in parentheses. Intermediate steps can be blown up in their own frames for a more detailed design. This methodology serves not only to document the conceptual model, but also to document the application design.

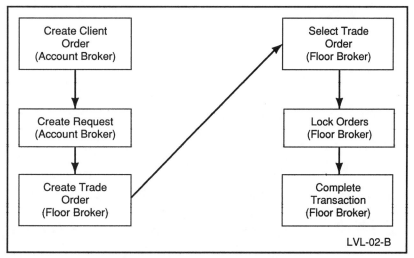

Sequence of Operations for Security Trading

Figure 8-28.   Security Trading Sequence Frame.

A number of other functions are described in the top-level frame in Figure 8-27. We will leave it as an exercise for the reader to develop the frames showing the data flows for all other functions, such as creating a new client account or printing periodic statements. The completion of this task will complete the conceptual model for the TMS application.

Top-level behavioral frames.   The first step in determining the top-level frames is to list the lowest-level menu functions for each operational group. Remember, our definition requires that the operations directly supporting menu (or function key level) functions are a part of the behavioral model. Consequently, each operation at this level will become a part of an object class. We will demonstrate an approach for developing the behavioral frames for the *Security Trading Functions* process. Let us first review the concepts of the relevant behavioral abstractions.

Securities trading functions.   Trading functions are concerned primarily with the sale or purchase of stocks at a client's request. The primary functions performed *sequentially* for trading are as follows:

- Accept client request for trade
- Create client order
- Create trade request (for floor broker to execute)
- Create trade order
- Lock trade order (no client changes allowed)

- Execute trade
- Record completed trades
- Perform follow-up functions

Note that it is possible to combine "create client order" and "create trade request" in one function. The "Create trade request" function checks the accounts for source or disposition of funds. The example in Chapter 16 combines the two functions in a *Request* object. A number of follow-up functions are performed automatically as a result of one of the above actions. These include the following:

- Account management for source of funds for a buy or disposition of funds from a sale
- Assign commissions according to broker and client profiles

A number of functions are available at any time and are not necessarily performed in a sequential manner. These are mostly user-activated functions for viewing and reporting or for changing status.

- View and print list of open trade orders and completed trades by day, week, month, year (or date range)
- View commissions earned by day, week, or month

A number of *choices* or *decisions* are made either by the user or automatically based on the results of a previous operations. For example, the following show some decisions:

- Unlock trade orders not executed.
- Modify client orders not executed.
- Update client accounts based on user request for source or disposition of funds.

Some functions are applied to all objects of a class in a *repetitious* mode. The following lists some examples of these functions:

- Aging of accounts requires aging to be applied to all account objects that have trade balances.
- Stop order expiration checks are similarly applied to all trade requests, and any trade *Request* objects that have expired are canceled (destroyed).
- Lists of trade requests require each trade *Request* object to be processed.

Now that we have seen how behavioral abstractions becomes very useful in understanding the process flow for an application segment, let us list all operations needed for that function. Figure 8-29 presents a sample behavioral frame for the operations for the Security Trading functions.

Note that by reducing the functions to frames in this manner it becomes much simpler to determine the lower-level functions that must be set up for the methods within the objects in the behavioral model.

Basic objects for the TMS application.   From the structural model, we know that a number of object classes have been defined. We now use the functions frame developed above and the transaction model to determine the methods for each object class involved in this function sequence. Figures 8-30 through 8-34 describe the frames for some of the basic objects required for the TMS application. Note that attributes are really not a part of the behavioral model, but are listed here only for convenience so that the readers do not need to keep flipping back to the structural definitions. You will also notice that the

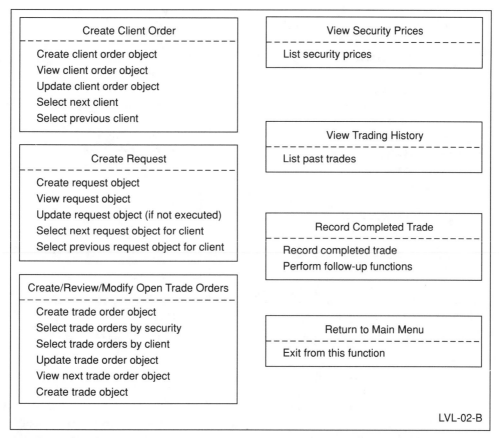

Security Trading Functions

Figure 8-29. Functions Frame for Security Trading Functions.

```
+-------------------------------------------------+
|                 Request Object                  |
|                                                 |
+- - Attributes - - - - - - - - - - - - - - - - --+
|        * AccountBroker                           |
|        * Client                                  |
|        * Security                                |
|        BuySellIndicator                          |
|        NumberOfShares                            |
|        StopPrice                                 |
|        ExpirationDate                            |
|        RequestDate                               |
|        FundsType                                 |
|        * Order                                   |
|        * Trade                                   |
|                                                 |
+- - Instance Methods - - - - - - - - - - - - - --+
|        Create Request Object                     |
|        Set Client (add to list)                  |
|        Set Security Level                         |
|        Set Buy Sell Indicator                    |
|        Set Number of Shares                      |
|        Set Stop Price                            |
|        Set Expiration Date                       |
|        Set Funds Type                            |
|        Mark Order Completed                      |
|        Destroy Request Object                    |
|                                                 |
+- - Class Methods - - - - - - - - - - - - - - - -+
|        Get Open Requests by AccountBroker        |
|        Get Open Requests by Client               |
|        Get Request List by Date                  |
|                                        LVL-01-B |
+-------------------------------------------------+
```

Object Request

Figure 8-30. Frame for object class *Request*.

```
+-------------------------------------------------+
|                  Order Object                   |
|                                                 |
+- - Attributes - - - - - - - - - - - - - - - - --+
|        * AccountBroker                           |
|        * Security                                |
|        * Exchange                                |
|        BuySellIndicator                          |
|        NumberOfShares                            |
|        StopPrice                                 |
|        ExpirationDate                            |
|        LockFlag                                  |
|        * Trade                                   |
|                                                 |
+- - Instance Methods - - - - - - - - - - - - - --+
|        Create Order Object                       |
|        Set Security Level                         |
|        Set Exchange (where traded)               |
|        Set Buy Sell Indicator                    |
|        Set Number of Shares                      |
|        Set Stop Price                            |
|        Set Expiration Date                       |
|        Lock Order                                |
|        Unlock Order                              |
|        TradeCompleted                            |
|        Destroy Order Object                      |
|                                                 |
+- - Class Methods - - - - - - - - - - - - - - - -+
|        Get Open Order List by AccountBroker      |
|        Get Open Order List by Exchange           |
|        Get Open Order List by Security           |
|        Get Order List by Date                    |
|                                        LVL-01-B |
+-------------------------------------------------+
```

Object Order

Figure 8-31. Frame for Object Class *Order*.

model does not attempt to define the calling sequences or datatypes. These issues are addressed during the system design phase in Chapter 9.

Figure 8-30 describes the object class *REQUEST*. You will notice that we have combined *Client Order* and *Trade Request* objects into one *Request* object. This object class is used for setting up requests for a trade. An AccountBroker uses this object to set up a request object when a customer places a buy or sell order.

```
┌─────────────────────────────────────────────┐
│                                             │
│  ┌───────────────────────────────────────┐  │
│  │             Trade Object              │  │
│  │                                       │  │
│  │ ─── Attributes ────────────────────── │  │
│  │       * FloorBroker                   │  │
│  │       * Exchange                      │  │
│  │       * Security                      │  │
│  │       BuySellIndicator                │  │
│  │       NumberOfShares                  │  │
│  │       Price                           │  │
│  │       TradeDate                       │  │
│  │       TradePartner                    │  │
│  │       OrderList                       │  │
│  │                                       │  │
│  │ ─── Instance Methods ──────────────── │  │
│  │       Create Trade Object             │  │
│  │       Destroy Trade Object            │  │
│  │                                       │  │
│  │ ─── Class Methods ─────────────────── │  │
│  │    Get List of Trades by FloorBroker & Date Range │
│  │    Get List of Trades by Exchange & Date Range    │
│  │    Get List of Trades by Security & Date Range    │
│  │    Get List of Trades by Date Range   │  │
│  │                                       │  │
│  │                          LVL-01-B     │  │
│  └───────────────────────────────────────┘  │
└─────────────────────────────────────────────┘
```

Object Trade

Figure 8-32.   Frame for Object Class *Trade*.

Note that some of the instance methods are actually performed in a sequential manner for setting up the order. This is a very simple case of sequential operations; it does not involve calling another object. The instance methods *Mark Order Completed* and *Destroy Trade Order* are not a part of that sequence. These two are performed as a result of a choice based on a determination that the trade has been completed. The more complex case of sequential action is the creation of an *Order* object on completion of the setup of a *Request* object.

The object class for all orders is class *Order*. Figure 8-31 describes the attributes and methods associated with the object class *Order*. The object class *Order* is used by the account broker for placing a trade order. The floor broker then executes the trade order when the conditions for the trade are appropriate.

Note that the methods within the *Order* object operate in a sequential manner. However, there is no automatic sequential operation calling another object. The object *FloorBroker* must get into the act at this point and execute the method *TradeCompleted*. This method calls for the creation of the *Trade* object.

The class *Trade* is the object class for all trades. Creation of a *Trade* object

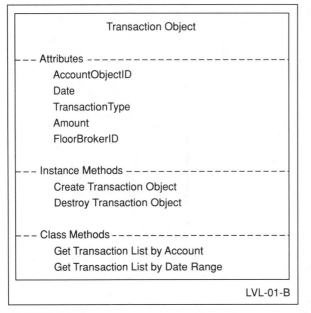

Object Transaction

Figure 8-33.   Frame for Object Class *Transaction.*

causes a number of functions to be executed depending on the nature of the trade. Other objects created may include *Transaction* object, *Invoice* object and *CreditMemo* object. The attributes and the methods for the class *Trade* are described in Figure 8-32.

The three object classes described above are the main object classes involved in the trading sequence. A number of other objects are created and are involved in the follow-up action resulting from a trade. We have described these briefly in the following.

Every transaction that takes place in the system such as a credit or debit to an account must be recorded. This information is recorded in a *Transaction* object and stored (as persistent object) for historical purposes. Figure 8-33 describes a *transaction* object.

A transaction may result in the creation of a credit memo if the account has a credit balance (after a sale) or an invoice if the account has insufficient balance to cover a purchase. Figure 8-34 illustrates the methods required for the *Invoice* and *CreditMemo* objects.

End of the month processing for every account causes a statement to be generated for each account. The statement is stored in an object that includes a complete list of all transactions applied to that account during the statement period. Figure 8-35 describes the object class for *Statements.*

Each broker object has associated with it a *CommissionPlan* object that describes the commission structure for the broker. Figure 8-36 describes the *Commis-*

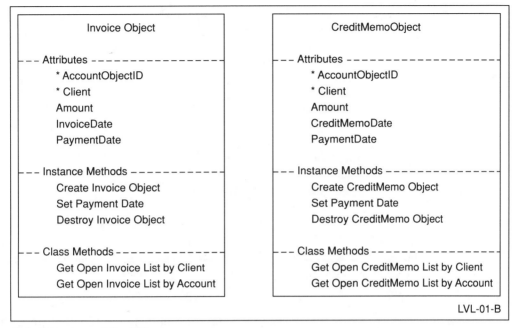

Objects Invoice and CreditMemo

Figure 8-34.   Frame for Object Class *Invoice* and *CreditMemo*.

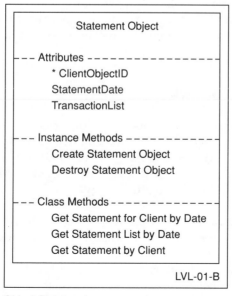

Object Statement

Figure 8-35.   Frame for Object Class *Statement*.

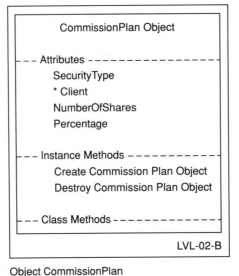

Object CommissionPlan

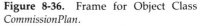

Figure 8-36. Frame for Object Class *CommissionPlan*.

sionPlan object. Note that there is no class method defined at this time since commission plans are read individually, and there are no operations defined that must be applied to the class.

We have developed the basic methodology for developing objects for the behavioral model of an application. Obviously, the model is incomplete as presented. It can be made more complete by performing a deeper analysis of the application and taking all nuances of processing into account. For readers interested in pursuing this further, developing the rest of the object frames would be a very rewarding exercise.

8.9 IMPLEMENTING AN OBJECT MODEL

In the previous two sections, we developed the concepts and the scope of the structural and behavioral perspectives of the data model, as well as the methodology for depicting the Object Model in Frame-Object Analysis diagrams. We will now define a systematic approach for developing an Object Model using the Frame-Object Analysis diagramming methodology.

Information depiction in Frame-Object Analysis.   In Part II of this book, we analyzed a number of approaches to modeling and presented an approach that we called Frame-Object Analysis diagrams. We have used this approach in our treatment of the Transaction Model and the Object Model, and the benefits of Frame-Object Analysis have become very evident. Let us recap some key characteristic of the Frame-Object Analysis methodology as follows:

1. A box in a frame represents a lower-level object.
2. A frame can be viewed as a single higher-level object that contains a collection of lower-level objects. The object represented by the frame is described in terms of its abstract data (attributes), as well as its abstract operations (methods). Both data and operations can be represented in the same frame.
3. Multiple objects can be described in a frame as a group of objects related by data abstractions or operations abstractions.
4. The relationship between the objects is depicted in a manner similar to the depiction of relationships in a semantic network.
5. Higher-level frames can be built to show the relationship between frames. Once again, each frame represents an object.

As in any other modeling methodology, Frame-Object Analysis is a disciplined approach for depicting a model. The characteristics noted above set it apart from most other methodologies in that it has the simplicity of abstraction as well as the flexibility to operate at a real-world depth of analytical detail.

Organized approach for advanced modeling.   A number of steps are involved in integrating the information collected during the various phases of information gathering and analysis. All data objects are identified (at least in broad terms) and all higher-level functions are identified.

The following describes potential stages and the sequence of tasks for each stage that would lead to the structural and behavioral models. Stage 1 gives us a set of basic objects as the building blocks for our models. Stage 2 applies the principles of association and stage 3 applies the principles of aggregation and of control abstractions. Finally, in stage 4, we perform the structural and behavioral mapping. You will notice that stages 1 and 2 produce structural frames and stages 3 and 4 produce behavioral frames. It may be feasible to perform stages 3 and 4 first if information on data objects is detailed enough.

STAGE 1

1. Each structural object is documented and its variables (or components) are determined. At the very basic level, the object may translate to a table and the variables or components to fields.
2. The principles of *classification* are used to determine if any objects have identical properties. If the objects differ simply by name and where they are used, they can be resolved into a single object.
3. The principles of *generalization* are used to determine similarities that lower-level objects must inherit. This step may lead to decomposing an object further through the principles of classification and creating common lower-level objects to replace some of the decomposed objects.

STAGE 2

4. The principles of *association* are used to group hitherto unrelated objects in related sets. The common properties of these sets are determined.
5. The differences in operations performed on component objects of the set are determined and documented.

STAGE 3

6. The principles of *localization* are used to *aggregate* objects to model each property of an application function independently in a localized manner. The result of this effort is a set of frames that combine the lower levels of objects into atomic subfunctions required for the application. For example, the subfunction of "aging" may be represented in this manner. Note that aging is a localized function that applies to all objects that have overdue account balances.
7. Frames are developed for each function of the application, thereby providing the first-level decomposition of the function. Each entity or object represented in this first-level decomposition frame is itself a frame.
8. The principles of control abstractions, *sequencing, choosing/decision making,* and *repetition,* are applied for grouping the operations in process flow diagram frames. This helps in understanding the relationships between methods across objects.

STAGE 4: STRUCTURAL AND BEHAVIORAL MAPPING

9. The objects of the high-level function frames are now broken down to further levels using the behavioral abstractions of transaction modeling until the lowest-level frames use only the objects defined in step 6.
10. The complete sequence of operations for each function is checked to ensure that each frame is correct and that the model fully meets the requirements.

At this point, we have an integrated structural and behavioral data model. A systematic approach of this nature ensures that all required objects are clearly defined in the hierarchy of objects and all functions are accounted for. The conceptual data model emerging from this approach is comprehensive and accurately represents the requirements.

8.10 SUMMARY

This chapter discussed our design methodology in detail. We divided the methodology into three main parts:

1. *Information System Model:* This describes the external view of the information system, the view that is visible to the user.

2. *Object Model:* This describes the internal view consisting of object class definitions (attributes, methods, and object relationships), a view largely visible to the designer but not necessarily to the user.

3. *System design:* The definition of the attribute datatypes, method datatypes, call parameters, constraints, and so on.

But before this part of the methodology can be applied, it is important to understand the requirements. An enterprise has a number of different operating entities with different functions. For developing an application set to support these functions, it is essential to understand the operations performed by each business unit, the interactions among the business units, and the information elements collected, processed, and disseminated by each business unit. The operations performed by a business unit are described in the Business Model. The business model describes the business of the corporation.

The information elements collected, processed, and disseminated by each business unit are described in the Business Information Model. An architectural recommendation is then prepared and a Technology Feasibility report is developed. This report, along with the Business Information Model, becomes the basis for the design of the information system.

The Information System Model presents a view of the system as perceived by the user. It describes the external view of the entities, their attributes, and the logical groupings and relationships among attributes and entities from a user perspective in the Entity Model. It further describes user functions and the user interface in the Transaction Model. The Information System Model is a complete external description of the functionality of the system. A partial Information System Model was developed as an example in this chapter.

The Object Model is the internal object view of the model. These two views of the model completely define the model to a point where it can be designed. It describes the underlying objects, the attributes of each object, relationships among objects, and descriptions of classes and inheritance in the Structural Model. It further defines the operations required to support each function described in the Transaction Model and describes the complete hierarchy of objects from an operations (methods) perspective in the behavioral model. We developed a partial Object Model for the trading management system in this chapter as an example.

The Information System Model and the Object Model describe the functionality and structure of the information and form the basis for the design. The effective use of the Frame-Object Analysis diagramming methodology is also presented in this chapter. The presentation of the model is made significantly more comprehensible when Frame-Object Analysis diagrams are used.

8.11 EXERCISES

1. Complete the frames for additional entities required for the financial information management system for the ITC corporation. Prepare the completed Entity Model as a formal document.

2. Complete the user forms for application components not described in this chapter. Using these, develop the additional frames describing all user functions. Prepare a completed Transaction Model as a formal document.

3. Redesign the objects based on the completed Entity Model. What kinds of changes are necessary to the existing frames? Prepare a completed Structural Model as a formal document.

4. Redesign the objects based on the changes to the Structural Model as well as the completed Transaction Model. What kinds of changes are necessary for the existing frames to adapt them to the completed Structural and Transaction Models?

5. Are additional Entity Relationship diagrams needed to describe the application? If so, explain why?

6. Are additional data-flow diagrams needed to describe the processes? If so, explain why.

7. How would you construct the Frame-Object Analysis diagrams on your system? What utility programs do you need?

8. Based on your experience, how would you improve on the Frame-Object Analysis methodology.

9

Object-Oriented Design

In the previous chapters we developed the logical model for an application. Now we must take these models and apply them to the design of an object-oriented database application. In Chapter 8, we also discussed the concepts of Frame-Object Analysis and used examples to demonstrate its application to database design (our case study in Chapters 15 and 16 demonstrates the use of this methodology for a complex distributed business application). Now that we have our model, we are ready to design the system. In our Object Model, we have frames containing objects. The structural frames themselves are representations of object classes. In our design, we need to take into account not only atomic objects, but also classes of objects, object hierarchies, and object inheritance. You may want to go back to Chapter 3 to review these basic concepts of object-oriented programming.

In the Object Model in Chapter 8 we described each component of the application in terms of an object, an entity with both structural and behavioral components. We described our requirements for the features of an object-oriented database management system in Chapter 5. These requirements play a significant role in this design exercise and include the following:

1. Capability to define persistent objects
2. Unique identification of each object

3. Object encapsulation (abstract data typing for classes)
4. Inheritance and multiple inheritance
5. Redefinition and dynamic binding
6. Polymorphism

In the Object Model, all of the application object classes were defined in terms of their structural attributes and the methods for accessing and manipulating objects of the class. In the object model we also defined the structural hierarchy of the object classes and the interactions among methods of different classes.

In this chapter we will discuss the issues involved in designing and coding actual class definitions for an object-oriented database. The steps involved include the following:

- Assigning datatypes to each object attribute
- Defining the interface to each object method and assigning datatypes to the parameters
- Writing code for each object method

We will discuss the datatypes available to the designer and programmer and the issues involved in choosing appropriate datatypes for each attribute and method parameter. We will also discuss the types of methods that can be developed for a class and the particular design issues for each type of method.

An object-oriented database provides an object-oriented programming language for the definition and manipulation of database objects. This programming language should be fully capable of being used for the development of the user interface components of the application. The implementation of the application objects defined in the logical design should be very straightforward using such a language. In the examples provided in this chapter, we have assumed an object-oriented database using the C+ + language or an extension.

9.1 OBJECT DEFINITION

In Chapter 8 we discussed the relationship between objects and created Frame-Object Analysis diagrams to illustrate these relationships. We will use the Structural and Behavioral models to formulate some definitions of objects, object classes, methods, and transaction classes. These definitions will help in representing the framework for the design of an application. (We can also call these definitions information groupings.)

The class definitions for each application object must be programmed in the object-oriented language of the application. Once this task is complete, these definitions must be loaded into the database. In a distributed environment the database resides in one or more database servers located in the local- or wide-area network. We will call these object servers. The database system should provide a tool for performing the task of loading object class definitions into the server. The process of loading object class definitions involves several steps, as follows:

- Transfer an object class definition to the server.
- Compile the object class definition on the server and report any errors to the user.
- If compilation is successful, build a set of RPC (remote procedure call) front-end routines that will be linked into the user interface component of the application to provide access to object methods.

As each object class definition is developed and loaded into an object server, code may be developed to test the class by creating objects and manipulating the objects using the defined methods.

We will first discuss the assignment of datatypes to objects and then the creation of object methods. These two actions are necessary for developing the code for defining the base objects.

9.2 ASSIGNING DATATYPES TO OBJECTS

The datatypes available for assigning to object attributes and method parameters include the following:

- Simple built-in datatypes such as *int*, *float*, and *char*.
- Additional utility datatypes that may be offered by the implementation language, such as:
  - *Money, String, Boolean*
  - *Pointers* to other datatypes, especially, other class objects
- *Arrays* may be used for storing a known fixed-size list of items.
- Set oriented datatypes for storing variable length list of objects (it is very useful to be able to define a *variable-length object list*.)

In the examples presented in this chapter, we have used a utility class called *Vec* to store an abitrary number of data items. Vec is an example of a parameterized class that takes a datatype as a parameter when a Vec object is declared. For example, a list declared as *Vec(Client)* will cause a *Vec* object to be created that may contain pointers to *Client* objects only. A good object-oriented database system may offer a built-in language feature for object set processing that includes the ability to add and delete set members and to iterate through each member of the set.

Objects in one class are linked to objects in another class in two ways, through *inheritance* and by including a *pointer* to an object as an attribute of another object. As defined in Chapter 5, inheritance allows one class to be derived from one or more existing classes; that is, the new class inherits all attributes and methods of the parent classes. The new class may add additional attributes and methods, as well as redefine any methods of the parent classes. Inheritance is often used when two or more object types defined in the Object Model share a large number of attributes and exhibit a common behavior. A parent class can be defined that contains the attributes and methods that the objects have in common, and two or more child classes can be defined that implement the unique characteristics of the object types. In the trading manage-

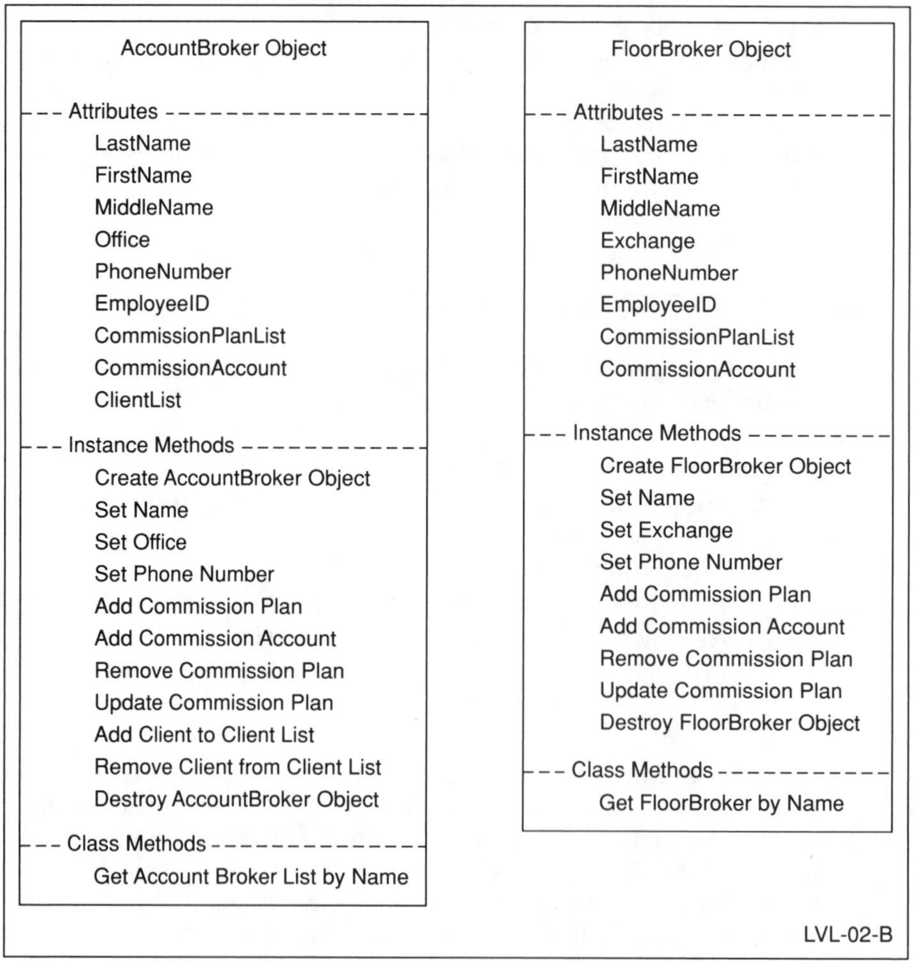

AccountBroker Object	FloorBroker Object
– – Attributes – – – – – – – – – – – –	**– – Attributes – – – – – – – – – – – –**
LastName	LastName
FirstName	FirstName
MiddleName	MiddleName
Office	Exchange
PhoneNumber	PhoneNumber
EmployeeID	EmployeeID
CommissionPlanList	CommissionPlanList
CommissionAccount	CommissionAccount
ClientList	
– – Instance Methods – – – – – – – – – –	**– – Instance Methods – – – – – – – –**
Create AccountBroker Object	Create FloorBroker Object
Set Name	Set Name
Set Office	Set Exchange
Set Phone Number	Set Phone Number
Add Commission Plan	Add Commission Plan
Add Commission Account	Add Commission Account
Remove Commission Plan	Remove Commission Plan
Update Commission Plan	Update Commission Plan
Add Client to Client List	Destroy FloorBroker Object
Remove Client from Client List	**– – Class Methods – – – – – – – – – –**
Destroy AccountBroker Object	Get FloorBroker by Name
– – Class Methods – – – – – – – – – – –	
Get Account Broker List by Name	

LVL-02-B

Objects AccountBroker and FloorBroker

Figure 9-1. Frames for AccountBroker and FloorBroker Objects.

ment system application, this method can be used to define the broker datatypes. Figure 9-1 shows the frame for the AccountBroker and FloorBroker objects.

As can be seen, most of the attributes of these objects are identical, and the methods for manipulating these common attributes are identical as well. The following code segment shows an implementation of these object classes using the object-oriented language C++. It defines a parent class called *Broker* and then defines two child classes, *AccountBroker* and *FloorBroker*, that are derived from Broker. Note that the class definitions for *AccountBroker* and *FloorBroker* are quite simple and only include the one or two attributes and associated methods that distinguish them from each other. The *Broker* class in this scenario is known as a *generic* class. No objects of the *Broker* class may be instantiated by a program; it exists only to provide a common basis for two or more real-world object classes. Note, however, that methods may be defined in the *Broker* class that take a *Broker* object as a parameter. This means that they may operate on either *AccountBroker* or *FloorBroker* objects, since both are derived from the *Broker* class.

```
class Broker {
    // Broker attributes. Note that in the absence of either the public or
    // private keyword, the attributes will be considered private. Private
    // methods may be declared as well; they may only be called by other
    // Broker methods.

    // Declare the character string fields using the String datatype.
    // The char datatype may be used as well; however, the String datatype,
    // if properly defined, will automatically allocate the appropriate
    // amount of memory to contain character strings assigned to String
    // objects.
    String last_name;
    String first_name;
    String middle_name;
    String phone_number;

    // A simple integer employee id.
    int employee_id;

    // A pointer to an Account object.
    Account * commission_acct;

    // A list of CommissionPlan objects. Initially this list is empty.
    Vec(CommissionPlan) commission_plan_list;

public:
    // The public methods for the class.

    // The first three methods are simple methods used to assign values to
    // the attributes.
    void SetName(String p_last_name, String p_first_name, String p_middle_name);
```

```
    void SetPhoneNumber(String p_phone_number);
    void SetEmployeeId(int p_employee_id);

    // This method is used to update a CommissionPlan object contained within
    // the Broker object.
    Money UpdateCommissionPlan(Security * p_security, int num_shares, Money  p_price,
                          DateTime p_trade_date);

    // These methods are used to add and remove CommissionPlan objects.
    void AddCommissionPlan(CommissionPlan * p_plan);
    void RemoveCommissionPlan(CommissionPlan * p_plan);
};
```

The class *AccountBroker* has the same attributes as the class *Broker* except for the attributes *office* and *client_list*. The following code segment shows the code for that class.

```
class AccountBroker : public Broker {
    // AccountBroker attributes that do not exist in the Broker object.
    String office;
    Vec(Client) client_list;

public:
    // Public AccountBroker methods.

    // The AccountBroker constructor method is used to initialize AccountBroker
    // objects. It takes as arguments values for each of the attributes
    // that must be defined in a valid object. Note that it initializes
    // the base Broker attributes as well as the attributes unique to the
    // AccountBroker object.
    AccountBroker (String p_last_name, String p_first_name, String p_middle_name,
                String p_phone_number, int p_employee_id, String p_office);

    // The AccountBroker destructor method is called automatically when an object
    // is destroyed to deallocate resources, in this case the CommissionPlan
    // objects.
    ~AccountBroker();

    // Methods to update the AccountBroker specific attributes.
    void SetOffice(String p_office);
    void AddClient(Client * p_client);
    void RemoveClient(Client * p_client);

    // A class method used to retrieve a set of AccountBroker objects that have
    // a last_name attribute matching a supplied value. The caller supplies
    // an empty AccountBroker vector; the method fills the vector with pointers
    // to each matching object.
    static void GetAccountBrokerByName(String p_last_name, Vec(AccountBroker) &
                          broker_list);
};
```

Inheritance, as we just saw, is one mode of linking one object to another object. The second mode in which one object may be linked to another object is by defining an attribute of one object to be a *pointer* to the second object. In fact, one object may include pointers to several different objects or even an array of pointers to other objects. In an object-oriented database these pointers will actually be object identifiers; however, it is easier to define and manipulate them as pointers in an object-oriented language like $C++$. Note in the code segment above that the definition of the *AccountBroker* object class includes a *vector* of *Client* objects. The vector object is a variable-length list of pointers to *Client* objects. This list is used to maintain for each *AccountBroker* object the list of clients managed by the account broker.

The following code segment shows the inheritance of the *FloorBroker* object class from the *Broker* object class.

```
class FloorBroker : public Broker {
    // FloorBroker attributes that do not exist in the Broker object.
    String exchange_name;

public:
    // Public FloorBroker methods.

    // A FloorBroker constructor method similar to that of the AccountBroker,
    // however specifying an exchange name instead of an office.
    FloorBroker(String p_last_name, String p_first_name, String p_middle_name, String
                p_phone_number, int p_employee_id, String p_exchange);

    // The destructor method is:
    ~FloorBroker( );

    // Method for setting the unique FloorBroker attribute.
    void SetExchange(String p_exchange);

    // A class method for retrieving a list of FloorBroker objects by last_name.
    static void GetFloorBrokerByName(String p_last_name, Vec(FloorBroker) & broker_list);

};
```

9.2.1 Public and Private Attributes

Object attributes may be defined in $C++$ as either *public* or *private*. Public attributes may be read or modified directly by an application function. Private attributes, on the other hand, are hidden from an application. They may be accessed only through an object's methods. By default, an attribute that is not listed as either public or private is considered to be private. When an attribute of an object is defined as private, it is generally necessary to provide two methods for accessing the attribute, one for reading the attribute value and one for updating it. If many attributes are defined for an object, then many methods will need to be defined for the object. One way of reducing the number of methods is to group certain attributes together and provide a single method for updating the group. In the previous example, the *Broker* class defined a method, *SetName,* which takes three arguments to assign values to each of the name attributes, *last_name, first_name,* and *middle_name.*

The following example shows the class definition for the *Client* class. We will be extending this example in the following section, where we will discuss in more detail each common type of object method and provide code examples of the actual method implementations. Note that the *Client* class also contains methods that update several attributes in a single call.

```
class Client {
    // Declare the Client attributes.
    // ClientType is an enumerator, defined elsewhere, that specifies whether the
    // object represents an individual or a corporate client.
    ClientType client_type;

    // The following attributes are dynamic character strings.
    String last_name;
    String first_name;
    String middle_name;
    String address;
    String city;
    String state;
    String zip;
    String day_phone;
    String eve_phone;

    // A pointer to an AccountBroker object representing the primary account
    // broker for this client.
    AccountBroker * primary_broker;

    // The list of all account brokers that may manage the client's accounts.
    Vec(AccountBroker) broker_list;

    // The list of Client portfolios.
    Vec(Portfolio) portfolio_list;

    // The list of accounts that maintain the balances of the Client's assets.
    Vec(Account) account_list;

public:
    // Declare the public methods for Client objects.

    // The Client constructor for initializing Client objects.
```

```
Client(String & p_last_name, String & p_first_name, String & p_middle_name,
        String & p_client_type, String & p_address, String & p_city, String &
        p_state, String & p_zip, String & p_day_phone, String & p_eve_phone,
        AccountBroker * p_primary_broker)

// The destructor method for deallocated Client object resources.
~Client( );

// Methods for updating Client attributes
void SetName(String & p_last_name, String & p_first_name, String & p_middle_name);
void Setaddress(String & p_address, String & p_city, String & p_state, String & p_zip);
void SetPhoneNumbers(String & p_day_phone, String & p_eve_phone);
void SetClientType(ClientType p_client_type);
void SetPrimaryBroker(AccountBroker * p_broker);

// Methods for adding or removing Portfolio objects
void AddPortfolio(Portfolio * p_portfolio);
void RemovePortfolio(Portfolio * p_portfolio);

// Methods for adding or removing Account objects
void AddAccount(Account * p_account);
void RemoveAccount(Account * p_account);

// Methods for adding or removing AccountBroker objects
void AddBroker(AccountBroker * p_broker);
void RemoveBroker (AccountBroker * p_broker);

// Method for applying the results of a Trade to Client accounts
void RequestCompleted(Request * p_request, DateTime p_trade_date, Money p_price,
        Money p_commission);

// Class Methods for retrieving Client objects
static void GetClientByName(String & last_name, Vec(Client) & client_vec);
}
```

There are several notable features in this class definition. They will be discussed in the following section, which deals with the coding of object methods. An important point to note here is that this class definition does not include methods for reading the private object attributes. One reason is simply for brevity and clarity in the presentation of the class definition. The methods for reading attributes, one for each attribute, are very trivial methods. A more important reason is related to the nature of a distributed object database system. Objects in a distributed object database system are stored on a remote object server. The methods defined for the object class are stored and executed on the object server as well. Everytime an object method is invoked a *remote procedure call* (RPC) is sent from the application (client) machine to the object server. The object server locates the object, performs the requested operation, and returns a result to the application. A level of optimization can be obtained by transferring a copy of an object to the client machine upon first reference and allowing the application to read the object's attributes directly without needing to create an RPC request for each access. We have defined methods for updating object attributes because all update requests must be routed through an object server to maintain integrity during concurrent updates.

9.3 CREATING OBJECT METHODS

Two general types of methods may be defined for an object class, *instance methods* and *class methods.* Instance methods manipulate individual objects of the class, whereas class methods manipulate the set of all objects of the class. In a database application, class methods are the primary means for retrieving a specific class object or set of objects, given some constraints on the object attributes.

9.3.1 Class Methods

Class methods may also be used to obtain information about the class as a whole, such as the current number of objects of the class. The following code example shows a class method that is used to retrieve a set of *Client* objects that match a given last name. In C++, class methods are generally defined using the type specifier *static* in front of the class definition.

```
static void Client::GetClientByName(String & p_last_name, Vec(Client) & client_vec)
{
        for Client * c in Client suchthat client_name = name
                client_vec += c;
}
```

The experienced C++ programmer will notice that this example contains constructs that are not regular C++ syntax. This is because C++ does not currently have any built-in mechanisms for iterating or searching through the list of all objects of a class. Such a mechanism could of course be implemented using a statically defined array or vector of object pointers. However, we have chosen to present a language feature offered by the object-oriented database language O++[1], which is derived from C++. In O++, the *for* statement has been extended to allow for iterating through all of the objects of a class. This mechanism is pro-

---

[1] R. Agrawal and N. H. Gehani, "ODE (Object Databases and Environment): The Language and the Data Model," AT&T Bell Laboratories Technical Memorandum, Murray Hill, N.J., 1989.

R. Agrawal and N. Gehani, "Rationale for the Design of Persistence and Query Processing Facilities in the Database Programming Language O++," *2nd International Workshop on Database Programming Languages*, Oregon Coast, June 1989.

vided with the "for object in Classname" clause. A further feature is that the range of objects returned may be constrained through the use of the *suchthat* keyword followed by a number of constraints on object attributes.

9.3.2 Instance Methods

Instance methods are the most common methods developed for a class as they provide the mechanisms for retrieving and manipulating an object's attributes. Several different types of instance methods may be developed for a class. Some of the more common ones are as follows:

- Constructors
- Destructors
- Methods for retrieving attributes
- Methods for updating attributes
- Methods for operating on linked objects
- Trigger methods

The first method invoked for most objects is the object constructor. A constructor initializes the object attributes. It is invoked automatically by the system when an object is created. If an object is derived from one or more parent object classes, then the constructors of the parent classes will be invoked as well to initialize the inherited attributes. The following example shows the *Client* object constructor:

```
Client::Client(String & p_last_name, String & p_first_name, String & p_middle_name, String &
        p_client_type, String & p_address, String & p_city, String & p_state, String &
        p_zip, String & p_day_phone, String & p_eve_phone, AccountBroker *
        p_primary_broker)
{
    /* Assign values to the simple attributes */
    last_name = p_last_name;
    first_name = p_first_name;
    middle_name = p_middle_name;
    client_type = p_client_type;
    address = p_address;
    city = p_city;
    state = p_state;
    zip = p_zip;
    day_phone = p_day_phone;
    eve_phone = p_eve_phone;
    primary_broker = p_primary_broker;

    /* Add primary broker to the Client's broker list */
    broker_list += primary_broker;
```

```
/* Create default account objects for the Client */
Account * margin_account = new Account(AT_CLIENT_MARGIN, 0.0, 0.0);
Account * mm_account = new Account(AT_CLIENT_MM, 0.0, 0.0);
Account * port_account = new Account(AT_CLIENT_PORTFOLIO, 0.0, 0.0);

/* Add these account objects to the account list */
account_list += margin_account;
account_list += mm_account;
account_list += port_account;

/* Create a default portfolio object and add it to the portfolio list */
dflt_portfolio = new Portfolio("Default", port_account);
portfolio_list += dflt_portfolio;
}
```

When an object is destroyed, a *destructor* method is invoked to free any resources allocated by the object and to sever any associations the object may have to other objects. For simple classes that are not derived from other classes and contain no links to other objects, the destructor method may often be omitted. The destructor method for the *Client* object, shown below, destroys each of the Account and Portfolio objects that were created for the Client object.

```
Client::~Client( )
{
    // Destroy the client account objects. It is assumed that the application
    // has already checked that the account balances are zero before destroying
    // the Client object.
    for (Account * account = account_list.First(); account; account =
        account_list.Next())
            delete account;

    // Destroy the client portfolio objects.

    for (Portfolio * portfolio = portfolio_list.First(); portfolio; portfolio = portfolio_list.Next())
    {
            delete portfolio;
    }
    // The AccountBroker objects in the broker_list will remain valid after the
    // client object is deleted, so they must not be destroyed. All remaining
    // attribute objects, such as the String and Vector objects, will be destroyed
    // when the Client object is destroyed. Therefore, the destructor method is
    // complete.
}
```

As discussed earlier, methods may or may not be provided for reading the values of each individual attribute. Whether they are provided depends on whether the attributes are declared as public or private and on the nature of the object-oriented database system. It may in any event be useful to provide methods that return values based on some combination of attributes or on calculations involving the attributes. It may also be useful to provide a full set of retrieval methods to shield the user from the underlying implementation of the attributes.

Most of the methods defined for a class provide mechanisms for updating one or more object attributes. The actions performed may range from the update of a single attribute to a complex operation that affects many attributes, creates links to other objects, and creates one or more new objects. In the following example a simple method is shown that takes three strings as parameters and uses them to set the name attributes of a *Client* object.

```
void Client::SetName (String & p_last_name, String & p_first_name, String &
                      p_middle_name)
{
        last_name = p_last_name;
        first_name = p_first_name;
        middle_name = p_middle_name;
}
```

In some cases it is useful to provide more than one method for updating a single attribute. For example, an *Account* object may provide one method for debiting an account and another method for crediting the account. Both methods update the *Account* object's *balance* attribute. The next code segment illustrates this point.

```
void Account::Debit(Money p_amount)
{
        balance + = p_amount;
}
void Account::Credit(Money p_amount)
{
        balance − = p_amount;
}
```

In the next code segment example, a method is defined to set the primary broker for a *Client* object. In addition to setting the *primary_broker* attribute, the method checks to see if the specified broker is contained in the Client's *broker_list* attribute. If not, the *Broker* object is added to the list.

```
void client::Set Primary Broker(AccountBroker * p_broker)
{
        primary_broker = p_broker;
        if (!broker_list.Contains(p_broker)) broker_list + = p_broker;
}
```

Note in the previous example the use of the "+ =" operator to add a *Broker* object to the broker list. This makes use of a powerful feature of the C++ language to define methods for a class that are invoked through the use of any of the C++ operator symbols. These include the simple operators such as +, −, *, and, /, as well as other operators such as [], −>, + +, and =. This feature allows new object classes to be defined that are nearly as integrated into the language as the built-in datatypes.

9.3.3 Trigger Methods

Triggers are a construct of database management systems that are executed upon certain constraints on attributes when a certain set of conditions is met. Triggers are executed at certain times or intervals or upon certain events such as changes to an attribute value. For example, a trigger method may be executed if a certain pre- or postcondition is met.

A condition may be set for an account attribute that prevents further trading when a margin account is overdrawn by a predetermined amount. When that amount is reached, the condition is met and a trigger method is executed that sets a flag to prevent further trading. A trigger used in this manner is analogous to a trigger in a relational database.

9.3.4 Complex Methods

An example of a much more complex method is the *RequestCompleted* method of the *Client* object class, shown below. It is at the bottom of a chain of methods invoked when a *Trade* object is created. It is used to update the client account and portfolio objects to reflect the purchase or sale of a security.

```
void Client::Request Completed(Request * p_request, DateTime p_trade_date, Money p_price,
                Money p_commission)
{
    Security * sec = p_request->security;
    Portfolio * port = p_request->client_portfolio;
    FundsType funds_type = p_request->funds_type;
    Boolean purchase = (p_request->buy_sell_ind == BUY);
    int num_shares = (purchase) ? p_request->num_shares : − p_request->num_shares;

    /* Locate the SecurityHolding object in the indicated client portfolio
     and update the number of shares owned. */

    for (SecurityHolding * sh = port->First(); sh; sh = port->Next())
      if (sh->security == sec) {
        sh->num_shares += num_shares;
        break;
      }

    /* If the security was not found in the portfolio, then add it. */
```

```
if (sh == (SecurityHolding *)0)
  port->AddSecurityHolding(sec, num_shares);

/* Calculate the net cost of the purchase (positive amount) or
   the net proceeds (negative amount) from the sale of the security */

Money net_amount = num_shares * p_price + p_commission;
Account * acct = (Account *)0;

/* Determine the correct Account to update according to the FundsType
   specified in the Request. */

switch (p_request->fund_source {

case FS_PORTFOLIO_ACCT:
        acct = port->account;
        break;

case FS_MM_ACCT:
        for (acct = account_list.First(); acct; acct = account_list.Next())
          if (acct->account_type == AT_CLIENT_MM) break;
        break;

case FS_MARGIN_ACCT:
        for (acct = account_list.First(); acct; acct = account_list.Next())
          if (acct->account_type == AT_CLIENT_MARGIN) break;
        break;

case FS_INVOICE:
        acct = port->account;
        Invoice * inv = new Invoice(acct, this, net_amount, p_trade_date);
          break;

case FS_CREDIT_MEMO:
        acct = port->account;
        CreditMemo * cm = new CreditMemo(acct, this, net_amount, p_trade_date);
        break;

default:
        acct = port->account;
        break;
}

/* Now Debit or Credit the account as appropriate */
if (purchase) {
        acct->Debit(net_amount);
} else {
        acct->Credit(net_amount);
}
}
```

9.3.5 Error Reporting

In designing object methods, consideration must be given to how methods will handle and report error conditions. There are two basic types of error conditions: errors that are a part of the design of the application, and errors that occur due to programming. The first type of error usually occurs as the result of improper input or actions on the part of the user. The application should detect these error conditions and report them gracefully to the user. The second type of error results from calling an object method with invalid parameter values; for example, passing a NULL object pointer where a valid object is expected, or passing a numeric value that is outside of the valid range required by the method. Thorough unit testing of each class and of the interface between the class and callers of the class will eliminate most of these unexpected errors, which typically result in program termination.

For error conditions that are designed into the application, errors will be detected by low level methods and propagated to higher level methods which can report the error conditions to the user. Users should be allowed to acknowledge the error condition and possibly modify input to correct the error.

In terms of implementation, errors can be communicated between methods in one of two ways:

- through method parameters
- through signalling

Generally, all functions return a value which indicates the success or failure of the operation. This value may be a pure status value or it may be a data value for which certain defined values indicate an error condition. In many cases additional information may be useful to describe the nature of the error. This information may be communicated by storing descriptive text in an *error_msg* parameter passed to the function. Alternately, this information may be stored in a global variable. In an object-oriented system a separate globally accessible *Error* class may be implemented to provide a common interface for reporting all error condition information. Any method that encounters an error would invoke an *Error* class method to describe the error and then return an error indication to its caller. The calling method would either pass the error up, possibly add additional information, or act on the error.

A signalling mechanism for reporting errors provides an alternate path for returning from a function. In the normal path, data is passed to a function through its parameters, and data is returned by the function through its return value and through updates to the supplied parameters. If an error occurs, it may be signalled to the calling function; this causes an abnormal exit from the function. A signalled error must be caught by an error handler which will either handle the condition or resignal the error to a higher level handler. If an error occurs in a method for which the calling function has not declared an error handler, then the error will be propagated up the chain of callers until an error handler is reached. If there is no error handler to deal with the error, then a system level error handler will print a generic error message and terminate the application.

9.4 IMPLEMENTING OBJECT CLASSES

So far, we have concerned ourselves with the design of the object classes. In this section, we will address implementation issues that must be kept in mind for the design of the system. In most object-oriented databases, user-defined objects will generally inherit a number of common properties from a base database object (that is, from the base class). These properties are used for the identification and management of each database object. The following describes the potential attributes of a base class that should be inherited by all objects:

BASE OBJECT ATTRIBUTES

Class identifier
Object identifier
Owner object server ID
Local copy address
Persistence flag
Version
Creation date/time
Modification date/time
Access date/time
Access control list
Distribution list
Transaction object list

These attributes are very useful for the management of the objects in terms of their location, type, access controls, and time of creation and last access and update.

9.4.1 Object Identification

As we described in Chapter 5, object identifiers are assigned by the object server when an object is created. Similarly, class identifiers are assigned when a class definition is first loaded into the system. Together, they uniquely identify an object and remain unchanged throughout the life of the object. The object server maintains an index of the class identifier/object identifier pairs stored within or known to the object server. Objects owned by another object server (identified by the owner object server ID attribute) may be accessed through the local object server. If a copy of the object is present on the server, read operations may be satisfied locally. All update operations will require communication with the object's owner to verify the object version and to process the transaction.

One object can locate and reference another object by including its object identifier and object class identifier as attributes within itself. For a complete reference, the object owner (location that created or retains the master copy of the object) must also be known. An object index can be used to identify the owner and address of an object, given its object identifier and object class identifier. Objects can then be located and accessed by the database using the object identifier, object class identifier, and object owner. Copies of the object may exist on other servers. If the local server is not the owner, but it has a local copy of the object, then the index should be able to provide the address of the local copy. The index must contain the following four parameters to locate an object:

1. Object identifier
2. Object class identifier
3. Object owner
4. Address (if not owned, address of a local copy, if any)

Note that once an object is created the object identifier and the object class identifier are permanently assigned and cannot be changed.

9.4.2 Object Persistence

Objects are created very often for short durations and are removed when they are no longer needed. These temporary objects also serve an important role in the design of an information system. The temporary objects do not find a home in the database and cannot be accessed by any client other than the owner (creator) of the object. One primary purpose of an object-oriented database system is to store objects created by an application for use by additional and future application instances. This property of maintaining objects across application instances is known as persistence. In a relational database system, all objects (rows) created in a database are persistent. However, in an object-oriented system, with a fully integrated object-oriented programming environment, an application may create temporary instances of an object defined in the database for use only by the application instance. Similarly, during the execution of an object method on the object server, temporary objects may be created for the life of the method only. The persistence flag in the base object attributes identifies whether an object is temporary or persistent. For an object to become persistent (or permanent), it must have a *method* in the object or base class that invokes a routine to make the object permanent by storing it in the database. Persistent objects stored in the database can then be accessed and updated by all authorized users or client applications.

9.4.3 Access Control Lists

An important aspect in a networked system is security. The security of the system is ensured by checking all access requests for user authorizations. An access control list defines what operations users or groups of users may perform on objects. In a relational database the *owner* of an object maintains an access control list that includes all users authorized to *create, read, update,* or *delete* a data object. If the user is not listed on the access control list, the data object owner may add the user to the access control list with the minimal read privileges allowed to all users on a global basis (that is, the user can read the object unless it has specific restrictions on *read* also). In an object-oriented database, permissions are granted or denied for the execution of each method defined for the object.

Access control lists may be associated with the class to provide default permissions for each object in the class. They should provide the capability to allow or disallow access to each object attribute and method. If, on attempt to access an object, the object does not reside on the local server and the owner server cannot be accessed (due to security restrictions or network congestion or failure), an error will be returned to the requestor.

9.4.4 Object Distribution

An attribute of the base object definition lists each server that currently contains a copy of the object. This attribute is initially null and is updated dynamically. When updates are performed on an object, notification messages must be sent to each of these servers, informing them that their copy is now obsolete. Distributed object management is discussed in more detail in Chapter 10.

9.4.5 Transactions and Object Updates

An attribute of the base object definition lists copies of the object being used for current transactions. All updates to an object are performed within the context of a transaction. The simplest transaction involves a single update to a single object. It executes immediately and, in general, it does not involve conflicts with other users. More complex transactions involve reads and updates of several objects; all updates must be performed completely or not at all. We will define in a later section a mechanism for managing transactions that involves the use of transaction objects.

9.4.6 Creating a New Object Class

Objects and object classes are defined and created using an object-oriented programming language such as C++. A module of C++ (or another object-oriented language provided with the database system) must be written for each application object class to denote the structural attributes and behavioral methods of the class. Each module must then be processed by a *class compiler*, which will check the module for correct syntax and load the class definition into the local object server. The object server will create the new class (or update an existing class) in the database and propagate the class definition to all other object servers in the network. The class compiler and object server will also implicitly define the new class as a subclass of the base class. Once an object class definition is successfully loaded into the database, the object class compiler will generate a front-end module of locally executable object method stub routines. These stub routines will handle the formatting of remote procedure call (RPC) requests, sending these requests to the object server and returning the result to the caller. This mechanism provides transparent access for application programs to remote object servers.

We have now covered most of the major aspects of object definition. Once defined, objects can be created and, if persistent, stored permanently in the database.

9.5 OBJECT USE AND MANIPULATION

Objects that have been created and are defined to be persistent are stored in the database. Any application using the objects must be able to access them uniquely. Objects in an object-oriented database system may be accessed uniquely in one of three ways:

- By class and object identifiers
- As a member of a set of objects
- An object satisfying specified constraints on its attributes

These three access methods are interrelated. The most direct means of accessing an object is by specifying its class and object identifiers. The object server will search for the object using its master object identifier index and return the object if it is present locally or forward the request to the object's owner if not. Objects may be grouped together in a number of ways. One object may store a list of other objects as one of its attributes. For example, a client object may contain the list of securities objects owned by the client. A given object server may own a subset of objects of a particular class. For example, the New York server may be responsible for the client objects representing all U.S. customers. And, finally, there is the set of all objects of a given class.

In accessing groups of objects, it is helpful if the object-oriented programming language and object server provide set-processing features. In the object-oriented database language $O++$[2], a named set of objects is denoted by the following construct:

---

[2]$O++$ is an extension of the $C++$ programming language and provides special constructs for object-oriented programming.

```
set_name          += new_object;          /* add object to set */
set_name          −= object;              /* remove an object from set */
set_name          += set2;                /* add set of objects to existing set */
```

Figure 9-2.   Example of Adding or Removing Objects from a Set in $O++$.

following construct:

ObjectType set_name<size>

Objects may be added to or removed from a set using the "$+=$" and "$-=$" operators, respectively, as shown in Figure 9-2. Iteration through the members of a set is made possible by an extension to the *for* statement, as illustrated in Figure 9-3.

To handle the grouping of large numbers of objects, for example, in the case of all U.S. client objects, it is useful if the object-oriented database supports *object clusters*. The ability to define object clusters allows the application developer control over where objects are stored in the system. Groups of objects that are typically referenced together may be associated with a particular named cluster. Such a cluster may then be assigned to a particular object server. The $O++$ language allows objects within such a cluster to be accessed using the same iteration statement used for set processing.

In most applications it is useful to be able to retrieve a particular object within a set based on certain specified values of its attributes. In $O++$ this

```
for Order * o in orders {
    int order_shares = o −>GetNumShares();
    Money order_commission = order_shares *
                        COMMISSION_PER_SHARE;
    money odd_lot_penalty = (100 − (order_shares %
                        100))*PENALTY_PER_SHARE;
    o−>TradeCompleted(this, trade_date, price, odd_lot_penalty,
                        order_commission);
    shares_ordered += order_shares
}
```

Figure 9-3.   Example of Manipulating Objects in a Set.

```
for Client c in Client:USClients
     suchthat c->GetLastName() = "Johnson"
{
    printf ("%s/n%s, %s/n%s/n", c->GetAddress(),
            c->GetCity(), c->GetState(), c->GetPhoneNumber());
}
```

Figure 9-4.   Example of Conditional Retrieval of an Object from a Set.

capability is provided by adding a *suchthat* clause to the for statement, as illustrated in Figure 9-4.

These set processing features allow an object-oriented database system to provide some of the useful functionality of a relational database system. The *for . . . suchthat* statement allows the object server to perform similar optimizations in accessing objects. For example, if an index is created for the client class on the *LastName* attribute, the object server could make use of it in the processing of the above example.

9.6 SUMMARY

We have now covered the complete methodology proposed in this text for designing an object-oriented database and an application using such a database. The primary functions involved in converting the definitions for object classes into designs include assigning datatypes to all attributes and methods and describing the calling sequences for the methods.

Attributes can be public or private. Private attributes are hidden from the application. An object with a large number of attributes requires a large number of methods unless attributes can be grouped and the group is addressed by a method. A logical grouping of this nature must be considered for large objects.

Object methods can be of a number of different types, including class methods, instance methods, trigger methods, and complex methods. Class methods are used to obtain information about a class as a whole. Instance methods provide the mechanisms for retrieving and manipulating an object's attributes. Trigger methods are special constructs of database management systems that are executed upon certain constraints on attributes when a certain set of conditions is met. They perform the same function as triggers in relational databases. Complex methods are methods that perform a number of complex functions.

Object identification is an important design consideration for any object-oriented database design. Identification may involve network-wide identification with programmable access control.

9.7 EXERCISES

1. Figures 8-33 and 8-34 depict object frames for *Transaction, Invoice,* and *CreditMemo* objects. For each of these objects, perform the following:
   a. Assign datatypes to each object attribute.
   b. Assign datatypes to the object methods.
   c. Create a C++ class definition for the objects.
   d. Write C++ code to implement each method.
2. Take one of the above class definitions and attempt to implement it on a computer. If you have access to an actual object-oriented database management system, modify the object definition to work within the constraints of the database management system, in particular, the procedures for object creation, storage, and retrieval. If you do not have access to an object-oriented database management system, write methods to emulate object storage. Specifically, add a method for making an object persistent (that is, storing it in the database). Implement object retrieval methods to retrieve the objects from storage; write a method to remove the object from permanent storage.
3. Write a test application that makes use of the objects implemented in Exercise 2. Test the object class by creating a number of objects, storing them, retrieving them, and manipulating the object attributes.

10

Distributed Systems Issues

Interestingly, the growth and profitability of business enterprises are becoming increasingly dependent on information systems. *Information Resource Management*, similar to the management of any other critical corporate resource, has become extremely complex and challenging for widely distributed corporate structures, especially when these structures span international boundaries. Poor planning and design often produce systems that do not provide integration of information as desired in a timely manner and, consequently, the information systems become a bottleneck rather than a real aid to the users. Linking of business strategy to information systems strategy, especially as it relates to widely distributed operations is crucial for the successful management of distributed data.

It is important to concentrate on the following four salient aspects of information systems design during the conceptual data modeling component of the design phase:

1. Focus on business and information strategies
2. Design for potential uncertainty and change in information systems
3. Facilitate centralized versus distributed control of data management
4. Facilitate economical and efficient operation of the entire system

Strategic and systems planning of this nature is essential as an integral component of the development life cycle. It ensures smoother systems integration leading to better integration of the business functions.

A company competing in a global economy must develop an information strategy that encompasses the whole business in a common corporate information strategy. Notable concerns that must be addressed include the following:

1. Ensure that the information systems strategy is derived from the corporate business strategy.
2. Create an information systems vision that not only elegantly meets current requirements but also provides for growth and transition to the future requirements.
3. Maintain required performance through growth and change as user needs change.

Change in information systems can happen for a variety of reasons and in a number of ways. The basic application must change as the corporate business environments change. The needs of the end users change because their local business requirements change (for example, the European Economic Community imposed a number of changes on the corporate functions in Europe but with no discernible effect on corporate functions in the United States). And user needs change as they develop a better understanding of the applications and determine alternate ways of performing the tasks.

This implies that, even though they may have started out with very similar applications and data requirements, over a period of time the needs will change. The information system must adapt gracefully to such change.

Supporting these diverse requirements is a challenging task. It requires careful management of a number of technological aspects of systems design. The design must be documented clearly for both current understanding and future use. The key technological aspects include the following:

1. Logical (data elements) and vertical (application) integration of the distributed information system.
2. Definition of formal structures (objects) for exchanging information.
3. Extraction of data elements from databases for modeling, decision support, and routine business functions.
4. Unification of software compatibility and data portability tools to facilitate development, portability of application, and data transfer.
5. Integration of a variety of communications and networking protocols and structures, including local-area networks (LAN), wide-area networks (WAN), Integrated Services Digital Networks (ISDN), ISO X.25, IBM SNA, and so on.

The overall systems architecture so designed includes the networking capabilities required for supporting the corporate business strategies. Let us at this point review some of the networking issues for a distributed system.

10.1 DISTRIBUTED SYSTEMS

Exchange of information between computers requires common information systems logic and a physical connection that supports this logic. Not only does this facilitate exchange of information, but this can also be extended to support centralized (or remote) backup and archival functions. The supporting network is the foundation of a successful distributed system. There are two major types of components of a distributed system that must be planned carefully. These include the following:

1. Local-area networks (LANs)
2. Long-haul networks (LHNs) and associated gateways (for heterogeneous connections) or bridges (for homogeneous connections)

LANs are based on the following major types of technologies:

- PBXs (private branch exchange)
- Baseband technology (primarily data)
- Broadband technology (for multimedia transmissions)

These technologies use a variety of media types, including coaxial cable, twisted pair, or fiber-optic cable.

Long-haul networks also come in a number of types, including the following:

- Private lines (dedicated)
- Leased lines (also dedicated)
- Value-added networks (VAN) such as, TELNET.

Dial-up telephone lines often included in WANs are not really considered for LHNs because of their inherently slow transmission rates.

LHNs provide a variety of choices in terms of network topology and access methods. Network topologies include national-area networks (for example, T1 lines and country-wide WANs) and international-area networks (for example, international T1 and T3 lines).

A number of protocols have been standardized for international networking, including X.3 (the terminal level), X.25 packet switching (to enter a packet distribution network, PDN), X.75 (to exchange data between PDNs), and others.

Developing the architecture of a complex, widely distributed information system requires considerable planning and careful analysis. The analysis should include not only the technical but also the sociological aspects of information management. The functional requirements of the users must be very carefully analyzed to determine their needs for access to the information. Similarly, the topological location must be considered. The architect must ensure that the various functional groups affected by the computer system are represented adequately and treated fairly through the logical distribution of data.

To understand the role and function of information for a user in a department, one must analyze the elements of that environment, including objects (such as materials, machines, products, and tools) and processes (such as social, economic, business, and technological) and understand the relationships between the components of that environment in a form of cognitive units, such as transactions, data, information, concepts, and knowledge. The cognitive relationships operate through the pragmatic process of communication, which conveys the meaning through transactions, data, information, concepts, and knowledge.

A *transaction* is an activity that reflects the nature of the organization. For example, a securities trade or a securities pricing management transaction reflects the nature of business of a stock trading corporation. Transactions describe sales, receipts, changes in personnel, changes in stock portfolios, and so on.

Information is a comparative unit of cognition that defines a change between the previous and the present state of objects as a result of operation of processes. Comparison of actual data from two different periods of business operations produces conclusions about the change in business.

A *concept* is a perceptive unit of cognition that generates thoughts or ideas that create intuition or intention and a sense of direction. It helps in making decisions, for example, buy or sell decisions for stocks.

Knowledge is a reasoning unit of cognition that creates awareness based on facts, rules, coherent inferences, and well-defined methods. This knowledge provides a point of reference for analyzing data, information, and concepts.

A valid question at this point is where this analysis is leading to. At the very basic level, the purpose of data processing is to process transactions and compare the results to produce a conclusion. Information processing, a more advanced concept than data processing, should lead to more advanced systems that can identify the state of an organization and analyze the changes to that state. A distributed system must take advantage of all four cognitive concepts, *transactions, information, concepts,* and *knowledge*. The hierarchy shown in Figure 10-1 is the fundamental basis for managing objects in a distributed system.

Figure 10-1 shows a hierarchy of cognition functions ranging from transactions to an analysis of changes in an organization. The higher the level in this hierarchy, the better is the understanding of the organization and its operations. An understanding of the full range of these cognition concepts is essential for effective information resource management. This understanding is decisive in the design of a distributed computing system.

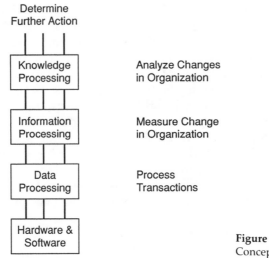

Determine
Further Action

Knowledge
Processing

Analyze Changes
in Organization

Information
Processing

Measure Change
in Organization

Data
Processing

Process
Transactions

Hardware &
Software

Figure 10-1.   Hierarchy of Cognitive
Concepts.

10.2 INFORMATION RESOURCE MANAGEMENT

The steady growth of information technology applications in business and the extent of resources allocated for these applications have caused a significant awareness of information as a resource. The processing of this resource is not a service any more; rather, it is an integral part of all business activity. A business may be viewed as consisting of six activity groups, as defined by Fayol[1]:

1. Technical (production, manufacturing, adaption)
2. Commercial (buying, selling, exchange)
3. Financial (optimum use of capital)
4. Security (protection of property and personnel)
5. Accounting (stocktaking, balance sheets, costs, statistics)
6. Managerial (planning, organizing, commanding, coordinating, controlling)

These activities have since been defined as processes. Additional business processes have been added to this list, including research and development, engineering, marketing, legal, public relations, and strategic planning. These processes are performed by a number of groups or departments that must share common data. This common data is the *information resource* for the company. The information resource has, in a sense, become the integrator of most or all business processes of an organization. The primary mission of information resource management is to serve all departments efficiently.

---

[1] H. Fayol, *Administration et Generale,* Dunod, Paris, 1916. First English translation 1929; second translation by Constance Storrs, Sir Isaac Pitman & Sons Ltd., London, 1949.

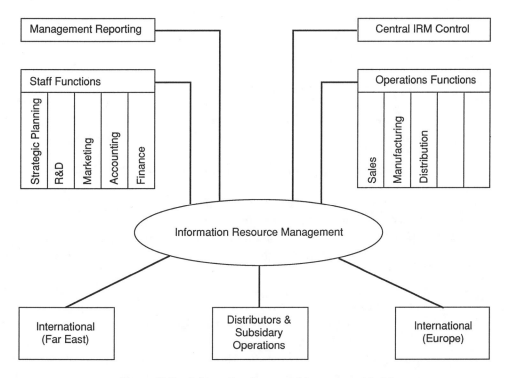

Figure 10-2.   Information Resource Management Model.

In an organization where departments are physically distributed across vast geographical distances, efficient service takes on a new meaning. The development of integrated enterprise-wide information resource management is based on a variety of methodologies and techniques that optimizes both the local operations as well as international access. The design of the database has to go beyond the primary database considerations. The information needs have to be viewed from the perspective of both the source of the information and the use of the information. A model of this is described in Figure 10-2. This model shows international access as well as local requirements. Each international group may include both operations as well as staff functions.

The ellipse in the middle of Figure 10-2 represents the shared information resource. The distributed functions supported by the shared resource include the following:

- Management reporting
- Decision support
- Planning and control
- Problem solving

- Information management
- Transaction processing and management
- Business operations support

Information resource management models support a number of different applications. This is especially true when departmental systems are linked via networks and potentially share information. Typical applications required by an enterprise and supported by this model include the following:

- Marketing management (forecasting, sales analysis, customer orders, and so on)
- Distribution management (control of distribution, warehouse planning, invoicing, delivery, and so on)
- Product development management (research and analysis, product requirements, product planning, product implementation, product testing, and so on)
- Production scheduling (production schedules, item forecasts, parts orders, and so on)
- Materials requirements planning (bill of materials, requirements calculations, and so on)
- Capacity planning (short-, medium-, and long-range planning)
- Purchasing (purchase orders, receiving and inspection, invoice validation, and so on)
- Inventory and processing management (inventory status, optimum order quantity, production pick lists, and so on)
- Finance and administration (budgeting and accounting, general ledger, accounts receivables, accounts payables, financial reporting, and so on)
- Payroll and human resources (payroll, time reporting, promotions, and so on)

Advanced *Information Resource Management* implies that information required for all activities is, ideally, a common shared resource accessible from any corporate facility. The information is managed as a corporate resource, rather than as a departmental resource.

10.3 DATA DISTRIBUTION BY CORPORATE HIERARCHY

In a large enterprise, there are many subsidiaries, divisions, and departments structured as both horizontal and vertical groups. A complex network for an enterprise must, at least to a certain extent, reflect this corporate hierarchy. This approach requires decomposing a complex system into more manageable subnetworks and systems. This decomposition task is made easier by studying and documenting the following:

- The fundamental entities of the organizational hierarchy
- Economy of information flow in decision making
- Knowledge and experience levels of the personnel in the subsidiaries, divisions, and departments
- Factors such as cooperation, competition, joint functions, and any other factors that affect organizational growth

Typically, enterprises are organized to provide strategic planning, management control, and operational control. The structures developed ensure reasonably clear definitions of authorities and responsibilities. These departmentalized structures also define the types, nature, and levels of decisions. Consequently, they also define the nature and extent of information needs for all classes of departmentalized structures. We can classify some of these structures by functional range (horizontal grouping), as described in Figure 10-3.

- Enterprise functions consisting of:
  - production,
  - sales,
  - finance and administration,
  - engineering,
  - personnel, and so on.
- Product or product lines consisting of:
  - conveyers,
  - inventory,
  - tools,
  - instruments,
  - parts, and so on.
- Territory:
  - offices,
  - sales territories.

Figure 10-3.   Functional Grouping for Enterprises.

Another means of classification is by functional hierarchy (vertical grouping), such as the following:

- World headquarters
- Subsidiary corporate headquarters
- Research and development facilities

- Manufacturing divisions
- Regional and district offices

As we have just seen, departmentalization can be horizontal, describing the span of authority, or vertical, defining the line of control. The departmentalization creates discrete organizational components that must interact for the day to day business.

The distributed database must cater to the diverse needs of the departments created through these two classes of departmentalization. The information must be presented to each department in the form most useful to them. For example, sales analysis information is used by the strategic planners, accounting staff and financial analysts (for forecasting), and sales groups. All three groups must access the same data, but in a presentation and encapsulation that must be customized for individual departmental requirements. Furthermore, they must combine this data with other data sets relevant to their perspective for preparing operational plans and reports.

10.4 DISTRIBUTED DATABASE SYSTEM ARCHITECTURES

The corporate requirements for database systems suggest a distributed database system that has independent databases connected via a network such that it appears as a comprehensive and centralized information resource management system. A client/server architecture is a prevalent approach for addressing distributed database management systems. In a client/server architecture, the database resides in and is managed by one or more servers. Multiple clients can run applications that access these servers, either individually or as a group.

The definition of distributed database systems, however, is not restricted to client/server architectures. C. J. Date[2] has defined a distributed database as consisting of "a collection of sites connected by a communications network, in which each site is a database system in its own right but the sites have agreed to cooperate so a user at any site can access data in the network as if the data were stored in the user's own site."

You will notice that some of the discussion in Chapter 1 on design issues for distributed systems is repeated here due to its importance to the subject matter in this section.

Single logical database view.   For a distributed database to present to the user a single logical view of the database and appear to the user as a centralized or local system, a distributed database must have the following types of *transparency* features (features transparent to the user):

---

[2] "Twelve Rules for a Distributed Data Base", C.J. Date, *Computerworld*, June 8, 1987.

1. Location transparency
2. Data partitioning and fragmentation
3. Data replication
4. Localized failures

Location transparency.   Location transparency is the capability of managing a database server distributed across a number of network nodes with potentially duplicated data components and automatically determining how data should be combined from these different nodes for a query or how a distributed update should be addressed. Location transparency signifies that users do not know and should not have to know where data objects are stored in the network. The users access data objects as if they are stored locally; the location of the data is transparent to the user and applications.

In a network that provides location transparency users should be able to log on from any workstation or terminal and be able to gain the same level of access to the distributed database; the system must address the differences resulting from display technology (that is, workstation or terminal) available to the user; and their custom working environment should be duplicated (or adapted depending on the class of the workstation or terminal) on their current workstation or terminal. Another perspective important for location transparency is the need for providing the same privileges to the user no matter which terminal or workstation is used by the user.

Data partitioning and fragmentation.   In a distributed database, the data elements can be fragmented and spread across a number of data servers for efficiency. The fragmentation should be fully transparent to the users. The users should neither be aware of the fragmentation or when the fragmentation takes place, nor should they be aware of the steps needed to access all components of the data objects. Furthermore, tasks such as backup and archival should transparently combine all data elements.

Data replication.   We have used the term data *replication* to signify that multiple copies of the data objects are replicated in a number of servers in a semipermanent manner to improve performance (note that we use *duplication* to mean creation of a temporary local copy for a specific function). The database system must ensure that the replicated copies are maintained in a synchronized manner. Synchronization is a complex task, especially for managing multiple concurrent transactions. The discussion on transaction management in the next section explores these issues further.

Localized failures.   In a nondistributed system, a user experiences failure when the database server fails. Failure of a node in a distributed system should not affect a user. This kind of transparency is called a *localized failure*, and it signifies that, if a node fails in a network or some database components become inaccessible at one node, other nodes in the network can continue to operate through replicated copies of the database. A key design issue to be noted here is proper and complete resynchronization of the databases on recovery of the failed network node. Resynchronization requires that all legitimate updates that took place while the failed node was out of service be applied to the database elements in that node in the proper sequence. Before the updates are applied, the database may need to run recovery so that all transactions not completed are backed off. The local transaction log must be compared with another update log to ensure that the distributed database components remain synchronized.

10.4.1 Distributed System Architecture

The architectural issues for a distributed database system include both the *network architecture* (media, protocols, and topography) connecting the database and application components (the servers and the clients in a client/server architecture), and the *database system architecture* (that is, the distribution of database components, communications between them, management of distributed data objects, and concurrent operations). Another major aspect of distributed database systems is the ability to manage multiapplication as well as multivendor database components and database access methods. The client/server architecture, using a combination of LANs and WANs, provides a potential solution.

Figure 10-4 describes an architectural approach designed to provide access to a variety of database types from any functional group within a geographically distributed enterprise.

You will notice the concept of an *OpenServer* allows common access to a relational as well as an object-oriented database. At the same time, the database can be accessed by any user who has authorization via the *communication agents.* In this architecture, each horizontal or vertical group within the enterprise can have its own local data server and at the same time have access to a corporate data server.

The definition of a distributed database varies significantly. We will consider a database fully distributed if it enables multiple clients to access multiple servers (very likely, separated geographically in different locations).

Database security.   Security is an important issue for an enterprise-wide distributed database system. The key to maintaining the security of a distributed access database system is proper *authentication* at all levels. Authentication is a generic problem for all applications and services in a distributed environment. Ideally, there should be a generalized scheme for authentication. A user logs on once into the network environment by *username* and *password.* An authentication server validates the username and password in such a way as to ensure the identity of the user to other network services. At this point, the issue of authentication comes into play. An administrative database would provide a list of services that each user is authorized to use. A hierarchy of services may be defined so that in the case of a database service the user may be authorized to use

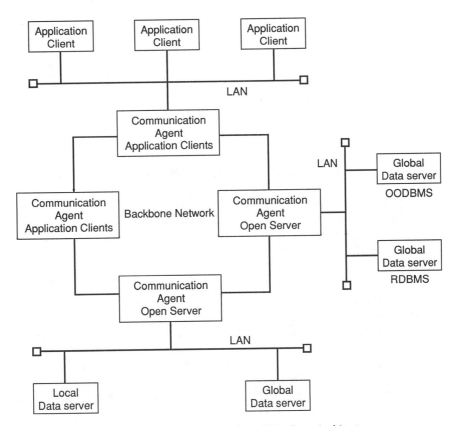

Figure 10-4. Example of Distributed Database Architecture.

a particular server or servers (or the database service in general), and the user may be allowed access to particular objects within the database.

One method of identifying authorized users to network services is to generate *tickets* when a user is approved for each service that the user is authorized to access. These tickets are supplied to the service provider when the initial connection is requested by the user. The approach to authentication must provide a fine balance between additional actions performed by the user and the depth of security necessary for the organization. Thought has to be given to the actions that users can perform from local terminals (being considered more protected than remote terminals) and reduced capabilities for remote dial-ups. Similarly, the abilities to copy data to remote workstations or other nodes on a network have to be taken into account.

A network-wide *access name server* can maintain an on-line distributed database of the log ons and passwords for every user, along with the servers that these users can access. Similarly, each server maintains a list of all users who can access data on that server. Under this scheme, a distributed query is checked against the access name server to determine if the user has access to all servers. Only on access confirmation is the query attempted.

Security can be applied at a number of programming levels. Security becomes a major design issue when it has to be applied at the *form, object, attribute,* and *function* level in a distributed-network-based database system. Most relational databases, as well as object-oriented databases, and their supporting 4GLs do not provide convenient programming mechanisms for achieving a high level of access control in a distributed environment.

10.4.2 Performance and Query Optimization

Fast transparent access to remote database objects requires fast local-area and wide-area networks. Response times become especially significant for remote object access, especially in the case of a complex distributed query that requires combining objects from a number of nodes. In a relational database, the same issue manifests itself in the form of *joins.* Joins require searching through multiple tables in the specified *join order.* The level of complexity for a join increases by an order of magnitude when a join is performed across multiple database servers in a distributed system.

A common scheme to address combining data elements from different servers is to locate the potential elements in each server, bring back the results of each individual query to the local system, and then compile the final result. Data elements (or objects) not needed are discarded. Another scheme is to combine the data elements at each successive server in turn according to the query plan (such as a join order in a relational database), using the previous result as one component. In this scheme, each successive result is transmitted to the next server in the sequence, and successive selections are performed at the servers. Optimization of a *distributed query* is a complex task that requires careful thought in designing the database and the application using the distributed database.

Query optimization.   *Query optimization* in both nondistributed as well as distributed environments has been a subject for significant research and development. Concepts of artificial intelligence and back-end expert systems have been utilized for query optimization. A primary task in query optimization is access path selection for joins and developing an optimal plan for joining n relations.

The performance of on-line distributed systems hinges to a large extent on the query optimizer's level of intelligence in the handling of dissimilar queries and remote data. Note that most systems store the access information for each query encountered, called the *query plan,* for future use. A good understanding of the optimizer's capability not only helps in understanding the potential performance issues, but also helps in determining how data objects should be distributed across servers and in hardware configurations to achieve the desired results.

Query execution plan.   A query execution plan describes the internal sequence of operations for executing a query. Depending on the implementation, it is either in the form of a tree, where the leaf nodes represent tables and nonleaf nodes represent operations, or it is in a canonical form (for example, in INGRES). In addition to optimizing the number of operations in a distributed environment, the query plan must also take into account the distribution of the data objects among different servers in the network.

In relational databases, reducing a query to its canonical form has a significant advantage in that the query takes on a unique representation of all equivalent queries regardless of the manner in which the query was written. The overall number of operations required to compare a new query with canonical versions of previous unique queries is much smaller due to the smaller number of unique queries stored and due to the reduced number of operations in canonical form. This method provides significant benefits in the speed of selecting a query plan. In an object-oriented database, reducing a query to a canonical form is inherently more difficult due to lack of a firm underlying structure and the flexibility available to the user for moving objects. The query plan becomes less predictable. This is especially true in the case of distributed queries, where the overall number of potential query plans can increase dramatically. It is possible to control the range of query execution plans by setting up evaluation criteria for specific operations. Obviously, this process is not as simple as it sounds, especially for distributed database servers. An expert system approach, based on artificial intelligence techniques, improves the selection process quite noticeably for the complex queries associated with distributed joins.

Use of AI techniques.   Some query optimizers, in addition to syntactic analysis, perform semantic analysis. *Semantic analysis* is especially useful in a distributed query because, no matter how the query is structured, it is always reduced to the same canonical structure containing a fixed order of operations. Very often, AI techniques are required for intelligent semantic analysis.

Heuristics can be used to evaluate execution plans without really performing a detailed cost analysis on them. This, obviously, saves processing time and affords the opportunity to determine the most promising paths in greater detail. In a distributed server, the number of potential execution plans can increase dramatically as the number of network nodes involved in the query increases. Heuristic elimination of unpromising execution plans reduces the task to a more manageable level.

Another important feature of AI systems is the capability to learn. An optimizer based on AI techniques can be implemented with a capability to learn from the following parameters:

1. Query statistics
2. Usage patterns
3. Frequency and quantity of updates
4. Impact of the organization of data

In conventional relational database management systems, even if the optimizer does manage to learn from these parameters, it may not be able to relocate data very easily due to the inherently rigid structure of a relational database. This, however, is not so in an object-oriented database. Due to encapsulation (a data abstraction that combines data, operations, preconditions, and constraints within the object), objects have a greater freedom to move. Consequently, AI-based optimizers present unquestionably greater benefits when applied to object-oriented databases.

Query optimization for distributed systems.   We have touched on a number of issues pertinent to query optimization in a distributed database server environment. Let us summarize the principal issues here as follows:

1. Is the optimization capability restricted to individual nodes (local) or can it optimize a distributed query globally?
2. If optimization is global, can the optimizer evaluating a query assess execution plans on remote nodes and assimilate an overall execution plan?
3. Can execution plans for different servers be performed in parallel and, if not, can the optimizer determine the most efficient execution order?
4. Are the results achieved by the optimizer consistent? Are these results predictable?

Query optimization is still in the formative stage for distributed object-oriented databases. It is a complex task and we urge the reader to analyze the issues to gain a better understanding of design considerations for distributed object-oriented systems.

10.5 DATA INTEGRITY IN A DISTRIBUTED ENVIRONMENT

Maintaining the integrity of the database in a distributed database system in which the network is operating normally is in itself quite a complex task. What happens when there is a communications link failure that partitions the network, thereby fragmenting a distributed database system into isolated partitions? Does the object-oriented database design provide adequate safeguards? How is an adequate design achieved? Can the architecture include slower links that can be used in an emergency?

These are all very interesting questions. Proper design of the database system and carefully thought out control mechanisms are essential for a reliable operation that maintains system integrity. We will try to address the following key design issues, related to transaction management, that have an impact on the operation of the database system:

1. Dynamic locking and concurrency control
2. Distributed transaction management
3. Distributed database management

It should be noted that the importance of these design issues is as great in object-oriented database systems as it is in relational database systems.

10.5.1 Dynamic Locking and Concurrency Control

It is essential to ensure that two users (or applications) do not update the same data object concurrently (that is, at the same time). The first user who requests the data object causes an update lock to be assigned to the data object. When another user requests an update of the same object, the update request is aborted. Locking provides the means for concurrency control; that is, it allows concurrent processing of transactions while database integrity is maintained and a consistent view of the database is provided to transactions.

In a typical locking system, a transaction requesting update of a data object that is already locked is *blocked* and waits until the lock is released. Typically, a two-phased dynamic locking approach is used. Locks are requested on demand (that is, locks are requested and applied when records are retrieved for update); lock releases are deferred until the completion of the transaction (that is, until the commit). This avoids the potential for cascading aborts caused by the failure of an update request. A cascading abort happens when one of a series of updates of a transaction fails, and every other update in progress must also be aborted. In a distributed database system with a large number of users accessing common data objects, a severe degradation in the performance of the system may be experienced if lock contention becomes very high. Transactions cannot proceed until the update requests are granted.

Another approach was presented by Ryu and Thomasian.[3] In this approach, transactions making conflicting lock requests are aborted, releasing all locks they currently hold, and are restarted after an interval (note that this is a concept similar to *collision detection* in LANs). This method removes the delays caused when a transaction has to wait for a lock to be released. However, this can cause a higher volume of network traffic. Retries become necessary when an update request fails due to lock contention. This presents an even greater problem of network congestion if the number of retries grows beyond anticipated network volumes.

Both methods have their own advantages as well as disadvantages. An ideal situation is one in which the distributed database system can determine the

---

[3] In Kyung Ryu and Alexander Thomasian, ''Performance Analysis of Dynamic Locking with No-waiting Policy,'' *IEEE Transactions on Software Engineering*, 16, No. 7, July 1990.

optimum method based on the current state of transaction management and change dynamically from one method to another. The objective of this approach is to provide the best possible performance under changing conditions.

Distributed commits.   To maintain consistency in a distributed database environment, one important requirement is that the transactions be executed atomically. Two-phase commit protocol and its variations are the well-known protocols employed for this purpose. Generally called *distributed commit* protocols, these protocols are characterized by successive sequences of message exchanges to ensure that all components of a distributed database that need to be updated by the transaction in progress are completed. The *atomic* requirement for a transaction implies that all actions required for completion of the transaction must be performed in entirety, or no action should be performed at all. If successfully completed, the transaction is said to be *committed*. If the transaction fails at any step, it is *aborted*. The distributed functions must take database as well as network failures into account to ensure that the consistency (or integrity) of the database is not adversely affected. Replicating copies of the database at each node greatly simplifies this process. However, it significantly complicates the process of keeping the entire database synchronized at all times.

A distributed commit protocol can be implemented in a centralized or decentralized fashion. In the centralized scheme, a single site is designated as the coordinator for all transactions generated in the network, and other participating nodes act as slaves. Once the coordinating site finishes its processing, it proceeds toward committing the transactions by executing the commit protocol. In this scheme the coordinating node can potentially become a bottleneck. The decentralized approach is more efficient due to lower overhead and is inherently fault tolerant. In the decentralized approach, every transaction-originating site can act as the coordinator for its transaction, and the rest of the sites act as slaves. Each site, at each step of the protocol, communicates with all other sites in the network to ensure synchronization.

Advanced transaction management.   An interesting approach based on the perspective of *advanced transaction management* has been provided by Pons and Vilarem.[4] The implementation of the principles presented by Pons and Vilarem leads to the organization of transactions in a serial order, using the conflicts as a means of determining the serial order. This task can be performed by a centralized transaction manager. The dynamic reconstruction of the serial order helps in minimizing update lock conflicts. This approach also addresses the need to minimize the duration for which objects participating in a transaction may remain locked.

---

[4] Jean-Francois Pons and Jean-Francois Vilarem, "A Dynamic and Integrated Concurrency Control for Distributed Databases," *IEEE Journal on Selected Areas in Communications*, 7, No. 3, April 1989.

10.5.2 Defining a Distributed Transaction

A *transaction* in database terminology is defined as a grouping of database operation predicates, such as SELECT and UPDATE, that must all be applied in the
proper sequence at the same time with no intervening operations. If the entire
group cannot be applied atomically (as a single logical action), then it must be
rolled back to the starting point to leave the database in a consistent state. A
transaction can be simple, with a few operations, or it can be complex, with a
number of SELECT and UPDATE predicates interspersed with calculations on
the values derived from the data objects selected.

In an object-oriented database application, similar to a relational database
application, a transaction involves multiple requests to one or more objects that
must be executed atomically as a group. That is, all operations must complete
entirely or they must all be rolled back to their starting point. To other users
accessing the objects, the effects of each of the operations will become apparent at
the same time, but only on completion of the full transaction. While the transaction is in progress, the previous values of each object involved will continue to
be presented to all other users.

In a distributed environment, the complexity involved in managing transactions can become quite high. This is especially true in the case of multiple
concurrent updates to the same object by two or more users. In the simplest of
implementations, multiple concurrent updates would simply be disallowed.
However, there are many cases where such updates would not conflict with each
other. Furthermore, preventing concurrent updates could have a significant
impact on performance.

Updating an object.   An object is updated whenever some variable (or
field) is modified. Objects can be updated only by the *instance method* or *class
method* (remember that the instance and class methods are routines for accessing
or manipulating the attributes of an object). The instance or class method is
invoked on the object, and the object version number is updated. In the interest
of maintaining consistency across the network, the *owner* copy of the object must
always be updated first. The owner then informs all servers maintaining a local
copy of the object that an update has taken place.

The synchronization of the local and the owner copy is maintained by
following a well-defined sequence of operations for an update. When the local
object server receives a request for the object, instead of updating the local copy,
it sends the request to the owner server for that object. The owner server performs the update and informs the local server. The local server can then get a
copy of the updated object for use by the client application. We indicated previously that the remote server can send an object directly to the user. It is
sufficient for the local server to be notified that an update has been performed so
that it can properly handle future object access requests.

An important question arises as to when the client application is informed of the update of an object. It is obvious that there is no clear answer to the question. The client who initiates an update knows that the update has occurred when the method returns successfully. Database systems do not normally provide a means of informing other clients who are using the affected object that the object has been updated. An optional feature may be included in a database system to solve this problem wherein a user may request to be notified when an object that it is currently accessing has changed. An attribute in the *BaseClass*, User NotificationList, may be used to maintain this information. Potential stages in the update process that are candidates for update notification to a client application include the following:

1. After the update request is accepted by the local object server
2. After the update request is accepted by the owner object server
3. After the update is complete and the local server receives a completion notification
4. After the local server receives a copy of the updated object

The criterion for selecting one of the four options noted above (we can call them classes of service) depends significantly on the application's required synchronization levels and on the performance requirements. It is conceivable that all four classes of service may be available to applications and the applications may determine the class of service that is most applicable to their requirements. How an update is managed is a major concern in any transaction management function.

Transaction management sequence.   Most database systems in current use employ a scheme known as a *two-phase commit protocol* to manage transactions in a distributed environment. The basic operations and parameters for this protocol are shown in Figure 10-5.

The typical sequence of messages for updating all copies of an object consists of the local server sending *update messages* to all owners of the objects that need to be updated. The owners examine the requests and verify whether the operation can be performed and return either a *update accepted* or *update rejected* message to the originating server. If the update can be performed, the server creates a copy of the object and performs the operation on the copy. If a server returns a *update accepted* message, then it must perform the operation when the prepare-to-commit message is received. If all owners respond with a *request accepted*, the local server sends a *commit object* message to complete the transaction. If even one of the object owners returns a *request denied* message, the local server sends a *rollback* message to all object owners. The rollback message causes each server to destroy any temporary objects created to process the requests and release any locks related to the transaction.

Update
- transaction_id
- object_id
- method
- arglist

Prepare-to-Commit
- transaction_id

Request Accepted
- transaction_id

Request Denied
- transaction_id

Commit Object
- transaction_id

Rollback
- transaction_id

Figure 10-5.   Transaction Management Operations for a Two-phase Commit.

10.5.3 Managing Distributed Transactions as Objects

Now let us look at the mechanics of handling transactions in a distributed environment from another perspective. A complex transaction can take an inordinate amount of time (in the CPU time scale) and would cause a number of object accesses locally as well as over the network. An uncomplicated scheme to manage transactions is to simply lock all objects for the duration that the transaction is in progress. However, in a shared environment where a number of application clients are attempting to access the same objects, a locking scheme of this nature would be very disruptive and disturbing to the users. To address this problem, the authors have developed a new approach for managing complex transactions in a distributed database system.

We have extended the basic concepts of Pons and Vilarem to a new approach, called *Transaction Object Management*, for managing transactions in a distributed environment. Transaction Object Management is based on the concept of treating transactions themselves as objects and using features of the *Base* object class to manage complex transactions. This approach is designed to address update contentions in a distributed database. The following describes the key aspects of this approach. Our scheme is decentralized in general. The Transaction Control Object (which functions as the transaction manager) is created on whichever object server is local to the application.

The Transaction Control object acts as a centralized transaction manager for transactions. A centralized transaction manager presents the opportunity for treating a transaction as an object that operates in two phases. During the first phase, the transaction reads all data objects that will be updated by it and it announces its write intentions. These write intentions cause the creation of a new version of each data object that is subject to an update. The transaction proceeds normally using copies (the new versions) of data objects in its own workspace. On completion, the second phase updates the new version it created and marks it current as the latest database version. By maintaining serialized operations, both lock conflicts and inadvertent loss of concurrent updates to the same data object can be avoided. If necessary, a time limit can be established that limits the duration between the two phases of a transaction if another transaction is waiting to update a common data object. Once the transaction exceeds that time limit, the entire transaction can be easily backed out, another key advantage of serial operation.

A centralized transaction manager also facilitates the *commit* operation. The two-phase commit is the most common approach for distributed database systems. A centralized transaction manager simplifies two-phase commit and the two phases are built into the transaction object itself. The second phase of the transaction, due to the serialized nature of transactions, does not need update request approval and can proceed directly with the update.

One issue that has not been addressed so far is the potential for a link failure that may make a centralized transaction manager ineffective. An alternative to this is the concept of a cooperating distributed transaction manager. The components of the transaction manager operate on each server and remain in constant communication using a *distributed transaction management* protocol to manage serialized transactions. Failure of a link may cause failure of transactions being managed by the server, which are then taken out of service; other servers and transactions can continue functioning. The failed transactions can be restarted on another transaction manager.

The concepts of object-oriented database management play a significant role in this architecture. Let us now expand on the concept of managing transactions as objects and discuss the mechanics for managing transaction objects and key issues as they relate to object-oriented systems.

Transaction object management.　Earlier we described how each object is owned by exactly one object server. Any updates to an object must be made to its owning object server. A transaction that involves updates to multiple distributed objects will require processing by several different object servers. To the user application, however, this should all be handled transparently by its local object server.

In our transaction management scheme, two types of objects will be used to process transactions, a *Transaction Control object* and a *Transaction object*. The Transaction Control object provides the interface to the user application and is the major control point for a transaction. A Transaction object is created by the Transaction Control object on each object server that participates in the transaction (that is, contains objects that are updated in the transaction). The Transaction object processes each application request that is a part of the transaction and handles the distributed commit protocol and interactions with any concurrent transactions.

Certain attributes and methods are required in Transaction Control objects and Transaction objects. Figure 10-6 shows the attributes and methods of the Transaction Control object. The data maintained by the Transaction Control object is a list of *object server Id/Transaction Object* pairs for each object server participating in the transaction. It has the standard methods for creation and destruction, a method for processing each user request, and methods for commiting or aborting the transaction.

The attributes and methods of the Transaction object are shown in Figure 10-7. All reads and updates performed during a transaction are performed on copies of the referenced data objects. This allows any changes to the data to be insulated from other users until the transaction is committed. The Transaction object contains the list of all object copies involved in the transaction. It has the standard create and destroy methods and a method for executing each user request on the object copies. A transaction is committed in a two-step process, which will be described below, and these steps are performed by the *Prepare-ToCommit* and *Commit* methods. The *Abort* method is used to cancel a transaction, either because of a conflict with another transaction or because of a user-specified rollback.

A number of attributes of the Base object class are used in the processing of a transaction. These attributes are listed in Figure 10-8.

Let us now review in detail the processes for creating and managing a transaction.

Transaction Control Object

    Attributes:
        List of Server Id/Transaction Object pairs

    Methods:
        Create
        Destroy
        ProcessRequest
        CommitTransaction
        AbortTransaction

Figure 10-6.   Attributes and Methods of a Transaction Control Object.

Transaction Object

Attributes:
    Object List
    (list of object copies involved in the transaction)

Methods: Create
        Destroy
        ExecuteRequest
        PrepareToCommit
        Commit
        Abort

Figure 10-7.   Attributes and Methods of a Transaction Object.

Base Object (attributes relevant to transactions)
        Copy Identifier
        Object Copy List
        Attribute Update Mask
        Transaction Invalidation Indicator
        Update Lock (Commit in Progress)

Figure 10-8.   Attributes of Base Object Class for Transaction Control.

Creating a transaction.   When a user makes a request to begin a transaction, the local object server creates a Transaction Control object and returns its object identifier to the user application for use in subsequent RPC requests. As the user invokes each object method in the transaction, an RPC request is generated and sent to the object server. The RPC request contains the information described in Figure 10-9.

When the object server receives an RPC request, it examines the Transaction Control *Object_Id* field. If this field is null, then the request is not a part of a transaction. In this case a Transaction Control object is created on behalf of the user, and the transaction is executed with the single request. During a transaction each requested operation must be carried out immediately since later requests may depend on data retrieved in earlier requests. As we have discussed, copies of the affected object must be created during the transaction so that none of the

Transaction Control Object Id
    Object Class Id
    Object Id
    Method Id
    Argument List

Figure 10-9. Contents of an RPC Request.

changes will be visible to other users. The requests of a transaction are performed by Transaction objects. The Transaction Control object maintains a list of Transaction objects for each object server participating in a transaction. Each Transaction object is owned by the object server for which it was created.

The *ProcessRequest* method of the Transaction Control object is invoked to identify the object server that owns the object indicated in the RPC request, to create a Transaction object if it is the first request for the server, and to invoke the *ExecuteRequest* message of the appropriate Transaction object to perform the operation.

The Transaction object's *ExecuteRequest* method performs a number of steps in processing a request. If the request is the first for a particular object, then a copy of the object must be created. A Base class method will create the copy and assign a Copy Identifier. (The Copy Identifier of the publicly visible version of the object is always zero.) The identifier of the object copy will be added to the Object Copy List of the public object. This identifier will also be added to the Transaction object's list of participating objects. Once a copy of the requested object is created, the requested operation may be performed on the copy. The Attribute Update mask of object copy will be updated to indicate which attributes have been modified during the transaction.

Committing a transaction.   When the user commits the transaction, the *CommitTransaction* method of the Transaction Control object is invoked. A two-step process is required to commit the operations that have been performed during the transaction. First, the *PrepareToCommit* method is invoked on each Transaction object. The Transaction object at this point will contain the list of all objects on a particular object server that have been affected by the transaction. The *PrepareToCommit* method inspects any other ongoing transactions involving these objects to determine if any attributes updated by the other transactions conflict with the ones updated in its transaction. Transactions commit on a first come, first served basis; this means that if there are any conflicts between transactions then the first transaction to commit will cause any objects that conflict with it to be invalidated. If none of the current transaction objects has been invalidated, then the transaction may be committed, and each object will be temporarily locked against any further updates by other transactions, and the *PrepareToCommit* method will return a success status to the Transaction Control object.

If all Transaction objects return success from the *PrepareToCommit* stage, then the Transaction Control object will invoke the *Commit* method on each of the Transaction objects to lock in the changes. This involves replacing the public version of each object that has been updated with the copies of the objects used in the transaction. For each object copy the Commit method will zero the Copy Identifier, inherit the Object Copy list (minus this copy) from the old object, update the version number, and destroy (or archive) the old object. Once the object is replaced, updates by other transactions will be allowed to continue.

If, on the other hand, any of the Transaction objects returned failure at the *PrepareToCommit* stage (indicating that another transaction has invalidated one or more updates to objects in this transaction), then the Transaction Control object must invoke the *Abort* method on each Transaction object to cancel the transaction. When a transaction is aborted, all object copies are destroyed. The user may also abort the transaction, in which case the Transaction Control object will immediately invoke the *Abort* method on each Transaction object.

10.6 DISTRIBUTED DATABASE MANAGEMENT

A comprehensive record-keeping and information management system for an enterprise with a large number of geographically distributed facilities presents two major challenges: a very large volume of data that must be maintained on line, and the need for a large portion of data to be globally accessible. For example, a financial services company has a number of applications that are closely related, including the following:

- Client account management
- Trading (stocks and other securities)
- Historical pricing data for securities
- Mutual fund management
- Portfolio accounting and management
- Accounting and general ledger management
- Administrative functions

While, in themselves, these applications are reasonably independent, they all have a basic financial and accounting link among them.

Any large corporation managing a variety of financial instruments and trading at a number of stock exchanges is likely to have a number of geographically distributed facilities. Distributed systems are a necessity for such an environment.

We have discussed a number of distributed issues in a number of different places in this text. A number of those issues relate to concurrency management and the reliability of the database. In this section, we will analyze the issues of object retrieval management and system administration in a distributed system.

Object-oriented database management plays a significant role in distributed systems. Three major aspects of distributed database management must be considered. First, remote access of objects must be considered. Second, the complexities of system administration must be understood. And, finally, the design of object servers should be adapted to make the system efficient and yet flexible.

10.6.1 Distributed Object Retrieval Operation

In a distributed system, objects may be dispersed among multiple servers to achieve optimum performance. An important issue in any distributed system is locating information. The objects dispersed around the network have to be tracked constantly so that they can be located rapidly. There are a number of methods for achieving this goal. Chief among them are central directories, data dictionaries, name service mechanisms, and so on. The most applicable model is a distributed object retrieval service where each object server is capable of providing a *retrieval service* to its users. In this scheme each object class is assigned to an object server. That object server has responsibility for tracking all master and replicated (and duplicated) copies of instances (objects) of that class. All object servers maintain a list of all object classes and which server each class is assigned to. Rather than giving the system administrator responsibility for updating these lists periodically, the object servers should operate in what we call a *learn* mode. As the object server uses objects on other servers, it retains information about them. Any updates to the list of object classes on a server are broadcast to all object servers. The learn mode allows capturing this broadcast information to keep the object retrieval services on different object servers synchronized at all times.

Remote object retrieval service.   The information retained in the *Service* objects of an object retrieval service includes a set of attributes that describe the status of each object. The following describes these file attributes:

- Access date.
- Modification date.
- Creation date.
- Access control.
- Size.
- Data.

The *Service* class has an attribute—*data* (with potential values of ImageClass or BlockList) that determines the data is of bit-map or character type.

Steps for object retrieval. A number of steps are involved in locating and accessing objects. First the *Service* object with the object definition has to be located. A method *locate_retrieval_object* (called by *object ID* and *membership in object class*) is invoked for this purpose. The structure passed to this method contains the *object_id* for the data object being searched. The return structure provided by the method contains the name of the *object_retrieval_list* object on the owner server and a list of the current locations of the object on all object servers that have copies of the object.

Read data object. Once the list of locations of the object on the owner server as well as its copies on the other servers is obtained, the object can be read. The object is read from the local server if it is resident on the local server. If not resident on the local server, it is read from the owner server and is copied to the local server for further action. Remember that in our definition, the local server is the server on the LAN where the client application requesting the object is located. The owner server may be a remote LAN. For example, in our case study, the owner server may be in New York, while the local server may be in Tokyo.

Another important consideration for reading the object is the nature of the information in the object and the size of the information being read in. The object instance may consist of the equivalent of a row from a table consisting of text fields interpreted by the database. Another type of object instance may consist of binary fields such as image data that is not interpreted by the database. If the object is image data, reading it will return contents of the entire image file (or binary object in the database). If the object is a *BlockList*, the Block objects can be read one at a time by calling a *BlockList* method with the virtual block number. Another BlockList method would provide a count of the blocks in the file. (It would probably be possible to provide an optimization mechanism wherein all Blocks could be read with a single request.) It may be useful to be able to read the list of Block object ids from the BlockList and read the block objects directly by object_id.

10.6.2 Distributed System Administration

System administration is by nature complicated when there are a wide variety of users and a number of applications in progress at any given time. When the users are distributed over a wide-area network and share a distributed database, the task of administering the WAN becomes an even more complex, two-layer proposition. Managing distributed services requires a number of capabilities, including the following:

- Establishing connections among the database and applications servers. The communications front-ends play an important role in this.
- Authentication of database access and schemes for maintaining security of the data. Authentication may become necessary at a number of levels. The

authentication should be reliable without being overly burdensome on the user.

- Automatic configuration management that dynamically updates the list of available database servers and other distributed network services available to a user.
- Backup and archival of distributed data.

While all these tasks can be performed by a highly trained systems administrator, the real goal should be to provide the tools that can automate the tasks and allow users to customize system administration to their individual needs and environments.

Object-oriented system administration offers a means of building a layer over the systems administration tools that present a simplified and customizable view to users. A user can define an object that consists of all files that the user wants to backup and includes the methods needed to perform the backup in a manner fully customized for the user. For example, a backup object can be defined as in Figure 10-10.

It is important to note that the major contribution of object-oriented operation is the transparent operation of the system administration tasks facilitated by customized objects. Objects can be created for each user and can be maintained by the user. The system administrator uses a class method that locates all *Backup* objects and executes the appropriate class method within the objects.

The use of objects becomes even more attractive when an advanced icon-based graphics user interface is employed. In our example above, we can define the icon to represent the class of objects for backup. Users can click on the icon to back up their own data objects. When the icon is activated, the tasks associated

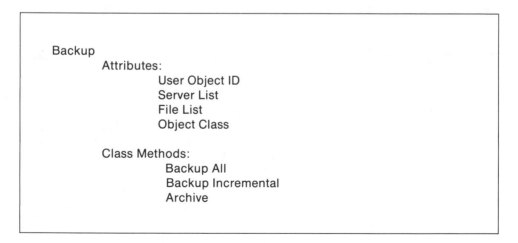

Figure 10-10.   Example of *Backup* Object

with the object, that is, the methods in the *Backup* object in our example, are performed.

10.6.3 Managing Distributed Objects

We will study the management of distributed objects for an architectural configuration consisting of workstations grouped in clusters within a LAN, LANs connected by high-speed wide-area networks (WANs), as well as low-speed international WANs. Within each cluster is a single object server. The object server should not, typically, reside on the same processor as the network gateway to achieve optimum performance. Each object server contains all class definitions (generally including all class methods) used within that LAN and knows the network address of each object server in all other clusters.

Object replication and duplication.   Data objects are distributed among multiple object servers in a local- or wide-area network. Each data object is owned by exactly one object server at any given time. However, objects may be moved from one server to another for efficiency, either automatically or through manual intervention. The location of objects should be transparent to most users.

At any given time an object is *owned* by exactly one object server. Other servers may have copies of the object, but any updates must be performed by the object's *owner*.

Object servers may maintain copies of objects owned by other servers. When a user program (or application) requests a local object server to access an object, a message is sent to the object's owner, via the available network link, to verify that the local copy is the current version of the object. If the local copy is an older version, the current version is retrieved from the owner. Versions of objects are recognized by comparing the version numbers stored within the copies of the object. This model of version control ensures that the application programs always operate with the latest version of the object and, to the extent possible, realize a performance benefit from the local copy. If the object is not on a local copy and is not on the owner server either, the object is considered unavailable even if it may reside as a local copy on some other node in the network.

Even though a server may have a local copy of an object, to maintain consistency, all updates must be forwarded to the owner server of each object. Servers with copies of an object must be notified when the object (for which it has a copy) is updated. This is called *update notification*. As a further protection, each time an access is made to a copy of an object, the server may send a message to the owner verifying that the object is current. This is called *version verification*. If only update notification is used, it is possible that an update message may fail to be delivered, so a server may not know that an object has been updated. However, update notification is generally much less costly than the version notification scheme. Ideally, both methods, *update notification* and *version verification*, should be used in combination for achieving a high level of data integrity, even if it is at the cost of performance.

We have defined replication as the case where a major component of the database is replicated on a semipermanent basis on other servers within the network. Duplication has been defined as the case where a temporary copy is duplicated locally for the duration of its use. Replication requires keeping track of the multiple copies and ensuring that the owner server can be identified for each copy.

Object identity.   Object identity is assigned on creation and remains unchanged. Object references must include the name of the server where the object resides. The attributes of the object should also indicate if it is an *owner server* or a *copy server*. Note that every object in the database must be uniquely identifiable. Consequently, two copies of identical objects must be uniquely identifiable. Prefixing a server name to the identity achieves this uniqueness for multiple copies of the same object.

Name servers and directories.   In a distributed environment, objects may be scattered across several object servers in a local- or wide-area network. An application may have knowledge of the location of a particular object and access directly via the appropriate object server. Most applications, however, will not know the exact locations of each object they access. They will connect to a single object server and rely on the object server to transparently route requests to the appropriate server.

Each server maintains a master index of objects that it owns. It may have copies of objects owned by other servers and will maintain an index of these objects as well. If a request is received for an object that is not present locally, then the server must determine where to forward the request for processing. Each object server will have within it or in tight association with it a distributed name service that maintains an up to date map of the locations of objects or object classes within the network. If a particular name service instance does not know the location of a particular object, it should at least know the location of a server that is responsible for objects of its class.

When a request is received for a remote object, the object server may handle it in one of three ways. It may simply forward the request to an appropriate server that has a copy of the object, which will process the request and return the results to the client. Or it may request a copy of the object from the remote server and process the request locally after receiving the object. Or it may do both, that is, forward the request to the remote server for processing and request that the remote server send it a copy of the object after processing is complete.

A version number is stored with each object that is incremented every time an object attribute is updated. In a distributed environment, version numbers are very important for determining whether a copy of an object is up to date. They are also very useful for managing concurrent updates to an object.

Distributed data dictionary issues.   Data dictionaries in an object-oriented database describe the object classes, much as data dictionaries in relational databases describe tables. Data dictionaries describe the datatypes for each attribute for each object class. The dictionary also describes each method in the object. An additional component in a distributed environment is on what servers the object is located and on which servers can the methods be executed.

Another issue of interest is that the dictionary itself must be distributed; either there are identical copies on each server or each server maintains a data dictionary that describes components on that server only. Vendors have approached designs from both perspectives. There are likely to be other options in this regard.

10.6.4 Communication Link Failures

A communication *link failure* occurs when a network link is broken such that individual LANs continue to operate but the overall network is divided into two parts. This partitioning of the network fragments distributed object database into isolated partitions. Some options for dealing with this are:

1. Maintaining a slower standby link for temporary use
2. Continuing limited operations until the link is restored
3. Duplicating all information to reduce operational impact

When a network is partitioned, all transactions involving objects not owned within the partition must be aborted. Similarly, all transactions initiated by a server in the lost partition must be aborted as well. Database accesses for copies of objects in the other partition may or may not be allowed.

Maintaining a slower standby link.   For a distributed object database to function successfully, an alternate access path is essential in case the main network path fails. The alternate path, even if it is slower, continues to provide access to all objects on all servers.

Limited operations.   If no link is available and the network is split, some components of the database will not be accessible. Transactions in progress may be blocked since objects cannot be written back, and other operations may not be feasible as object accesses fail. Duplicate copies of objects help avoid failure conditions of this nature. Obviously, bringing the database to the level of full synchronization is a complicated task in a case where operations continue in a divided network. The transaction management architecture presented in Section 10.5, using transaction objects, overcomes some of these limitations.

Duplicating the object database.   We have defined the mechanism for maintaining multiple copies of objects in a database. Multiple copies not only help in case of network failure, but also improve performance by reducing access across the network for objects.

10.7 SUMMARY

Distributed computing networks are a major consideration for an enterprise-wide information system. This chapter started out by analyzing organizational complexities in large corporations with geographically distributed operations. This background was used to present a set of requirements for distributed database systems.

Distributed database requirements were studied from the aspects of database and system architectures, data integrity in distributed environments, distributed transaction management, and system administration of complex distributed database networks.

We presented a new approach for transaction management in distributed database systems that manages transactions as objects. Database synchronization and transaction management are probably the most complex issues for a distributed database system. Closely linked to transaction management are the issues of dynamic locking and distributed commit protocols. The readers will find it worthwhile to explore these areas further, especially with respect to the current research in progress for addressing these issues for object-oriented databases.

10.8 EXERCISES

1. Describe a corporation that you are very familiar with and explore the corporate hierarchy: the operating divisions, manufacturing plants, remote offices, and so on, for that corporation.

2. Explore the information needs for this corporation. What kinds of information systems are needed to satisfy all activities in all divisions?

3. How frequently do these divisions share information? Do two or more organizations within the corporation update the same information at the same time? How do they accomplish that at present?

4. Explain the hierarchy of cognitive concepts in relation to the corporation selected for Exercise 1.

5. Explore potential hurdles in achieving location transparency with relational database systems you are familiar with. How can these be overcome? What design changes would you recommend?

6. Explore the same issues as in Exercise 5 for an object-oriented database. Explain inherent differences in the two approaches as they relate to location transparency.

7. Evaluate the various data object locking schemes and explain the pros and cons of each.

8. Why is a two-phase commit necessary for managing a transaction? Is a single-step commit acceptable?

9. Explore the issues of system administration for a geographically distributed enterprise-wide information system. What issues must be addressed to ensure synchronization of database servers that are geographically dispersed?

10. Extend the concept of managing transactions as objects into a practical solution. Build a small database system to demonstrate the practical use of this concept.

11. Describe the pros and cons of using objects to manage transactions based on your experiences in Exercise 10.

12. Compare the pros and cons of the relational model versus the object model for a distributed database system.

11

Designing for Performance

Generally, three practices are employed for improving performance:

1. Faster and more capable hardware and networks
2. Performing more operations in parallel
3. Software optimization

All three approaches have been drawn on by database vendors to improve performance. More and more implementations work on multiprocessor systems and support multiple servers linked via high-speed LANs, as well as high-speed WANs (such as those based on T1 and T3 lines).

Another aspect of improved performance is the separation of back ends and front ends so that separate CPUs can be dedicated to each individual function. This separation has also played a role in enhancing the performance of the individual software components by optimizing their dedicated operating environments.

While database vendors are making notable strides at maintaining or improving performance while increasing functionality, the database designer and application developer can have a major impact on the performance of the application.

Performance is never obtained by accident. Frequently, a good design helps in achieving optimum performance. A number of steps are necessary to ensure that a design is based on a sound foundation leading to good performance. Some key issues that must be analyzed in detail for relational and object-oriented database systems include the following:

1. Performance issues and monitoring for performance
2. Role of indexing in database design
3. Dynamic denormalization and restructuring of databases
4. Object programming techniques for performance realization
5. Distributed object-oriented database issues

In a relational database, an operation that requires careful design to achieve high performance is a *join*. A complex join can result in a very large volume of data that must be processed. Obviously, the functionality achieved by a join will remain a requirement for any database, be it relational or object oriented. Normalization leads to an increase in the number of tables, thereby causing an increase in the number of joins required for views and reports. While normalization is not quite as stringent an issue for an object-oriented database, the consequent update issues are and must be addressed. Before trying to analyze what affects performance and how to deal with it, let us first determine the performance issues and how performance is monitored.

11.1 PERFORMANCE ISSUES AND MONITORING FOR PERFORMANCE

Performance and the monitoring of performance have always been complex issues. Performance depends on the specific task being performed. A database application can be optimized for a particular set of functions. It is not necessary that all potential database queries be fully optimized. However, monitoring the database application to determine performance under different conditions is essential to fine tune the organization of the database and the physical disk layout.

Benchmarks have been used as a real quantitative means of measuring performance. It is important to realize that benchmarks have to be used with care and with clear goals in mind. Benchmarks can be customized to check special aspects of the database. A combination of benchmarks that tests various aspects of performance is necessary to determine an overall perspective. Some benchmarks should test very simple queries, while others test complex joins. Still others should test the use of memory arrays and disk access speeds under different disk organizations.

A performance study of the database system must include the following topics to allow examining various aspects of the database organization:

1. Change in performance going from a single query to a complex join
2. Issues related to multiple processes (for example, single process server in SYBASE versus multiple process server in ORACLE)

3. Network traffic impact due to queries

4. Database organization

5. Physical disk organization

6. Methodology for ongoing monitoring

Performance change: single query to complex join (relational databases).   Performance depends on two factors: the database architecture in terms of overhead for a query and the number of tables involved in a join. The extent of optimization performed in the database engine and the architectural approach have a very direct impact on potential degradation in performance as the query increases in complexity. A complex join may cause a large volume of data to be sifted through for the final result. The manner in which this volume of data is handled determines the overall database performance.

Server architecture.   In database systems (especially relational) the prevalent server architectures fall into three classes:

- Process per user (each application program requires its own server process to provide database access).
- Main server process and process per user (the main server process performs common control functions).
- Single server process (multi-threading server process supports a large number of applications).

Obviously, a process per user architecture results in a large number of processes in the database server host system and may lead to significant overhead for process management. This issue becomes more complex when users on multi-window terminals and workstations open a number of connections to the same or different servers. A process per user architecture can benefit from a multiprocessor system.

A notable approach to server architecture consists of a single process that performs its own multitasking for multiple users. There is no code duplication and no process management overhead. In fact, the complete CPU system can operate with only the database server process, in addition to the system processes, with virtually no context changes or process swaps to disk. This architectures provides inherently better performance.

Another means of improving performance is to distribute the database over multiple servers connected to a LAN. As long as the issues of managing distributed transactions, keeping databases synchronized, and adjusting data distribution according to usage patterns can be addressed, distributing the data can improve performance.

Network traffic issues.   In a distributed database, a large amount of data must travel over the LAN from the server to the client. The network can potentially become a bottleneck and can affect performance. Even if the network is not a bottleneck, excessive data traffic can cause performance problems. Some key approaches to reducing network traffic include the following:

1. *Query organization* to ensure that the joins can be performed in the least expensive manner (from a network traffic perspective). This can be significant if multiple servers are involved in the join.

2. *Stored procedures* (or methods in object-oriented databases) can be used (if available) to subselect data in the server. Note that very often a query is used to select a set of records, and a subset of these records is then used to select data from another table. Intermediate copying of results to the client system can be avoided if procedures in the server can perform the intermediate selections. Stored procedures also reduce the need to transmit lengthy SQL code across the network. The code is stored in the server and invoked by name and a list of arguments.

3. *Replication of data* in multiple servers can help in constraining the database access to a limited number of servers.

Database organization (or organization of objects).   Relational databases are organized in data tables and indexes. The organization of indexes (or object lists) determines to a large extent how data will be accessed. We will study the issue of indexes and object-oriented database optimization in greater detail in the following sections.

Disk organization.   The physical location of tables or objects on one or more disks has a notable impact on performance. Most database systems provide utilities to customize disk organization. The physical layout of related elements of data must be optimized on the basis of the accesses required for specific applications supported by the database. Many database systems use raw disk partitions and set up their own file structures for data tables. Use of multiple disk drives and careful placement of data and indexes are used commonly to improve performance.

Clustering (keeping close together information that is generally accessed together) is used for both relational as well as object-oriented databases. Other approaches include *nondense* index structures (the records are maintained sequentially for that index, so the index needs pointers to blocks only).

Ongoing monitoring and redesigning for performance.   Dynamic monitoring tools are essential for tracking database performance on an ongoing basis under different load conditions. These tools should give the following types of information:

- Kinds of data accesses used most frequently
- Number of disk accesses needed for each type of data access

- Network distribution of data most commonly called for together
- Excessive table scans (or searches through an object class)
- Memory usage by server and application processes
- Size of server data and procedure cache
- Sizes of shared memory segments

A detailed analysis can provide good pointers on database usage for optimizing the design.

11.2 ROLE OF INDEXES IN DATABASE PHYSICAL DESIGN

Data can be accessed in a variety of ways depending on the requirements of the application. The logical and physical database design should be optimized for data retrieval and the functions the database needs to support. Specific queries and reports also confer their own requirements on the database design. Some fundamental types of data retrieval consist of the following:

1. Accessing records based on a range of values, or using partial or inexact keys
2. Accessing records randomly using an exact key
3. Accessing all records in a table sequentially starting from a specific key
4. Keyed access for producing a record that consists of a *join* of records from two or more tables

The different types of data retrieval require, for best results, different types of access methods. Each method is optimized for a certain type of data access. Most relational database vendors use more than one specific method to improve query performance. The most common access methods in current use include the following:

1. Buffered sequential access
2. Indexed sequential access method (ISAM)
3. B-trees (balanced trees)
4. Hashing
5. Explicit relationships
6. Direct access

The different data retrieval methods speed up access to records specified in the search criteria (that is, in the WHERE clause of a SELECT statement). Each access method has its own advantages and disadvantages. In the following sections, we will study the access methods in detail and assess the advantages and disadvantages relative to the nature of specific types of data access.

11.2.1 Sequential and Buffered Sequential

The *sequential* access method has been long recognized as the simplest record access method. This method does not really use any keys. Instead, the search is started at the beginning and continues until the required record is located (also known as a table scan) or the search fails. For obvious reasons, this access method is fast for sequential search, but is extremely slow for random searches.

Buffered sequential is very similar to sequential search except for buffering disk blocks in memory for fast access. If continuous sequential access or update is desired, buffering of corresponding disk blocks in memory speeds up access to the successive records. The buffers can be located in the system area or directly in the user area. The buffers can be set up to be much larger than buffers typically set up by the operating system.

11.2.2 Indexed Sequential Access Method

The indexed sequential access method (ISAM) is probably the earliest commercially used access method for database systems. It is simple to develop and administer. In this method, records are stored in a sequential manner according to the search key. The search key index is maintained in a separate file to allow fast look-up of the appropriate block in the main data file. If the main data file is ordered sequentially, the index can be maintained in a *nondense* form (that is, the index contains pointers to the start of each block in the main data file). If the main data file is not ordered, the index must have pointers for every data record (this is usually called an *inverted file*). Generally, ISAM implementations provide binary search algorithms to search through the index.

ISAM files were used quite extensively for COBOL programs using hierarchical databases. ISAM is not a prevailing methodology for database organizations for relational and object-oriented systems.

11.2.3 B-Trees

The B-tree (otherwise known as balanced tree) is the most common access method used for indexes in contemporary database management systems. It is a significant improvement over indexed sequential access methods and provides predictable performance.

B-tree indexes use a modification of the *binary search* technique. A binary search can be performed effectively on a sorted list only. The list is divided into two halves and the first decision is determining in which half the key being searched is located. The other half of the list is discarded for the search. The remaining half is in turn divided into two quarters, and one quarter is similarly discarded. After two decisions, the search list is reduced to a quarter the size. The next decision reduces the list to an eighth and then to a sixteenth, and so on, until the key is located. The binary search technique can locate one value out of 1024 (that is, 2^{10}) using no more than 10 decisions. In other words, it takes n decisions to locate a value in a list containing 2^n entries. As we can see here, a binary search is very effective for lists such as customer names that are typically used in a sorted manner.

Instead of using a binary search technique, if the search space is divided into three parts (that is, a tree with three branches) the first time, then 3^n entries in a list can be searched in n decisions. In other words, 1458 entries can be searched in seven decisions. And if a factor of 4 is used, then 1024 entries can be searched in only five decisions. Each decision level creates another level of subbranches in the decision tree. The B-tree method implements a 1-of-N search mechanism, where N is chosen based on certain characteristics of the data to be searched, on the length of the fields to be indexed, and on the disk block size to provide an optimum search factor. B-trees are the most efficient when the search objects are spread evenly across the N parts after each decision; that is, the branches of the decision trees are fully balanced and each branch, at a specific level, points to an equal number of objects. B-trees are therefore dynamically reorganized as items are added to maintain this balanced nature of the access tree.

A good example of a B-tree is a customer card catalog. Typically maintained in alphabetical order, a tray may be used for each letter in the alphabet. This may result in a tray containing names starting with a Y or a Z being relatively empty, while one with an A or S is relatively full. A balanced approach would make all trays equally full so that a smaller number of trays need to be searched and a search through each tray is fully predictable. As new cards are added, some cards may need to be moved from one drawer to another to balance the drawers again.

The key advantage of B-trees lies in their always being balanced. Balancing makes every search take the same number of disk accesses and therefore the same amount of time. As the index grows, the increase in search time is relatively much slower. As more index entries are added, the tree structure is reorganized dynamically so that it is always optimized for retrieval.

B-trees can be added or dropped without reconfiguring the database. This allows creating new indexes for applications using the same database, but with a different set of requirements. B-trees are also well suited for accessing all records in a given table based on the values of the indexed fields and rapidly accessing a large number of records in a sorted order. B-trees outshine access methods, other than hash methods, for queries that require exact matches or well-defined ranges and wild-card searches where the initial part of the key is known.

B-trees can also be used for joins to rapidly locate records in a *one to many* relationship by creating a B-tree with nonunique indexes. All instances of a key point to the *many* side of the relation.

Some key disadvantages of B-trees lie in the complex algorithms for balancing and searching through the tree structure, and the additional disk storage required to maintain the index tree structures. While B-trees are predictable, other access methods may be faster in any specific search.

Despite the disadvantages, the B-tree access method has become very common due to its significant advantages relative to the most common types of data access searches.

11.2.4 Hashing

Hashing is a method of calculating a random number based on the data in a key. Hashing is frequently used for alphanumeric keys that are in no particular sequence. The *hash algorithm* uses a formula for calculating the random number. The random number is then used for accessing the record. It becomes clear right away why this method is most suited for unique keys. It also becomes clear that hashing can be used only if the complete key is known.

Hashing is very appropriate for fast random access to records when the primary key is known. The hash algorithms are especially fast if the key is short, 8 bytes or less. Since the random number calculation is based on the size of the key, and not on the number of records, hash access is independent of database size. It takes no longer to search through 1 million records than it does to search through 1000 records. Hashing, unlike B-trees, does not require disk storage for index tree structures. However, space for a hash table must be preallocated and is usually large, whereas a B-tree can grow dynamically.

The hashing method has some key disadvantages that make it a poor choice for many applications. If a range of values is to be located, the hash algorithm has to be applied to every potential value in that range. This can be an extremely slow process. And it is not possible to access data sequentially through hashing once the first record is determined. The third, major disadvantage is that the complete key must be entered. This can be not only time consuming or uncomfortable for the user, but also irritating, because the user has to remember the full keys even if they are very long and is unable to use wild-card searches based on the first few characters of the key.

Hashing is a very useful access method for looking up any kind of identification number, such as customer number, invoice number, or model number. A combination of fields can be used to derive a unique key. For example, line items on a purchase order can be accessed by locating purchase orders for specific customers using a hash key. Alternatively, both customer number and purchase order numbers can be hashed individually and the purchase order can be accessed using the two indexes separately.

Characteristics of hashing method.   When a primary key is specified for a table, entries must be reserved in the hash table to point to each record stored in the database. The hash table entry consists of a table identification and a record number. Depending on the implementation, the hash table entries will be 4 to 6 bytes long. A hash table is typically most effective when it is not more than 50% full. Many hashing schemes employ buckets such that one hash value may exist for several records. However, the hash table size should be calculated such that the hash table size is balanced with the bucket size. In other schemes the hash table has to be created for the maximum number of records that will be hashed. In other words, hashing presents a preset limit on the maximum number of records in the database for the key being hashed. This can prove to be a rather severe limitation for databases that may need to grow substantially. For this reason, hashing is good for master tables that have a predefined maximum number of records; for example, a master table for customers contains name and address information for customers and assumes a maximum number of customers that can be handled by the database.

11.2.5 Explicit Relationships

The term *explicit relationship* applies to an access method that supports a *one to many* relationship between two tables. If two tables have to be joined frequently, for example for a report, an explicit relationship will allow the join faster than any other access method. This is a common approach to *master-detail* table relationships.

An explicit relationship also provides the basis for enforcing relational integrity. An explicit relationship between a master and detail table can be used to ensure that a master record is not deleted if a corresponding detail record exists. This feature can, alternatively, be achieved by placing the primary key of the master table as a nonkey field in the detail table and then building a B-tree index on that field. Thus, once the master record is identified, all related detail records can be located. While this approach gives flexibility to change the master-detail relationship without changing the database, explicit relationships provide a much more effective and performance-intensive method for maintaining master-detail relationships.

11.2.6 Clustering and Direct Access

The basic concept of clustering is to store records that are logically related and frequently used together physically close together on disk. Clustering implies that logically related records are stored on the same page or adjacent pages in the database.

In a relational database, an index contains pointers to rows in a table. If the index is the primary means for accessing the rows, the index and the rows can be clustered. This is known as a *clustered index*. The row pointed to by the index is stored in the same database page as the index. In other words, the data is also available as the final leaf in the index tree. Another form of clustering allows data from two or more tables that are usually accessed by a common key to be stored together on the same data page. A single cluster index would be used to access data in both tables. The index points to pages instead of rows.

Clustering is also used in object-oriented databases to enhance performance. Clustering in object-oriented databases consists of storing an object and its subobjects on the same storage extent, such as a disk page. For example, a *ClientAccount* object contains *PortfolioList* and *AccountList* objects. Since these objects are typically accessed together, the performance can be enhanced by clustering these objects.

11.3 DENORMALIZATION AND RESTRUCTURING OF DATABASES

It is well known that a fully normalized database is an inefficient database. Denormalization is essential for reducing the number of potential joins that must take place for data entry as well as for complex reports. In a typical design methodology, the database is partially denormalized to improve performance and is rarely restructured after the initial implementation. It is assumed that the initial structure provides the best compromise among the diverse requirements for data access. Dynamic database restructuring is not considered an option; it is rarely available as an option.

Dynamic denormalization is, however, a subject of intense research. The greater flexibility of object-oriented databases makes dynamic restructuring a strong potential option for improving performance. Before evaluating the operation and benefits of dynamic denormalization, let us first establish what we mean by optimizing joins.

11.3.1 Join Optimization

In relational databases, joins are necessary for views or reports that require information from two or more tables. A (mathematically) robust database is one that is fully normalized (that is, it is in third normal form). The application must be reviewed in detail to determine all views and reports that require joins. The tables must then be studied to determine potential denormalization to reduce the number of joins. Finally, all update procedures that affect those tables must be reviewed to determine potential anomalies. The database, partially denormalized in this manner, is optimized for joins.

Most database systems automatically resequence the *join order* to achieve the most efficient join. In other words, the database systems calculate the number of rows created by each potential join order and select the one that is most efficient.

In object-oriented bases, there are no joins. However, there is a concept of a *join class*. A join class is one that has two or more superclasses and is created through multiple inheritance. The design of the join class is, in effect, conceptually similar to denormalization. The intention of creating a join class is to create an object class that has attributes (and methods) common to two distinct object classes and can potentially be used to relate the two.

11.3.2 Dynamic Denormalization

One of the lesser explored methodologies for improving performance is the concept of denormalization of a database dynamically while in use and relocating its components based on usage patterns. Manual operations for restructuring databases help to some extent, but are both time consuming and labor intensive. The results of manual operations attempt to average the requirements of specific access conditions to provide an overall improvement. There is really no capability to adjust the database to all potential situations when restructuring is performed on a manual basis.

Automatic (and dynamic) denormalization, on the other hand, can restructure the database on the basis of a rules database managed by an expert system. The rules are stored in a rules database and can be changed as enterprise-wide operational conditions and business rules change. The denormalization and restructuring rules define a set of parameters based on the experience of database designers. These rules determine when tables in a relational database (or objects in an object-oriented database) should be combined to improve performance. The operational performance of the database is measured, especially the joins in a relational database (and interobject messages in an object-oriented database). When these parameters exceed predetermined limits, the data objects in question are analyzed by the expert system against the detailed rules database.

The expert system checks to determine the common fields (or attributes) and ensures that updates to the combined table (or object) will not cause update anomalies. It ensures that the integrity of the database will be maintained after combining the data objects.

A good expert system-managed dynamic denormalization utility would have the capability to add code modules automatically for ensuring appropriate integrity checks.

A properly implemented and correctly used dynamic database restructuring utility can improve the functioning of the database very effectively in a dynamic manner. It allows a fully normalized database to be used for the base set of tables. The denormalization is performed on the basis of current applications in use and the data entry and reports required for these. As applications change, and consequently the database usage patterns change, the measured parameters will fall below their thresholds. The previously combined data objects are returned to their fully normalized state, while new data objects are combined. An important advantage of this approach is that data objects can be moved from server to server, not only on the basis of their current activity, but also to perform dynamic restructuring of the database for optimized performance.

An interesting side effect of this in terms of design is that it potentially obviates the need for temporary tables. The design can assume that if the frequency of use is high, the system will combine data objects dynamically; in a sense, all combined data objects are the equivalent of temporary tables.

11.4 OBJECT DESIGN TECHNIQUES FOR PERFORMANCE REALIZATION

While rows in a table are closely linked physically and must usually remain together in disk storage, the use of objects in an object-oriented database removes this limitation. This flexibility is a double-edged sword. It allows structuring the database in a very flexible manner. However, since each object is addressable independently, performance can suffer when a number of objects are to be combined in a *select* statement.

A number of potential issues that affect the performance of object-oriented databases need to be examined. The design may be adjusted based on this analysis to optimize the usage of objects, disk accesses, or the algorithms for accessing objects. The following lists potential areas where design optimization can be performed:

1. Class management (for managing a large number of objects).
2. Indexing objects (as is the case for relational database tables).
3. Clustering objects (to optimize disk accesses for searches).
4. Object storage optimization (a copy of the methods is also stored in the database).
5. Distributed objects management (optimum organization of the database, especially in a distributed environment).
6. Intermediate objects (optimization by maintaining intermediate results in objects).

Class management.   Classes are defined based on the principles of *generalization* and *aggregation.* The principles of multiple inheritance also provide the concept of a *join class* for relating classes. Object instances are related to a class by object type. A class descriptor (provided by some object-oriented programming environments) describes the class itself and lists all attributes and methods for the class.

Object instances are members of a class, and even though a class is not a runtime entity, the object instances of a class can be organized according to class membership. For example, just as all rows are stored as a part of a table extent in a relational database, all object instances of a class can be stored together in a class extent to facilitate rapid searches. The distribution of members of a class on one or more servers can be tracked by *class location descriptors.*

Another potential means of improvement is adding join classes to form redundant associations. As in denormalization, join classes provide additional associations designed to reduce disk accesses for searches.

It is usually important to examine all classes to determine if they can benefit from rearranging. Rearranging classes may be beneficial where inheritance and redefinition have made very slight changes. Slight redesign of the operations (methods) to adjust for different conditions may allow recombining classes that had been separated during initial design. As an extension of this approach, abstracting out common behavior among classes may help in restructuring the classes for more efficient operation. A superclass can be created (or updated if one exists) to contain all common attributes and methods, while the subclasses contain only the differences. Some reorganization along these lines improves the modularity and extensibility of the database.

Indexing objects.   Many implementations of object-oriented languages and databases provide a collection of generic data structures, including arrays, lists, queues, stacks, sets, dictionaries, trees, and so on, as predefined class libraries. Arrays, lists, and dictionary classes can be used for building indexes to object classes. These indexes can be maintained as ordered lists, B-trees, or hashed sets. An index is a qualified *association*. The derived association does not add new information but only speeds up access.

To create an index, the designer should examine each operation and determine what associations are traversed and how frequently this happens. All such operations are listed, and the ones that present the highest returns from creating index associations are selected for indexing.

Clustering objects.   Clustering in the object-oriented world has acquired at least two definitions. At the modeling and design level, a *cluster* is defined as a group of classes, associations, and generalizations that can be abstracted to a single entity for presentation to a higher level. In this sense, a frame may be viewed as a cluster.

At the implementation level, clustering is involved with locating classes, associations (especially aggregations), and generalizations close together on disk (usually on the same or adjacent disk pages) for fast access. All operations should be examined to determine the frequency of use of class associations and generalizations to arrive at the optimum cluster layouts.

Object storage optimization.   Objects can be stored either as whole (that is, the attributes and the methods are stored in the same disk area) or in logically organized components. Attributes are very different in structure and in the size of storage required. Methods, on the other hand, can require large amounts of storage, even though methods are stored only once for the class definition and may have significant duplication for similar classes. A carefully organized storage methodology would separate the attributes from the methods and use different storage methodologies as well as storage locations for them.

Distributed object management.   We discussed this issue at some length in Chapter 10. Distributed object management is inherently complex and requires careful design. An analysis of associations is important for determining what application subsets access which object classes. The attempt should always be to minimize the number of servers that must be accessed for an application subset.

Intermediate objects.   Operations that involve many calculations and intermediate processing may be improved if intermediate results are stored in special class libraries for the duration that the object is in memory. In some cases it may be worthwhile to make intermediate persistent objects.

11.5 SUMMARY

A database application must always be designed with the ultimate performance in mind. Redesigning an application is not only expensive, but can destroy the very basis of the original design. It is essential to understand the parameters that affect performance, the acceptable levels of performance, and how performance will be monitored on an ongoing basis.

Procedures for analyzing and improving performance in relational databases are well understood. Denormalization and join optimization, indexing, database organization, and disk organization are some of the primary approaches for optimizing the performance of a relational database.

While the general conceptual approaches are similar, object-oriented databases have a very different architecture and, consequently, very different solutions for database optimization. Classes and inheritance are the most fundamental concepts in object database design and form the basis for most optimization activity. Optimizing associations and generalizations for classes provides the most effective avenues for optimization. Increased definitions of associations and tightened generalizations for increased modularity are preferred approaches to improving the design of the object database.

Storage of objects, while much more flexible than storage of tables, is also more challenging from a performance point of view. The flexibility in the manner objects can be stored provides opportunities if the database system provides a good set of utilities for managing object storage. If not, the designer may have to develop utilities using container classes provided with the database system.

11.6 EXERCISES

1. For the application modeled in Chapter 8, describe tables that are fully normalized. What kinds of denormalization would you recommend for that?

2. What fields would you index? Would you use cluster indexes for any of the tables? Explain.

3. For the application in Chapter 8, complete the definitions of all objects. Analyze the model and determine if the associations can be tightened (that is, more attributes and methods combined in superclasses). What is the performance impact of these changes?

4. Use the operations listed in Chapter 9 as templates for this application and complete the design for all operations. Then analyze all operations and develop a matrix describing all associations for each operation.

5. Use the matrix developed for Exercise 4 and determine what improvements can be made to the design to achieve better performance.

IV

DESIGN APPROACHES TO ADVANCED INFORMATION SYSTEMS

Looking back over the recent history of database management technology, the progress has been impressive. Powerful on-line transaction processing applications, some hosting hundreds of users, are being provided by a wide range of networked architectures consisting of a variety of computer systems. High performance, fault tolerance, high data integrity, and security are some of the capabilities now available even on small- and medium-sized corporate networks. Fourth-generation languages, sophisticated database management systems, and window-based user interfaces have paved the way for powerful applications.

We defined advanced information systems as systems that have the following characteristics:

1. They consist of distributed architectures based on high-performance networks.
2. The size of data objects that can include multimedia information can be very large.
3. The information system caters to all corporate needs, and the number of data objects distributed around the network is very large.
4. Both data and the users of data are distributed around the network. Data is distributed among a number of servers, and users operate through a number of application servers.

5. The systems support high-performance, on-line distributed transaction processing.

The limitations of databases that allowed them to share only short alphanumeric pieces of information have been removed by new concepts such as binary large object datatypes (commonly known as BLOBs), text-retrieval systems (also called hypertext systems), and geographic information systems (GIS) databases. The availability of all three means of storage and retrieval of a variety of new information combinations leads to new applications that require advanced means of data management. The demands on information systems, due to these technological advances, are growing at a very rapid rate as new technologies increase the computing power of systems and new software techniques increase the flexibility and capabilities of software for managing and displaying information rapidly.

The development of office computing, so far, has been a process of automating functions performed by traditional desktop tools: typewriters, paper and pencils, calculators, and so on. The workstation is the new tool that is changing the manner in which information is used at all levels of an organization, especially by the knowledge workers. Due to the variety of tasks performed by professionals (such as doctors, lawyers, and engineers) and managers and the infrequent nature of their database access, they need a simple user interface for performing complex tasks. Advanced technologies make it possible to achieve the level of functionality that is essential for professionals and managers. In this part, we will consider a number of design issues for adapting these advanced technologies for building complex systems.

12

Advanced User Interfaces

The rapid advances in relational databases during the late 1980s and the start of the 1990s have been fueled by new display and user interface technologies. These technologies have given rise to a new generation of databases with versatile engines capable of storing and retrieving all types of computer-based data, from long documents to graphical and audio information. These storage and retrieval options serve as the basis for a wide variety of applications software for diverse business requirements.

A quick inventory of a typical modern office illustrates the diversity of information we deal with. There are books, articles, memos, and reports. Many of them contain charts, diagrams, graphs, pictures, and maps. In addition, there is voice communications using digitized voice techniques, document image storage and retrieval, and high-resolution facsimile machines integrated with computer systems.

Database products must come to terms with all of these information types and must provide the means for cataloging and storing all information types. The workstation has evolved to the extent that it has high-capacity storage, high-resolution monitors for crisp graphics, digitized audio storage and retrieval, voice synthesis and recognition capabilities, document scanning and digitizing for storage in highly compressed format, display interfaces for high-speed decompression and display, and techniques for combining a variety of these on a single user screen.

The database evolution is on the path of a complete multimedia database. Applications based on a multimedia database can efficiently present users with all of the sources of information they require. Not just alphanumeric fields, but also scanned photos and forms, text documents, spreadsheet, digitized voice and other audio tracks, three-dimensional holographic images, and any other objects that can be digitized and stored in a computer system are important components of advanced applications. These applications must continue to operate in demanding, shared multiuser environments where multiple users can take concurrent advantage of the application. For success, the database must unite several important database management functions, especially providing fast on-line transaction processing in a multimedia display environment.

An advanced user interface consists of a number of technologies, including the following:

1. Multiwindow display with dynamic window management
2. Simultaneous multimedia output
3. Two- and three-dimensional pointing device (such as mouse, trackball, and three-dimensional pointer)
4. Use of natural language interfaces
5. Voice command recognition and voice synthesis
6. Use of SQL for non-alphanumeric data

Items 1 and 2 are concerned with both display characteristics and operational control of the user's application environment. It determines the variety of functions that can be performed simultaneously by the user. Items 3 through 6 are primarily concerned with user-machine dialog. Advancing technologies will have an impact on the extent to which complex tasks can be simplified for the end users.

Characteristics of a good user interface.   A successful user interface must have the following important characteristics:

1. Intuitive interface
2. Flexibility across platforms
3. Confirmation of function completion
4. Underlying protocol benefits

A user interface supporting these features helps in making the user very productive. It provides the information the user needs during any activity that requires the user to interact with the system and allows the user to customize the working environment according to the application needs of the user. Graphical User Interfaces (GUIs) are a major step forward in achieving these objectives.

12.1 GUIs/MULTIMEDIA USER INTERFACES

Users have turned to GUIs because they provide an intuitive interface and a personalized organization of tasks and data. A GUI allows a user to organize applications and data in a logical manner. A user who runs many applications can organize them without constantly closing files and terminating them. Applications can be minimized to an icon, or they can stay partially hidden behind the currently active window. Users can run different applications related to different projects and have uniform access to a variety of networked application servers.

The Apple MacIntosh Computers with their point-and-click approach to user interface started a trend towards GUIs. The basic concepts of GUIs are similar for Apple, MS-DOS and UNIX systems.

GUIs are in use for all classes of systems, from microcomputers to mainframes. For contemporary enterprise-wide database-based applications, GUIs such as X Windows (and its derivatives, such as DECwindows) are becoming the user interface of choice. A number of derivatives (called tool kits) have been implemented. A number of other GUIs are in use for other operating platforms. They all have similar basic concepts and provide similar functionality. We will look at X Windows in some detail for a better understanding of the architecture and common desirable features of a contemporary GUI. We will also briefly discuss the OS/2 Presentation manager and MS-DOS Windows as other common GUI implementations.

12.1.1 The X Windows Architecture

As its name suggests, X Windows provides a means of dividing a computer screen into multiple areas called *windows*. Different applications can run in each window and users can cut and paste data among windows. Compared with text-based interfaces, X Windows' graphical user interface provides measurable gains in user productivity, accuracy, and task completion. It is not just the capability to run multiple windows that makes X Windows so important. It is X Windows' capability to support graphics-based applications. Many applications, especially multimedia database output, can benefit from the addition of the bit-mapped and icon-based graphics display capabilities.

Another important facet of the capabilities of X Windows is the ability to allow a user to simultaneously run applications across a number of different systems across a network. These application hosts can be from a variety of manufacturers and potentially running on different operating systems. X Windows' independence from any specific hardware or software architecture offers users a means of tying together heterogeneous computer systems and designing consistent GUIs across various applications.

The X Windows capability is extremely useful for applications where a simultaneous visual display of detailed as well as summarized tabular data or graphical display showing the current state or a trend is very useful. For example, network throughput and error rates in a network management system (along with a network schematic), pictures of real estate with descriptions of the estates in a real-estate agency, and creation of brochures, are applications that have benefited measurably from the graphics capabilities, To clearly understand the benefits provided by GUIs, it is important to analyze the architecture and understand the operation of X Windows as a representative GUI.

The X Window system has been designed as a client/server-based network protocol and not as a programming environment consisting of procedure calls. It should be noted that the X protocol actually defines most of the characteristics of X. Xlib, the low-level C language programming library for X, is really just a thin veneer over the protocol. This explains why programming with Xlib or any higher-level library, such as the X toolkit, requires understanding the X protocol.

Xlib is the underlying library that all X clients call to talk to an X server. X toolkit is a higher-level library that employs Xlib to implement features such as menus, scroll bars, command buttons, and so on. These features are commonly known as *widgets*.

The client/server architecture for X-Windows is almost a reverse of what one would expect; the host running an application is a client and the workstation is the server. The X server is a program that manages a screen, keyboard, and mouse, and the X client is an application program. The X protocol is bidirectional, whereby keyboard and mouse input from the user is sent from the server to the client, and requests to draw on the screen are sent from the client to the server. Because several clients can connect with a single X server and display on its screen, the server has to mediate the demands of these clients for screen space and access to user input. The following should be noted about the X protocol:

- The server and client can run on separate machines.
- Both local and network connections can be operated in a similar manner using the protocol, thereby making the network transparent from both the user's and application programmer's point of view.
- When the client and server are on the UNIX-based machine, the connection is typically based on local interprocess communication (IPC) channels.
- The X protocol is layered on top of an existing low-level network transport protocol, such as TCP/IP or DECnet.

Message types.   The X protocol specifies the following four types of messages that get transferred over the network:

Request: This message type is generated by the client and sent to the server, for example, a specification for drawing a line, changing the color value in a cell in a color map, or an inquiry about the current size of a window.

Reply: This message type is sent from the server to the client in response to certain requests.

Event: An event message is sent from the server to the client and contains information about a device action or about a side effect of a previous request.

Error: An error message is like an event, but it is handled differently by clients.

Windows management issues.   It should be kept in mind that when X is running a window manager is always running, with the reponsibility to manage the windows on the screen (initial placement, iconify, deiconify, move, resize, and so on). If only one window is required, a window manager need not be invoked. However, if multiple windows are in operation, the window manager arbitrates between the server and the clients.

Note that the client sends requests and the X server returns a reply. Frequently, the return information from the X server is event driven. Anything that happens on the server (pointer motion, key press, and so on) produces a (potentially unsolicited) event that is returned to a client, typically to the one that created the window the cursor is in. The client tells the server which events it is interested in. The client can wait (block) for an event, or it can poll the event queue.

The mouse can be moved beyond the current window and *clicked* on an underlying (or partially hidden) window to make it current. The window manager then sends a request to raise the window to the top. The Expose event is returned by the X server when a window is first made visible or it is reexposed on screen after being partly obscured. This makes that window the currently active window.

X toolkits and database interfaces.   The MIT X Windows distribution includes the MIT X toolkit. This is a basic tool kit that views an application as a collection of widgets. Commonly used object definitions such as pushbuttons, labels, toggle switches, and so on, are referred to as widgets. Widgets are associated with routines that can change the state of a widget. Widgets can be resized and/or relocated on the screen. They can also undergo priority changes and hide behind other widgets. The basic MIT X toolkit has been enhanced by OSF to produce OSF Motif and by AT&T to produce Open Look. Since all of these graphical user interfaces (GUIs) are based on Xlib and the X toolkit, they retain significant similarities even though they may appear different due to different handling of scroll bars and menu functions. Since DEC Windows is an adaptation of MIT X Windows that provides extensions to ULTRIX, VMS, and DOS operating systems, it appears very similar to the standard GUIs.

Most contemporary relational and object-oriented databases operate on UNIX, VMS, MS-DOS, and OS/2 operating systems. They generally provide application development or programming support to interface with one or more GUIs, such as OSF/MOTIF (based on X Windows), Presentation Manager (for OS/2), and MS Windows.

The GUIs allow users to use the same screen, keyboard, and pointing device to interface with multiple applications at the same time. Alternatively, they can have two or more views of the same application visible simultaneously. By moving the mouse pointer on the screen, the user can move from the screen image (or window) of one application to that of another by sending an event to the appropriate client.

12.1.2 Presentation Manager

The Presentation Manager is a GUI designed primarily as a user interface for the OS/2 operating system. Its graphical capabilities, though different in detail, are similar in function to X Windows. A network version of Presentation Manager provides client/server capability analogous with that of X Windows.

12.1.3 Microsoft Windows

Microsoft's Windows product has been enhanced in every release and is designed to have a very similar look and feel to that of the Presentation Manager. Besides providing a nice window- and icon-based graphical interface, Windows allows users of PCs running MS-DOS or PC-DOS to open and run multiple applications simultaneously. The Windows product also facilitates moving information from one program to another.

The interest in icon-based desktops is also obvious in the Windows environment. A number of supporting products are aimed at taking Windows functionality a step further to provide full icon-based desktop (and files) emulation functionality. Windows is supported by a wide variety of products, including relational databases, object-oriented databases, imaging systems, and expert systems. The ability to run multiple applications on a PC, especially in concert with a database server, demonstrates the new paradigm for user interfaces and workstation class functionality.

12.2 CHARACTERISTICS OF PROGRAMMING TOOLS FOR GUIs

Graphical user interfaces should allow for both iconic and textual interfaces and should adapt quite readily for user preferences. Bit-mapped displays and pointing devices such as a mouse are common requirements for GUIs and must be supported by any programming tool for GUI development. Research on Inter-Views performed by Linton, Calder, and Vlissides[1] has attempted to develop a

---

[1] Mark A. Linton, Paul R. Calder, and John M. Vlissedes, "The Design and Implementation of InterViews," *Proceedings of the USENIX C++ Workshop*, Sante Fe, New Mexico, November 1987;
Mark A. Linton, Paul R. Calder, and John M. Vlissedes, "InterViews: A C++ Graphical Interface Toolkit," Stanford University, Stanford, Calif., 1987;
John M. Vlissedes, Mark A. Linton, and Paul R. Calder, "Composition Mechanism for Graphical User Interfaces," Stanford University, Stanford, Calif., 1987.

set of programming abstractions that is used as the basis for driving the requirements for InterViews. Some of their key findings are as follows:

1. All user interfaces need not look alike. Users have different preferences and need the ability to customize their environments.
2. User interfaces need not be purely graphical. For some applications, a textual rather than iconic interface may be more appropriate for a given context.
3. User interfaces should be object oriented. Objects are a natural way of representing elements of a user interface and for directly manipulating them. For maximum advantage, an object-oriented language should be used to manipulate the objects.
4. Object-oriented does not necessarily mean better. Bad code can be written in object-oriented languages too.
5. Interactive and abstract objects should be separate. Interactive objects are called *views* and abstract objects are called *subjects*. Separating the user interface defined by views from the underlying application functionality provided by subjects makes it possible to change the interface without modifying the functionality.

Some definitions are used by Linton, Calder, and Vlissides to explain the concepts of InterViews better. These are as follows:

- *Interactor:* base class for interactive objects.
- *Scene:* base class for composite objects.
- *Box:* a composite object that tiles its components.
- *Tray:* a composite object that allows its components to overlap.
- *Deck:* a composite object that stacks its components so that only one is visible.
- *Frame:* a border.
- *Viewport:* an object that shows only part of a component.

Predefined components include *menus, scroll bars, buttons,* and *text editors.* These predefined components are instances of classes derived from the interactor base class. InterViews also includes classes for *structured text* and *structured graphics. Graphic* and *text* are base classes for structured graphic and structured text. Another interactor used frequently is a *message* (string of text). InterViews further defines resources such as *painter, sensor, cursor, color, font, brush,* and *pattern.*

InterViews is based on the X Windows system. InterViews is implemented for X in C++ such that a small number of primitive object classes of the InterViews system completely encapsulates the X protocol. This approach to object-oriented programming of the X system makes the user interface programming very flexible. The object classes defined for the InterViews system form the basis for defining a very flexible user interface to support a variety of applications, including multimedia applications.

12.3 SIMULTANEOUS MULTIMEDIA OUTPUT

Image handling is already appearing in RDBMSs. However, applications based on bulk image scanning and retrieval require some changes to RDBMS architectures. This section evaluates some of these potential evolutions in the RDBMS architectures for storage and retrieval of images, voice, and text as data objects. Stored as binary large objects in some relational databases and within objects in object-oriented databases, images, voice, and text can be retrieved as data objects for presentation on GUI-based display systems. Furthermore, voice synthesis allows simultaneous display of images and data along with the presentation of voice messages.

While a number of relational databases have been used for applications requiring multimedia output, object-oriented databases are inherently well suited for multimedia applications. An interesting example of a multimedia application is one of managing a part in a manufacturing process. The data describing the dimensions of the part, a graphic image (or images) describing the schematics (or isometric drawings of the part), text (or hypertext) describing the machining or annealing process, and a voice module emphasizing the care and special handling for the machining or annealing process can all be presented simultaneously on one workstation. A number of applications are emerging where multimedia output provides significant benefits, such as descriptions of properties (or houses) for sale, inventories of cars for sale at car dealerships, product lists prepared for distributors, and so on.

12.4 MULTIDIMENSIONAL POINTING DEVICE

The invention of the mouse as a pointing device started an innovative evolution in the manner users interact with the computer. The GUIs took advantage of this to the extent that a user can reduce keyboard entry to the bare minimum of real data entry, that is, to items that are not (and cannot be made) available on a *point and click* basis. A number of other pointing devices, including light pens, digitizers, and track balls, are currently in use.

Another development likely to have a significant impact in database technology is a three-dimensional (or spatial) pointing device. A device such as this becomes extremely useful for three-dimensional holographic displays. The initial implementation of three-dimensional holographic displays can be found in CAD/CAM modeling. Nonetheless, the technology is making headway in three-dimensional spreadsheets and three-dimensional tabular displays of data from a database. Two-dimensional tabular displays have long been a serious limitation of the display technology for modeling and other related applications. The ability to use the Z coordinate, view it spatially in three dimensions, and point to any element within this three-dimensional display will dramatically enhance the use of databases.

12.5 USE OF NATURAL LANGUAGE INTERFACES

As database systems gain increasing acceptance and understanding in an organization and innovative users find uses for information beyond those planned in the original design of the application, the need will arise for collection, dissemination, and presentation of information in a different manner. This may include different combinations of data objects and a different set of detail and summary reports. An obvious approach is the use of interactive SQL to permit users to perform ad hoc queries to produce simple tabular reports. Unfortunately, programming in interactive SQL requires users to learn the language itself as well as understand the structure of the database (that is, discern the organization of the data objects). For an infrequent or noncomputer literate user, this can be a daunting task. An alternative to this learning is provided by technology that has the learning already built into it; the user can perform the queries and print simple reports and charts using simple instructions in English, such as the following:

Show me all Sales over $100,000

Collectively called *natural language interfaces*, these ad hoc interfaces (or access windows) for the user into the database are an offshoot of the artificial intelligence technology. The comprehension of English phraseology depends on the extent of the dictionary and the programming of the language construction rules defined in the AI component of the product that parses and evaluates the query. Most current interfaces work well if the queries are simple and direct. Further development will allow the capability to interpret complex queries structured in complex sentences.

Before a natural language interface can work, it (rather than the user) needs to understand the organization of the data objects in the database. The extent of its capabilities to interpret and perform a desired query action depend on its ability to understand the organization of the underlying data objects. While most current implementations require developers to describe the organization in terms that the natural language product can interpret, future generations of natural language products will provide utilities for scanning the database and automatically maintaining a description of the organizational structure of the database. Dynamic adjustment of this description will be necessary for databases that feature dynamic restructuring and denormalization.

A good natural language interface provides additional capabilties for sorting and reorganizing the output from a query to the extent of converting it to complex reports and charts (such as pie charts, bar graphs, and so on).

12.6 VOICE COMMAND RECOGNITION AND VOICE SYNTHESIS

The use of natural language can be extended one major step to recognizing a natural language query as a voice command rather than as a typed query. A voice query removes the one last impediment for most users who find themselves uncomfortable in touching a keyboard or whose hands are tied up in other tasks they are performing. The voice query interpreter becomes a front-end to the natural language query interface. An inherent extension to this approach is the computer response also being in the form of voice (synthesized voice). The result of the query is synthesized (note that one has to be careful to ensure that the voice mode is controllable and does not overwhelm the user in describing a result consisting of a large volume of data). Users should be able to specify what part of the query result (for example, totals only) should be synthesized as voice.

As the reader may well know, voice synthesis is significantly easier than voice recognition. Nonetheless, voice recognition systems with limited vocabularies are making notable headway. A learning mode in the voice recognition unit adjusts its reception to the user's accent, cadence, and style of command input.

It is obvious that this is an area of significant new research. It will help bring database systems to users who are not very inclined to use a keyboard.

12.7 USE OF SQL FOR NONALPHANUMERIC DATA

Structured Query Language (SQL) has become the primary interface for relational database systems and has a good chance of becoming an interface of choice for object-oriented systems as well. SQL has worked well with data that is typically interpreted by the database. For a multimedia database, all data in a database (alphanumeric, text, graphics, or audio) must be made an integral part of the established database framework. Most programmers use a language such as C++ for implementing multi-media user interfaces. Enhancements to SQL are required to provide multi-media capability.

A multimedia user interface should provide all of the features required not only by users, but also by programmers. In other words, programmers must be able to write and manipulate nonalphanumeric data using standard SQL. All features provided by the multimedia user interface must be accessible through the SQL.

12.8 SUMMARY

Graphical user interfaces are making a significant impact on how users interact with a computer system. The technical challenge faced by a multimedia database supporting imaging as well as audio and voice is the sheer size of the data objects it must handle. In contrast to the few bytes needed to describe conventional data fields, a spreadsheet, text document, voice, or full color graphics may require 50 kilobytes to several megabytes per data element. The database must provide the capability to manage storage and retrieval mechanisms to handle such large data elements.

In this chapter we studied X Windows to examine the issues involved in the design and implementation of GUIs. We surveyed the requirements for multi-media user interfaces and presented the characteristics of multi-media user interface development tools. We also looked at related issues such as pointing devices and the use of natural languages. Storage and presentation of voice messages was another topic of interest in this chapter.

12.9 EXERCISES

1. Explain the concept of *client/server* as used for X Windows display systems.
2. What role can X terminals and workstations play in a distributed enterprise network.
3. What problems do advanced user interfaces pose for relational database systems?
4. How do object-oriented database systems address the problems posed by advanced user interfaces?

13

Rapid Development
Methodologies

Application development has always been the most significant cost for the development of new applications. From the task of data modeling to implementation and testing of code, any effort to make the task more efficient is welcomed. Most relational database management systems provide tools for application development and management and maintenance of the code. The tools tend to be somewhat independent of the database system. For example, most relational database systems provide forms development utilities that automatically generate the required 4GL (fourth-generation language) code. A precompiler is usually a part of the relational database system, but the rest of the development system, including editors, C language compilers, and linkers is not.

While many database systems provide interactive application development tools, these tools are not very useful for complex applications. A number of tasks are involved in information systems analysis, data modeling, conceptual database design, and overall system design. An integrated development environment must provide an integrated set of tools that address all of the development requirements, even for large, complex applications.

A key feature that characterizes integrated development environments is ease of use based on advanced user interface technologies. In addition, support for rapid prototyping is a major contribution of these tools. They should be able to build an executable version of the design of a user interface for an application.

In addition to features that support an integrated development methodology, an integrated development environment must have an open architecture to be adaptable to a variety of development disciplines. Similarly, an integrated development environment must be portable to a variety of operating systems and hardware platforms.

Generally called CASE tools, the integrated development environments have advanced beyond the basic definition of CASE. CASE tools were initially designed to manage the front-end modeling tasks, primarily the data modeling and data dictionary development. The scope of CASE tools has since been extended to a much wider range of functions related to the application development process. CASE tools are not only development aids, but they are, in fact, complete application development environments. Hence they fall into a class of software known as *advanced application builders.*

The comprehensive interactive application development environments present a user-friendly and efficient graphical interface for full application development, including the functions of data modeling and design, automatic code generation, and full application development repository management. In this chapter, we will review some key aspects of these development environments.

13.1 ADVANCED APPLICATION BUILDERS

A new generation of tools based on object-oriented programming techniques has made its way into the mainstream programming environment. Generally known as *advanced application builders,* these tools are comprehensive application development environments consisting of graphical editors, a fully interactive optimizing incremental compiler, an automatic code generator, an interactive object-oriented symbolic debugger, an object repository, a comprehensive object-oriented database with a graphical schema generator, an extended SQL with a symbolic debugger, and a documentation editor. In this section we will survey the components of tools designed primarily for relational database systems.

Graphical editors.   An integrated application builder may use standard editors or it may provide its own set of editors for custom functions. Examples of graphical editors include one or more of the following types of editors:

Graphical Forms Editors: Typical forms editors allow the developer to move the cursor to the location where a field is to be placed. The developer can add the field tag and define the field—all of this in a character mode. Graphical forms editors, on the other hand, use pointing devices such as a mouse to allow developers to select and place objects: edit boxes for text, buttons for data windows (look-up windows) and function keys, pop-up and pull-down menus, and so on. Attributes such as color, font, reverse video, blinking, and show/hide can be defined for each object defined in the form. Any special actions needed for a field can also be coded right away.

Editing a form developed in this manner consists of selecting the objects with a mouse (such as field tags or fields themselves) and dragging them to a new location. Note that this is a significant improvement over deleting the field, reentering it in the new location, reestablishing the field attributes and the field order, and recoding special actions. Similarly, buttons, pull-down and pop-up menus, and other objects can be edited. Not only does this provide high productivity in development, it also provides an excellent means for rapid prototyping.

Icon Editors: Also known as bit-map graphics editors, these editors allow users to develop bit-mapped graphics that can be used as icons or as data. For example, a picture can be drawn to illustrate a part that is described in the database. Similarly, the picture of the part can be used as an icon for a function that provides parts look-up operations. Graphics editors for bit-mapped graphics typically allow freehand drawing, scanned images, and even still video images.

Dataflow Editor: A dataflow editor is set up with standard diagramming objects for the most common data-flow diagramming techniques, such as Gane & Sarson and Yourdon/DeMarco flow diagrams. This allows users to create data-flow diagrams for applications in a structured manner. The concept of layering information using clearly defined decomposition techniques has become well established for data-flow editors. Advanced data-flow editors provide a library of objects for developing data-flow diagrams. In addition, once a diagram is drawn, the connections established between objects are maintained even when objects are relocated in the diagram. The connection must be deliberately broken to change linkages. The concept of frames has been used effectively in some implementations. As object-oriented databases make further headway, new tools are emerging that adapt better to the Transaction Model and Object Model depiction methodologies described in Chapter 8.

Entity Relationship (ER) Diagram Editors: ER diagrams have long been used for modeling database structures. Advanced graphical editors provide all basic elements and entity connection lines as selectable objects that can be manipulated to quickly develop entity relationships. Advanced tools also have the capability to show object classes on a screen (which acts as the frame) and to show the relations between object classes; for example, they can show pointers linking objects.

In addition to these two diagramming methodologies, a number of new approaches, including methodologies very similar to Frame-Object Analysis, are being developed and used. The editing tools must go beyond the basic well-known methodologies and provide library capabilities consisting of predefined objects to facilitate easy development of diagrams.

Fully interactive optimizing incremental compiler and code generator.   In an advanced application builder, methods are developed at the field (attribute) or the menu function item (operation point) level. An interactive incremental compiler allows testing each method as it is integrated into the application. This step by step integration provides an excellent means for debugging an application as it is programmed, rather than waiting for the full application to be programmed and tested. Side effects can be determined more easily from this stepped approach.

On completion of development, an automatic code generator can run the application through an optimizing compiler and code generator to produce an effective runtime application.

Interactive object-oriented symbolic debugger.   Fully integrated debugging utilities are essential for systems that do not have the traditional code structure (these systems link a significant volume of code at runtime). The utilities help in pinpointing and correcting (by providing context-based guidance) logic errors. Since user-written code can occur at any field or menu step (as a method associated with an attribute or a function step), the debugger must allow setting breakpoints graphically in the code objects associated with the fields providing incorrect results. When the breakpoint is reached, the user has the option of tracing (again graphically by moving to the appropriate field objects) the values of variables and data elements that affect the field (attribute) in question.

Object repository.   A good object repository is necessary for the application builder to make the best use of the utilities described above. This repository acts as the dictionary for all functional elements of the application and provides cross referencing between different parts of application development. The object repository may be part of the database system being used, or it may be independent. Developers must have access to browse through the object repository and print information about objects stored in the repository. The repository becomes an important component of program documentation.

Documentation editor.   A powerful documentation editor uses object libraries (used for application development) consisting of forms, field definitions, database object classes and attribute definitions, methods (code objects), icons, and so on. This ready reference library can be integrated in text descriptions of the functions to produce a complete design specification.

13.1.1 Advanced ODMS Development Environments

Engineers and programmers are starting to view object-oriented databases as the next database technology for complex engineering data analysis. While the object-oriented databases are designed to support existing development environ-

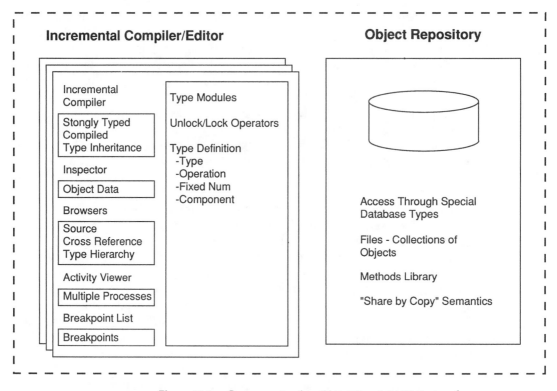

Figure 13-1. Components of an Object Based CASE System.[1]

ments, such as C and Pascal languages, and networked client/server operation, the most notable advance is in the area of graphical development tools.

A graphical *schema generator, database browser,* and a *source-level debugger* provide a comprehensive graphical development environment. The graphical input from the user is converted to C++ object-oriented code.

Object-oriented databases, such as ObjectStore and ONTOS, provide such graphical schemas. When users generate the schemas graphically, they can also create the inheritance relationships graphically instead of writing them separately in textual form. This approach allows engineers to easily view their underlying data models and helps them eliminate database creation errors.

Digital Equipment's TRELLIS Object System is an advanced application builder. The TRELLIS system consists of an advanced object-oriented programming language, an optimizing compiler, a fully interactive incremental compiler, an object repository, and a comprehensive object-oriented database with a graphical schema generator and an extended SQL with a symbolic debugger. Figure 13-1 describes the components of an application builder for an object-

---

[1] "Object-oriented SW Goes Mainstream," courtesy of Digital Equipment Corp. and *Electronic Engineering Times,* Oct. 20, 1990 p. 20. 10/29/90.

oriented database system. The components listed in Figure 13-1 are harbingers of the new crop of tools for object-oriented development environments. Typical utilities in these advanced application builders for object-oriented databases include the following:

User interface.   The most common approach to a user interface for comprehensive object-oriented development environments is to use a graphical user interface (GUI) such as X Windows (including Open Look, Motif, and SunView), DECwindows, SUNwindows, and Microsoft Windows. The GUI supports all functions required for application development, including project setup, object repository management, program development, graphical editing, and documentation.

Incremental compiler.   Interactive and incremental compilers act almost in real time. The code is edited in one window and is executed in another window. This allows the user to see the impact of the code change. The new behavior of the code may lead to further changes to it. Typically, the compiler comes with an additional feature to produce the final optimized code for the production version of an application.

Browsers.   Browsing is probably one of the more important features of an object-oriented development environment. Using browsers requires the use of multiple windows. Browsers come in a number of flavors. The following describes the various types of browsers and their primary functions:

Program structure browsers allow the developer to look at a list of directories used for an application and the files loaded from them. The browsers can be used further to view the object classes, member functions (methods), and variables loaded for the application. Note that the browsers operate in a dynamic environment rather than in a static environment. The browser has complete information on all directories and files required for an application and provides a dynamic snapshot of what is in use at any given time.

Call inheritance browsers (also known in short as class browsers) show the currently selected classes (a list of all currently loaded classes) and the attributes and methods for each class currently loaded. The better browsers also show the class inheritance hierarchy in a visual manner for the entire application or for a selected class as desired. A class inheritance hierarchy can be selected by pointing to the class in the complete tree.

Source browsers allow users to view the source code stored in folders and files. Note that the source code is typically a method in an object class. Source browsers typically operate with multiple windows (similar to the more sophisticated text editors). One window shows the class inheritance hierarchy and the folders and files associated with each level of the hierarchy. Other windows are used to narrow the search down to specific limbs of the hierarchy tree to list the header files, object classes, member functions (methods), and libraries. Still other windows are used to expand specific methods selected from the class detail windows.

Function call cross-referencing browsers provide information about which functions (or methods) are called by a currently selected method. If a function calls an overloaded member of a class (that is, a virtual member defined at runtime), all functions that could be called are listed and grouped. The function call referencing is displayed as a tree, and in a manner similar to the class inheritance hierarchy, the user can pick the point from where the tree must be developed. Note that in both cases the details become more easily visible as smaller and smaller limbs of the trees are viewed.

The list above is not exhaustive. Depending on the implementation, various other kinds of browsers perform a variety of other, similar program information retrieval tasks.

Debuggers.   Debuggers are essential for all types of programming. Object-oriented programming provides special benefits in that an object can be debugged in isolation from the other objects, thereby making debugging less complex. Generally, three major components are used for debugging functions:

The *activity viewer* provides a window display that changes dynamically as the application program moves from one object class to another. The activity viewer can be recorded to show the sequence in which object methods are executed. This dynamic display of the program activity is extremely useful for determining if the application is moving through the correct sequence of operations.

The *breakpoint list* window lists all the breakpoints set by the user. As each breakpoint is approached, the system checks if the user just wants to trace the value or if the system should stop. The window also shows the cases where the user wants a breakpoint to become effective after a predefined number of passes; the number of passes executed is displayed and is updated dynamically.

The *process inspector* works with the activity viewer and the breakpoint list to provide the user a means for controlling execution and for debugging. The process inspector displays the source code that is currently being executed, terminal I/O in progress, a list of active variables, controls, and contexts. The context refers to the execution stack. The execution stack can be viewed to observe the context of the stack at that point—the function calls and their variables.

In memory database.   Persistent objects used in the application are loaded in memory. Additional objects may be created on a temporary basis in memory. Unfortunately, memory is a limited resource with many demands upon it. Frequently, objects must be removed from memory to make space for more objects that must be loaded for continued operations within the application. The in-memory database maintains the objects in an orderly manner and removes objects that have been used least recently to optimize performance.

Object repository.   An object repository is a collection of information objects that describe the various components of the data objects. The repository maintains objects that describe the object classes, and the runtime and debugging environments such as menus, forms, fields, and breakpoints.

13.2 ADVANCED CASE-BASED SYSTEMS

While significant advances have taken place in the development of CASE systems, the advances in graphics and image processing and in the use of artificial intelligence are creating new demands for CASE systems. Increasing developer productivity and end-user programming capability have become important goals for the developers of application development environments. The following section discusses a few issues that are candidates for further CASE development effort.

13.3 EXPERT-SYSTEMS-BASED DEVELOPMENT TOOLS

Expert systems capture the knowledge of an expert and allow a computer to make decisions based on heuristics. Increasing the capability of the CASE tool to make programming decisions removes the development load from the programmers. Similarly, the more complex the decisions the computer can make, the easier it becomes for the end user to perform development tasks. Hence expert systems will play an increasing role in the development of advanced application builders.

AI logic-based query design.   Users have to really understand the structure of the database to develop appropriate queries. If an application builder can perform this task using an artificial intelligence logic-based query design by using simple graphical input provided by a user, the task of application development becomes significantly easier for the user. As graphical user interface-based development tools gain higher levels of maturity, the programming methodology will undergo a significant change. Artificial intelligence is destined to play a major role in making it feasible to develop applications from graphical models of the applications developed by the user.

Data dictionary portability.   Data dictionaries have been the least portable in relational databases. They continue to thwart efforts to create a seamless integrated network containing servers based on different relational database products. Object-oriented databases are not as tightly coupled as relational databases and are more adaptable to data dictionary portability. Furthermore, there are efforts afoot to attempt to standardize data dictionary interfaces to allow coexistence of a variety of object databases on the same network.

User-configurable databases.   Users like to have full control of their environments. Dynamic windowing capabilities provide the users with a lot of control. Advanced information systems must coexist in these environments.

13.4 SUMMARY

Systems and application development undergo ongoing change as technologies change and newer tools become available with greater capability. Application development using third-generation programming tools remained tedious despite rapid improvements in languages, compilers, and degbugging utilities.

The GUI capabilities and multiple-window capabilities of X11 terminals and workstations, coupled with advances in database technologies, present a new and more efficient environment for application development. In this chapter we reviewed some of these technologies and trends for advanced application development environments.

The new generation of application builders is based on the object paradigm and tends to provide a comprehensive set of tools such as browsers, debuggers, incremental compilers, and program structure documentation. Advancing technologies in the area of artificial intelligence and expert systems are also starting to make headway in providing significant improvements in programmer productivity.

13.5 EXERCISES

1. Study an advanced application builder. How is it better than the last application development environment you have used? What kinds of tools did it provide?
2. Describe an ideal application builder and its complete tool set. What are the advantages of its specialized components? What are the disadvantages?
3. What role can expert systems play in advanced application builders? Is the cost of developing an expert-system-based tool justified?
4. Is it possible to capture the knowledge of application development experts in an expert-system-based application builder? Will such a tool be really useful? Who could use such a tool?

14

Design Issues for Imaging, CAD/CAM, and Cartography

The relational database technology, known as the database management system technology of the 1980s, solved a number of problems as corporations migrated from dedicated batch COBOL programs to interactive enterprise-wide solutions. However, the relational technology does not provide a level of abstraction or even of modeling of objects necessary for storage and manipulation of multimedia components. The basic relational technology does not support full integration of multimedia data, such as text fields, raster and vector screen images, animation, and video input. These are a few of the multimedia objects necessary for CAD/CAM and geographic information systems (GIS), as well as cartographic systems.

As we saw in Chapter 3, multimedia types are stored as text or binary datatypes. These two datatypes are, for all practical purposes, long strings of bytes or bits that are not interpreted by the relational database. Beyond fetching and storing these special fields, the relational database has no capability of accessing these fields on an associative retrieval (that is, based on a relation to the contents of the field).

Furthermore, relational tables depict simple unchanging relations and are incapable of dealing with complex, multidimensional relations between objects. Relational algebra has not been designed for complex relations, and consequently SQLs based on this algebra are incapable of accessing and manipulating data stored in more complex relationships. Imaging, CAD/CAM, and GIS require capabilities beyond the basic relational databases to store the entire repository of information in the same database. Typically, the relational databases used for CAD/CAM and GIS store only the attribute information but not the graphic information.

An object-oriented information model is capable of effectively handling all of the datatypes used for CAD/CAM and GIS. More importantly, CAD/CAM systems use advanced technologies such as group technology (for searching equivalent parts) and expert systems for factory floor decision making. GIS also uses expert systems in a number of applications to assist the decision-making process. In this chapter we will look at the data structures needed to support CAD/CAM/CAE and GIS, the potential for integrating technologies such as expert systems and group technology in the database, and the key design issues for managing such systems.

14.1 REQUIREMENTS FOR IMAGING

A guiding principle for image management systems is a belief that users want imaging capability to be an extension of their standard computer system platforms. In other words, organizations want to continue using their existing workstations, computer systems, and applications software. They want to add document management as a fully integrated add-on capability to existing systems and applications. Integration of document management with existing applications provides significant dividends toward the business efficiency of the administrative staff.

14.1.1 Image Data Storage and Retrieval

Statistics show that less than 20% of all strategic information is automated, while more than 80% typically resides on paper. Paper records are difficult to integrate, control, search and access, and distribute. Locating paper documents requires searching through massive storage files, complex indexing systems understood only by a few key staff personnel (who become a bottleneck in the flow of information), and a major organizational effort to ensure that they are returned in proper sequence to their original storage locations.

Storage technologies.   Organizations can manage the information that originates on paper using the same computerized information systems that already handle data, text, and graphics. The result is an integrated strategic information base that is accessible by many people simultaneously, quickly, and easily. Any office or organization that must manage large volumes of paperwork can benefit from image processing. Image systems provide benefits in the following ways:

1. Significantly reduce the time and space needed to file, store, and retrieve documents
2. Increase productivity by eliminating lost or missing file conditions
3. Provide simultaneous document access to multiple users
4. Improve paper flow within the organization
5. Reduce time and money spent on photocopying
6. Increase client satisfaction by providing rapid access to files
7. Facilitate rapid and correct responses to requests for information
8. Convert paper-based information into a manageable, strategic asset

On-line optical disk storage systems are emerging as the dominant new technology for the storage of images. A few optical disk platters can store vast amounts of information. An average compressed CCITT Group IV image requires on average 50 Kbytes of storage for an A size ($8\frac{1}{2}$ by 11 inches) page.

Location of document images.   Storage of document images in optical media serves a real purpose only if the document's images can be located rapidly and automatically. A large number of images can be stored on one optical disk, up to 128,000 compressed A-size images on a strandard 12-inch disk platter. The simplest form of identifying an image is by platter identification and its relative position on the platter (file number). These images can then be grouped in folders (replicating the concept of paper storage in file folders).

14.1.2 Indexing Images

Applications typically need to access documents by a number of fields. For example, the record for a felon's personal bio data or fingerprints may have to be located by the felon's social security number, court docket number, file identification, name, alias, and so on. As another example, securities filings such as 10K forms can be identified by company name, company ID, and so on. Relating an image of a document to a suspected felon or a company, as the case may be, may require the capability of recording these relations when the image of the document is added to the optical disk storage. The process of creating this relationship is called *indexing.*

Image access.   The capability to access   record using fields stored in a database, such as company name, requires a capability in the database to perform the required query functions. Such ad hoc access to document images must be available by any of the selected index fields. The flexibility of an efficient database is ideal for performing such ad hoc access.

14.1.3 Current Trends in Database Systems

New computer architectures generally produce more efficient information storage and retrieval. Optical disk storage technology has reduced the cost of image storage by a significant factor. Distributed architectures have opened the way for a variety of applications distributed around a network to access the same database.

Flexible access by a number of applications requires that the data be independent from the application so that future applications can access the data without constraints related to a previous application. Key features of data-independent designs are the following:

1. Storage design is independent of a specific application.
2. Explicit data definitions are independent of application programs.
3. Users need not know data formats or physical storage structures.
4. Integrity assurance is independent of application programs.
5. Recovery is independent of application programs.

This kind of insulation between application and data, automatically provided by relational databases management systems, is especially important for an imaging database, given the long shelf life of image-based data and the potential for a variety of future applications that may access the data.

Common distributed database architecture.   The insulation of data from an application and access to it by users and applications distributed on a number of client workstations present the opportunity to employ common distributed database architectures. Key features to note are as follows:

1. Multiple data structures in the system (servers)
2. Uniform distributed access by clients
3. Single point for recovery of database
4. Convenient data reorganization to suit requirements
5. Tunability and creation of new joins and views
6. Expandability

The flexibility and the data independence provided by a relational database are very significant features for a document image management system. A further important aspect is that composite keys allow a very flexible mechanism for accessing image documents in a number of different combinations, and the database provides complete adaptability in this regard.

A datatype, called a binary large object, is supported by relational databases such as INFORMIX ON-LINE, INGRES, and SYBASE. This is a special data type such that the relational database management system makes no attempt to interpret the contents of this field. In other words, unlike normal data fields such as character or currency fields, the binary datatype field is not interpreted. Its characteristics are defined completely externally to the field. The field is therefore treated as binary data.

The binary large object implementations allow for very large data objects sufficient to store an image or voice data object. As a field in a table, the image becomes an integral data component of the database and can be retrieved along with the data record.

14.1.4 Object-Oriented Databases for Imaging

Object-oriented database systems offer an interesting alternative to the relational architecture for imaging. Since images are associated with other attribute information about a data object, it is logical to include the images as another set of attributes within the data object. If the storage management system is designed such that the physical storage can be managed at the level of attributes, it would be possible to store the information attributes of the object on magnetic disk and the image attributes on optical disk. Image retrieval will become automatic, that is, whenever the image attribute is retrieved in a query, the image will be retrieved from optical disk.

14.2 DATA STRUCTURES FOR CAD/CAM/CAE AND GIS

The data structures necessary for these applications present two kinds of problems. One of them originates from the wide variety of data structures necessary to store and manipulate the different kinds of information, such as graphics, geometric descriptions of entities treated as a group (for example a "bolt" or a "land parcel"), subassemblies, and versions.

The second problem arises from the large volumes of data. An average machine shop deals with hundreds of different nuts and bolts and thousands of parts and subassemblies. An auto parts manufacturing shop, for example, has parts lists from different suppliers, from the manufacturer of the automobile, standard equivalent parts, and so on. Let us review the key aspects of the data structures required to address the needs of CAD/CAM/CAE and GIS.

14.2.1 Data Structures for CAD/CAM/CAE

A significant amount of data stored in CAD/CAM/CAE databases consists of entity definitions for two-dimensional (2D) and three-dimensional (3D) entities. Complex figures or entities are composed of the basic building blocks used for CAD/CAM/CAE. These basic building blocks consist of the following:

- Lines
- Arcs
- Circles
- Polygons
- B-splines
- Nonuniform rational B-splines

A single curve may consist of a number of B-splines and arcs. A single object such as a "machine screw" may consist of hundreds of different entities. An automobile may require hundreds of different nuts and bolts, with the count of total parts running into four figures. A commercial airliner has parts running into 1 million or more. The key point to note here is that not only is the database for CAD/CAM/CAE very large, but it is also very complex. This is especially so if one adds the issue of maintaining versions of old drawings for released parts as new versions are created for maintaining older equipment already deployed.

Data manipulation requirements.   The basic building blocks stored in the database undergo a wide range of potential geometric manipulations before they are combined into a part. These geometric manipulations can include the following:

- Translation
- Rotation
- Scaling
- Mirroring
- Intersection
- Offsetting
- Trimming
- Selection
- Projection
- Linear approximation
- Tangent evaluation
- Curvature determination
- Fill patterns (shading)

There are other actions related to grouping and treating the basic objects as a group. These include the following:

- 2D objects
- 3D objects
- Animation
- Light source (shadow) analysis

Relating objects to manipulation.   Obviously, not all entities (or objects) can be manipulated in all potential ways listed above. Furthermore, the same type of manipulations may not apply in the same manner to all objects capable of being manipulated in that manner. In other words, not only is it necessary to store with the object the information regarding all potential types of manipulations applicable but also to define the specific scope of each potential manipulation. A relational database design can get very complex trying to address all these issues. Object-oriented databases present some interesting solutions. We encourage readers to develop their own views on this subject and we will come back to it shortly in Section 14.4. In the meantime, let us also look at the requirements of GIS.

14.2.2 Data Structures for GIS

Most cartography or geographic information systems consist of two kinds of data: the geographic data describing a parcel of land or a physical structure, such as a river, building, or mountain, and the attributes of the land or the physical structure. Depending on the nature of cartography or the GIS, the geographical data can consist of one or more of the following:

- Contour maps
- Area maps
- Physical coordinates
- Addresses
- Land parcel codes

Note that the latter three types may have the graphics of the land parcel or the digitized maps stored separately from the address or the coordinate descriptions.

The attribute data depend on whether the geographic information system is being used for applications such as urban or rural development, forest conservation, groundwater mapping and water conservation, wildlife conservation, sales tracking by territories, product distribution plans, public safety management, real-estate and property tracking and management, and so on. Obviously, a number of applications can use effective GIS databases, both in the industry and the federal, state, and local governments.

In any of these applications, there is a signficant amount of attribute data that must not only be accessed alongside the geographical data, but must be dynamically related to it and displayed. This close integration of attribute data to geographic data is essential for a system that supports dynamic changes to any kind of data. The change to one kind of data must be immediately reflected in the other kind of data.

Relational databases provide an excellent means of storing attribute data. Without the binary datatypes, relational databases had to resort to separate nonrelational GIS databases. Establishing effective links between the attribute data and geographical data has been a significant task. Furthermore, maintaining the accuracy of these links in changing environments is a complex task. The use of the binary datatypes allowed the graphics of the geographic data to be stored in the same row as the attribute data. However, relational databases are incapable of interpreting the information within the binary datatypes. A new technology is essential where this interpretation can be coded and stored as a part of the data object. As in CAD/CAM/CAE, the logical conclusions is that an object-oriented database can provide the solution to this problem.

Tiling GIS data.   An approach to handling GIS data is to divide a map into tiles. Each tile is a complete object that has the geographic data for the portion of the map represented by the tile, as well as the attribute data for that portion. This makes the geographic and attribute data highly accessible and fully interpretable by the methods stored within the object. A full map or parts of it can be recon-structed by recombining neighboring tiles. The close link of the attribute data and the geographic data ensures that any changes to the one are directly reflected in the other.

14.2.3 Managing Large Data Volumes

As we have seen, both CAD/CAM and GIS are highly data intensive and require large volumes of data to be stored. Some of this data is static, such as older versions of parts, and can be stored on mass storage media such as optical disk subsystems. Where performance is a concern, the data may be distributed over multiple servers connected via a LAN.

A concept promoted by some database vendors (such as SYBASE), called an *Open Server,*[1] facilitates management of large, complex databases. This concept provides for access to different databases across multiple servers from a single SQL query. For example, separate databases can be maintained for maps (as vectors or bit maps), attributes for objects located on the maps, and other general information about the objects. For example, a financial research database may use a national map to project the manufacturing base of a nation. The different types of data can be used for the purpose. The map information and the attribute information can be a part of an object-oriented GIS database, while general information is maintained as a part of a relational database. An Open Server allows retrieval information about a corporation, and the physical attributes of its plants and viewing the locations of its manufacturing plants on a map all as a part of a single SQL procedure that accesses all three databases.

14.3 INTEGRATION OF ADVANCED TECHNOLOGIES

The two main advanced technologies of interest are expert systems and group technologies. These two technologies provide significant benefits in the areas of searching and selecting objects in a database. Expert systems assist in making

---

[1] Open Server is a trademark of SYBASE, Inc.

best-fit decisions, for example, in determining what stocks provide the best combination for a portfolio.

Group technologies, on the other hand, are designed to select the most likely match based on some characteristics of the item being searched. A good example of the use of group technologies is in finding the most likely match for a part, given some characteristics. The grouping of characteristics and using this grouping for the selection process determine the ability of group technologies.

Obviously, both expert systems and group technologies sift through large volumes of information at high speeds in real time and tend to be very demanding. Integrating these technologies requires addressing the special considerations for their use.

14.3.1 Integrating Expert Systems

A marriage of the RDBMS and expert systems technologies appears to be almost a given. An RDBMS stores data, and expert systems make decisions based on rules acting on data. This section presents the authors' ideas on potential evolutions combining the two technologies. (Readers not familiar with expert systems may wish to consult a detailed text on expert systems for a more elaborate description.

The major component of an expert system is an *inference engine*. Figure 14-1 illustrates the architecture for a back-end expert system. Note that the key components in this figure are *inference engine* and *data and knowledge management*. An expert system consists of a rules database, an inference engine, and data.

The inference engine applies appropriate rules from the rules database to the data. An inference engine is software that provides a methodology for reasoning about information in the knowledge base and for formulating decisions for solutions. The inference engine makes decisions based on the rules estab-

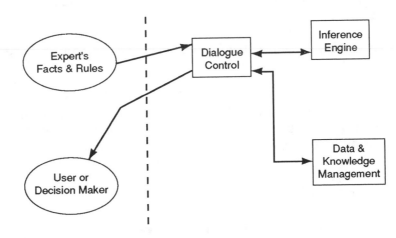

Figure 14-1.   Use of Expert System in a Database.

lished through the expert system shell. The inference engine is designed to perform the following functions:

1. Make decisions on the basis of a set of rules programmed into it
2. Solve problems on the basis of partial information
3. Deduce decisions on the basis of facts and learn new facts

Inference engines use control procedures to ensure correct reasoning. These control procedures include the following:

- Backward and forward chaining of reasoning operations in selecting applicable rules.
- Depth-first versus breadth-first search strategies for attacking problems using the bottom-up or top-down approach.
- Monotonic reasoning (reasoning based on one fact) versus nonmonotonic reasoning (reasoning based on multiple facts where facts can change during the reasoning process).

The key to an expert system is information based on an expert's manner of reasoning. This also includes recorded facts and rules. The facts and rules are stored in the expert system database. The data to which these facts and rules are applied is stored in the distributed database or is derived from the data in the distributed database. For example, the average growth rate of a stock over the previous five years may be a decision fact for the expert system.

The types of reasoning described above can be applied to data retrieved from a relational database. The reasoning is applied before the data is presented to the user. The typical relational database view of this process is described in Figure 14-2. This figure shows the relational database and the inference engine as two distinct entities that function almost independently. Expert systems used in this manner can help in conceptualizing solutions. They can function in a learning and advising mode. The expert system can request the database for facts and then apply the inference engine to the facts to arrive at a recommendation.

This method of operation is even more important in a business environment where most decisions are based on business principles rather than on rigorous rules. With the exception of accounting, where the rules are more rigorous and the expert systems can be used to provide firm and automatic recommendations, most business applications can use expert systems to provide a computer-assisted answer or a set of potential recommendations that the user can accept or reject. This implies that back-end expert systems' assistance can be applied right down to the field level.

Encapsulation of inference engines.   When we use the object paradigm, this figure can be changed substantially. The inference engine (now much

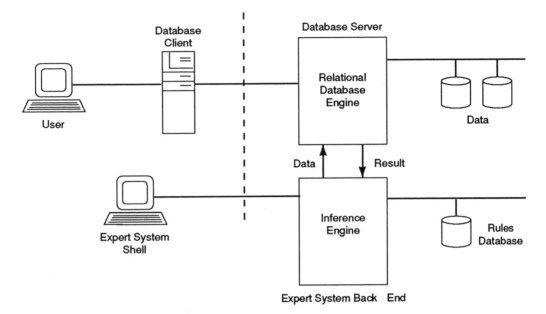

Figure 14-2.   Expert Systems with Relational Databases.

smaller in size since it is dedicated to one type of data) is an integral part of the database. This is depicted in Figure 14-3.

The algorithms for the basic logic of the inference engine for the expert system are encapsulated in the object classes. That is, the object methods are a part of the objects they act on. A major advantage of this organization is that rules can be changed selectively and relatively independently. Note that this allows the decision logic to be customized right down to the object level.

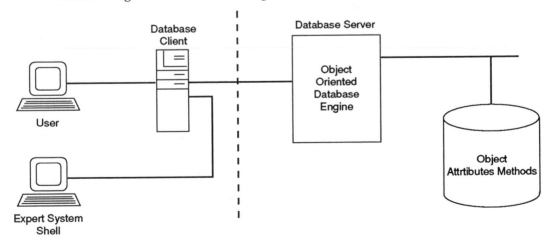

Figure 14-3.   Expert Systems in Object-oriented Databases.

14.3.2 Group Technology Integration

Interestingly, group technology has been used in a similar manner. Figure 14-4 illustrates the typical relational database view. Note that the logic and rules for selection are, typically, built into the group technology engine. Consequently, there is no separate database for group technology.

A major disadvantage of this organization is that a large volume of data has to be moved to the group technology engine to satisfy the requirements of a selection query. Transfers of large volumes of data over networks may cause performance degradation of major parts of the enterprise network.

Encapsulation of group technology.   This problem can be addressed by moving the group technology engine to the database server. An object-oriented database system provides a much better alternative for this organization. Figure 14-5 illustrates the modified organization of the systems.

Similar to the case of expert systems, the group technology engine can be encapsulated in the object database in the form of methods. These methods perform the logic operations of sifting through objects (right in the server) for selecting objects that have attributes that fall within the group technology criteria called out in the query and applied by the method. Not only does this speed up the performance of the search, but it also allows the customizing of selection criteria for each object class.

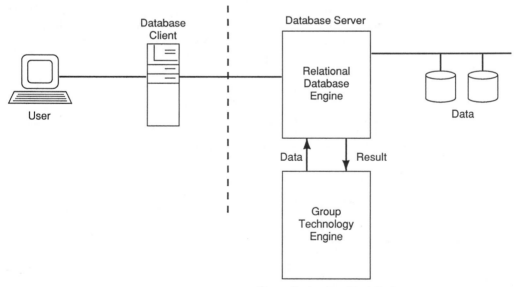

Figure 14-4.   Traditional Use of Group Technology.

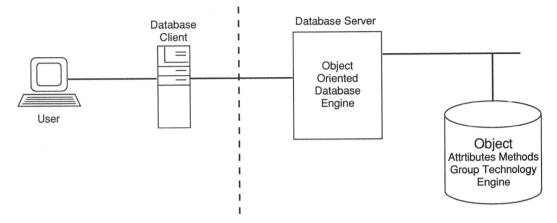

Figure 14-5. Use of Group Technology in Object-oriented Databases.

14.4 DESIGN ISSUES FOR OODBMS-BASED CAD/CAM AND GIS SYSTEMS

As we have seen from the technology discussion above, the requirements for integrating these technologies into an object-oriented database present special challenges. We will discuss the following three special requirements as they apply to these advanced technologies:

- Storage management and access optimization
- Transaction management
- Multimedia coordination

14.4.1 Storage Management and Access Optimization

In a large, enterprise-wide system, managing such complex applications would require the use of multiple database servers. An obvious question is what information should reside on each server. The system administrator (or database administrator) can attempt to set up information on servers so as to optimize usage. However, complex distributed transaction management and the movement of persistent objects dynamically present a challenge that demands a better solution.

In Chapter 3 we discussed the issues of moving persistent objects independently or as object clusters. We also discussed the use of name-servers and directories that tracked the permanent ("owner") and temporary locations of persistent objects. A storage management and access optimization manager would work in concert with the transaction manager to achieve the most effective overall system-wide performance.

In addition to tracking objects on a dynamic basis, the storage and access optimization manager would also maintain statistics on object location and object use by application servers. These statistics can be used to optimize persistent object storage algorithms. Similarly, these statistics can be used to build a pattern of access algorithms and can recommend building indexes to support faster access.

14.4.2 Transaction Management

CAD/CAM and GIS systems may have transactions that are much larger than those typically associated with debit and credit transactions of accounting systems. The development of a part or the definition of a geographic land parcel may be treated as a transaction. A transaction of this nature can last days or even weeks. A transaction management mechanism is essential for tracking and coordinating transactions in progress. The issues of concurrent updates on the same objects, location of objects, and managing distributed transactions become very important for large distributed systems of this nature.

Another important issue is the storage of intermediate stages of a transaction. The concept of versions developed initially in Chapter 9 provides a significant solution to this problem. A transaction manager can be defined that tracks transactions and maintains a database of transactions in progress. All intermediate stages of transactions are tracked also. Transaction snapshots are stored at the intermediate stages. Any database objects that have been updated since the last intermediate transaction snapshot are given a new version number and the intermediate step is stored. This provides a means of rolling back a transaction that does not complete and must be backed out.

The transaction manager also performs the role of ensuring that concurrent updates, if allowed, are managed in a controlled manner. A scheme can be developed using the "dirty object" concept. All objects retrieved for update are given a new version number. The object at the old version number remains available for shared read access as long as the update version of the object has not been modified. Once the update version of the object has been modified at an intermediate transaction level, the original version is marked as having been partially updated (that is, the transaction is still in progress). Any user who has read access to the object can use it, but is informed that a partial update is in progress. Any user requesting update access to the same object is warned that a partial update is in progress and changes may be in conflict or can get lost. This allows the user to coordinate changes with the other update if the first user did not opt for an exclusive update. This may sound complex, but the point here is that in this scheme the transaction manager can allow the second user to share the object that has been partially updated. For example, one user may be working on the graphic aspects of the update and the other may be working on the attributes of the land parcel. While the same object is being updated, the two users are not really in conflict. A well-designed transaction manager can facilitate both users working with the same version of the object. Another way of solving this is that, rather than copying the full object, only the object attributes that have changed are copied back on completion of the transaction. The version of the object that is the current operational version is updated to the extent of the changes only, so concurrent updates work fine as long as they do not affect the same object attributes.

The transaction manager can be designed to allow a number of users working concurrently with partially updated objects. As intermediate steps are stored, all users see the effect of the partial changes. Obviously, such a scheme requires a notable amount of programming, as well as application management coordination.

14.4.3 Multimedia Coordination

The information storage requirements have a variety, but a controlled one, of potential forms of storage. These can include the following:

- CHAR and VARCHAR
- SHORT and LONG INTEGER
- DATE(& TIME)
- MONEY
- TEXT fields
- BINARY information

While these field types have become standardized for most relational databases, they do not really define the full variety. The BINARY field types can include any of the following types of information:

- Raster and vector screen images
- Animation
- Voice and audio
- Video input

The key issues to be addressed then are the form of storage and how this should be translated from input medium or for target output medium. The input medium can consist of digitizers, scanners, and a variety of transducers. The output medium can consist of display systems, laser printers, electronic metering devices, and output transducers. The input or the output can be directly from or to the device, from or to disk storage, or from or to a network.

The last paragraph presents a wide range of data transformation options that must be addressed by the database. The database needs a multimedia management capability and a means of storing transformation information. Standard object templates can be created for the translations, and the translation control methods can be become a part of the information object. The multimedia manager can then be driven by the data translation method within the object to perform the appropriate translation and prepare the information for the target medium. Similarly, on input it can use the object templates to perform the appropriate incoming translations.

14.5 SUMMARY

Imaging, CAD/CAM, and cartography have been in use for a long time. With the advent of the bit-mapped graphics capability of personal computers and more recently X terminals (and workstations), imaging, CAD/CAM, and cartography have changed from being highly specialized applications to more mainstream applications. Rather than operating in a stand-alone mode as they have done in the past, these applications are becoming a part of overall enterprise-wide applications.

In this chapter we looked at the special requirements of each of the three main areas of applications. A common factor among the three applications is the need to store and retrieve binary data. Traditional relational database systems were not designed to address binary data. Consequently, this led to the development of object-oriented databases, as well as object datatypes in relational databases. Other technologies such as expert systems have also made an impact, and we looked at how they are integrated to assist in the management of CAD/CAM design information. Finally, we considered the multimedia environment and its use in database systems.

14.6 EXERCISES

1. Study the architectures of some of the leading relational database systems. How have they adapted to the need for storing images, voice, still video, mapping information, parts drawings, and so on?
2. How would you change their architecture to function better with the binary data described in Exercise 1?
3. What advantages do object-oriented databases provide for managing binary data? What disadvantages would make it difficult to use them?
4. If you were to design an ideal database for managing both business applications (such as financial applications), as well as imaging, CAD/CAM, and mapping information, what would be the primary architectural features?

OBJECT-ORIENTED DESIGN EXAMPLE

We have developed a sample application to demonstrate the design principles we have described in the book. We would like to show how object-oriented principles allow for a more direct representation of the problem and therefore yield a more simple and efficient design.

Chapters 8 and 9 presented the basic foundations of our modeling and design methodology. We will present the design of an application using the methodology presented in Chapters 8 and 9. This methodology consists of the following major steps (represented by the models applied at each step):

1. *Business model:* describes the company and its markets, products, locations, and operations.
2. *Business Information Model:* describes the information requirements for the corporation. These requirements, in turn, determine the functionality for the applications provided by the corporate information system. The business information model describes the following:

   - Who will be using the application,
   - What operations each type of user will be performing
   - Availability requirements
   - Performance requirements

- Data storage requirements
- User interface for the application

3. *Architectural Recommendation and Feasibility Report:* describes the architectural approach and the selection of hardware and software technologies that make the solution feasible. The key issues that are addressed in this report include the following:

- Distributed hardware
  —Location of database servers
  —Workstations
  —Networks used
- User access
  —Access capability limitations
  —Security issues
- Database management
  —Backup
  —Archival
- Database synchronization

4. *Information System Model:* describes the structural and transactional components of the information system. It consists of two models as described in the following:

- *Entity Model:* describes the entities and their attributes and relationships.
- *Transaction Model:* describes the functions of the information system visible to the user.

5. *Object Model:* describes the underlying objects that support the user-visible functions and the externally visible data elements. The Object Model consists of two models, as follows:

- *Structural Model:* describes the structural components: the underlying objects, their attributes, and the relationships between objects. This is derived primarily from the Entity Model.
- *Behavioral Model:* describes the behavioral components: the methods (operations) contained within the objects. This is derived primarily from the Transaction Model.

6. *System design:* converts the models into a design that can be used by a programmer to code an application. Key aspects of the design effort include the following:

- Describing datatypes and data element sizes for all attributes for every object.
- Describing the calling sequences for each method, including the attributes used as input parameters, return values from the methods, and error returns from the methods.

It is important to point out that even though this design is based on well-recognized financial concepts, it is neither intended in its current form to be complete nor necessarily applicable to a financial institution. Rather, the intention is to demonstrate the concepts for designing complex distributed applications using new approaches for data modeling and object-oriented database techniques.

You will notice that we have taken liberties with sound accounting practices on occasion to make a point or to demonstrate a concept. We have, similarly, left out obvious actions to maintain the simplicity of the explanation. Our primary goal is to improve comprehension of the concepts that we have presented here.

A very important and useful exercise for the reader is to fill in the gaps and build this into a complete and viable financial application (a task that is well beyond the intended scope of this text).

15

Designing a Financial Application

For our design example, we have created an imaginary corporation. Any resemblance to an existing corporation is purely accidental. It is obvious that many corporations do perform the functions we have noted in this chapter, and the design we have presented here can be the basis for the design of a security management system for many corporations.

We have called our imaginary corporation the International Trading Corporation (ITC) and the securities management application the Trading Management System (TMS).

We will start this chapter by introducing the corporation itself and developing the *business model* and the *Business Information Model*. The business model describes the organization and business of the corporation, the products marketed by the corporation, and its market share and operations.

The Business Information Model describes the information needs of the corporation, including the sources of information, what information needs to be stored, information outputs, and the functions of the users, brokers, and clients. This information is the major source for determining the applications required for the corporation.

We will then present some key architectural and design issues. Typically, an *Architectural Recommendation and Feasibility Report* is prepared to describe the network topology, location of data servers and workstations, hardware and software technologies, and related design issues.

With the information in these two models and the report as the basis, we will define the structural and behavioral components of the objects. Numerous coding examples have been presented to demonstrate how to create and use objects.

15.1 BUSINESS MODEL FOR THE INTERNATIONAL TRADING CORPORATION

The International Trading Corporation (we will call it ITC) is a multinational stock and bond trading corporation with worldwide headquarters in New York City. It has major regional headquarters in Chicago, Frankfurt, and Tokyo. It also maintains business offices in Boston, Houston, and Los Angeles in the United States, in London and Paris in Europe, and in Hong Kong, Taiwan, and Singapore in the Far East. These business offices tie into the regional headquarters.

The International Trading Corporation deals predominantly in stocks, bonds, mutual funds, and futures options as the primary financial instruments. Trading is performed on all major stock exchanges, and ITC uses its own agents on the trading floors, who have access to the computers at the business office. All trades performed during the day are matched by the clearinghouses at the stock exchanges and are electronically reported to the business office at night. The report also includes all unmatched trades (that is, trades recorded but that actually did not take place, usually due to improper tracking and recording at the trading floor).

The business offices also maintain current prices on all stocks, bonds, mutual funds, and options. The prices are received and updated via electronic feeds at periodic intervals during the day. However, only the opening price, day's high, day's low, and current price are maintained in history records for reporting to clients. ITC maintains daily price history information online in a distributed manner for three years for all stocks, bonds, mutual funds, and options that were traded through its offices. The price history information is based on the daily closing securities information feeds received from the stock exchanges. This allows adjusters to look up any prices in question when clients raise doubts about their accounts. This information is also used for statistical analysis on the performance of stocks or for a basket of securities. Projections developed from this analysis can present a view of the potential performance of a portfolio. Due to the multinational nature of some of their clients, account brokers may have to address questions about a trade in New York from an office in Europe or the Far East. This requires worldwide access to the price history information.

Due to the international nature of their operations, ITC also maintains foreign exchange information for all currencies in which securities tracked by ITC are traded. The daily foreign exchange information is also maintained for a three-year period.

The ITC clients consist of a mix of business and individual investors. Margin accounts are maintained for all clients. Usually one client is handled by a single broker. The commissions are split between ITC, the stock broker, and the pit broker (the floor broker on the stock trading floor). The commission structure is fully programmable by broker. In addition, a bonus structure is set by the size of the trade.

The price information, as well as foreign exchange information, is available to ITC through regular data feeds from the stock exchanges and can be recorded from these. For our purposes, we will use the closing price from the daily trade information tape for the price history file. The company trades an estimated 10 million shares a day spread over 5000 transactions of sizes ranging from 100-share blocks to 1 million-share blocks. Trades originating in Europe or the Far East may actually be carried out in New York. On-line database information is required in the office where the trade originated, the regional headquarters, and the world headquarters in New York. All offices are networked.

We will use ITC as our case study for the data modeling and design discussion in the chapters in this part of the book. Note that a complete business model covers all aspects of a business. We have restricted the business model to the securities trading components of ITC's business. We have further restricted it to trading in stocks and bonds.

15.2 BUSINESS INFORMATION MODEL FOR ITC

The Business Information Model describes the information needs of the corporation. Consequently, the Business Information Model describes the required applications and the functions, the data elements that must be captured and stored, and output in the form of reports. The requirements of the application are based primarily on the following factors that reflect the functions for which this application is designed:

1. Corporate and individual client requirements
2. Types of client accounts and accounting plans
3. The types of securities traded
4. Geographical distribution of the offices and users
5. The variety of currencies the stocks are traded in
6. Commission structure

There are, obviously, other factors that affect application requirements. However, a majority of them will fall into one of the categories noted above. It is important that a number of issues related to these factors be addressed before a design can be started. In trying to address this, we will also point out our self-imposed limitations on the scope of the applications and design simplifications for the design exercise in Chapter 16.

There are a number of operational factors that place a second set of requirements on the design of the application. These operational requirements for the application will be addressed under the following topics:

- Application functional overview
- Roles of clients and brokers
- Users of the application and what their profiles look like
- Functions provided by the application
- Descriptions of operating environments

We would like to point out once again that this information is based on an imaginary corporation and, therefore, may not appear appropriate for a real operating corporation.

15.2.1 Application Functional Requirements Overview

The Trading Management System (we will call it the TMS) is being designed to address the business information requirements for ITC as noted above. Toward that goal, TMS includes the following major application functions:

1. Client account management

   - Client information consists of the client name, address, phone numbers, and other static information about the client.
   - Client account management consists of managing security holdings, creating and executing transactions, handling dividend and interest earnings, reinvestment planning, stock purchases and sales, maintaining trading history, and so on.

2. Broker account management

   - Broker information includes broker name, location, phone numbers, employee ID, database access restrictions, and other employee information.
   - Broker account management consists of handling commissions, bonuses, client history, and current trading authorizations.

3. Management of trades

   - Management of purchase and sale of stocks, bonds, mutual funds, options, trades, and open buy and sell orders.

4. Security pricing information management

- Loading and retrieval of current stocks, bonds, and options pricing status.
- Pricing history information for stocks, bonds, mutual funds, and options. (This is referred to as time-series data because it is daily securities pricing for a period of three years.)
- Loading and retrieval of current foreign exchange rate information.
- Foreign exchange rate history information. (This is also time-series data similar to the security pricing data.)

5. Clearinghouse accounting management

- The clearinghouse activity consists of managing unmatched trades. Unmatched trades are trades that cannot be traced back to a client order. This is a very complex account management issue. Unmatched trades become a liability of ITC. When trades are not matched to existing orders, there is significant accounting activity to resolve it.

While the company itself trades in a variety of securities and financial instruments, for our design purposes, we will concentrate on stocks trading. The database is designed to be capable of handling bonds and stock options, in addition to stocks. The application design will ignore these functions, thereby reducing the potential complexity of financial operations that may overwhelm the reader and hide the design concepts. The application design will also ignore the *clearinghouse accounting management* function to simplify the modeling and design exercise.

15.2.2 Roles of Clients and Brokers

Clients and stockbrokers (or agents) have very specific roles. In the real world, the large fund managers have the capacity to directly execute trades via their own computers. For the purposes of ITC, we will assume that all trades are executed via stockbrokers and that there is no direct trading access by clients. The following spells out the exact roles of clients and stockbrokers.

Role of clients. The corporation has both individuals and corporations as clients. Generally only one agent (or account broker) is assigned to a client. A client may have more than one account for trading in different types of financial instruments. For each such account, the client is assigned an account broker. Different account brokers may be assigned to different accounts for the same client.

A number of types of trade orders can be requested by clients. The following lists the different types supported for this application:

1. Current order: immediate buy or sell at market price
2. Stop order: buy or sell at given value within the next n (30) days
3. Program trading orders (not discussed in the application design)

For the most part, the design example will concentrate on current orders, that is, on client requests to buy or sell stock at the current market price for that stock. Stop orders are open orders or requests to buy or sell stock when it reaches a certain price (called the stop price). A pending orders list is used in the design, and the design is capable of handling stop orders.

Due to the inherent complexities of programmed trading, the design does not address that mode of trading. It may be an interesting exercise for the reader to extend this design to determine the impact of programmed trading on the logical sequence of operations and the conceptual data model and to then determine the changes to the relevant objects.

Role of brokers.   The company maintains its own set of trading staff at the stock exchanges. We will use the following names to differentiate between the different classes of brokers:

1. Account brokers: financial advisors and account brokers who take client buy or sell orders. The account broker (also called an agent) creates the trade request.
2. Floor brokers: the brokers who perform the trades on the floor of the stock exchange.
3. Options brokers: the brokers who perform the trades on the options stock exchange floor.

We separated the categories of floor brokers at stock exchanges from options brokers at options exchanges due to the differences in the manner in which they operate and their commission structures. Note that we will not deal with options brokers in this application. The following design does not really cover options trades.

15.2.3 Users of Application

The Trading Management System (TMS) is a distributed application that will allow company staff at all ITC worldwide locations to access client and broker information, access current securities information, initiate and create trades, and review trade and security pricing histories.

The primary users of this application will be the company stock brokers. There are two types of brokers for common stock trading: account brokers and floor brokers. The account brokers interface directly with the company clients (purchasers and sellers of securities), and they create orders that the floor brokers execute (to buy or sell specific securities at current or specified prices). When a floor broker executes a trade, the information is entered into TMS and the account brokers are notified that the orders have been fulfilled.

TMS will also perform certain functions in support of the account and floor brokers. These functions include maintaining current security price information and notifying brokers of certain events, such as trades executed and security price changes that affect stop orders.

While stock brokers are required to learn and use TMS effectively, they are not very computer literate. The system must have a simple and intuitive user interface that prompts users to perform the required functions.

15.2.4 Functions Provided by the Application

Section 15.2.1 described a functional requirement overview of the TMS system. To address these requirements, the TMS system is designed with the following function groups that provide the functionality stated in Section 15.2.1:

1. Client account management
2. Broker account management
3. Securities trading functions
4. Securities pricing history management
5. Accounting functions
6. Reference information
7. System administration functions

The functions noted above manage trades and provide information for statistical analysis on stocks. Each function provides reports relevant to the function. The clearinghouse function is not noted here as it is an independent and rather complex function. Even though the clearinghouse function for comparing unmatched trades uses components of the same database, we will treat it as an independent application.

Client account management.   This function sets up the general information about clients, including account brokers handling the client account. All requests for trades are also managed through this function. Client management functions include the following:

- Create and update a client account
- Manage client portfolios
- View or print client holdings (portfolios)
- View or print recent client transaction history
- View and print invoices and periodic account activity statements

- View security pricing information
- Accept client orders to sell or buy securities
- Record client payments

You will notice that some functions are duplicated under trading functions and accounting functions. It is useful to have some functions accessible from different menu items for user convenience.

Broker account management.   The broker account management function identifies a broker to the system, establishes security access privileges for the broker, and manages the commission accounts for the broker. Broker account management will consist of the following functions:

- Create and update broker accounts
- Establish broker commission structure
- Manage security access codes and broker's level of security authorizations
- View or print current clients managed by broker
- View or print recent transaction history
- View or print periodic activity statements

Note that the cross references between brokers and clients allow listing all clients for a broker as well as all brokers for a client. It is also notable that there is great similarity between the accounting functions for brokers and clients.

Securities trading functions.   Trading functions are concerned primarily with the sale of purchase of stocks at a client's request. The primary functions for trading are as follows:

- Take buy and sell orders from clients
- Place buy and sell orders in a request queue for the floor broker to execute
- Review (and/or change) current buy or sell orders (orders not yet executed can be changed)
- Track and resolve completed trades
- Assign commissions according to broker and client profile
- View and print a list of open trade orders and completed trades by day, week, month, year (or date range)

This is the most complex operation in a distributed system because all functions must happen in real time, and conflicts can be expensive for clients as well as the company (for example, a trade is executed after the client requests the trade to be canceled). Interestingly, this topic also demonstrates the strengths and weaknesses of object-oriented programming. This is a major topic for which detailed design and coding examples are provided in later sections.

Securities pricing management.   This function not only tracks the master records for securities that describe the type of security (and includes general security information), but also tracks daily pricing information on securities. The general information component of this consists of the following functions:

- Adding, updating, and deleting securities from the master file
- Changing securities information due to capitalization changes and dividends
- Updating and viewing current prices and foreign exchange information

For each security the securities pricing history function maintains the high, low, open, close, bid, and asked information at the close of each business day at the stock exchange. Obviously, this will become a very significantly large storage requirement for a company tracking 10,000 securities (for example, 10,000 × 260 days × 3 years = 7.8 million records) to store just three years of data. The types of functions required for managing these data are as follows:

- Storing and retrieving pricing information
- Normalizing this information based on foreign exchange rate changes as well as capitalization changes (for example, stock splits) if any
- Performing statistical analysis for client newsletters (or to address client phone inquiries)

Due to the complexity of storage and access, especially for a relational or an object oriented database, we have chosen these as key topics for which we will demonstrate design and coding examples.

Foreign exchange pricing history.   This function records the daily foreign exchange prices for all major currencies at all exchanges that ITC trades in. The securities pricing history function maintains, for each security, the high, low, open, and close information at the close of each business day at the stock exchange. The types of functions required for managing this data are as follows:

- Storing and retrieving pricing information
- Normalizing security prices based on foreign exchange rate changes

Foreign exchange pricing information also needs to be stored as time-series data. We have not discussed this topic in detail as the security pricing history topic covers most of the key aspects.

Accounting functions.   The account management functions are basic to any trading system. The details of these functions may differ from one system to another, but generic functions remain the same. The accounting functions of interest for TMS include the following:

- Create invoices for stock purchases and credit memos for stock sales
- Print periodic activity statements
- Print client disbursement and broker commission checks
- Manage client payments and current account balances

An accounting function requires a number of additional tasks, such as aging, accounts receivables, and accounts payables. For the purposes of this design exercise, we will concentrate on the functions noted above that are directly related to stock trades.

Reference information.   Reference information refers to information that is frequently used as reference data. For example, this may be a list (and descriptions) of all currencies for which securities are traded. Another example is the types of broker commission plans used by the corporation. Rather than hard code such information, it can be built into objects (or database tables) that can be updated by the clerical staff as new securities are added and commission plans change. As another example, we can build a reference table for all stock exchanges. Using these reference tables ensures that the users make no typing mistakes, especially if any of these fields are index fields. All fields where reference information is required force the user to select a value from a window that displays the list of possible choices (the choices are the set of values entered in the table or the objects related to it). The functions required for reference tables are the following:

- Adding or updating reference data
- Viewing or printing reference data

A key advantage of using reference tables is that users can select reference information on the basis of their local contexts and even in their local languages, while the database has entries that are common worldwide.

System administration.   The system administration function is involved with the following major functions:

- Maintaining user log on, password, and worldwide security access codes
- Backup and recovery of databases that may be distributed
- Archival of databases that may be distributed

While system administration is generally quite straightforward for most operations, the concept of system administration on systems that may be distributed worldwide is an important issue. The role of object orientation in this context needs further explanation to determine the benefits and problems associated with it.

15.2.5 Application Data

The following general data provide the details about the operations of ITC. This data will be used as the basis for the design exercise. It is important to note that this data is purely imaginary to demonstrate the methodology and may not be reasonable from a financial operational point of view.

While the overall system can be made much more comprehensive, we will limit the functionality of our system to improve comprehension of the design process. We will further make assumptions as and when needed for our imaginary corporation (these assumptions may not be fully realistic, but will assist in understanding the design process).

Financial instruments.   ITC is a widely diversified international corporation and manages a variety of financial instruments for its clients. The financial instruments that will be managed by the proposed application include the following:

- Stocks
- Bonds
- Mutual funds
- Options

As mentioned earlier in the ITC overview, we will design the system primarily for management of stocks or bonds (even though it is sufficiently general in nature to handle the other types).

Office locations.   ITC is an international corporation with world headquarters in New York City. The following lists all business offices involved in the trading of the financial intruments noted in the previous section.

New York	World headquarters	(stock exchange)
Chicago	Full services	(stock and options exchange)
Boston	Feeder system (to NYC)	
Houston	Feeder system	
Los Angeles	Feeder system	
London	Full system	(stock exchange)
Paris	Full system	(stock exchange)
Frankfurt	Full system	(stock exchange)
Tokyo	Full system	(stock exchange)
Hong Kong	Feeder system	

It should be noted that all offices in cities that host a stock exchange have a full system configuration, while the cities with business offices but no stock exchanges (that ITC trades in) have smaller feeder systems.

Communications infrastructure.   ITC has invested a significant amount of capital in setting up a worldwide network for communications. This communications infrastructure consists of the following major communications links:

- High-speed T1 links within the continental United States
- High-speed satellite links worldwide at 56 Kbps to all offices with full systems
- Slower X.25 links to offices with feeder systems
- Local-area networks within offices (10 Mbps or higher)

All high-speed links are backed up by slower links, such as X.25 and dial-up lines within the continental United States and X.25 lines for international access. The high-speed links operate at a minimum of 56 Kbps both nationally and internationally. X.25 links operate at 9.6 to 64 Kbps depending on location.

Design assumptions.   We will make a number of simple design assumptions to illustrate the methodologies. These assumptions are designed to set parameters in ranges that force certain design constraints. Some of these issues will be more apparent as we progress through the design.

Trade volume assumptions.   The following describes the trading volume for stocks:

- We will assume that the company trades in 10,000 different issues of common stock.
- We will assume that multiple trades can take place per day for each active stock traded by ITC.
- Stock prices will be continuously tracked from exchange service feeds, but the database will record only the prices at the time of the trades in the trade record and at the close of the business day in the price history.
- Estimated number of trades per day is based on the following:

   ITC claims 6% market share for trading in the United States and Europe
   NY Stock Exchange trades approximately 200 million shares per day
   ITC trades 12 million shares spread over 5000 trades per day

15.3 ARCHITECTURAL RECOMMENDATION AND TECHNOLOGY FEASIBILITY

A sound, well thought out, and carefully designed architecture is crucial for a large and complex enterprise-wide network running a distributed real-time database application. Distributed database servers allow the creation of vital networking and shared database resources throughout an organization. The networks and database servers must be fine-tuned so that the two crucial components are loaded appropriately (and not stressed) and can handle the packet transmission loads without any bottlenecks. Proper configuration and careful distribution of data are essential for maximizing access to the data and minimizing network traffic. Some key architectural issues include the following:

1. Number of user sessions and network connections to the database that determine the potential overhead
2. Types of networking protocols
3. Impact of server degradation on the servers in the network
4. Access security considerations
5. Database synchronization overhead

Recommendations for proposed architecture, selection of technologies for constructing the network, and the implementation strategies for hardware and software components are described in the architectural recommendation and technology feasibility report.

15.3.1 Architectural Recommendations

Architectural recommendations include the topology of the network, location of database servers and clients, communications and networking protocols, security considerations, and database integrity considerations. Each of these issues is analyzed and documented, and a recommendation is prepared for the proposed architecture.

Location of database servers, workstations, and networks. An enterprise-wide system typically requires multiple LANs, WAN connections, and a number of database servers located close to the clients. Each server is likely to have its own LAN that supports the database server, application servers, and user workstations, in addition to the WAN traffic. The LAN carries network connections from users to the application server. For each user, the application server would maintain at least one or two connections to the database server. This overhead is significant if the server supports a couple of hundred users. It may become necessary to have more than one database server on the LAN and, consequently, the database software must provide for directing user traffic to the appropriate server. Even more complicated is the task of keeping the multiple servers in a LAN synchronized in real time.

Impact of networking protocols.   The networking protocol provides a number of standard features, but also has an overhead associated with it. Ideally, the same networking protocol should handle the LAN as well as the WAN (in this case international WAN) requirements. A major issue that must be a strong consideration for the architectural recommendation is standardization of the networking protocols and support of the protocols by the database server systems. Network speeds and overheads associated with the networking protocols must also be considered.

Impact of server degradation.   When a server gets congested due to unexpectedly high network traffic or user load, it fails to keep up with the packet transmission load on the network. Because it is unable to receive all packets transmitted by another server (database or application server), retransmissions become necessary. Retransmissions, in turn, cause increased congestion on other servers. This can continue in an increasing spiral unless stopped by the system. The system must be architected with appropriate capacity, as well as threshold checks, to prevent this kind of thrashing.

Access security considerations.   A widely distributed database open to access by a large number of users requires flexible, multilevel security authorizations. For example, brokers need access to securities (for example, stocks) information worldwide but need access to client records for their own clients only. Brokers should not have access to client information for clients managed by other brokers. Similarly, brokers should have no access to commission structures and other personal information about other brokers. This implies that the system must have worldwide access control mechanisms. These mechanisms should be flexible and, at the same time, should not become a hindrance for the users.

Database synchronization overhead.   Distributed databases are increasingly becoming essential for enterprise-wide information systems. A major consideration is ensuring that all components of the database remain synchronized if more than one copy of any data element is maintained on the network. Handling of distributed transactions is also a major architectural consideration.

Backup and archival of database network.   Backup and archival become important architectural issues for distributed database systems. The key questions that need to be addressed are the locations where backups and archival must be performed and if backups and archival can be performed for remote database servers via the network.

15.3.2 Technology Feasibility

The technology feasibility component of this report describes how available technologies will be utilized to address the information system requirements. It is essential that all major design issues be addressed relative to the selected technologies.

We have selected a number of design issues that should be addressed in a design exercise. These design issues have been selected not because they are the most important issues for ITC (even though they may meet that criterion), but because they will help us in emphasizing certain aspects of the design process.

Designing for high availability.   Clients must be able to request purchases and sales of securities at all times. Under most circumstances they will contact their local account broker to request transactions. The account broker will enter an order into the system using a local workstation connected to the company network. If the connection between a business office and the nearest regional headquarters is down, the broker can call an account broker at another office over the telephone to have the order entered into the system.

When orders are entered into the system, they must be made available to all floor brokers at the active exchanges so that trades may be executed as soon as possible. Before executing a trade a floor broker must be able to lock an order so that another floor broker, possibly at another exchange, will not process the same order. These two requirements lead to a requirement that the connections between floor brokers' workstations and regional headquarters be very highly reliable. This can be achieved by having multiple dedicated network connections to one or more regional headquarters and by having the capability of using an asynchronous connection over normal phone lines when the network connections fail. It further implies that the connections between the regional headquarters be very reliable in order to support the distributed locking of trade orders. In the event that connections are disrupted, the company must decide whether to allow floor brokers to go ahead with trades that may result in duplicate trades or to delay service to the clients.

Designing for performance.   The major areas where performance is a factor are very similar to the areas requiring high availability. When a client makes a request to buy or sell securities, the request and resulting trade orders must be entered into the system and distributed to floor brokers as quickly as possible so that clients may be provided with fast, efficient service. This implies that access to client account information and security and price information be readily available to the account broker's workstation, that the client requests and trade orders be entered into the regional database quickly, and that the regional system be able to distribute the orders to floor brokers' workstations with very little delay.

Floor brokers will need to view and lock orders, execute trades, and enter the trade information into the system at a rapid pace. The process of locking orders will require updating the database at the regional headquarters, waiting for the update to be distributed to the other regional headquarters, and sending a confirmation back to the floor broker's workstation. When a floor broker enters trade information into TMS the information may be stored locally and transmitted later to the regional headquarter's database in order to reduce delay to the broker. This would, however, require that reliable backup mechanisms be in place so that trade information is not lost.

There are two other major performance issues in the TMS system: the ability to manage a significant volume of information maintained by the system worldwide (due to security information and daily security pricing updates arising from a large number of securities), and the ability of the system to rapidly locate and manipulate information such as security prices and trade orders.

In addition to performing trades, the TMS would be expected to provide statistical information about stock performance. Such statistical analysis, especially when performed for a basket of stock, presents a significant performance challenge for a system with data distributed on a worldwide basis.

Data storage considerations.   All current client and broker information, outstanding orders, and recent trades must be immediately available at each regional headquarters. Histories of client and broker transactions, security prices, and trade information for a one-year period must be immediately available in at least one regional headquarter's database and be capable of being distributed to brokers' workstations on request. Longer-term histories should be available on slower optical storage systems, with the capability of being distributed to any broker's workstation without much delay.

These requirements imply that current and yearly information be stored in mirrored or distributed fashion and be accessible from more than one processor. Current information, which has the highest availability requirements, will be duplicated at each regional headquarters and may be mirrored as well. It is sufficient for yearly history information to reside at one site on mirrored disks. Note that all information of a given type need not reside at the same site. Long-term history information may reside unmirrored on optical disks at a single site. All information will be backed up daily onto off-line storage media.

The bulk of the data maintained by the Trading Management System is security information, pricing history, and trading history. The current orders and trades, while needing fast access, do not constitute a major percentage of the overall data storage. Security information and pricing history are maintained on line for several years and must be designed to be accessible from any ITC office in the world.

Distributed storage.   The database is distributed among database servers at the major worldwide office. Pricing and trading data is distributed among database servers based on the origin of the data. This implies that data is stored closest to the exchange that is generating the data. Similarly, client account information, as well as broker information, is maintained at the office closest to the broker or the account.

This method of distribution provides for full distribution and fully distributed access to data, while at the same time minimizing the movement of data over the international network. The most salient aspect of designing for performance is ensuring that the network traffic is minimized without a corresponding reduction in functionality.

Database synchronization.   A major design consideration in any distributed data storage is the management of concurrent transactions and maintaining a synchronized database where data is copied to various locations for expediency. Two such examples of data that may be copied are as follows:

1. The daily stock pricing information for all stocks that are traded internationally. This may be useful because the information changes only once a day and can be applied as a bulk data update.
2. Reference information describing corporations (underlying securities that are being traded), exchange information, dividend information, and tax information. This information is relatively stable and needs to be updated only when it changes.

Even though the need to synchronize is controlled and can be managed effectively, database synchronization is still a significant design issue. The distribution of the database must take this issue into consideration.

Advanced user interface.   All functionality provided by TMS is through a common user interface on high resolution color graphics workstations. The common user interface will reduce training time as well as development time. It is anticipated that there will be a mix of ASCII terminals, X-terminals and workstations for users. The design should handle the full variety of terminals and workstation clients in a transparent manner.

Any functionality provided through backup communications mechanisms such as asychronous phone lines shall appear to the user exactly as though normal communications facilities were in use. The only difference may be a perceptible delay in response time.

15.4 SUMMARY

An enterprise has a number of different operating entities with different functions. For developing an application set to support these functions, it is essential to understand the operations performed by each business unit, the interactions among the business units, and the information elements collected, processed and disseminated by each business unit. The operations performed by a business unit are described in the Business Model. The business model describes the business of the corporation.

The information elements collected, processed, and disseminated by each business unit are described in the Business Information Model. The model describes the sources, the uses and the disposition of each information element entered into the information system database.

We also touched upon the Architectural Recommendation and Technology Feasibility issues. These issues form the basis for a formal report.

15.5 EXERCISES

1. Expand the Business Information Model to cover all aspects of the applications required for ITC.
2. Describe the level of information exchange across various departments.
3. Prepare an outline for an Architectural Recommendation and Technology Feasibility Report.
4. What are some of the key issues that must be addressed in the report of Exercise 3? What additional information is required to address these issues?

16

Data Modeling and Design

We developed the business model and the business information model for the International Trading Corporation (ITC, our imaginary corporation) in Chapter 15. These two models are somewhat general in nature and, consequently, we did not apply any specific depiction methodology to these models. Nonetheless, more detailed models, such as the ones described in this chapter, do require a rigorous methodology for clearly depicting the organization of data and functions.

We presented the Frame-Object Analysis methodology in Chapter 8. We encourage the reader to review that methodology in detail at this time. In the following sections we will develop models using the Frame-Object Methodology. Chapter 8 also described the Information System Model and the Object Model. You may recall that the Information System Model represents the user perspective of the system and the Object Model represents the design of the system. We will review these two models and present a more detailed practical example of how the Frame-Object Analysis methodology is used for depicting these models.

We will show how a system design is derived from these models. Numerous coding examples are provided to help the reader understand the transformation from the models to the system design.

Finally, we have evaluated and presented our perceptions of the benefits of the object-oriented design approach and how it applies to both relational as well as object-oriented databases.

16.1 INFORMATION SYSTEM MODEL

The Information System Model was described in detail in Chapter 8. In this section we will exemplify the concepts developed in Chapter 8 by developing an Information System Model for the Trading Management system (TMS) for International Trading Corporation (ITC). Let us briefly revew the definition of the components of the Information System Model.

> *Information System Model:* in our approach to modeling, the Information System Model replaces parts of the conceptual data model and consists of the Entity Model and the Transaction Model. It presents the user's perspective of the information system.
>
> *Entity Model:* describes the entities, individual attributes, and logical groupings of attributes as seen by the user. It also describes the logical relationships between entities. The Entity Model describes the structural components visible to the user.
>
> *Transaction Model:* describes the interactions among application objects from the user's point of view. It describes the user-level operations (such as insert, query, update, and delete) in terms of the behavioral relationships among each application object. The transaction model describes the behavioral components visible to the user.

The Information System Model depicts the entities, their attributes, and the functions visible to the user. The Information System Model also depicts the relations between entities and operations performed on the entities, but does not describe objects. The objects are not visible to the user; only their external representation is. The underlying objects are derived from the Information System Model and are described in the Object Model.

Figure 16-1 duplicates Figure 8-2 and describes the structural and behavioral components of the Information System Model. The Entity Model represents the structural components, and the Transaction Model represents the behavioral components of the information system. It is important to note that what may be visible to the user may not necessarily map to the actual internal structure of objects. The user is primarily concerned with the data elements stored in the system and the behavior of the system with respect to manipulating these data elements in the most efficient manner.

The models developed in the following discussion are based on the Business Information Model developed in Chapter 15. All assumptions and limitations noted in the Business Information Model are applicable to this discussion.

16.1.1 Entity Model

The Entity Model describes the real-world relations for the information system. The entities, attributes, and the logical grouping of attributes can be converted to

Entity Model (as seen by user)	Transaction Model (as seen by user)
* External view of entities (but these entities may or may not map directly to data objects). * Individual attributes as seen by the user (but the user may have no perception of their link to physical entities). * Logical groupings of attributes (such as address, city, state, zip). * Logical relationships among groups of entities. * Output results of manipulating attributes as seen by the user (such as in reports).	* A set of menu hierarchies that defines user visible functions. * Data input forms that may cause certain operations to be performed. * Data outputs (such as screen displays of data and printed reports). * May include other user-initiated functions such as backup and archival. * Description of the nature of access to lower-level transactions (that is, to operations within objects).

Figure 16-1. Components of the Information System Model.

tables for a relational database or to objects for an object-oriented database. In the limited version of the application presented here, the structural frame for the highest level includes the entities visible to the user as shown in Figure 16-2. Note that this is a representative, not an exhaustive, list.

The entity *Brokers* can be decomposed to the next level of entities visible to the user. While *Brokers* is a generalized class of entities, *AccountBroker* or *FloorBroker* are specific entities (Figure 16-3).

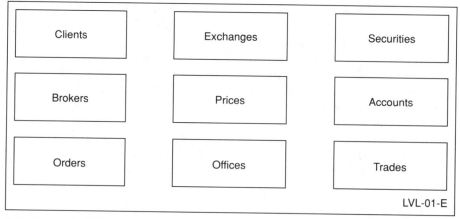

Basic Entities for TMS

Figure 16-2. Entity Frame with Basic Building Blocks.

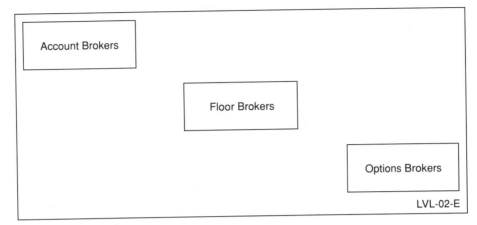

Class Hierarchy for BROKERS

Figure 16-3.   Subclass Decomposition of Class *BROKERS*.

A similar decomposition can be performed for some of the other entities, such as *Securities, Clients,* and *Requests.* The reader may find it worthwhile to decompose the other entities to lower levels and develop the lower-level frames to assist the study of the design and coding examples presented in Section 16.3

Note that we are really interested in entities that are used for specific component applications within the overall enterprise-wide information system. We will therefore create only the frames that show the entities for the trading management application. We can break the frames down further for specific processes within this application, for example, for a trade as shown in Figure 16-4.

Figure 16-4 also illustrates how logical relationships between the entities are described by employing the Entity Relationship diagramming conventions within the frame. We have used arrows to indicate the *one to one, one to many,* and *many to many* relationships.

Attributes in a frame.   Figure 16-5 describes the use of frames to show attributes for one or more entities. The name of the object class for the model is used as the heading of the object box. This is followed by a broken line and then by the object identifier. The object identifier is indicated by a # sign. For example, each client object instance is identified by a *Client Object ID.* In a relational database, this is the equivalent of the *primary key.* An object class is characterized by a number of attributes as shown in Figure 16-5. Note that the attributes that are candidates for establishing a relationship with attributes in other entities, called *link attributes,* are indicated by an asterisk (*). Link attributes can be viewed as being the equivalent of *foreign keys* in a relational database.

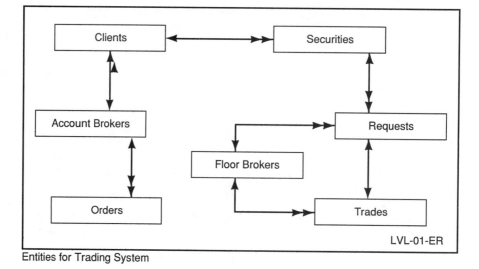

Entities for Trading System

Figure 16-4. Entity Relationships in an Entity Frame.

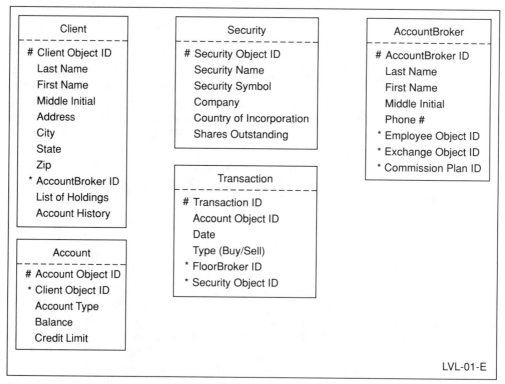

Entities for TMS Application (1)

Figure 16-5. Description of Entities for TMS Application.

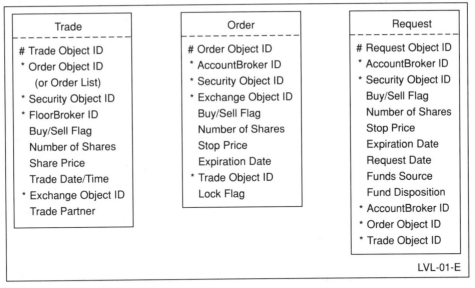

Entities for TMS Application (2)

Figure 16-6.   Other Entities for TMS Application.

Generally, it will not be practical to fit all entities in one frame. The entities can be depicted in multiple frames for clarity and to ensure that there is enough room to describe all attributes. Figures 16-5 and 16-6 show some of the entities required for the TMS application. We suggest as an exercise that the reader determine which additional entities need to be defined and then build the frames for these entities. For example, a frame is needed for the entities *Invoice*, *Credit-Memo*, and *Statement*. It is advisable, for convenience and clarity, to group entities with some level of commonality in the same frame. For example, *Invoice*, *Credit-Memo*, and *Statement* are all part of reports for the accounting function.

Our methodology for depicting entities with just the object identification and link attributes (or primary and foreign keys in a relational database) is illustrated in Figure 16-7. This methodology allows showing a larger number of entities and their relationship within a frame. The link attributes are the only ones shown with the entity name since they are the only ones that contribute directly to the relationship. Note that *AccountBrokers* can service multiple *Clients*, and a *Client* may be serviced by a number of specialized *Brokers* (for example, specialized by types of securities—options, commodities, stocks, bonds, and so on). The frames showing the relations are created as a separate group from the frames showing the full list of attributes of entities. Together, these two groups of frames define the entities structurally.

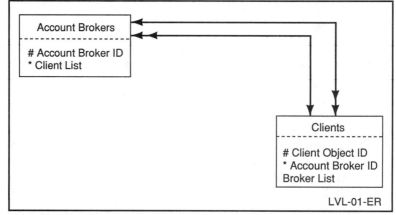

Entity Relationships

Figure 16-7.   Representing Relationships between Entities in Frames.

Outputs from trading application.   The outputs from a trading management system include summary reports and specific printouts such as statements. The following lists the types of outputs planned for our TMS application:

- Invoices
- Credit memos
- Statements
- Daily list of trades (by client, broker, exchange, and so on)
- Trading summary (by security type, exchange, broker, and so on)
- Open order list
- Open request list

Figure 16-8 illustrates how outputs are shown using frames. Note that this frame can be translated to a reports submenu during application design. The entity model is concerned primarily with the attributes of intermediate data objects created for reports, that are visible to the user, and the additional relationships between data objects required for reports. The frame in Figure 16-8 is analyzed to determine if additional entities should be created and if new relationships between existing entities should be defined. *Invoice, CreditMemo,* and *Statement* are the entities we mentioned earlier that are added to the entity list to support the output functions.

Multilevel frames can be generated by decomposing these *output* objects further. For example, *Statements* can include *Client Account Statements* as well as *Broker Commission Statements.* Similarly, *Daily List of Trades* and *Trading Summary* can have a number of subobjects.

We have now completed the Entity Model. The Entity Model consists of the frames describing the entities and their relationships and explanations of the frames and the relationships.

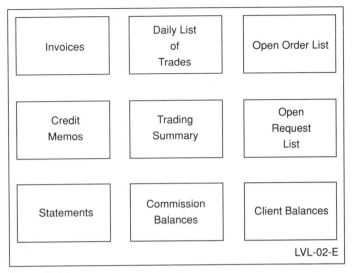

Output Entities

Figure 16-8.   Representing Output Entities in Frames.

16.1.2 Transaction Model

The Transaction Model describes menu hierarchies, input forms, and reports from an operational perspective. A menu hierarchy determines the grouping of functions and the sequence in which these functions are performed. Some menus are vertical menus with a line describing each function. Other menu items, usually at the lowest level, are selected via function keys, buttons, pop-up windows or pull-down menus. Most menu items open screen forms for data entry, display, and modification.

Before the menu items can be determined, all operations performed by the system that are visible to the user must be listed. This list is then broken down into logical groupings of functions and into a function hierarchy. This hierarchy determines the menu hierarchy.

The Transaction Model uses frames to describe menus. In addition to frames, the transaction model also describes the screen forms required for the application. In this section, we have presented a transaction model for the trading management system for ITC and show some of the screen forms. This model has been deliberately simplified to clearly demonstrate the methodology. A number of aspects of a real trading management system that do not contribute to understanding of this methodology have not been addressed in this example. The user would find it an interesting exercise to expand this model to cover all aspects of a real trading management system.

The authors have proposed a top-down approach to developing a Transaction Model. We believe that this is the most appropriate approach for developing a logically sound information system.

Operations descriptions for the Transaction Model.   A complex system has many functions at a number of functional levels. The TMS system for ITC is a complex financial application and, consequently, has a large number of functional levels. For simplicity and to ensure clarity in the presentation of the design concepts, we have taken into account only a subset of the functions to develop the frame-object analysis diagrams. These functions also become the basis for the creation of the objects required to perform this limited set of functions. We encourage the reader to enlarge this set as a design exercise. The functions covered in this design exercise are as follows:

1. **Client actions:** Client actions are the functions that are performed (usually by an account broker) on behalf of a client. The following lists a useful subset of client functions:

   - Buy shares in security at current price, at specified price
   - Sell shares in security at current price, at specified price
   - Get current value of holdings
   - Create account request
   - Delete account request
   - Create or update portfolios
   - Add primary broker and update broker list
   - Record payments for purchased securities
   - Receive money from sale of securities
   - Get account history
   - Get security information or current price

2. **Account brokers actions:** The account brokers interface with the client and place buy and sell orders with the exchange floor brokers on behalf of clients. The account broker performs the following functions:

   - Create or delete client accounts
   - Accept client buy or sell requests
   - Create orders
   - Receive notification of trades (resulting from orders)
   - Get list of client requests
   - Get list of current orders
   - Get list of stop orders
   - Get value of client holdings
   - Get client account history
   - Receive money from client for securities purchases
   - Send money to client from sale of securities (actually, money may be to/from a cash account, with security purchases/sales from/to same account)

3. **Floor brokers actions:** The floor broker operates on the trading floor of the exchange and actually carries out the sale or purchase of stock by monitoring the pending stock order list and the current price of each stock listed for a buy or sell on the pending order list. The floor broker is responsible for recording a trade when it takes place. The floor broker performs the following functions:

- Get list of current orders
- Get list of stop orders
- Get notification of trades that would satisfy stop orders
- Create trade

4. **Security trading functions:** These are functions performed primarily by the brokers for executing a trade. The full sequence of functions includes the following:

- Accept client's buy or sell requests
- Create order
- Create (trade) request
- Record trade on execution
- Notify client of trade execution
- Complete accounting tasks

5. **Security pricing history management:** Pricing history is maintained for client information with reference to portfolio or stock performance as well as for resolving disputes. Functions include the following:

- Record daily prices for all securities
- Retrieve prices by security and date

6. **Accounting functions:** The accounting functions include some functions performed automatically by the system (such as aging of account balances), some functions performed by floor brokers, and some functions performed by account brokers on behalf of clients. These functions include the following:

- Recording payments by clients
- Recording invoices for stock purchases
- Printing periodic statements
- Viewing invoices and credit memos
- Performing interaccount fund transfers
- Processing broker commission payments

- Processing client payments
- Maintaining (and aging) delinquent client accounts

7. **Reference code management:** Reference codes are used to simplify data entry by providing routine look-up information for a variety of information objects. For example, lists of exchanges and types of securities can be stored as codes referring to the appropriate exchange- or security-type objects so that searches are much faster.

- Adding initial reference codes
- Updating reference codes

8. **System administration:** System administration (including database administration) is performed for updating the database and maintaining the integrity of the system. The functions include the following:

- Backing up and restoring database
- Archiving data
- Storing data feeds into databases (daily stock prices)
- Database recovery actions

For the purposes of this design exercise, we will concentrate on the primary function of stock trades. Consequently, a large number of other functions one associates with a complete financial securities trading management system will not be addressed. The stock trade function by itself is, however, quite comprehensive and is very useful for illustrating the design concepts. Note that the functions listed above do not necessarily define the menu hierarchy. To develop the menu hierarchy, these functions must be grouped into logical higher-level operations. The grouping of functions follows simple rules of tree traversal; that is, common functions are grouped together as the next level limb of the tree. Let us start with the top-level frame and follow through the development of the menu hierarchy.

Top-level frame.   Figure 16-9 shows the results of the grouping of functions as a top-level frame. These functions will be the menu items for the top-level menu (or rather the subset we are concerned with) for TMS. You will notice that no links are shown between the functions at this time. The functions (or menu items) are treated as objects in this Frame-Object Methodology diagram. Links can nonetheless be shown to describe the data flows between the functions.

Note that the entry at the lower-right corner of the frame identifies it to be a level 1 transaction frame. A similar entry is used in all frames to identify them. Also note that the name of the frame (describing its primary function as well as for

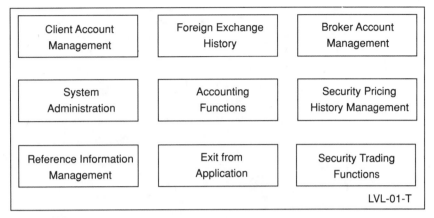

Top-level Menu

Figure 16-9.   Top-level Behavioral Frame.

identification of the frame) is tagged at the lower-left corner. This frame is called *Top-level Menu*. The menu items of the top-level menu include the following:

1. Client account management
2. Broker management
3. Security trading functions
4. Security Pricing History Management
5. Accounting functions
6. Reference code management
7. System administration
8. Exit trading management system application

The top-level menu screen is shown in Figure 16-10. You will notice that there is a direct one to one mapping between the objects in the frame and the menu items in Figure 16-10. Each of these main-menu items can be decomposed to the next-level menu item. In some cases, the next-level menu items may not require a menu form; rather they are achieved by the use of push buttons. Let us decompose the top-level frame into its constituents.

Decomposition of the top-level frame.   When the top-level frame is decomposed, we get eight new frames, one for each function. Each of these can be decomposed further to illustrate the functions at the next level. Similarly, the next level can be decomposed further until the frame is reached that shows the lowest level. The lowest-level frame may have to be backed off if the functions described by that frame are encapsulated within an object.

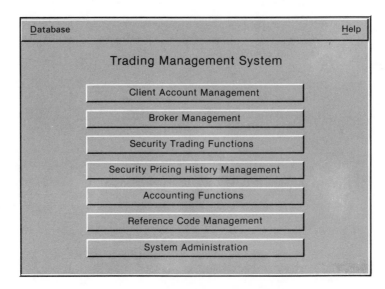

Figure 16-10.   Main Menu for TMS Application

The key to understanding the required level of decomposition is to determine the level of menus a user will see. The Transaction Model frames should cover all the menus a user will see. Let us use some examples to demonstrate the methodology.

1. **Client account management:** Figure 16-11 illustrates an example of decomposing the top-level frame. In this figure, the next level frame, that is, the frame for *Client Account Management* functions, is described.

    The frame in Figure 16-11 can be decomposed to one more level for the functions that can be defined at the next lower level. For example, Figure 16-12 illustrates the next-level frame (level 3 frame) for the *Create, Review,* or *Modify Account* function. You will notice that all functions listed in Figure 16-12 will become pull down menus or push-button selections (rather then menu items).

    Note that the functions shown in Figure 16-12 do not need to be further decomposed. This frame depicts the lowest level of functions visible to the user. We will build objects with encapsulated methods that perform the functions at the next lower level. These objects are described in the Object Model and system design (Sections 16.3 and 16.4).

    From this example, it becomes obvious that a frame is very useful to show a collection of related objects. A frame can be used further to show attributes and methods within an object. As a final step in this process, we can develop the screen forms for "Review/Modify Existing Client" function. Figures 16-13A through 16-13C describe sample screen forms for this

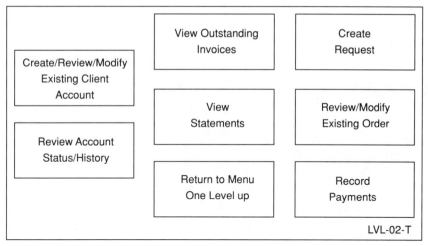

Client Account Management

Figure 16-11.   Client Account Management Frame.

function. Note that the pull down menus (top line of the screen) and push buttons (usually last line of the screen) describe the lowest-level menu items for this function such as creating, updating and deleting portfolio objects.

The *Portfolio List* column displays a list of all portfolios being managed for this client. The *Portfolio Detail* columns describe the details (a list of securities and the number of shares) for a portfolio currently highlighted by the cursor in the *Portfolio List* column.

The subaccounts window functions in a manner similar to the portfolio window. The subaccounts list is displayed in the left column and the

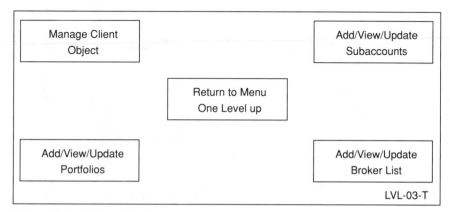

Review/Modify Existing Client

Figure 16-12.   Create, Review or Modify Account Frame.

| Database Edit View | Help |

Client Account Information

Last Name

First Name

Middle Initial

Telephone (Work)

Telephone (Home)

Address

City

State   Zip

Client Type   ◇ Corporate
                     ◇ Individual

Primary Broker

[Accounts]   [Portfolios]   [Brokers]

Figure 16-13A. Client Account Screen Form.

| Database Edit | Help |

Portfolio List   Portfolio Detail

                      Security   Shares

Figure 16-13B. Client Portfolio Form Window.

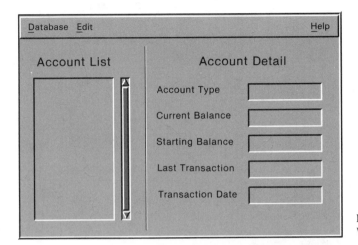

Figure 16-13C.   Client Subaccounts Form Window.

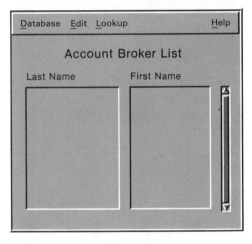

Figure 16-13D.

current selection is highlighted. The right column displays the details about the highlighted account. Similarly, Figure 16-13D shows the Account Broker list window.

2. **Broker account management:** Figure 16-14 shows the frame for the *Broker Account Management* function. This function includes all actions that can be taken relative to a broker account. These actions may or may not be performed by the broker. Some of these actions may be performed by the clerical staff or the supervisory staff.

   One may wonder why printing commission checks is a function not included in this frame. Logically, printing checks is an accounting function and is, therefore, not included in the frames depicted in Figures 16-15A and 16-15B.

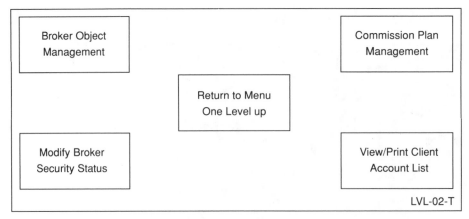

Broker Account Management

Figure 16-14. Broker Account Management Frame.

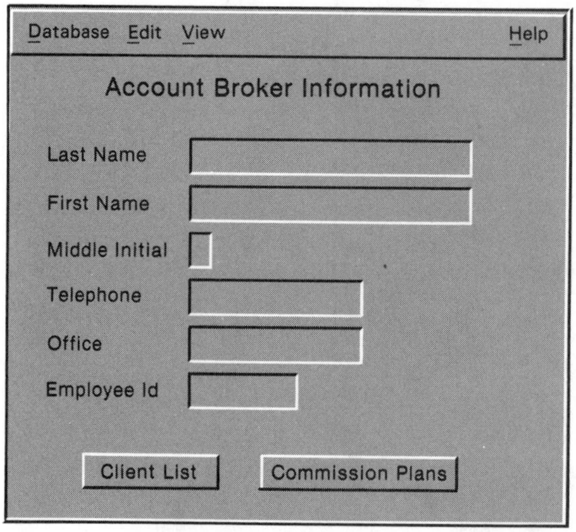

Figure 16-15A. Broker Account Management Screen Form.

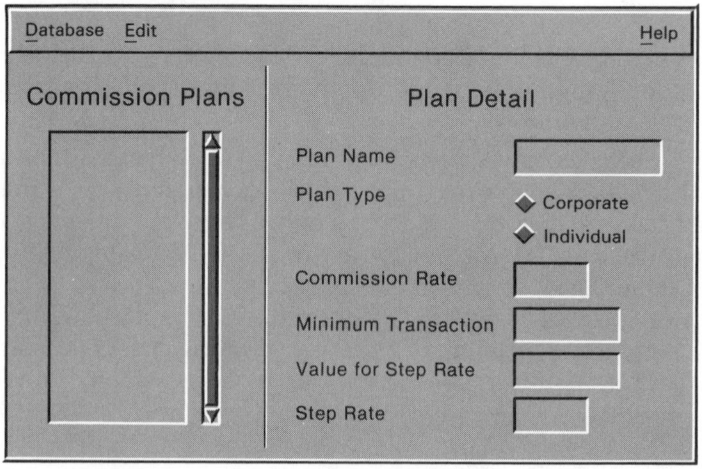

Figure 16-15B. Broker Commission Structure Form Window.

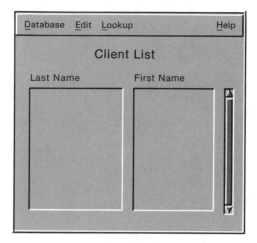

Figure 16-15C. Broker Client List
Window.

There can be a number of corporate commission plan structures. The basic information describing these commission plan structures can be maintained as reference information (in reference tables or commission plan description objects). The commission plan window is described in Figure 16-15B. The left column of the window shows the various types of commission plans applicable to the selected broker, while the right column shows the details for the plan selected by the cursor in the left column. Note that the same window can be used for maintaining reference information for all commission plans.

Each broker manages the accounts for a number of clients. The client list maintains the authorization of the broker to access the client account. This window lists all clients managed by the selected broker (Figure 16-15C).

3. **Security trading functions:** Figure 16-16 portrays the frame for the *Security Trading* functions. The functions described by this frame cover all activities related to sale or purchase of a security once a customer request has been entered by the account broker. Note that this frame is designed to depict the functions and does not directly translate to a menu.

The frame in Figure 16-16 is decomposed further as shown in Figure 16-17 to determine the menu operations. Note that figure 16-17 describes a methodology for better organization of the documentation. The subfunctions are described on the same frame as operations within the subobjects. This basically indicates that these subfunctions are activated by function keys or buttons rather than by separate menus. You will note that this methodology is based on the contents of the box being in the order of object name, attributes, and functions. Consequently, the area reserved for attributes is left blank.

Figures 16-18A through 16-18G describe the screen forms for the security trading functions.

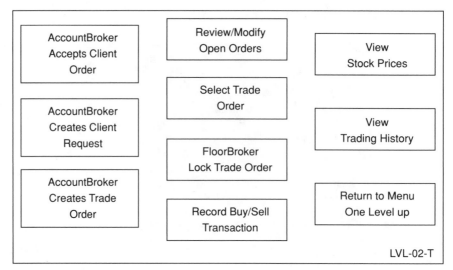

Security Trading Functions

Figure 16-16. Security Trading Functions Frame.

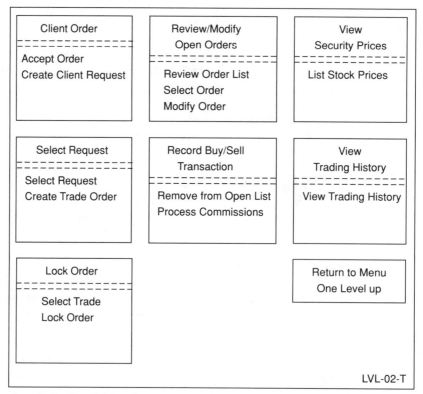

Security Trading: Subfunctions

Figure 16-17. Subfunctions of Security Trading Functions.

Figure 16-18A shows the screen form for creating a new *Request*. Figure 16-18B shows the screen form for listing outstanding requests.

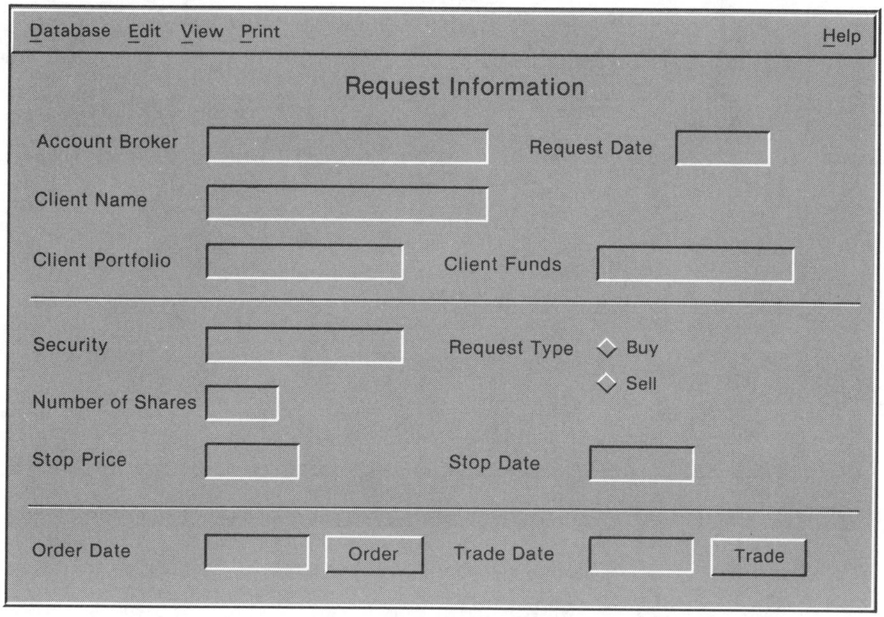

Figure 16-18A.   Screen Form for Creating a New *Request*.

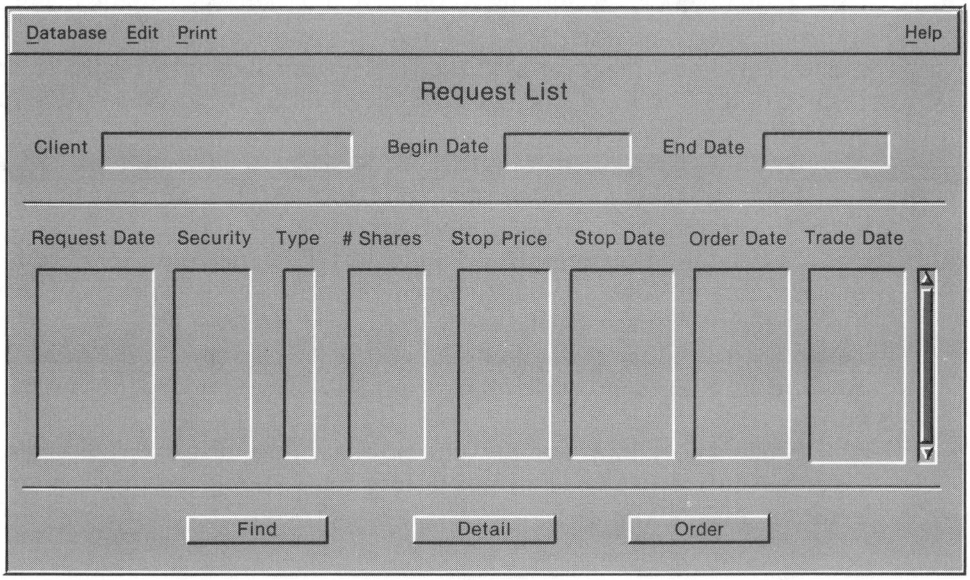

Figure 16-18B.   Screen Form for Listing Outstanding Requests.

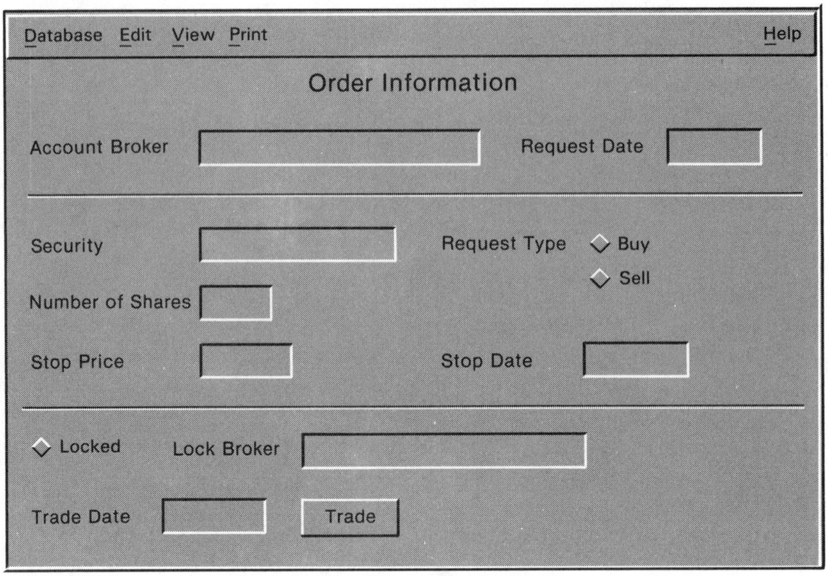

Figure 16-18C. Order Information Screen Form.

When the *Order* push-button is pushed, a new screen form shown in Figure 16-18C is displayed.

Figure 16-18D describes the open order list screen. The column on the left lists all open orders and the columns on the right display the detail for the each order. Note that the screen form for reviewing or modifying open requests is almost identical with the screen form shown in Figure 16-18B. Instead of the *Order List*, the window on the left is set for *Request List* and shows all open requests.

On completion of a trade, the order is marked completed on the completed trades window described in Figure 16-18E, and the system performs the necessary accounting functions.

The trading history screen, Figure 16-18F, allows the user to look at recent trades (by date range) for a specific FloorBroker or a specific security. The cursor rests on a specific entry in the *List of Trades* window, and the details for that trade are highlighted in the detail columns on the right. The cursor control keys or the scroll bars (and a mouse) are used to move the cursor.

Brokers need to frequently look up share price history. The screen in Figure 16-18G is used to look up history for a specific security or for all securities in an exchange.

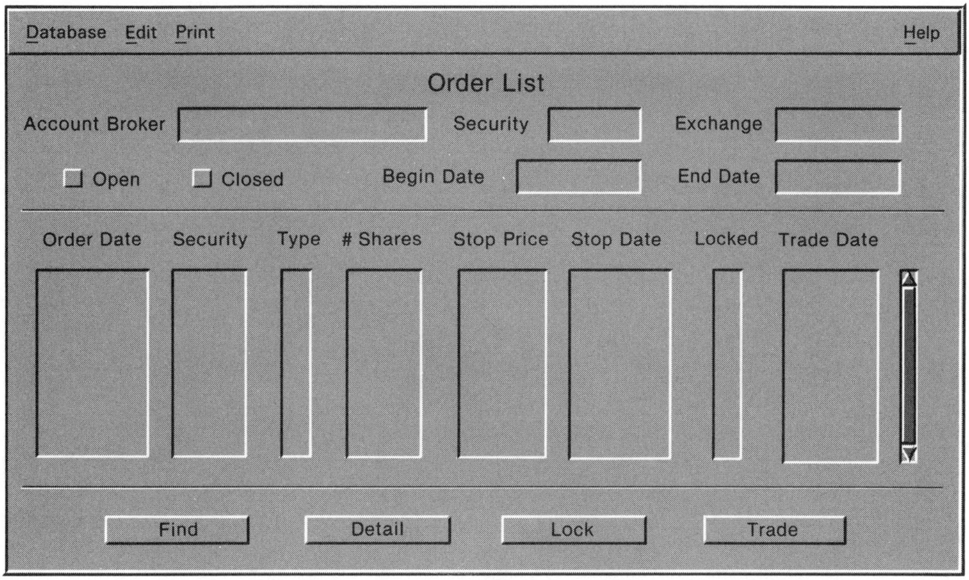

Figure 16-18D.   Review or Modify Open Orders Screen Form.

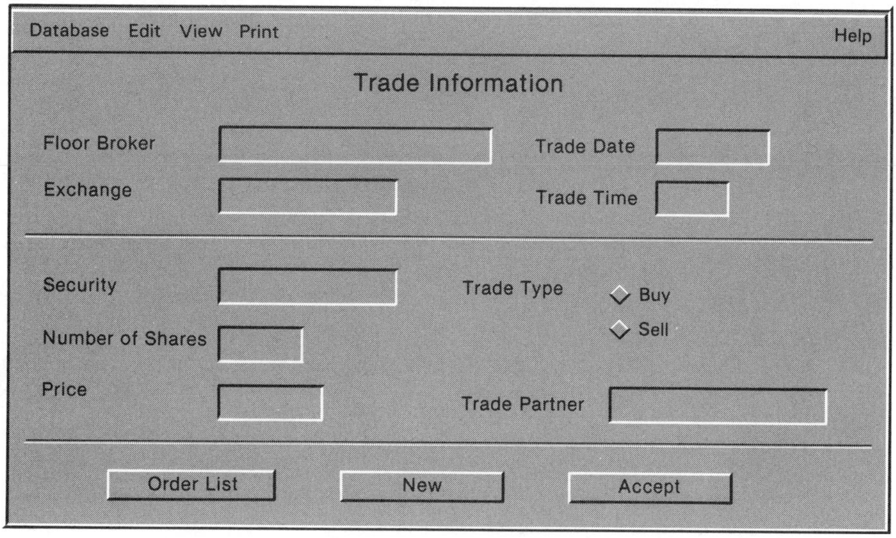

Figure 16-18E.   Form Window for Recording a Trade.

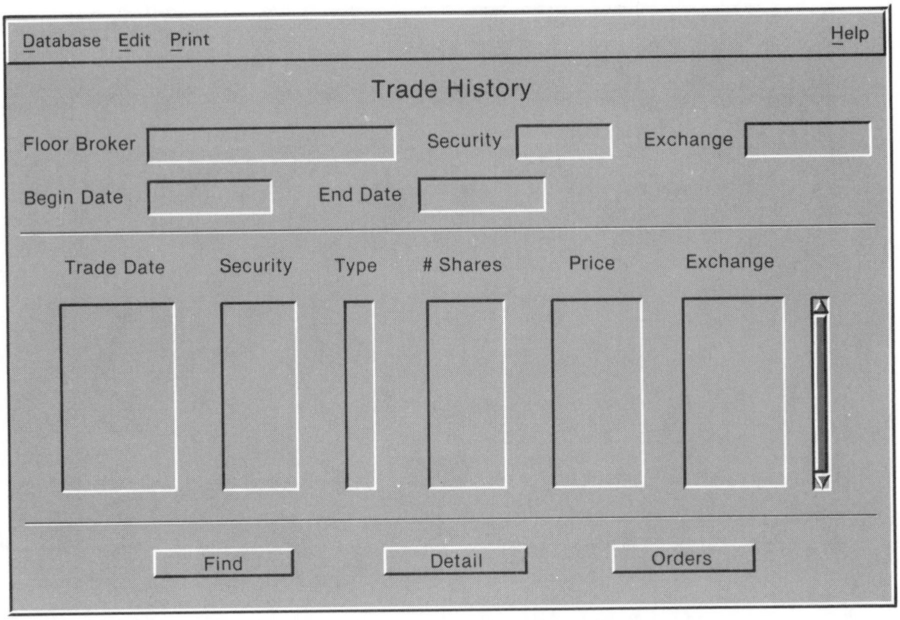

Figure 16-18F. View Trading History Screen Form.

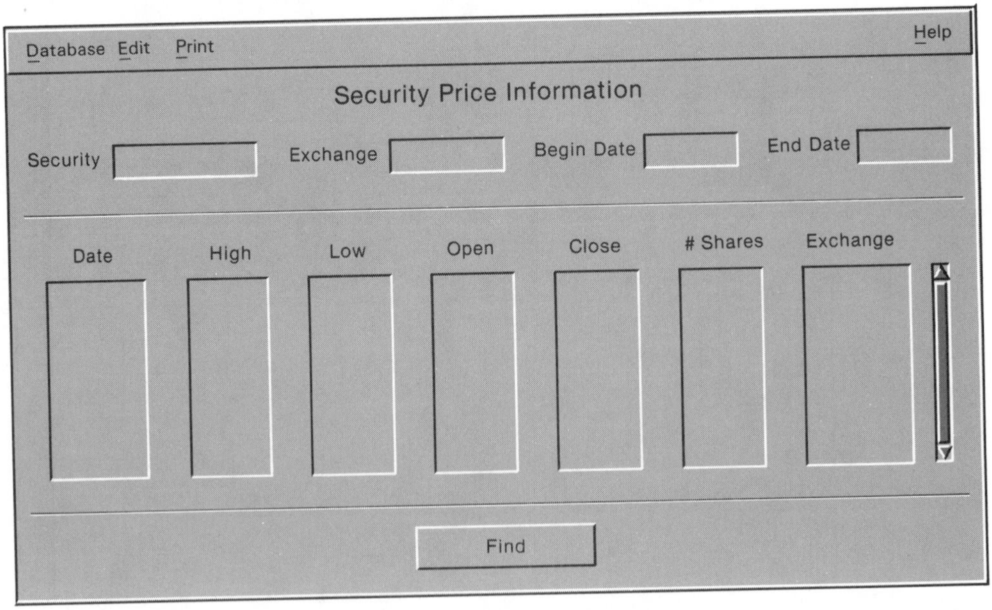

Figure 16-18G. View Security Prices Screen Form.

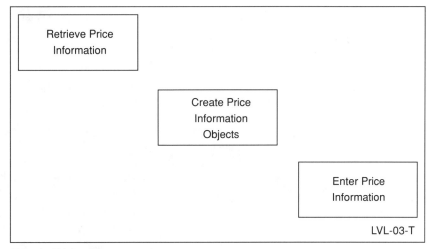

Security Pricing Management

Figure 16-19.   Security Pricing Management Frame.

4. **Security pricing management:** A major activity of the TMS application is managing daily security price updates. Figure 16-19 depicts the frame for Security Pricing Management. This frame, although very simple, is important for evaluating the performance of client portfolios over a period of time. Note that Section 16.3 presents code to address the functions noted in this frame. Obviously, this function by itself only creates and stores the pricing information objects. These objects, as we have just seen in the trading functions example, are accessed from other functions within the application.

You will notice when you study the code examples in Section 16.3 that a number of methods are associated with each object in the frame. Figure 16-19 describes one approach to using the next level of decomposition as a means of describing the methods as the components within an object.

We have now covered some of the key functions in the examples above. We leave it as an exercise to the reader to use this model and complete the frames and screen forms for the rest of the application functions (including Accounting Functions, Reference Code Management, and System Administration).

16.2 OBJECT MODEL

As defined in Chapter 8, the Object Model (Figure 16-20) is used to describe the underlying objects that provide the functionality visible externally to the user.

Structural Model	Behavioral Model

* Description of the underlying objects.
* Listing of the attributes of each under-
   lying object.
* Relationships among objects including
   links, hierarchy, and inclusion within
   other objects.
* Descriptions of classes and inheritance.
	* Representation of every function defined
	   in the transaction model.
	* Descriptions of higher-level operations
	   that invoke the low-level operations of
	   one or more objects for performing a
	   complex task (possibly recursively).
	* Descriptions of low-level operations that
	   can be performed on each object type.
	* Descriptions of functions at the Transac-
	   tion Model level that may directly invoke
	   a low-level operation at the lower-level
	   objects.

Figure 16-20.   Components of the Object Model.

The objects, in themselves, are not necessarily visible to the user. The following describes the components of the Object Model:

Object Model: while there are other definitions for the term Object Model, in our view it describes the structure and the behavior of objects that are constituents of an application. The Object Model consists of the Structural Model and the Behavioral Model.

Structural Model: describes the structural properties of objects from a static perspective. These properties include the logical elements of the objects required for the application.

Behavioral Model: describes the behavioral abstractions, that is, the set of rules for combining abstract operations into higher-level abstract operations.

Note that the Structural Model can be used for both relational and object-oriented databases. The Behavioral Model, while being directly applicable to object-oriented databases, can shed some important perspectives in the design of the 4GL or 3GL code in a relational database application.

Object Design Methodology.   The structural part of the objects is somewhat straightforward for designers very familiar with database schema designs. One must nonetheless remember that objects also include methods, and in some cases direct translations from entities in the Information Model to objects in the

Object Model may not be totally applicable. The detailed object design methodology was presented in Chapter 8. The methodology for designing objects as presented in Chapter 8 must be applied to the TMS application at this stage for classifying attributes and operations. The key steps are summarized here for convenience (we recommend that readers go back and review the detailed methodology at this time).

- Each structural object is documented and its attributes are determined.
- The principles of *classification* are used to determine if any objects have identical properties and can be resolved into a single object.
- The principles of *generalization* are used to determine similarities that lower-level objects must inherit and if objects can be decomposed through the principles of classification.
- The principles of *association* are used to group hitherto unrelated objects in related sets (or classes).
- The principles of *localization* are used to *aggregate* objects to model each property of an application function independently in a localized manner. Frames are created that combine the lower levels of objects into atomic subfunctions required for the application.
- Frames are developed for each function of the application.
- Structural and behavioral mapping is performed to create objects and describe them, along with their attributes, instance methods, and class methods.
- Each frame is checked to ensure that it is correct and that the model fully meets the requirements.

In the following two sections, we will illustrate how the Information Model developed in Section 16.1 is used as a basis for developing the Object Model. The information collected and categorized for the Information Model is analyzed, and based on the analysis steps noted above, the application objects are derived from the real-world objects. They are abstractions of the real-world objects.

Readers will find it very useful to perform the analysis steps noted above as an exercise for the TMS application. For the most part, we will present the results of our analysis (rather than the analysis itself). Note that classifications and aggregations can be subjective and can lead to potentially different results for the same application.

16.2.1 Structural Model

Section 16.1.1 described a number of entities as seen by the user. Using this information, we will define the underlying object classes that support these high-level entities. For the most part, the entities can be translated almost directly to objects. One must nonetheless remember that objects also include methods, and in some cases direct translations may not be totally applicable.

The structural definitions of the data model consist of definitions of all main object classes. These are the primary entities that will be used in the system. The objects at the lowest level can then be defined using the concepts of inheritance. For the TMS application, the following lists some of the major classes of structural objects:

- Trade
- Order
- Request
- Broker (account brokers as well as floor brokers)
- Client
- Security
- Transaction

These object classes and their attributes are defined in this section. The classes of objects can then be decomposed further. The methods for the objects are defined in the next section.

Figure 16-2 has been reproduced here as Figure 16-21. While not always the case, in this example, the entities defined in Figure 16-2 can be logically translated to the object classes described in Figure 16-21. Each entity described in this frame is a basic object class. Some of these object classes can be decomposed further as shown in Figure 16-22. This, in fact, demonstrates the class hierarchy for the

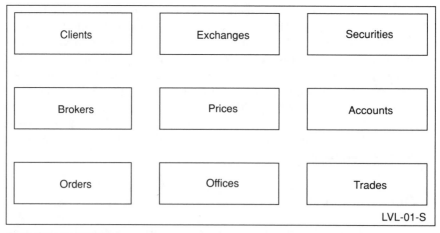

Basic Objects for TMS

Figure 16-21.   Basic Building Blocks Structural Frame.

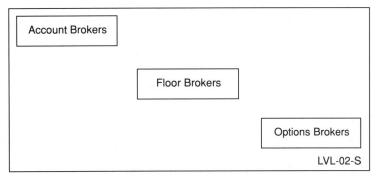

Class Hierarchy for BROKERS

Figure 16-22. Decompositon of Object Class *Brokers*.

object class *Brokers*. Multiple levels of class hierarchy can be depicted in a similar manner using multilevel frames. Note that this is a replication of Figure 16-3.

As in the case of entities, we can show the relationship between objects. Once again, we have replicated Figure 16-4 as Figure 16-23. One may wonder why this process of replication is being used. You may recall that relational databases address primarily the structural components. Consequently, the procedures used for describing a relational database are very similar to those for the structural components of an object oriented database. Furthermore, entities are defined from a user perspective, while object classes are defined from a design

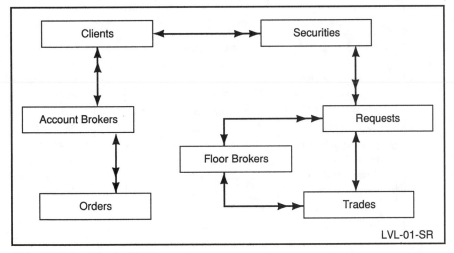

Object Relationships for TMS

Figure 16-23. Representing Object Relationships.

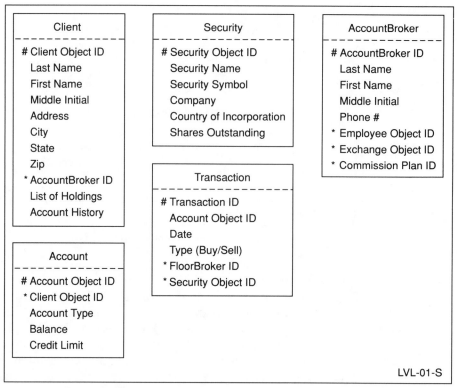

Objects for TMS Application (1)

Figure 16-24. Object Classes for the TMS Application.

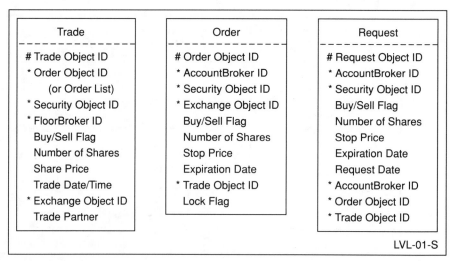

Objects for TMS Application (2)

Figure 16-25. More Object Classes for the TMS Application.

perspective. Usually, there is a high level of correspondence, though not necessarily so.

Define object classes.   To define object classes, we go back to Figures 16-5 and 16-6, where we defined the attributes for some of the important entities required for the TMS application. We will again use frames to depict the object classes. Figures 16-24 and 16-25 describe some of the object classes required for the TMS application. We encourage the reader to develop the frames for the rest of the object classes as an exercise.

Note that during the modeling phase we do not need to determine the attribute characteristics (such as datatypes). These characteristics are determined as a part of the design phase (described in Section 16.3).

Figure 16-26 describes the next level in the hierarchy for object class *Client.* Note that the *List of Accounts* and *Portfolio List* are aggregated to the *Client* object. These two object classes are contained within the *Client* object.

The examples above were intended to present the methodology and are neither complete nor exhaustive in terms of attributes necessary for real-world objects. We encourage the reader to add the objects and attributes necessary to make this example a more realistic application.

The Structural Model will be complete when all objects and their attributes at all hierarchical levels required for the TMS application have been defined. The frames developed are grouped and cataloged to complete the documentation for the Structural Model.

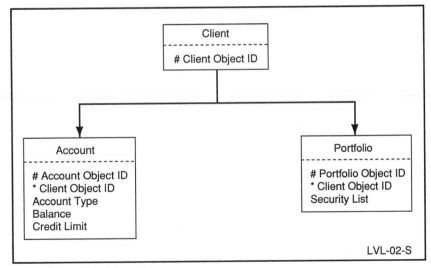

Client Object Class Hierarchy

Figure 16-26.   Representing Object Hierarchies.

16.2.2 Behavioral Model

The Behavioral Model is the second component of the Object Model. The Behavioral Model consists of the following main components:

- Description of every function at the lowest menu level. These functions invoke methods in objects.
- Descriptions of the methods of the base-level objects.
- Descriptions of higher-level operations that invoke the low-level operations of one or more objects for performing a complex task (possibly recursively). This describes the hierarchy of objects in terms of the methods within the objects.

The *behavioral* Frame-Object Analysis diagrams describe the functions of the application system (that is, how the system behaves). The top-level frame therefore describes the methods that directly support the lowest-level menu functions. The basic analysis necessary to determine the frames at this level consists primarily of determining the lowest-level menu function for each operational group of functions.

All information systems have processes that are followed from start to finish. For example, the *trading process* consists of the account broker taking the request from the customer and creating an order, and the floor broker selecting and locking an order, and creating a trade object on completion of trade to record the transaction. Similarly, there are other processes, such as creating a new client account, creating a new broker account, and performing month-end accounting functions. All these processes must be analyzed in detail for developing the behavioral model. Frames can be used to describe process flows. These frames help in determining the operations needed at each stage of the process.

Process flows.   The frame described in Figure 16-27 can be used to actually show the sequence of trading functions, as depicted. This new frame presents the most powerful feature of the Frame-Object Analysis methodology, the ability to show structural and behavioral objects and the relationships among them. This shows how a frame can be used to describe a process. The use of this capability is crucial for data-flow analysis. Figure 16-27 actually shows the complete sequence of operations from the creation of a client order until the trade is completed. All major intermediary steps are described in the frame. The entity performing the function is shown in parentheses. Intermediate steps can be blown up in their own frames for a more detailed design. This methodology serves not only to document the conceptual model, but also to document the application design.

A number of other functions are described in the top-level frame in Figure 16-2. We will leave it as an exercise for the reader to develop the frames showing the data flows for all other functions, such as creating a new client account or

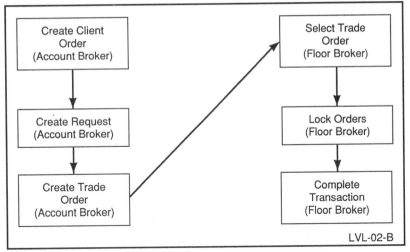

Sequence of Operations for Security Trading

Figure 16-27.   Security Trading Sequence Frame.

printing periodic statements. The completion of this task will complete the conceptual model for the TMS application.

Top-level behavioral frames.   The first step in determining the top-level frames is to list the lowest-level menu functions for each operational group. Remember, our definition requires that the operations directly supporting menu (or function key level) functions are a part of the Behavioral Model. Consequently, each operation at this level will become a part of an object class. We will demonstrate an approach for developing the behavioral frames using the *Review/ Modify Existing Client (Client Account Management)* and *Security Trading Functions* processes.

1. *Review/Modify Existing Client:* These functions set up the general information about clients and brokers. Client management functions include the following:

   • For "Manage Client Object"
        —Create client object (for *Creating New Account*)
        —View client object
        —Update client object
   • For "Add/View/Update Subaccounts"
        —Add new subaccount
        —View client subaccount
        —Update client subaccount

- For "Add/View/Update Portfolios"
  —Add new portfolio
  —View client portfolio
  —Update client portfolio
- For "Add/View/Update Broker List"
  —Add primary account broker
  —Add broker to list
  —View broker list
  —Update broker list
- For "Return to Menu One Level Up"
  —Exit current function

The client account management functions are basic to any trading system. The details of these functions may differ from one system to another, but generic functions remain the same. The functions listed above can be listed in a frame as shown in Figure 16-28.

The top-level frame for *Broker Management* functions is very similar to the frame for *Client Account Management*. We leave it as an exercise for the reader to build that frame.

2. *Securities Trading Functions:* Trading functions are concerned primarily with the sale or purchase of stocks at a client's request. The primary functions for trading are as follows:

- Create client request
- Create trade order (for floor broker to execute)
- Modify orders not executed
- Record completed trades

Other actions are performed automatically as a result of one of the above actions. These include the following:

- Account management for source of funds for a buy or disposition of funds from a sale
- Assign commissions according to broker and client profiles
- View and print list of open trade orders and completed trades by day, week, month, year (or date range)

Figure 16-29 presents a sample frame behavioral frame for the operations for the Security Trading functions. Note that by reducing the functions to frames in this manner it becomes much simpler to determine the lower-level functions that must be set up for the methods within the objects in the Behavioral Model.

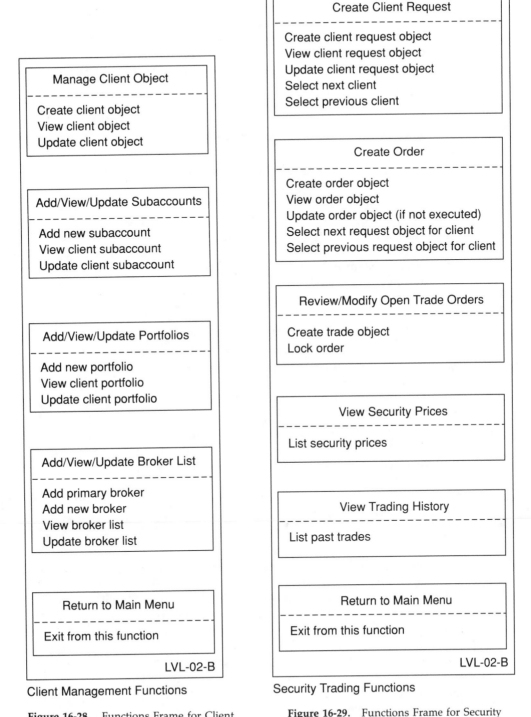

Manage Client Object
- - - - - - - - - - - - - - - - - - - -
Create client object
View client object
Update client object

Add/View/Update Subaccounts
- - - - - - - - - - - - - - - - - - - -
Add new subaccount
View client subaccount
Update client subaccount

Add/View/Update Portfolios
- - - - - - - - - - - - - - - - - - - -
Add new portfolio
View client portfolio
Update client portfolio

Add/View/Update Broker List
- - - - - - - - - - - - - - - - - - - -
Add primary broker
Add new broker
View broker list
Update broker list

Return to Main Menu
- - - - - - - - - - - - - - - - - - - -
Exit from this function

LVL-02-B

Client Management Functions

Figure 16-28. Functions Frame for Client Management Functions.

Create Client Request
- - - - - - - - - - - - - - - - - - - -
Create client request object
View client request object
Update client request object
Select next client
Select previous client

Create Order
- - - - - - - - - - - - - - - - - - - -
Create order object
View order object
Update order object (if not executed)
Select next request object for client
Select previous request object for client

Review/Modify Open Trade Orders
- - - - - - - - - - - - - - - - - - - -
Create trade object
Lock order

View Security Prices
- - - - - - - - - - - - - - - - - - - -
List security prices

View Trading History
- - - - - - - - - - - - - - - - - - - -
List past trades

Return to Main Menu
- - - - - - - - - - - - - - - - - - - -
Exit from this function

LVL-02-B

Security Trading Functions

Figure 16-29. Functions Frame for Security Trading Functions.

3. *Securities Pricing History Management:* This function not only tracks the master record for securities that describes the type of security (and includes general security information), but also tracks daily pricing information on securities. The general information component of this consists of the following functions:

- Adding, updating, and deleting securities from the master file
- Changing securities information due to capitalization changes and dividends
- Updating and viewing current prices and foreign exchange information

For each security, the securities pricing history function maintains the high, low, open, close, bid, and asked information at the close of each business day at the stock exchange. Obviously, this will become a very significantly large storage requirement for a company tracking 10,000 securities (for example, 10,000 × 260 days × 3 years = 7.8 million records) to store just three years of data. The types of functions required for managing this data are as follows:

- Storing and retrieving pricing information
- Normalizing this information based on foreign exchange rate changes as well as capitalization changes (for example, stock splits) if any
- Performing statistical analysis for client newsletters (or to address client phone inquiries)

Due to the complexity of storage and access, especially for a relational or an object-oriented database, we have chosen this as one of the key topics for which we will demonstrate design and coding examples.

We suggest that the reader use the list of functions described above and build the behavioral frame for this function.

Basic objects for the TMS application.   From the Structural Model, we know that a number of object classes have been defined. We now use the functions frames developed above and the Transaction Model to determine the methods for each object class. The following figures describe the frames for the basic objects required for the TMS application. The attributes are really not a part of the Behavioral Model, but are listed here only for convenience so that the readers do not need to keep flipping back to the structural definitions. You will also notice that the model does not attempt to define the calling sequences or datatypes. These issues are addressed during the system design phase (Section 16.3). You should also note that the base object ID is not included in these frames as they are a basic attribute in an ODBMS.

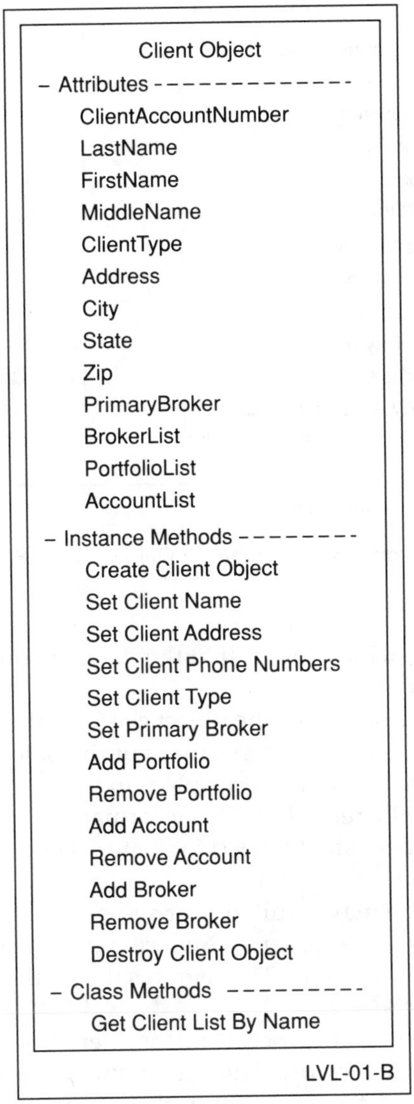

```
                    Client Object
    - Attributes - - - - - - - - - - - -
        ClientAccountNumber
        LastName
        FirstName
        MiddleName
        ClientType
        Address
        City
        State
        Zip
        PrimaryBroker
        BrokerList
        PortfolioList
        AccountList
    - Instance Methods - - - - - - - -
        Create Client Object
        Set Client Name
        Set Client Address
        Set Client Phone Numbers
        Set Client Type
        Set Primary Broker
        Add Portfolio
        Remove Portfolio
        Add Account
        Remove Account
        Add Broker
        Remove Broker
        Destroy Client Object
    - Class Methods  - - - - - - - - -
        Get Client List By Name

                                 LVL-01-B
```

Object Client

Figure 16-30.   Frame for Object Class *Client.*

The *Client* object frame is described in Figure 16-30. You will notice that the *methods* are separated into *instance methods* and *class methods*. The class methods perform operations on many object instances of the class at the same time. Instance methods, on the other hand, perform functions on individual objects.

Similarly, we can develop the frames for the general classes for *Account* and *Portfolio* object as illustrated in Figure 16-31. Note that Figure 16-26 presented the

Account Object

– Attributes – – – – – – – – – – – –

    ClientObjectID

    AccountType

    Balance

    CreditLimit

– Instance Methods – – – – – –

    Create Account

    Debit Charges

    Credit Payments

    Set Credit Limit

    Destroy Account Object

Portfolio Object

– Attributes – – – – – – – – – – – – .

    ClientObjectID

    SecurityHoldingsList

    Description

– Instance Methods – – – – – – – .

    Create Portfolio

    Add Security Count (Holdings)

    Modify Security Count

    Remove Security

    Destroy Portfolio Object

    Set Description

LVL-02-B

Objects Account and Portfolio

Figure 16-31.   Frame for Object Classes *Account* and *Portfolio.*

object hierarchy, which shows that the *Account* and *Portfolio* objects are contained within the *Client* object.

Figure 16-32 describes the object class for all securities. Note that, as before, operations such as listing all instances of the object class are class methods.

Every transaction that takes place in the system, such as a credit or debit to an account, must be recorded. This information is recorded in a transaction object and stored (as a persistent object) for historical purposes. Figure 16-33 describes a transaction object.

A transaction may result in the creation of a credit memo if the account has a credit balance (after a sale) or an invoice if the account has insufficient balance to cover a purchase. Figure 16-34 illustrates the methods required for the *Invoice* and *CreditMemo* objects.

End of the month processing for every account causes a statement to be generated for each account. The statement is stored in an object that includes a complete list of all transactions applied to that account during the statement period. Figure 16-35 describes the object class for *Statements.*

We have discussed the roles of the *AccountBroker* and *FloorBroker* objects quite extensively already. Figure 16-36 describes the object classes for the two subclasses of the object class *Broker.*

Each broker object has associated with it a *CommissionPlan* object that describes the commission structure for the broker. Figure 16-37 describes the *CommissionPlan* object. Note that no class method is defined at this time since commission plans are read individually and no operations are defined that must be applied to the class.

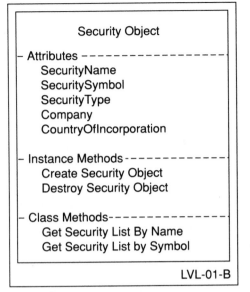

Object Security

Figure 16-32.   Frame for Object Class *Security*.

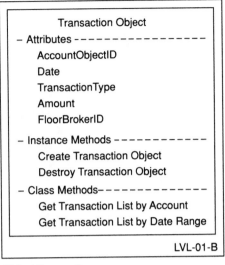

Object Transaction

Figure 16-33.   Frame for Object Class *Transaction*.

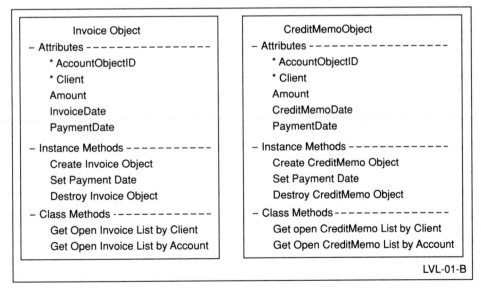

Objects Invoice and Credit Memo

Figure 16-34.   Frame for Object Classes *Invoice* and *CreditMemo*.

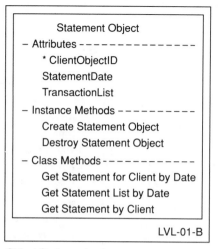

```
         Statement Object
  – Attributes – – – – – – – – – – – –
      * ClientObjectID
      StatementDate
      TransactionList
  – Instance Methods – – – – – – – – –
      Create Statement Object
      Destroy Statement Object
  – Class Methods – – – – – – – – – – –
      Get Statement for Client by Date
      Get Statement List by Date
      Get Statement by Client

                              LVL-01-B
```

Object Statement

Figure 16-35. Frame for Object Class *Statement.*

```
      AccountBroker Object                        FloorBroker Object

  – Attributes – – – – – – – – – – – –        – Attributes – – – – – – – – – – – –
      LastName                                     LastName
      FirstName                                    FirstName
      MiddleName                                   MiddleName
      Office                                       Office
      PhoneNumber                                  * Exchange
      EmployeeID                                   PhoneNumber
      CommissionPlanList                           EmployeeID
      ClientList                                   CommissionPlanList


  – Instance Methods – – – – – – – – –        – Instance Methods – – – – – – – – –
      Create AccountBroker Object                  Create FloorBroker Object
      Set Name                                     Set Name
      Set Office                                   Set Office
      Set Phone Number                             Set Exchange
      Add Commission Plan                          Set Phone Number
      Remove Commission Plan                       Add Commission Plan
      Add Client to Client List                    Remove Commission Plan
      Remove Client from Client List               Destroy FloorBroker Object
      Destroy AccountBroker Object             – Class Methods – – – – – – – – – –
  – Class Methods – – – – – – – – – – –           Get FloorBroker by Name
      Get AccountBroker List by Name

                                                                      LVL-02-B
```

Objects AccountBroker and FloorBroker

Figure 16-36. Frame for Object Classes *AccountBroker* and *FloorBroker.*

420

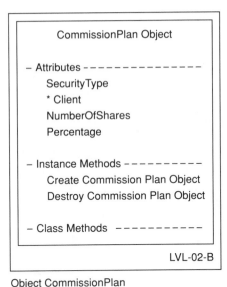

Object CommissionPlan

Figure 16-37.   Frame for Object Class *CommissionPlan.*

Figure 16-38 describes the object class *Request.* This object class is used for setting up requests for a trade. An account broker uses this object to set up a request object when a customer places a buy or sell order.

The object class for all orders is class *Order.* Figure 16-39 describes the attributes and methods associated with the object class *Order.* The object class *Order* is used by the account broker for placing a trade order. The floor broker then executes the trade order when the conditions for the trade are appropriate.

The class *Trade* is the object class for all trades. The attributes and the methods for the class *Trade* are described in Figure 16-40.

We have developed frames for a number of objects for this Behavioral Model. The primary purpose of this exercise was to demonstrate the methodology. Obviously, this model can be made more complete by performing a deeper analysis. For readers interested in pursuing this further, developing the rest of the object frames would be a very rewarding exercise.

We will now use this model in the next section to demonstrate how the Behavioral Model and the structural components included in the frames for the Behavioral Model are translated into a design.

16.3 SYSTEM DESIGN

As we said in Chapter 8, modeling provides a visual perspective about the structural and behavioral components of an information system. The intermediate step of system design is necessary to convert a model into code for an information system. The system design describes the datatypes, calling sequences for functions (or methods), returns from functions, and management of

```
┌─────────────────────────────────────┐
│  ┌────────────────────────────────┐  │
│  │        Request Object          │  │
│  │                                │  │
│  │  - Attributes - - - - - - - -  │  │
│  │      * AccountBroker           │  │
│  │      * Client                  │  │
│  │      * Security                │  │
│  │      BuySellIndicator          │  │
│  │      NumberOfShares            │  │
│  │      StopPrice                 │  │
│  │      ExpirationDate            │  │
│  │      Request Date              │  │
│  │      FundSource                │  │
│  │      FundDisposition           │  │
│  │      * Order                   │  │
│  │      * Trade                   │  │
│  │                                │  │
│  │  - Instance Methods - - - - -  │  │
│  │      Create Request Object     │  │
│  │      Set Client (add to list)  │  │
│  │      Set Security Level        │  │
│  │      Set Buy Sell Indicator    │  │
│  │      Set Number of Shares      │  │
│  │      Set Stop Price            │  │
│  │      Set Expiration Date       │  │
│  │      Set Fund Source           │  │
│  │      Set Fund Disposition      │  │
│  │      Mark Order Completed      │  │
│  │      Destroy Request Object    │  │
│  │                                │  │
│  │  - Class Methods - - - - - - - │  │
│  │      Get Open Requests by AccountBroker │  │
│  │      Get Open Requests by Client │  │
│  │      Get Request List by Date  │  │
│  │                                │  │
│  │                      LVL-01-B  │  │
│  └────────────────────────────────┘  │
└─────────────────────────────────────┘
```

Object Request

Figure 16-38.   Frame for Object Class *Request*.

```
┌─────────────────────────────────────┐
│  ┌────────────────────────────────┐  │
│  │        Order Object            │  │
│  │  - Attributes - - - - - - - -  │  │
│  │      * AccountBroker           │  │
│  │      * Security                │  │
│  │      * Exchange                │  │
│  │      BuySellIndicator          │  │
│  │      NumberOfShares            │  │
│  │      StopPrice                 │  │
│  │      ExpirationDate            │  │
│  │      LockFlag                  │  │
│  │      * Trade                   │  │
│  │                                │  │
│  │  - Instance Methods - - - - -  │  │
│  │      Create Order Object       │  │
│  │      Set Security Level        │  │
│  │      Set Exchange (where traded) │  │
│  │      Set Buy Sell Indicator    │  │
│  │      Set Number of Shares      │  │
│  │      Set Stop Price            │  │
│  │      Set Expiration Date       │  │
│  │      Lock Order                │  │
│  │      Unlock Order              │  │
│  │      TradeCompleted            │  │
│  │      Destroy Order Object      │  │
│  │                                │  │
│  │  - Class Methods - - - - - - - │  │
│  │      Get Open Order List by AccountBroker │  │
│  │      Get Open Order List by Exchange │  │
│  │      Get Open Order List by Security │  │
│  │      Get Order List by Date    │  │
│  │                                │  │
│  │                      LVL-01-B  │  │
│  └────────────────────────────────┘  │
└─────────────────────────────────────┘
```

Object Order

Figure 16-39.   Frame for Object Class *Order*.

exception conditions. The system design guides the programmer at a very detailed level and ensures that the information system will meet the expected
requirements.

Using frames for design.   We have so far looked at frames from the
behavioral and structural perspectives. Real designs consist of both structural

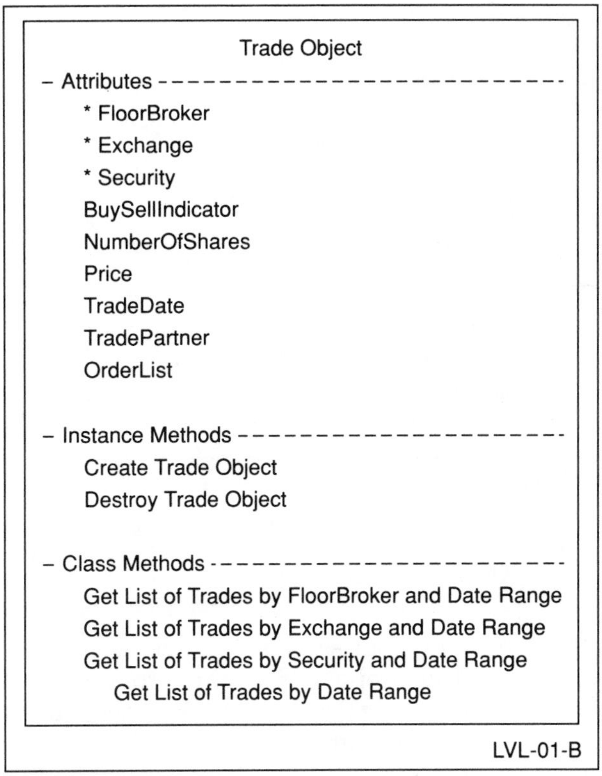

```
+-----------------------------------------------------------+
|                      Trade Object                         |
|  - Attributes - - - - - - - - - - - - - - - - - - - - -   |
|          * FloorBroker                                    |
|          * Exchange                                       |
|          * Security                                       |
|          BuySellIndicator                                 |
|          NumberOfShares                                   |
|          Price                                            |
|          TradeDate                                        |
|          TradePartner                                     |
|          OrderList                                        |
|                                                           |
|  - Instance Methods - - - - - - - - - - - - - - - - - -   |
|          Create Trade Object                              |
|          Destroy Trade Object                             |
|                                                           |
|  - Class Methods - - - - - - - - - - - - - - - - - - -    |
|          Get List of Trades by FloorBroker and Date Range |
|          Get List of Trades by Exchange and Date Range    |
|          Get List of Trades by Security and Date Range    |
|             Get List of Trades by Date Range              |
|                                                           |
|                                                LVL-01-B   |
+-----------------------------------------------------------+
```

Object Trade

Figure 16-40.   Frame for Object Class *Trade.*

and behavioral components. The Frame-Object Analysis diagrams can also be used to provide the design perspective, in addition to the structural and behavioral perspectives of the Object Model.

The frame depicted in Figure 16-41 illustrates the use of Frame-Object Analysis diagrams for this purpose. It shows the objects involved in a trade and shows the functional flow associating these objects. This frame can obviously be decomposed further for more detailed design descriptions.

Figure 16-42 describes the components of an information system design. As in the case of the Information System Model and the Object Model, the design also has structural and behavioral components. However, the structural and behavioral components must be designed at the same time. For example, the attributes and methods must be designed for an object at the same time to fully define an object. Designing structural and behavioral components separately can become very confusing.

Rather than perform a full-scale detailed design here, we will design the objects and demonstrate how code is developed from the design. The layout of

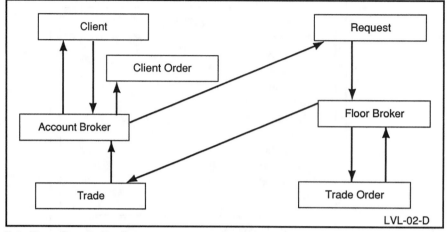

Data Flow - Security Trading

Figure 16-41.   Security Trading Design Frame.

menus, screen forms, and reports was developed in the Transaction Model. The design of menus, forms, and reports is primarily concerned with determining the processing of the contents of attributes within objects that satisfy the requirements of the application. For example, the processing may consist of calculations of percentage change in the value of a portfolio over a specific period of time. The design is performed by relating the processing information determined in the Transaction Model (as it related to entities and data elements within entities) to objects and attributes within objects. The algorithms used for this translation are documented in a design specification describing the forms and reports.

Design of Structural Part of Objects	Design of Behavioral Part of Objects
* Descriptions of object attributes in terms of low-level datatypes. * Definition of data objects by combining attributes and operations into real database objects. (This sets up the objects for object creation.) * Detailed definition and relationships among classes.	* Definition of each operation and its input and output parameters. * Denotation of what functions and operations are called by other functions and operations. * Representation of all messages between objects.

Figure 16-42.   Design of Object-oriented Database.

16.3.1 Designing Objects

There are two parts to designing objects: determining the size and datatypes of attributes and designing the behavioral components of objects. We could have presented the design in the form of pseudocode using some of the classical design methodologies. However, we have chosen to show the design by using code examples to make this methodology more readily usable by a large majority of programmers.

The examples of class definitions are depicted using the object-oriented programming language C++. It is assumed that all the object method code will be executed on the object server and that all objects created are persistent objects; that is, they permanently reside on the object server. The definitions of the parameters passed to and returned by the object methods depict an interface as might exist in a standard C++ application running on a single machine. In a distributed environment, the interface may differ somewhat depending on the nature and transparency of the remote procedure call implementation.

The class definitions assume the existence of several common utility objects. The *String* object represents variable-length character strings and contains methods for creating string objects from quoted strings, existing string objects, and concatenations of string objects, updating string objects, retrieving substrings and string lengths, and destroying string objects. *Vec* objects (or vector objects) contain variable-length lists of other objects. The notation *Vec(Class)* is used to indicate the types of objects contained by a particular Vec object. This is an example of a parameterized object class. Vec objects use the operators + = and − = to add and remove objects from the vector. The vector object is automatically resized to accommodate new elements. Methods are provided for returning the number of elements in a vector and for iterating through the elements of a vector.

In C++, object attributes can either be publicly readable and writable or completely private, accessible only through object methods. In these examples, we are assuming the ability to allow public read access to all object attributes (unless declared in a private section), while requiring that all updates to attributes be performed through an object's methods.

In the C language, the /* . . . */ combination is used for comments. The C++ language allows this C language structure for comments and also adds a new type of comment structure as // . . ⌐ENTER⌐. In this new comment type, the comment line is terminated by a line terminator (usually the ENTER key). The code examples used in the following use this type of comment extensively. The comments within the code are intended to make the code self-explanatory.

Object class hierarchies and instances.   In the examples above, we have seen three cases of object class hierarchies. These can be described as shown below in Figure 16-43, which illustrates how a hierarchy of object classes can be set up.

Class	Subclass	Subclass
Client	Individual	Regular Margin account
	Business	Regular Special commission Electronic trading
Broker	Account broker	Individual Business
	Floor broker	Stocks Bonds Options
Security	Stocks	NYSE NASDAQ
	Bonds	Annuity Null coupon Fixed interest
	Warrants	
	Options	Call Put
Transaction	Purchase	
	Sale	

Figure 16-43.   Object Class Hierarchies.

Client object.   The *Client* object consists of the general information about a client. In addition, it embodies arrays containing portfolio lists, account lists, and broker lists. No private methods are defined for the *Client* object. You will notice that this design follows directly from Figures 16-30 and 16-31. The datatypes for the attributes are defined. For each method within the *Client* object, the attributes passed to the method are defined.

The following C++ code demonstrates the creation and use of the *Client* Object:

```
CLIENT OBJECT
enum ClientType {CT_UNDEFINED, CT_INDIVIDUAL, CT_CORPORATE};

class Client {
    String Last_name;
    String first_name;
```

```
                String middle_name;
                ClientType client_type;
                String address;
                String city;
                String state;
                String zip;
                String day_phone;
                String eve_phone;
                AccountBroker * primary_broker;
                Vec(AccountBroker) broker_list;
                Vec(Portfolio) portfolio_list;
                Vec(Account) account_list;

        public:
                // Create a new Client object
                Client(String & p_last_name, String & p_first_name, String & p_middle_name,
                        String & p_client_type, String & p_address, String & p_city, String &
                        p_state, String & p_zip, String & p_day_phone, String & p_eve_phone,
                        AccountBroker * p_primary_broker)

                // Destroy a Client object
                ~Client();

                // Methods for updating Client attributes
                void SetName(String & p_last_name, String & p_first_name, String & p_middle_name);
                void Setaddress(String & p_address, String & p_city, String & p_state, String & p_zip);
                void SetPhoneNumbers(string & p_day_phone, String & p_eve_phone);
                void SetClientType(ClientType p_client_type);
                void Setprimary_broker(AccountBroker * p_broker);

                // Methods for adding or removing Portfolio objects
                void AddPortfolio(Portfolio * p_portfolio);
                void RemovePortfolio(Portfolio * p_portfolio);

                // Methods for adding or removing Account objects
                void AddAccount(Account * p_account);
                void RemoveAccount(Account * p_account);

                // Methods for adding or removing AccountBroker objects
                void AddBroker(AccountBroker * p_broker);
                void RemoveBroker(AccountBroker * p_broker);

                // Method for applying the results of a Trade to Client accounts
                void RequestCompleted(Request *p_request, DateTime p_trade_date, Money p_price,
                                Money p_commission);

                // Class Methods for retrieving Client objects
                static void GetClientByName(String & last_name, Vec(Client) & client_vec);
        }
```

Once we have defined the object attribute datatypes and the methods with all parameters, the design of the object is complete. In other words, the code above shows the design of the object. In the following C++ code segments, we have used this design to show additional code examples to illustrate how the objects are created and destroyed. You will notice that additional setup code is required for calling each method defined in the design. The next code segment illustrates the creation and destruction of an object.

```
Client::Client(String & p_last_name, String & p_first_name, String & p_middle_name,
          String & p_client_type, String & p_address, String & p_city, String &
          p_state, String & p_zip, String & p_day_phone, String & p_eve_phone,
          AccountBroker * p_primary_broker)
{
    last_name = p_last_name;
    first_name = p_first_name;
    middle_name = p_middle_name;
    client_type = p_client_type;
    address = p_address;
    city = p_city;
    state = p_state;
    zip = p_zip;
    day_phone = p_day_phone;
    eve_phone = p_eve_phone;
    primary_broker = p_primary_broker;

    broker_list += primary_broker;

    Account * margin_account = new Account(AT_CLIENT_MARGIN, 0.0, 0.0);
    Account * mm_account = new Account(AT_CLIENT_MM, 0.0, 0.0);
    Account * port_account = new Account(AT_CLIENT_PORTFOLIO, 0.0, 0.0);

    account_list += margin_account;
    account_list += mm_account;
    account_list += port_account;

    dflt_portfolio = new Portfolio("Default", port_account);
    portfolio_list += dflt_portfolio;
}

Client::~Client()
{
    // Destroy the client account objects. It is assumed that the application has
    // already checked that the account balances are zero before destroying the
    // Client object.
    for (Account * account = account_list.First(); account; account =
        account_list.Next())
        delete account;
```

```
// Destroy the client portfolio objects.
for (Portfolio * portfolio = portfolio_list.First( ); portfolio; portfolio = portfolio_list.Next( ))
    delete portfolio;

// The AccountBroker objects in the broker_list will remain valid after the
// client object is deleted, so they must not be destroyed. All remaining
// attribute objects will be destroyed when the Client object is destroyed.
// Therefore, the destructor method is complete.
}
```

The following code segment illustrates the coding of the update of the attributes of the *Client* object after the *Client* object has been created.

```
void Client::SetName(String * p_last_name, String & p_first_name, String & p_middle_name)
{
    last_name = p_last_name;
    first_name = p_first_name;
    middle_name = p_middle_name;
}
```

The code segment above is used to update the client name as the three attributes in the *Client* object. Similarly, we can update all other attributes in the *Client* object.

```
void Client::SetAddress(String & p_address, String & p_city, String & p_state, String & p_zip)
{
    address = p_address;
    city = p_city;
    state = p_state;
    zip = p_zip;
}

void Client::SetPhoneNumbers(String & p_day_phone, String & p_eve_phone)
{
    day_phone = p_day_phone;
    eve_phone = p_eve_phone;
}

void SetClientType(ClientType p_client_type)
{
    // Actually this may be an immutable attribute, but assuming it's not . . .
    ClientType = ¬ client_type;
}
```

Note that the following code segments maintain the lists for brokers, accounts, and portfolios. The key difference to note here is that the parameter passed is an address rather than a variable, for example, * *p_broker*.

```
void Client::SetPrimary Broker(AccountBroker * p_broker)
{
    primary_broker = p_broker;
    if (!broker_list.Contains(p_broker)) broker_list += p_broker;
}


voidClient::AddPortfolio(Portfolio * p_portfolio)
{
    portfolio_list += p_portfolio;
}


void Client::RemovePortfolio(Portfolio * p_portfolio)
{
    portfolio_list -= p_portfolio;
}


void Client::AddAccount(Account * p_account)
{
    account_list += p_account;
}


void Client::RemoveAccount(Account * p_account)
{
    account_list -= p_account;
}


void Client::AddBroker(AccountBroker * p_broker)
{
    if (!broker_list.Contains(p_broker)) broker_list += p_broker;
}


void Client::RemoveBroker(AccountBroker * p_broker)
{
    if (broker_list.Contains(p_broker)) broker_list --= p_broker;
}
```

When a client order is executed, the *Trade* object causes some operations to take place to update the *Client* object. The following describes the operations on the *Client* object on completion of a trade request.

```
void Client::RequestCompleted(Request *p_request, DateTime p_trade_date, Money
                              p_price, Money p_commission)
{
    Security * sec = p_request->security;
    Portfolio * port = p_request ->client_portfolio;
    FundsType funds_type = p_request -> funds_type;
    Boolean purchase = (p_request -> buy_sell_ind == BUY);
    int num_shares = (purchase) ? p_request ->num_shares : - p_request ->num_shares;
```

```
/* Update holdings in client portfolio */
for (SecurityHolding * sh = port -> First(); sh; sh = port -> Next())
    if (sh -> security == sec) {
            sh -> num_shares += num_shares;
            break;
        }
/*Calculate net cost of purchase (positive amount) or
    net proceeds (negative amount) from sale of security */
Money net_amount = num_shares * p_price + p_commission;
Account * acct = (Account *)0;

switch (p_request ->fund_source) {
case FS_PORTFOLIO_ACCT:
    acct = port -> account;
    break;
case FS_MM_ACCT:
    for (acct = account_list.First(); acct; acct = account_list.Next())
                if (acct ->account_type == AT_CLIENT_MM) break;
    break;
case FS_MARGIN_ACCT:
    for (acct = account_list.First(); acct; acct = account_list.Next())
        if (acct->account_type == AT_CLIENT_MARGIN) break;
    break;
case FS_INVOICE:
    acct = port->account;
    Invoice * inv = new Invoice(acct, this, net_amount, p_trade_date);
    break;
case FS_CREDIT_MEMO:
    acct = port->account;
    CreditMemo * cm = new CreditMemo(acct, this, net_amount, p_trade_date);
    break;
default:
    acct = port ->account;
    break;
}
if (purchase) {
    acct -> Debit(net_amount);
} else {
    acct -> Credit(net_amount);
}
}
```

The following code segment describes a class method for listing a client by name. This operation requires searching through all objects in the database. It returns a vector containing pointers to all client objects that match the supplied name.

```
static void Client::GetClientByName(String & p_last_name, Vec(Client) & client_vec)
```

```
{
    // This operation requires that the database system have built-in capabilities
    // for iterating through or retrieving a subset of the entire set of objects of
    // a given class. For purposes of example, we will assume the set processing
    // capability of O++.
    for Client * c in Client suchthat last_name = p_last_name
        client_vec += c;
}
```

We have gone rather deep in showing the coding for the *Client* object to set a framework for translating the design into code. Only the design but not the code has been shown for the rest of the objects. We recommend that readers try to develop the code as an exercise and study the operation of real, persistent objects.

Account object.   You may recall that the *Account* object is the generic class for all accounts, including portfolio accounts, margin accounts, and so on. The following *C++* code describes the creation and usage of the *Account* object:

ACCOUNT OBJECT

```
enum AccountType { AT_UNDEFINED, AT_CLIENT_TRADE, AT_CLIENT_MARGIN,
                   AT_CLIENT_PORTFOLIO, AT_CLIENT_MM };
class Account {
    AccountType account_type;
    Money balance;
    Money credit_limit;
public:
    Account(AccountType p_account_type, Money p_balance, Money p_credit_limit);
    ~Account();
    void Debit(Money p_amount);
    void Credit(Money p_amount);
    void SetCreditLimit(p_amount);
};


Account::Account(Type p_account_type, Money p_balance, Money p_credit_limit)
{
    AccountType = p_account_type;
    balance = p_balance;
    credit_limit = p_credit_limit;
}


Account::~Account()
{
}


void Account::Debit(Money p_amount)
{
    balance += p_amount;
}
```

```
void Account::Credit(Money p_amount)
{
     balance −= p_amount;
}

void Account::SetCreditLimit(p_amount)
{
     credit_limit = p_amount;
}
```

Portfolio object.   The *Portfolio* object is used to track client portfolios (that is, securities grouped together for account management purposes. Note that a client can have a number of portfolios and each portfolio can have a number of securities. It would be useful to refer back to the portfolio component of the code for the *Client* object and study the relationship between the *Client* and *Portfolio* objects. The creation and usage of the *Portfolio* object are described by the following C++ code:

PORTFOLIO OBJECT

```
// Define a public structure that contains the Security and number of shares owned
struct SecurityHolding {
     Security * security;
     int num_shares;
};

// A Portfolio object is simply a set of SecurityHoldings
class Portfolio {
     String description;
     Account * account;
     Vec(SecurityHolding) security_holdings;

public:
     Portfolio(string * p_description, Account * p_account);
     ~Portfolio();
     void SetDescription(String * p_description);
     void AddSecurityHolding (Security * p_security, int num_shares);
     void ModifySecurityHolding(Security * p_security, int num_shares);
     void RemoveSecurityHolding(Security * p_security);
};

Portfolio::Portfolio(String * p_description, Account * p_account)
{
     description = p_description;
     account = p_account;
}
```

```
Portfolio::~Portfolio()
{
    for (SecurityHolding * sh = security_holdings.First(); sh; sh = security_holdings.Next())
        delete sh;
}


Portfolio::SetDescription(String * p_description)
{
    description = p_description:
}


Portfolio::AddSecurityHolding(Security * p_security, int num_shares)
{
    SecurityHolding * sh = new SecurityHolding;
    sh -> security = p_security;
    sh -> num_shares = num_shares;
    security_holdings += sh;
}

void Portfolio:ModifySecurityHolding(Security * p_security, int num_shares)
{
    for (SecurityHolding * sh = security_holdings.First(); sh; sh = security_holdings.Next())
        if (sh -> security == p_security) {
            sh -> num_shares = num_shares;
            break;
        }
}

void Portfolio::RemoveSecurityHolding(Security * p_security)
{
    for (SecurityHolding * sh = security_holdings.First(); sh; sh = security_holdings. Next())
        if (sh -> security == p_security) {
            security_holdings -= sh;
            break;
        }
}
```

Security object.   The *Security* object describes each security such as a common stock, bond, or option. For simplicity, we will use the case of common stock (shares) only and create the security object to handle only one class of securities. The following describes a security object.

SECURITY OBJECT

Attributes
    SecurityName
    SecurityType

Company

. . .

Instance Methods
    Create(SecurityName, SecurityType, Company, . . .)
    Destroy

Class Methods
    GetSecurityByName(SecurityName) returns SecurityList

As you may notice, we have actually reproduced the information from the Behavioral Model, but have not really described the C++ code for the *Security* object. It would be a good coding exercise for the reader to do so now, using the previous examples as templates.

Transaction object.   We described the transaction object in detail in the Behavioral Model. Every transaction (credit or debit) to any account results in a *Transaction* object instance to be created and stored. These persistent instances of the *Transaction* object are used for creating end of the month statements. The following C++ code describes the creation and usage of a *Transaction* object:

TRANSACTION OBJECT

```
enum TransactionType {T_DEBIT, T_CREDIT};

class Transaction {
      Account * account;
      DateTime date;
      TransactionType transaction_type;
      Money amount;

public:
      Transaction(Account * p_account, Datetime p_date, TransactionType p_trans_type,
                  Money p_amount);
      ~Transaction();
      static void GetTransactionsByAccount(Account * p_account, Vec(Transaction) &
                                  trans_vec);
      static void GetTransactionsByDate(Datetime p_start_date, Datetime p_end_date,
                                  Vec(Transaction) & trans_vec);
};

Transaction::Transaction(Account * p_account, Datetime p_date, TransactionType
                  p_trans_type, Money p_amount)
{
      account = p_account;
      date = p_date;
      transaction_type = p_trans_type;
      amount = p_amount;
};
```

```
Transaction::~Transaction()
{
}

static void Transaction::GetTransactionsByAccount(Account * p_account, Vec(Transaction) &
                                                  trans_vec)
{
    for Transaction * t in Transaction suchthat account  == p_account trans_vec += t;
}

static void Transaction::GetTransactionsByDate(Datetime p_start_date, Datetime p_end_date,
                                               Vec(Transaction) & trans_vec)
{
    for Transaction * t in Transaction suchthat date >= p_start_date && date <= p_end_date
        trans_vec += t;
}
```

Invoice object.   A purchase of a security causes an invoice to be generated for the amount of the purchase. The invoice defines the amount due from the client for that trade. An *Invoice* object instance is created for every security purchase. The following C++ code describes the *Invoice* object and its usage:

INVOICE OBJECT

```
class Invoice {
      Account * account;
      Client * client;
      Money amount;
      Datetime invoice_date;
      Datetime payment_date;

public:
      Invoice(Account * p_account, Client * p_client, Money p_amount, Datetime
            p_invoice_date);
      ~Invoice();
      void SetPaymentDate(Datetime p_payment_date);
      static void GetOpenInvoicesByClient(Client * p_client, Vec(Invoice) & inv_vec);
      static void GetOpenInvoicesByAccount(Account * p_account, Vec(Invoice) & inv_vec);
};

Invoice::Invoice(Account * p_account, Client * p_client, Money p_amount, Datetime
                 p_invoice_date)
{
      account = p_account;
      client = p_client;
      amount = p_amount;
```

```
        invoice_date = p_date;
        payment_date = Date(NULL);
}


Invoice::~Invoice()
{
}


Invoice::SetPaymentDate(Datetime p_payment_date)
{
        payment_date = p_payment_date;
}

static void Invoice::GetOpenInvoicesByClient(Client * p_client, Vec(Invoice) & inv_vec)
{
        for Invoice * inv in Invoice suchthat client = p_client
            inv_vec += inv;
}


static void Invoice::GetOpenInvoicesByAccount(Account * p_account, Vec(Invoice) & inv_vec)
{
        for Invoice * inv in Invoice suchthat payment_date = Date(NULL) inv_vec += vec;
}
```

CreditMemo object.   A credit memo is issued when a client sells a security. A client may have a number of credit memos open. These may be paid out or applied to a trading account according to client instructions. Note that a class method is used for listing all open credit memos by client or account number. The following C++ code describes the creation and usage of the *CreditMemo* object:

CREDITMEMO OBJECT

```
class CreditMemo {
        Account * account;
        Client * client;
        Money amount;
        Datetime credit_memo_date;
        Datetime payment_date;
public:
        CreditMemo(Account * p_account, Client * p_client, Money p_amount, Datetime
                    p_credit_memo_date);
        ~CreditMemo();
        void SetPaymentDate(Datetime p_payment_date);
        static void GetOpenCreditMemosByClient(Client * p_client, Vec(CreditMemo) &
                                            memo_vec);
        static void GetOpenCreditMemosByAccount(Account * p_account, Vec(CreditMemo) &
                                            memo_vec);
};
```

```
CreditMemo::CreditMemo(Account * p_account, Client * p_client, Money p_amount, Datetime
                    p_credit_memo_date)
{
    account = p_account;
    client = p_client;
    amount = p_amount;
    credit_memo_date = p_credit_memo_date;
}

CreditMemo::~CreditMemo()
{
}

void CreditMemo::SetPaymentDate(DateTime p_payment_date)
{
    payment_date = p_payment_date;
}

static void CreditMemo::GetOpenCreditMemosByClient(Client * p_client, Vec(CreditMemo)
                                                    & memo_vec)
{
    for CreditMemo * cm in CreditMemo suchthat client = p_client
        memo_vec += cm;
}

static void CreditMemo::GetOpenCreditMemosByAccount(Account * p_account,
                                                    Vec(CreditMemo) & memo_vec)
{
    for CreditMemo * cm in CreditMemo suchthat account = p_account
        memo_vec += cm;
}
```

Statement object.   An account statement is issued at the end of every statement period (usually end of the month). The statement consists of all transactions during the statement period and the account balances at the start and end of the statement period. Intermediate statements to show activity to date may also be created (usually to address client questions about account activity). The following C++ code describes the creation and usage of the *Statement* object:

STATEMENT OBJECT

```
class Statement {
    Client * client;
    Datetime statement_date;
    Vec(Transaction) transaction_list;
```

```
public:
     Statement(Client * p_client, Datetime p_statement_date, Vec(transaction)
               p_transaction_list);
     ~Statement();
     Statement & GetStatement(Client * p_client, Datetime p_date);
     void GetStatementsByDate(Datetime p_date, Vec(Statement) & statement_vec);
     void GetStatementsByClient(Client * p_client, Vec(Statement) & statement_vec);
};

Statement::Statement(Client * p_client, Datetime p_statement_date, Vec(Transaction)
               p_transaction_list)
{
     client = p_client;
     statement_date = p_statement_date;

     // Create copy of transaction list
     for (Transaction * t = p_transaction_list.First(): t; t = p_transaction_list.Next())
          transaction_list += t;
}

Statement::~Statement()
{
}

Statement & Statement::GetStatement(Client * p_client, Datetime p_date)
{
     for Statement * s in Statement suchthat client = p_client and statement_date = p_date
          // there should be only one
          return *s;
}

void Statement::GetStatementsByDate(Datetime p_date, Vec(Statement) & statement_vec)
{
     for Statement * s in Statement suchthat statement_date = p_date
          statement_vec += s;
}

void Statement::GetStatementsByClient(Client * p_client, Vec(Statement) & statement_vec)
{
     for Statement * s in Statement suchthat client  = p_client
          statement_vec += s;
}
```

Broker object.   The object class *Broker* may be viewed as a superclass for the objects *AccountBroker* and *FloorBroker*. While the attributes for the two objects are almost identical, the methods for the two are very different due to the difference in the nature of functions performed by the two brokers. The attributes include personnel information, location of work, and commission on bonus structures for the brokers.

Obviously, a more comprehensive design will include a number of other method definitions. The *class hierarchy* of *Brokers* would also include *OptionsBrokers*. The objects at the lower levels of the hierarchy are the actual instances of the class. For example, there will be an object for every *AccountBroker*. These objects are called instances of the class *AccountBroker*. As you may recall, a class is the means of coding an object and, for most object-oriented systems, does not exist at runtime. On the other hand, the instances of the class, or objects, only exist at runtime (or as persistent objects residing on disk).

The following *C++* code describes methods for the creation and usage of the class *Broker*. The methods for the *subclasses* of *AccountBroker* and *FloorBroker* are also described separately.

BROKER OBJECT

```
struct CommissionPlan
{
     SecurityType sec_type;
     Client * client;
     int num_shares;
     double percentage;
};

class Broker {
     String last_name;
     String first_name;
     String middle_name;
     String phone_number;
     int employee_id;
     Vec(CommissionPlan) commission_plan_list;
     Account * commission_acct;
public:
     void SetName(String p_last_name, String p_first_name, String p_middle_name);
     void SetPhoneNumber(string p_phone_number);
     void SetEmployeeId(int p_employee_id);
     Money UpdateCommissionAccount(Security * p_security, int num_shares, Money
                              p_price, DateTime p_trade_date);
     void AddCommissionPlan(CommissionPlan * p_plan);
     void RemoveCommissionPlan(CommissionPlan * p_plan);
};

void Broker::SetName(String p_last_name, String p_first_name, String p_middle_name)
{
     last_name = p_last_name;
     first_name = p_first_name;
     middle_name = p_middle_name;
}
```

```
void Broker::SetPhoneNumber(String p_phone_number)
{
     phone_number = p_phone_number;
}


void Broker::SetEmployeeId(int p_employee_id)
{
     employee_id = p_employee_id;
}


Money Broker::Update CommissionAccount(Security * p_security, Client * p_client, int
                                       num_shares, Money p_price, DateTime
                                       p_trade_date)

{
     // Brokers can receive commissions based on the type of security traded,
     // the client who requested the trade, and on the number of shares traded.
     // The commission_plan_list is searched first for a match on the specific client.
     // If not found, then the list is searched for the security type. For simplicity
     // in the example, we will assume that the same commission rate will apply
     // regardless of the number of shares traded.
     CommissionPlan * cp;
     Money commission_amount;
     for (cp = commission_plan_list.First(); cp: cp = cp-> Next()) {
          if (cp -> client == p_client) {
               commission_amount = num_shares * p_price * cp -> percentage:
               commission_account ->Credit(commission_amount);
               return commission_amount;
          }
     }
     for (cp = commission_plan_list. First(); cp; cp = cp -> Next ()) {
          if (cp ->sec_type == p_security -> type) {
               commission_amount = num_shares * p_price * cp -> percentage;
               commission_account -> Credit(commission_amount);
               return comission_amount;
          }
     }
}

void Broker::AddCommissionPlan(CommissionPlan * p_plan)
{
     commission_plan_list += p_plan;
}


void Broker::RemoveCommissionPlan(CommissionPlan * p_plan)
{
     commission_plan_list -= p_plan;
}
```

AccountBroker object.   Having designed the class *Broker*, we can now turn our attention to the design of the subclass *AccountBroker*. Note that the key difference between the *AccountBroker* and the *FloorBroker* is the office location and client list versus the exchange location in terms of the attribute. The following C++ code will show that an *AccountBroker* has additional methods to add and remove clients, define an office location, and so on.

ACCOUNTBROKER OBJECT

```
class AccountBroker : public Broker {
    String office;
    Vec(Client) client_list;

public:
    AccountBroker (String p_last_name, String p_first_name, String p_middle_name,
                   String p_phone_number, int p_employee_id, String p_office);
    ~AccountBroker();
    void SetOffice(string p_office);
    void AddClient(Client * p_client);
    void RemoveClient(Client * p_client);
    static void GetAccountBrokerByName(String p_last_name, Vec(AccountBroker) &
                                       broker_list);
};

AccountBroker::AccountBroker(String p_last_name, String p_first_name, String
                             p_middle_name, String p_phone_number, int p_employee_id,
                             String p_office)
{
    last_name = p_last_name;
    first_name = p_first_name;
    middle_name = p_middle_name;
    employee_id = p_employee_id;
    office = p_office;

    commission_acct = new Account(AT_BROKER_COMMISSION, 0.0, 0.0);
}

AccountBroker::~AccountBroker()
{
    for (CommissionPlan * cp = commission_plan_list.First(); cp;
        cp = commission_plan_list.Next())
        delete cp;
}

void AccountBroker::SetOffice(String p_office)
{
    office = p_office;
}
```

```
void AccountBroker::AddClient(Client * p_client)
{
     for (Client * c = client_list.First(); c; c = client_list.Next())
          if (c == p_client) return;
     client_list += p_client;
}

void AccountBroker::RemoveClient(Client * p_client)
{
     for (Client * c = client_list.First(); c; c = client_list.Next())
          if (c == p_client) {
               client_list -= c;
               break;
          }
}

static void AccountBroker::GetAccountBrokerByName(String p_last_name,
                                        Vec(AccountBroker) & broker_list)
{
     for AccountBroker * b in AccountBroker suchthat last_name = p_last_name
          broker_list += b;
}
```

FloorBroker object.   The following C++ code describes the methods for
the object class *FloorBroker*. The difference in the methods has been kept very
simple to point out the advantages of object-oriented programming. As we noted
earlier, the definitions for the *AccountBroker* and the *FloorBroker* can be inherited
from the class *Broker* and then redefined to make the required changes that
distinguish the two subclasses.

FLOORBROKER OBJECT

```
class FloorBroker : public Broker {
     String exchange_name;

public:
     FloorBroker (String p_last_name, String p_first_name, String p_middle_name, String
                    p_phone_number, int p_employee_id, String p_exchange);
     ~FloorBroker();
     void SetExchange(String p_exchange);
     static void GetFloorBrokerByName(String p_last_name, Vec(FloorBroker) & broker_list);
};


FloorBroker::FloorBroker(String p_last_name, String p_first_name, String
                    p_middle_name, String p_phone_number, int p_employee_id,
                    String p_exchange)
```

```
{
    last_name = p_last_name:
    first_name = p_first_name;
    middle_name = p_middle_name;
    phone_number = p_phone_number;
    employee_id = p_employee_id;
    exchange_name = p_exchange;

    commission_acct = new Account(AT_BROKER_COMMISSION, 0.0, 0.0);
}

FloorBroker::~FloorBroker()
{
    for (CommissionPlan * cp = commission_plan_list.First(); cp;
        cp = commission_plan_list.Next())
        delete cp;
}

void FloorBroker::SetExchange(String p_exchange)
{
    exchange_name = p_exchange;
}

static void FloorBroker::GetFloorBrokerByName(String p_last_name, Vec(FloorBroker) &
                                              broker_list)
{
    for FloorBroker * b in FloorBroker suchthat last_name = p_last_name
        broker_list += b;
}
```

Request object.   A *Request* object is created by the account broker. When the information is filled in for a client order by the account broker, a function is executed to send a message to the data server with the information to create the *Request* object. The message invokes the *Request constructor* method to create the new *Request* object.

After creating one or more *Request* objects to purchase or sell a particular security, the account broker must create an *Order* object that will be sent to floor brokers for a trade to be executed.

After the account broker selects one or more *Request* objects, the *CreateOrder* function will be selected to bring up a window for entering order information as illustrated in the code for the *Order* object. Note that each *Request* object results in an *Order* object.

REQUEST OBJECT

```
enum BuySell { BUY, SELL };
enum FundsType { FT_PORTFOLIO_ACCT, FT_MM_ACCT, FT_MARGIN_ACCT, FT_INVOICE,
                FT_CM };
```

```
class Request {
        // Account Broker who created Request object
        AccountBroker * broker;

        // Client who made request
        Client * client;

        // Security to be traded
        Security * security;

        // Client portfolio containing (or that will contain) the security
        Portfolio * portfolio;

        // Whether to buy or to sell
        BuySell buy_sell_ind;

        // Number of shares
        int num_shares;

        // Stop Price (if zero, then trade at current price)
        Money stop_price;

        // Expiration Date (if goal price specified)
        DateTime exp_date;

        // Date or request
        DateTime req_date;

        // Source/Dispositions of funds
        FundsType funds_type;

        // Order object (set when Order is created)
        Order * order;

        // Trade that satisfied request (set by OrderCompleted method when Trade is
        // created)
        Trade * trade;

public:
        // Create a new Request object
        Request(AccountBroker * p_broker,
                Client * p_client,
                Security * p_security,
                Portfolio * p_portfolio,
                BuySell p_buy_sell,
                int p_num_shares,
                Money p_stop_price,
                DateTime p_exp_date,
```

```
        DateTime p_req_date,
        FundsType p_funds_type);

// Destroy a Request object (cancel request)
~Request();

// Complete a Request (called from Order::TradeCompleted method)
void OrderCompleted (Trade * p_trade, DateTime p_trade_date, Money p_price, Money
                    p_commission);
// Methods for modifying requests (A request can be modified only if a Trade
// has not yet been executed for it. The functions return 0 if the update
// was allowed, −1 otherwise.)
int SetOrder(Order * p_order);
int SetClient(Client * p_client);
int SetSecurity(Security * p_security);
int SetBuySellIndicator(BuySell p_buy_sell);
int SetNumberOfShares(int p_num_shares);
int SetStopPrice(Money p_amount);
int SetExpirationDate(DateTime p_exp_date);
int SetFundSource(FundSource p_fund_source);
int SetFundDisposition(FundDisposition p_fund_disp);

// static Class methods for retrieving Request objects
static void GetOpenRequestsByAccountBroker(AccountBroker * p_broker, Vec(Request)
                                          & request_list);
static void GetOpenRequestsByClient(Client * p_client, Vec(Request) & request_list);
static void Get RequestsByDate(DateTime p_start_date, DateTime p_end_date,
                              Vec(request) & request_list);
};
```

The design of the *Request* object described above has been used to develop the following code. We start with the routines for the creation and destruction of the *Request* object.

```
Request::Request(AccountBroker * p_broker,
        Client * p_client,
        Security * p_security,
        Portfolio * p_portfolio,
        BuySell p_buy_sell,
        int p_num_shares,
        Money p_stop_price,
        DateTime p_exp_date,
        DateTime p_req_date,
        FundsType p_funds_type)
{
    broker = p_broker;
    client = p_client;
    security = p_security;
```

```
            portfolio = p_portfolio;
            buy_sell_ind = p_buy_sell;
            num_shares = p_num_shares;
            stop_price = p_stop_price;
            exp_date = p_exp_date;
            req_date = p_req_date;
            funds_type = p_funds_type;
            order = (Order *)0;
            trade = (Trade *)0;
}


Request::~Request()
{
}
```

We defined a number of methods that manipulate the attributes of the *Request* object. The following code for these routines describes the specifics of how the attributes are handled.

```
int Request::SetOrder(Order * p_order)
{
       if (trade == (Trade *)0) {
           order = p_order;
           return 0;
       } else {
           return −1;
       }
}


void Request::OrderCompleted(Trade * p_trade, DateTime p_trade_date, Money p_price,
                             Money p_commission)
{
       trade = p_trade;
       client −>RequestCompleted(this, p_trade_date, p_price, p_commission);
}


int Request::SetClient(Client * p_client)
{
       if (trade == (Trade *)0) {
           client = p_client;
           return 0;
       } else {
           return −1;
       }
}


int Request::SetSecurity(Security * p_security)
```

```
{
    if (trade == (Trade *)0) {
        security  = p_security;
        return 0;
    } else {
        return -1;
    }
}

int Request::SetBuySellIndicator(BuySell p_buy_sell)
{
    if (trade == (Trade *)0) {
        buy_sell_ind = p_buy_sell;
        return 0;
    } else {
        return -1;
    }
}

int Request::SetNumberOfShares(int p_num_shares)
{
    if (trade == (Trade *)0) {
        num_shares = p_num_shares;
        return 0;
    } else {
        return -1;
    }
}

int Request::SetStopPrice(Money p_amount)
{
    if (trade  == (Trade *)0) {
        amount = p_amount;
        return 0;
    } else {
        return -1;
    }
}

int Request::SetExpirationDate(DateTime p_exp_date)
{
    if (trade == (Trade *)0) {
        exp_date = p_exp_date;
        return 0;
    } else {
        return;
    }
}
int Request::SetFundsType(FundsType p_funds_type)
```

```
{
    if (trade == (Trade *)0) {
        funds_type = p_funds_type;
        return 0;
    } else {
        return −1;
    }
}
```

The next three routines are class methods that allow listing of all open requests for trades; that is, they list all *Request* objects that have not been selected for trading as yet. The *Request* objects can be listed by AccountBroker, Client, or Date.

```
static void Request::GetOpenRequestsByAccountBroker(AccountBroker * p_broker,
                                                    Vec(request) & request_list)
{
    for Request * req in Request suchthat trade = (Trade *)0 and broker = p_broker
        request_list += req;
}

static void Request::GetOpenRequestsByClient(Client * p_client, Vec(Request) & request_list)
{
    for Request * req in Request suchthat trade = (Trade *)0 and client = p_client
        request_list += req;
}

static void Request::GetRequestsByDate(DateTime p_start_date, DateTime p_end_date,
                                       Vec(Request) & request_list)
{
    for Request * req in Request such that request_date between p_start_date and
        p_end_date
        request_list += req;
}
```

Order object.   *Order* objects are used by the floor broker to select the requests that will be acted on during the trading period. The floor broker must lock *Order* objects before executing a trade to satisfy the requirements of the order. This is accomplished by calling the *Lock method* of each Order object to be locked.

Once an Order has been locked, the floor broker can execute a real-world trade to satisfy the order. A single trade can also be used to satisfy multiple orders to buy or sell a particular security.

When the floor broker has completed a trade, information about the trade must be entered into the system. This is accomplished by creating a *Trade* object. The following C++ code sequence illustrates the methods for creating and managing *Order* objects.

ORDER OBJECT

```
typedef OrderError { OE_OKAY, OE_LOCKED, OE_NOTLOCKED, OE_READONLY };

class Order {
        // Account Broker who created the Order
        AccountBroker * account_broker;

        // Request object associated with Order
        Request * request;

        // Security to be traded
        Security * security;

        // Exchange on which security should be traded
        String exchange;

        // Whether the security should be bought or sold
        BuySell buy_sell_ind;

        // Number of shares to be traded
        int num_shares;

        // Price at which security should be traded
        Money stop_price;

        // Date by which security must be traded at stop_price
        DateTime exp_date;

        // Date at which Order was created
        DateTime order_date;

        // Is Order locked?
        Boolean lock_flag;

        // Broker who locked Order
        Broker * lock_broker;

        // Time at which order was locked
        DateTime lock_time;

        //Trade object (when order is completed)
        Trade * trade;

public:
        // Create a new Order object
        Order (AccountBroker * p_broker, Request * p_request, Security * p_security, BuySell
                p_buy_sell, int p_num_shares, Money p_stop_price, DateTime p_exp_date,
                DateTime p_order_date);
```

```
    // Destroy an Order object (cancel order)
    ¯Order();

    // Lock Order
    OrderError LockOrder(Broker * p_broker);

    // Unlock Order
    OrderError UnlockOrder(Broker * p_broker);

    // Complete an Order
    // Executed by the Trade object constructor to unlock the Order, update
    // the Account Broker's commission account, and execute the
    // OrderCompleted method on the Request object.
    void TradeCompleted (Trade * p_trade, DateTime p_trade_date, Money p_price, Money
                           p_fb_commisson);

    // Methods for updating Order objects (prior to Trade)
    OrderError SetSecurity(Security * p_security);
    OrderError SetExchange(String p_exchange);
    OrderError SetBuySellIndicator(BuySell p_buy_sell);
    OrderError SetNumberOfShares(int p_num_shares);
    OrderError SetStopPrice(Money p_price);
    OrderError SetExpirationDate(DateTime p_exp_date);

    // static Class methods for retrieving Order objects
    void GetOpenOrdersByAccountBroker(AccountBroker * p_broker, Vec(Order) & order_list);
    void GetOpenOrdersByExchange(String p_exchange, Vec(Order) & order_list);
    void GetOpenOrdersBySecurity(Security * p_security, Vec(Order) & order_list);
    void GetOrdersByDate(DateTime p_start_date, DateTime p_end_date, Vec(Order) &
                           order_list);
};
```

The code segment above describes the design of the *Order* object. We will now show how the *Order* object is created and destroyed.

```
Order::Order(AccountBroker * p_broker, Request * p_request, Security * p_security,
           BuySell p_buy_sell, int p_num_shares, Money p_stop_price, DateTime
           p_exp_date, DateTime p_order_date)
{
    account_broker = p_broker;
    request = p_request;
    security = p_security;
    buy_sell_ind = p_buy_sell
    num_shares = p_num_shares;
    stop_price = p_stop_price;
    exp_date = p_exp_date;
    order_date = p_order_date:
}
```

```
Order::~Order()
{
// No cleanup required.
}
```

Before a trade is executed, the *Order* object must be locked so that no changes can be made to it while the trade is in progress.

```
OrderError Order::LockOrder(Broker * p_broker)
{
      if (lock_flag) return OE_LOCKED;

      lock_flag = TRUE;
      lock_broker = p_broker;
      lock_time = DateTime("NOW");

      return OE_OKAY;
}

OrderError Order::UnlockOrder(Broker * p_broker)
{
      if (!lock_flag) return OE_NOTLOCKED;

      lock_flag = FALSE;
      lock_broker = (Broker *)0;
      lock_time = 0;

      return OE_OKAY;
}
```

On completion of the trade, a number of actions must take place, such as recording broker commissions, recording of the trade, and updating other objects.

```
void Order::TradeCompleted(Trade * p_trade, DateTime p_trade_date, Money p_price,
                           Money p_fb_commisson)
{
    // Unlock the Order
    lock_flag = FALSE;
    lock_broker = (Broker *)0;
    lock_time = 0;

    // Set Trade object
    trade = p_trade;
```

```
    // Apply Account Broker's commission
    Money ab_commission =
            account_broker −> UpdateCommissionAccount(security, num_shares, p_price,
                                                      p_trade_date);
    Money total_commission = p_fb_commission + ab_commission;

    // Invoke OrderCompleted method of Request object
    request −> OrderCompleted(trade, p_trade_date, p_price, total_commission);
}
```

The following methods are used to update an *Order* object prior to a trade.

```
OrderError Order::SetSecurity(Security * p_security)
{
    if (trade == (Trade *)0) {
        security  = p_security;
        return OE_OKAY;
    } else {
        return OE_READONLY;
    }
}


OrderError Order::SetExchange(String p_exchange)
{
    if (trade == (Trade *)0) {
        exchange = p_exchange;
        return OE_OKAY;
    } else {
        return OE_READONLY;
    }
}


OrderError Order::SetBuySellIndicator(BuySell p_buy_sell)
{
    if (trade == (Trade *)0) {
        buy_sell_ind = p_buy_sell;
        return OE_OKAY;
    } else {
        return OE_READONLY;
    }
}


OrderError Order::SetNumberOfShares(int p_num_shares)
{
    if (trade == (Trade *)0) {
        num_shares = p_num_shares;
        return OE_OKAY;
```

```
    } else {
        return OE_READONLY;
    }
}


OrderError Order::SetStopPrice(Money p_price)
{
    if (trade == (Trade *)0) {
        stop_price = p_price;
        return OE_OKAY;
    } else {
        return OE_READONLY;
    }
}


OrderError Order::SetExpirationDate(DateTime p_exp_date)
{
    if (trade == (Trade *)0) {
        exp_date = p_exp_date;
        return OE_OKAY;
    } else {
        return OE_READONLY;
    }
}
```

The next four methods are class methods for listing all open orders by AccountBroker, Security, Exchange, and Date. The concept of subselects allows listing all orders by date for a specific Security and AccountBroker for a specific Exchange.

```
void Order::GetOpenOrdersByAccountBroker(AccountBroker * p_broker, Vec(Order) &
                                         order_list)
{
    for Order * o in Order suchthat account_broker  = p_broker and trade = (Trade *)0
        order_list += o;
}


void Order::GetOpenOrdersByExchange(String p_exchange, Vec(Order) & order_list)
{
    for Order * o in Order suchthat exchange = p_exchange and trade = (Trade *)0
        order_list += o;
}


void Order::GetOpenOrderBySecurity(Security * p_security, Vec(Order) & order_list)
{
    for Order * o in Order suchthat security = p_security and trade = (Trade *)0
        order_list += o;
}
```

```
void Order::GetOrdersByDate(DateTime p_start_date, DateTime p_end_date, vec(Order) &
                            order_list)
{
    for Order * o in Order suchthat order_date >= p_start_date and order_date <=
        p_end_date
          order_list += o;
}
```

Trade object.   The following C++ code describes the attributes of the object class and the *public methods* for this object class. (Note that public methods are the methods that are known to other objects, while private methods are used only by this object class.) A *Trade* object is created every time an *Order* object is executed and a security trade takes place. A trade also results in commissions for the brokers, and the *Trade* object contains methods to apply commissions.

TRADE OBJECT

```
class Trade {
        // Floor broker who created the trade
        FloorBroker * floor_broker;

        // Security that was traded
        Security * security;

        // Exchange where trade occurred
        String exchange;

        // Was trade a Buy or a Sell
        BuySell buy_sell_ind;

        // Number of shares traded
        int num_shares;

        // Price of security as traded
        Money price;

        // Date of Trade
        DateTime trade_date;

        // Broker or firm with whom the FloorBroker traded
        String trade_partner;

        // List of Orders satisfied by Trade
        Vec(Order) order_list;
```

```
public:
        // Create a new Trade object (this constructor will call the
        // UpdateCommissionAccount method of the FloorBroker object and the
        // TradeCompleted method of each of the Order objects.
        Trade(FloorBroker * p_broker, String p_exchange, Security * p_security, BuySell
                p_buy_sell, int num_shares, Money p_price, DateTime p_trade_date, String
                p_trade_partner, Vec(Order) & order_list);

        // Destroy a Trade object
        ~Trade();

        // static class methods for retrieving Trade objects
        static void GetTradesByFloorBroker(FloorBroker * p_broker, DateTime p_start_date,
                                    DateTime p_end_date, Vec(Trade) & trade_list);
        static void GetTradesByExchange(String p_exchange, DateTime p_start_date, DateTime
                                    p_end_date, Vec(Trade) & trade_list);
        static void GetTradesBySecurity(Security * p_security, DateTime p_start_date,
                                    DateTime p_end_date, Vec(Trade) & trade_list);
        static void GetTradesByDate(DateTime p_start_date, DateTime p_end_date,
                                    Vec(Trade) & trade_list);
};
```

The design depicted by the code segment above is used for developing the routines for creating and destroying the *Trade* object as follows (note that the attributes are defined in the create routine and that the *Trade* object is created only when a trade actually takes place):

```
Trade::Trade(FloorBroker * p_broker, String p_exchange, Security * p_security, BuySell
        p_buy_sell, int num_shares, Money p_price, DateTime p_trade_date,
        String p_trade_partner, Vec(Order) & p_order_list)
{
    floor_broker = p_broker;
    exchange = p_exchange;
    security = p_security;
    buy_sell_ind = p_buy_sell;
    num_shares = p_num_shares;
    price = p_price;
    trade_date = p_trade_date;
    trade_partner = p_trade_partner;
    for (Order * o = p_order_list.First(); o; o = p_order_list.Next())
            order_list += o;

    // Apply Floor Broker commission
    Money fb_commission =
            floor_broker - > UpdateCommissionAccount(security, num_shares, price,
                                            trade_date);
    // Keep track of actual number of shares traded. After calling each Order's
    // TradeCompleted method, we'll have to do something with any excess shares.
```

```
        int shares_ordered = 0;

        // Iterate through the orders, calling the TradeCompleted method of each.
        // Distribute the floor broker's commission among all the orders
        // according to the fraction of shares requested by each order.
        for (Order * o = order_list.First(); o; o = order_list.Next()) {
                dist_commission = fb_commission * ((double)o->num_shares / num_shares);
                o->TradeCompleted(this, trade_date, price, dist_commission);
                shares_ordered += 0->num_shares;
        }
        // Now do something with any excess shares traded. (Like apply the
        // shares to some company account)

        int excess_shares = num_shares - shares_ordered;
}


Trade::~Trade()
{
}
```

The next four methods are class methods for listing *Trade* objects by Floor-Broker, Security, Exchange, and Date. These methods help in comparing trades against trade orders, as well as follow-on actions such as broker commissions.

```
static void Trade::GetTradesByFloorBroker(FloorBroker * p_broker, DateTime
                                          p_start_date, DateTime p_end_date,
                                          Vec(Trade) & trade_list)
{
        for Trade * t in Trade suchthat floor_broker = p_broker and trade_date >=
           p_start_date and trade_date <= p_end_date
           trade_list += t;
}


static void Trade::GetTradesByExchange(String p_exchange, DateTime p_start_date,
                                          DateTime p_end_date, Vec(Trade) & trade_list)
{
        for Trade * t in Trade suchthat exchange = p_exchange and trade_date >=
           p_start_date and trade_date <= p_end_date
           trade_list += t;
}


static void Trade::GetTradesBySecurity(Security * p_security, DateTime p_start_date,
                                          DateTime p_end_date, Vec(Trade) & trade_list)
{
        for Trade * t in Trade suchthat security = p_security and trade_date >=
           p_start_date and trade_date <=p_end_date
           trade_list += t;
}
```

```
static void Trade::GetTradesByDate(DateTime p_start_date, DateTime p_end_date,
                        Vec(Trade) & trade_list)
{
        for Trade * t in Trade suchthat trade_date >= p_start_date and trade_date <=
            p_end_date
              trade_list += t;
}
```

We have discussed a number of objects in the code examples shown here. As we said at the outset, these examples were intended to show primarily the design and how the design is used to develop the actual methods. However, not all objects have been covered above, and this may be a good time for the reader to use the methodology presented above to complete the rest of the objects. Furthermore, the readers can actually try to build some components of the application using the code modules above as templates to build and manipulate objects.

Security pricing management.   Security pricing management was the other major application component of interest. We will see in the following how objects are useful in solving an interesting problem. Prices of securities (stocks, bonds, and stock options) change on a daily basis. Pricing management requires storing the price information for every trading day for every security. The trade management system (TMS) receives security pricing information from all the major trading exchanges around the world. The primary storage site for information from a particular exchange is the database server host in the ITC regional office nearest the exchange.

Two kinds of pricing information are maintained by the system. Real-time security price information is received and stored in the TMS database so that brokers will have up to the minute prices to quote to clients and so that brokers may determine where the best price can be obtained for trading a particular security. The TMS system keeps up to one day's worth of real-time price information for each security that is traded. This allows brokers to obtain the current price, as well as to chart the activity of a particular security throughout the day. The other kind of pricing information stored by TMS is daily summaries of security prices obtained from each exchange at the end of trading. This information is useful for historical tracking of prices for analysis and verification. The TMS system maintains up to two years of daily price information on line for each security and up to ten years of information in archived storage.

Two major types of operations are performed on pricing data in the TMS system: retrieving pricing information for a particular security for a given date or range of dates, and inserting pricing data into the database as they are received from the exchanges. Both operations are very straightforward in an object-oriented database environment. We will assume that the reader is familiar enough with the relational environment to make a meaningful comparison of how this would be done in a relational environment.

Retrieving price objects.   The TMS database maintains a class of Security objects for each security that it trades. A Security object contains basic information about the security, including one or more names or symbols by which it is known in the real world. To obtain pricing information for a particular security, an application must first obtain a pointer to the corresponding *Security* object in the database. This pointer is used as part of the key into the *PriceHistory* objects in the database. If the application needs to obtain the price of a security at a particular exchange, then an exchange identifier must also be obtained. Both operations are very fast since copies of Security and Exchange objects are maintained on every server.

To locate price information for a particular date or range of dates, the application must retrieve the *PriceHistory* object(s) whose *start_date* and *end_date* span the given date(s). There are then two methods provided for obtaining the desired price data. Both methods are named *GetPriceInfo(X)*; however, the arguments to each method differ. (This is a standard practice in C++ programming known as function overloading.) One method allows extraction of a single PriceRec record, while the other method allows the extraction of multiple records.

Creating price objects.   When new pricing information is to be added for a security, the application must first determine in which *PriceHistory* object the data will be added. This is accomplished by querying the database for the object with the matching security identifier, exchange identifier, and nearest date. It must then determine if there is sufficient room in the *PriceRec* array for an additional price record. If so, then the *AddPriceRec* method is invoked on the object to add the new price information. Otherwise, a new *PriceHistory* object must be created with an empty*PriceRec* array to which the new price record will be added with *AddPriceRec*.

The large volume of pricing information that must be maintained by TMS puts tremendous demands on the amount of disk space that is needed on the database servers. In our example, our approach to addressing this issue is to partition the data among each of the database servers in the ITC network. The data from each exchange will be assigned to a particular server. Brokers at any company office may access the data, which may result in data being temporarily copied to another server, but in general data for a particular exchange will exist at a single site.

In a relational database the huge number of individual price records would put an enormous strain on database performance. One method of increasing performance would be to group a set of price records, say one month's worth, into a single undifferentiated block of data (commonly known as a binary large object, or BLOB) and to store a pointer to this data block with a header record in the security price table. This would greatly reduce the size of the index (and increase the speed of access) required to locate a particular day's price. This also has the benefit of reducing the amount of actual data since the information maintained in the header (such as the security id, exchange, currency, and date range) does not have to be repeated with each price record. This approach works well in a relational database environment. A good question at this point is whether this approach will work well in an object-oriented database. More appropriately, the question is whether there is a better way of handling this information.

In an object-oriented database the need to reduce the access time to a particular price record is still a valid issue, and a method similar to the one described above can be used. The following $C++$ code (note that the $O++$ is an extension of $C++$ and we have generally used $O++$ only where standard $C++$ does not support the desirable feature) presents a definition of a *PriceHistory* class that is simply a header for a set of price information records stored as a separate array of contiguous data.

The following describes the structure for the price record. This structure is a part of the object that defines price history management.

PRICEREC OBJECT

```
// Define types and enums used in PriceHistory class
typedef long DateTime;
enum CurrencyType { CT_DOLLAR, CT_DM, CT_YEN, CT_POUND };

enum SPError {
    SP_OKAY,            // Success
    SP_BAD_DATE,        // Date out of range
    SP_FULL,            // Price array is full
    SP_TRUNCATED,       // User array size too small
    SP_ARCHIVED         // Price data has been archived
    };

// Define structure containing single price record
struct PriceRec {
    active : 1;         // Was stock active on date?
    float open;         // Opening price
    float high;         // High price
    float low;          // Low price
    float close;        // Closing price
    float bid;          // Final Bid price
    float ask;          // Final Asking price
    int volume;         // Volume of shares traded
};
```

The *PriceRec* object stores the pricing information for all securities, one *Price* object for each security for each day. The following code describes an object class method for manipulating the price history data. The *PriceHistory* object maintains an array of *PriceRec* objects for a given security and exchange over a certain date range.

```
class PriceHistory {
private:
    persistent Security * security;        // Security Identifier
    persistent Exchange * exchange;        // Exchange Identifier
    DateTime start_date;                   // Start Date in price_recs
    DateTime end_date;                     // End Date in price_recs
    CurrencyType currency;                 // Currency of prices
    short price_rec_count;                 // Count of records in price_recs
    short price_rec_size;                  // Allocated size of price_recs
    persistent PriceRec (*price_recs) [ ]; // Array of price records
    persistent ArchiveInfo *archive_info;  // Archive Information

public:

    // Create a PriceHistory object
    PriceHistory(persistent Security * p_security, persistent Exchange * p_exchange,
            CurrencyType p_currency, short p_price_rec_size);

    // Destroy PriceHistory object
    ~Price History();

    // Get object attributes
    persistent Security * GetSecurity();
    persistent Exchange * GetExchange();
    DateTime GetStartDate();
    DateTime GetEndDate();
    CurrencyType GetCurrencyType();
    short GetRecCount();
    short GetRecSize();

    // Get Price data for a given date
    SPError GetPriceRec(DateTime date, PriceRec & p_rec);

    // Get Price data for a given date range
    SPError GetPriceRec(DateTime s_date, DateTime e_date, PriceRec p_array[], short &
        p_array_size);

    // Add new price data to price_recs array
    SPError AddPriceRec(DateTime, PriceRec &);

    // Delete price_recs array and set Archive information
    void SetArchiveInfo(persistent ArchiveInfo *);
}
```

Note that one difference between an object-oriented database that uses
C++ (or a derivative) as its programming language and a typical relational
database is that the individual price records can actually be referenced and
manipulated by an object method executing on the server. A procedure written in

the extended SQL of relational databases is unable to manipulate data stored within a BLOB; the data within a BLOB is not interpreted by the database, and the database can only transfer the contents of the BLOB to a user buffer. The user has to manipulate this data (typically via C language routines).

16.4 BENEFITS OF OBJECT-ORIENTED DESIGN APPROACH

This is a book about advanced information systems—what consitutes a distributed and advanced information system and how to design and implement one. As we see it, there are three primary components in a modern information system: an advanced user interface using a graphics workstation or PC with the capability of integrating text, graphics, pictures, and possibly sound and video; a distributed environment where multiple workstations are connected to a network along with one or more database servers providing transparent access to multiple sources of data; and an object-oriented data management system that provides fast and flexible access to many classes of data objects.

Having sophisticated presentation technology assumes that there is sophisticated data. Simple text and numbers, graphics, animation, video, sound—all of this information must be collected and stored in a manner that is easy to organize and manage and to integrate and manipulate. Relational databases arose primarily to service tabular information such as financial data. Various extensions to its basic structure have been proposed and implemented, but there are inherent limitations to the usefulness of the classical relational model that do not fully meet the requirements of contemporary information systems. We can summarize the requirements for a contemporary database management system by the following:

1. Data is more complex, both in terms of datatypes as well as in the interrelationships between entities.
2. More types of data to manage, especially, in multimedia applications.
3. Progress from centralized to decentralized data in distributed environments as enterprises attempt to link all operating entities to a common database.
4. User has access to many sources of data on a network and, consequently, accesses a number of data servers.
5. Workstations and user interface standards provide greater understanding and ease of use and reduce training time for new applications, thereby placing further strains on the database resources.
6. Users at workstations use several application windows to connect to a variety of databases simultaneously.
7. An enterprise consists of a network with users and information sources spread across the various facilities of the enterprise.

Object oriented data management is necessary to deal with the new data complexity. Contemporary information systems design requires simplifying principles to be able to cope with data complexity, development schedules, enhancement requirements, and maintenance.

Let us now review the key benefits of the object oriented database design in light of these issues. Object oriented databases offer the following important benefits, especially, as compared to relational databases:

1. Object oriented databases offer the ability to store more complex objects.
2. Window toolkits are a collection of objects that can be used to build applications with a common look and feel.
3. Object orientation allows these complex objects to be manipulated in a more organized (rather than restricted) fashion.
4. Object orientation allow building new objects by combining properties of previously existing objects.
5. Object oriented design principles allow applications to be built that are easier to maintain and enhance than with previous design principles.
6. Object oriented design principles provide for clearer and more robust implementations and allow applications to be built on top of other applications.
7. New applications can build on old object oriented applications without the need for restructuring the database schema and access methodologies, thereby saving development time.

16.5 SUMMARY

This chapter presented an operational perspective on the methodologies for modeling and designing an information system. We started out with the Information System Model that defined the external, user-visible entities and the user visible functions or transactions. It described the external view of the entities, their attributes, and logical groupings and relationships among attributes and entities from a user perspective in the Entity Model. It further described user functions and the user interface in the Transaction Model. The Information System Model is a complete external description of the functionality of the system. A partial Information System Model was developed as an example in this chapter.

This was followed by the modeling of objects in the Object Model, where the structural components (attributes) of the objects are defined in the Structural Model and the behavioral components (functions or operations) are defined in the Behavioral Model. The Object Model is the internal object view of the information system. It describes the underlying objects, the attributes of each object, relationships among objects, and descriptions of classes and inheritance in the

Structural Model. It further defines the operations required to support each function described in the Transaction Model, and describes the complete hierarchy of objects from an operations (methods) perspective in the Behavioral Model. We developed a partial Object Model for the Trading Management System in this chapter as an example.

The Information System Model and the Object Model describe the functionality and structure of the information and form the basis for the design. The user visible external view and the internal object view completely define the model to a point where a complete application can be designed. The effective use of the Frame-Object Analysis Diagramming methodology is also presented in this chapter. The presentation of the model is made significantly more comprehensible when the Frame-Object Analysis diagrams are used.

We also looked at a number of examples of converting the models defining the objects to an actual design of the objects. The examples further showed how these objects are manipulated, and how they are used to solve real-world problems.

16.6 EXERCISES

1. Explain the difference between instance attributes and class attributes.
2. Explain the difference between instance methods and class methods.
3. Develop the design for all objects that have not been described in this chapter.
4. Examine the instance and class methods for each class. Apply the rules of aggregation and generalization. How would you improve upon this design?
5. Redesign the objects to achieve improved modularity.
6. Redesign the objects to achieve improved performance.
7. What kinds of changes would you recommend to associations to achieve better indexing?
8. Develop the Business Information Model for the following functions:

   • Accounting Functions
   • Reference Code Management
   • System Administration

   Describe the top level functions in a frame.
9. Develop an Entity Model for the functions listed in Exercise 8. The Entity Model should contain a description and frame object diagrams for the user visible entities related to the application function. It should also include entity relationship frames.

10. Develop a Transaction Model for the functions listed in Exercise 8. Provide detailed operational descriptions for the functions. Develop the top-level functional frame and second level functional frames. Develop screen layouts for the menus and lower level operational functions.

11. Develop the Structural Model for the functions listed in Exercise 8. Expand the Entity Model to create a detailed structural model that includes any additional entities necessary to the proper functioning of the application. Create structural frames showing the list of entities, entity relationships, and object attributes.

12. Develop the Behavioral Model for the functions listed in Exercise 8. Define the methods for the objects in the Structural Model that may be used to implement the low-level functions of the Transaction Model. Describe the high-level operations in terms of the low-level operations and object methods they invoke. Draw frames depicting these operations. Also show frames for each object that list both attributes and the methods.

13. Are additional data flow diagrams needed to describe the processes? If so, explain why.

14. Based on your experience, how would you improve upon the Frame-Object Analysis Methodology.

Glossary of Database Terms

We have presented two major streams of database technologies in this book, relational database systems and object-oriented database systems. These two technologies use a variety of terms both in the descriptions of the basic technologies and in the development methodologies presented. This glossary is provided to ensure that these terms are interpreted in the manner we intended. This glossary provides a ready reference for a variety of terms.

3GL interface (third-generation language interface) is also known as *embedded SQL*. Most relational databases and an increasing number of object-oriented databases provide the capability for querying and updating a database from 3GLs, such as C or FORTRAN languages, using standard SQL statements.

4GL (fourth-generation development language), especially a good 4GL, provides a complete development environment with full screen management, windowing, combination of procedural and nonprocedural (SQL) code, and high-level debugging capabilities. A good 4GL should provide programming power and flexibility without the need for resorting to third-generation languages. High performance for OLTP requires at least partial compilation capability.

abstract class is a class that can have only subclasses but no instances. The subclasses may have instances.

abstract datatype is a data structure definition that describes only the services offered to the outside world. This level of abstraction allows reusing the data structure in all cases that require exactly the same set of services.

abstract operation is an operation defined for an abstract class but implemented only in the subclasses.

abstraction is defined as a mental activity or a mental concept. In the object-oriented programming world, abstraction is defined to be a mental activity that allows conceptualizing of a problem to a level of detail necessary for the current context.

aggregation is a relationship between objects where objects representing constituent components are associated with an object representing the complete assembly.

architecture has synonyms such as planning, designing, construction, and structure. In the computer systems sense, it refers to the manner in which the system is divided into subsystems and how these subsystems interact with one another. Similarly, software architecture, and more specifically database architecture, is concerned with the layout of the components of the software and the interaction among the components.

archival is an activity in which data that is not current but may need to be accessed occasionally, such as historical data, is selectively transferred to off-line media for permanent storage. Note that the intent of archiving is different from the intent of a backup.

assertion is a declaration or affirmation about a condition or relationship being either true or false.

association is a relationship among instances of two or more object classes described by a semantic statement within a frame.

attribute is a property of an object class for which each object instance contains a data value. Note that this is analogous to a field in a table (in a relational database).

automatic integrity control is used in databases for maintaining integrity of the data. In a database, maintaining integrity becomes critical as more and more users and developers gain access to the database. Most relational databases require the developer to include integrity constraints at the application level. This puts the burden on the developer to ensure that all potential risks to integrity are addressed. Another approach to data integrity is to include the rules in the database itself. Both referential integrity and data validation rules are stored centrally in the data dictionary. Built-in validation rules and procedures provide two advantages; no application can be built that circumvents these rules, and the rules can be programmed once and stored centrally. This not only improves programmer productivity, but it also makes maintaining rules much easier.

automatic network configuration capability is a complex feature supported by very few databases. The databases that support this feature have the capability of effectively managing a network and reconfiguring nodes out of the network when they fail. In case of failure of the node running the database server, the tasks of the database server are assigned to another node.

backup and restore—frequent backups, that is, transferring current data to off-line media, is essential to recover from disk failure or database corruption. A restore utility allows reloading the complete database from off-line media (also refer to *recovery*). Most database systems provide utilities for automatic backups and restore.

Behavioral model describes the behavioral abstractions, that is, the set of rules for combining abstract operations into higher-level abstract operations.

business information model describes the information objects that a business collects, uses, and stores. It details how the information objects are stored.

business model describes what business a corporation is in and how it conducts its business. It describes a corporation's business needs.

business rules are the norms of the business that must be checked for every action that updates or deletes any objects in the database to ensure that incorrect actions are not performed inadvertently. Triggers and stored procedures (or user-defined functions or the equivalent) are used in relational databases for programming these norms.

class is an implementation of an abstract data type supporting a designated set of properties. A class describes a group of objects with similar properties; note that a class definition provides the means of programming the properties of an object; only the object exists at runtime.

class attribute is an attribute for which every instance of that class has the same value.

class descriptor is used in some programming languages as an instance of a metaclass that describes the attributes and methods of the class. In other words, it is an object that describes the class itself.

client is a system component in a network responsible for handling user-specific database access tasks, and the server is responsible for managing shared data. The applications functions run on the client machines (usually a mini or a workstation), and the data access and manipulation functions run on one or more server machines. The functions performed by the client include user interface management, validation of user data entry and interpretation and display of query results.

client/server model—most DBMS vendors have implemented distributed processing by separating the DBMS into a front-end and a back-end component (generally called the *client/server* model), each of which can run on a different system in the network. The front end consists of the user interface and the application (client), while the back end is the database engine itself, which processes a query and accesses data (server). The front end and back end communicate across a network via SQL. A single back end can support multiple front ends, and a single front end can access multiple back ends.

conceptual data model describes an integrated view of all data employed within the business in graphical terms as well as in the form of a database schema (conceptual schema). It includes the external schema, the conceptual schema, and the internal schema. In our approach to modeling, the conceptual data model consists of the Transaction Model, Structural Model, Behavioral Model, and the database schema.

conceptual schema provides the mapping between the internal schema and the external schema. Also known as the *conceptual business model* or the *integrated model*, the conceptual schema is almost always the most important component of the business modeling and design activity. As an integrated description of the business's data, the conceptual schema is, effectively, a consolidation of multiple logical data models. The conceptual schema helps to ensure consistency of multiple logical data models defined to support a variety of user groups and different functions and areas of the business. The conceptual schema also helps in designing a shared database supporting a number of user applications.

concurrency control is required for multiuser databases. There are two primary and conflicting goals of a multiuser database system: to allow many users to rapidly access and update data whenever they want (concurrency) and at the same time give each user the impression that no one else is changing the database at the same time (control). The design of the database system should ensure that there are no lost updates, that queries can be reproduced between viewing them on screen and printing a report, and that only committed records can be viewed by other users. Operating systems typically provide record and file locking mechanisms for concurrency control. Distributed databases typically provide their own record locking at the row, page, or table level.

concurrent tasks or events are those that are occurring simultaneously.

constraint is a condition or relationship that must remain true; constraints restrict operations on objects that may violate these conditions.

constructor is a C++ operation that initializes a newly created instance of a class.

data definition languages (DDL) are provided by most database vendors for creating and maintaining a database (usually a time-consuming task). Some databases allow developers to write 4GL (or SQL) code for creating a database. The 4GL code is then modified for any updates to the database. The DDL allows creation of catalogs (system-defined tables) that describe tables (or relations) for user data within the database.

data dictionary is a manual or automatic repository of information, usually managed by the database, describing applications, databases, logical data models and constituent objects, users and user access authorizations, and any other information useful for defining the organization and use of data within the database. These tables (which store the data dictionary) consist of the following information:

1. Definition of tables, columns, and datatype attributes for each column.
2. Information about primary and foreign keys relating different tables. (Note that foreign keys are used to maintain master-detail relationships between records.)
3. Definition of physical schema concepts, including data locations and utilization of disk volumes.
4. Definition of views, including information on what tables and columns are included in the view.
5. List of authorized users and their levels of authorization (that is, access restrictions on certain functions).
6. Domain information and business rules information.

A data dictionary is a critical component for a distributed database, providing location transparency for the user/developer in viewing data dispersed around the network. When the user asks to see what data are available, the appropriate information on tables and fields from each local and remote database must be somehow captured, consolidated, and presented to the user in a format consistent with what the user is accustomed to seeing.

data flow diagram (DFD) is a graphic functional representation of a system. DFDs are used for structured systems analysis. A high-level DFD presents a system overview depicting its overall purpose and its interaction with external objects. A DFD provides a general picture of data transformation in the system. Decomposition techniques are used to divide the system into individual processes. The decomposition technique is carried down to as many levels as necessary to fully define the system. Every process in a DFD transforms incoming data and passes its output data to another process or a data store. The transformation of data is identified by a control flow tag. Any primitive process that is not decomposed further is tagged with a control specification. A completed DFD is particularly useful in identifying the functions of a system and the ensuing data transformation. From the diagrams, users can determine if the inputs to the system reflect the real business model, if the outputs from the system are appropriate, that the data structures represent the information as it is currently stored (or should be stored), and that the processing logic takes into account all business rules and practices.

data integrity ensures that the data remain in a consistent state while providing concurrent access to a number of users. Data integrity in shared environments is an increasingly important and complex issue. Data integrity in a distributed database is particularly complex and only a few vendors have successfully implemented the capability to update data stored on multiple servers of a network in a single transaction. Data integrity in a tightly coupled system is generally achieved via two-phase commits and careful journaling.

data security has been an important issue due to confidential information (such as customer/employee records and financial information) in the database system. In a shared networked environment, there is less control on who may log in. Password security is provided by most operating systems and database systems at field and action level. Once set up properly, a good security scheme can be very effective in preventing unauthorized access to the database.

database is a permanent repository of data organized for ordered retrieval. The database management system manages all access to the data and maintains its own descriptive information about the organization and location of data.

database architecture describes layouts and interactions among database components. The client/server architecture, for example, is based on the concept of distributed processing, with the front end of the DBMS being the client and the back end, the server. The applications functions run on the client machines (usually a mini or a workstation), and the data access and manipulation functions run on one or more server machines.

database management system is a set of programs that manages and provides access to a permanent, self-descriptive repository of data organized for ordered retrieval.

database schema describes the organization of the database as tables and fields within tables. It includes the definition of tables, columns, and datatype attributes for each column and information about primary and foreign keys relating different tables. (Note that foreign keys are used to maintain master-detail relationships between records.) Also referred to as the *internal schema*, it describes the storage structures within the database and the retrieval strategies for accessing and retrieving data from the database.

data server, also called a database server, performs the following functions:

1. Centralized data management
2. Data integrity and database consistency
3. Database security
4. Concurrent operations (for multiuser access)
5. Centralized processing (for example, stored procedures)

A data server is typically a separate computer system in a network. There can be more than one data server in a network.

decision support systems are designed to provide management with information for making decisions and consequently have database requirements that are different from information systems that perform traditional data processing.

destructor (a C++ method) removes an instance of a class that is no longer needed.

development languages provide the means for programming applications. The most important reason for using a database management system is productivity; and the most important aspect of programmer productivity is elimination of mechanical detail without loss of flexibility and program flow control management capability. 4GLs, the most common development languages for database systems, allow data access algorithms and complex relations to be expressed in a high-level language. The development tools provide the environment to develop custom applications that utilize the full potential of the available 4GL languages and the database management system. For object-oriented systems, C++ and O++ have been used for programming. Other 4GL-level development environments are also emerging.

development tools are tools provided by the database system for the developers of applications. These tools typically include a database creation and maintenance utility, forms editor, a 4GL programming environment, and debuggers.

discriminator is an attribute that describes which property of a class is being abstracted by a generalization.

distributed database consists of two or more database servers connected on a network; that is, the data is distributed. Performance is a major factor that experiences significant impact from distributed system architectures. A distributed database is a means to provide parallel functions concurrently. A good distributed database can automatically handle concurrency control, integrity requirements, transaction management, and recovery across the network; it makes both the user's task and the developer's task significantly easier.

distributed network computing implies that processing (rather than or in addition to data) is distributed. The emphasis on distributed network computing has been the impetus for the database vendors to implement distributed database architectures. The database processing is split among two or more logical CPUs connected by a network. These CPUs may be geographically dispersed.

domain is a set of legal values that an attribute may assume.

domain integrity governs the allowable values that each attribute within the logical data model can assume. This check includes both a datatype check and a data range check.

domain integrity rules govern the types and ranges of values that attributes may assume. For example, a column defined to be CURRENCY (or MONEY) can contain only currency values. Some databases allow users to define their own datatypes. The domain integrity rules are applied in these cases also.

dynamic (or late) binding—the capability to bind the variables dynamically to objects at runtime (after selecting the method). Dynamic binding is used in object-oriented programming.

encapsulation (or information hiding) separates the external services of an object from its internal implementation (attributes and methods) and allows for cleaner modeling and implementation.

enterprise-wide systems support the diverse information needs of the entire enterprise. Enterprise-wide systems are characterized by heavy demands on data servers by geographically distributed users across towns, cities, states, countries, and continents sharing the same data and processing resources. Decentralization is a major step forward in bringing the data closer to the user and providing improved performance, while still maintaining the communication links for uniform access to all data across the enterprise.

entity integrity implies that no attribute that is a part of a primary key of a relation can be a NULL. This implies that not only is an object identified uniquely by its primary key, but also that it has a unique relation and a unique reason for existence. In other words, the object can be referenced unambiguously by one of its attributes.

Entity-Relationship (ER) diagram is a graphical representation of data objects (or entities) that shows the structural relationships between them.

event is an occurrence at an instantaneous point in time.

extensibility is a property of software that allows it to be enhanced with new data objects and functionality with little or no modification to existing code.

external schema defines the perspective of a relational database from an application point of a view. It is the view of the database that is visible to the users. The external schema defines the manner in which the data organization is presented to the user. The external schema may be different depending on the application and the programming interface used to access the data. A single database can support a large number of applications. Each application may have its own view of the database that is concerned only with the data items required for that application. Consequently, there can be a number of external schemas supported by a single internal schema.

firing of triggers happens when a field (or attribute) attains a value specified in the trigger. The trigger causes 4GL code to be executed that may change fields (or attributes) in other tables (or objects).

first normal form defines all relations (under normalization theory) that contain atomic values (therefore, every potential relation is included in first normal form).

foreign key is a key in a table in a relational database that is a primary key for another table.

Frame-Object Analysis—a good analysis and design for an information system require that both structural and behavioral properties be modeled to a level of detail sufficient for accurately defining each entity and each process within the system. Frame-Object diagrams combine the features of object definitions of information analysis, relation depiction of semantic networks, and the structured/layered concepts of frames. Frames can depict both structural and behavioral properties of objects. A frame in a behavioral perspective represents a function (or an operation).

frames are used to collect information components (which we will call objects for this discussion) that define an aspect or an area of an application. The representation of these objects can also include the relationship between these objects. A database can be described using the concept of frames. Each object in the frame defines a component of the database that may be resolved into a single field, a group of fields, or even a table. The database description is further enhanced by descriptions of relationships between the objects.

generalization is the relationship between a class and one or more refined versions of that class.

identity (as in object identity) is an identifier of an object that uniquely identifies the object and remains unchanged through the life of the object.

index is an ordered data structure that maps one or more keys in a table (or attribute values into objects) to provide rapid optimized access to the data record.

Information Analysis (IA) was developed as a methodology for depicting relations between objects by G. M. Nijssen of the University of Brussels. Based on the concepts of natural language, this methodology produces a data model that clearly, accurately, and unambiguously presents the design of the information system to the user and guides the implementation of the system. The concepts of IA are based on objects. The objects are classified and identified for an accurate description and depiction of data. Natural language constructs are then developed to depict the relations between objects. The information collected is then converted to diagrams that follow very specific data and relation representation guidelines.

information engineering is a methodology for designing information systems. Successful implementation of database systems requires the application of sound analytical techniques to ensure data integrity and reliable operation. The database design should provide flexibility for creative application development and should be laid out to perform efficiently. A good design should take into consideration current as well as future requirements to minimize database redesign as the needs of the business change.

information hiding (see *encapsulation*)

Information System model describes functions and data elements from a user-level perspective.

inheritance provides the means for building new classes on top of an existing, less extensive hierarchy of classes instead of redesigning the class of objects in totality. The new class inherits both characteristics of the parent class: object attributes (as defined by instance variables) and the methods (or operations).

instance is an object that has been described by a class; the object is called the instance of that class.

instance variable (as used in SmallTalk terminology) is an attribute in an object instance.

instantiation is the process of creating an object in a class.

interactive development tool typically provides a complete interactive graphical (or GUI) development environment. An interactive development tool consists of graphical editors, incremental compilers, interactive debuggers, and database browsers. The success of any development project depends to a large extent on the tools used. This is not only true but is crucial for very large projects where a number of programming groups are involved in development. Quality can be introduced early to the development cycle by ensuring clear communications with and among the project team and documenting not only the design but all other relevant project information at every step of development. A common tool set and consistent methodology go a long way in achieving this.

interprocess communication (IPC) is a scheme, usually within an operating system (such as UNIX) for passing messages or signals between two processes (or applications). Message queues, semaphores and shared memory are examples of IPC in UNIX.

internal schema describes the storage structures within the database and the retrieval strategies for accessing and retrieving data from the database. This consists of multiple occurrences of *internal records* (an ANSI/SPARC term equivalent to a row in a table). The internal schema views the data space as being contiguous logical space. The physical implementation of pages and physical records per page is defined one level below the internal schema level. The internal schema is commonly referred to as the database schema.

invariant—a statement about a condition or relationship that does not change and that is therefore always true.

join is the concatenation of rows from one database table to rows from another table.

join order is the sequence in which rows from one table are concatenated to rows from another table when more than two tables are being joined.

Concatenation produces a product, and adjusting the join order to minimize the product improves performance.

journaling—full transaction management is achieved through features called before-image and after-image journaling and rollback and roll-forward. Rollback is used if a complex transaction fails to complete; all incomplete updates are rolled back to reach a system state as it existed before the start of the transaction. Rollforward is used after a database failure to bring up an archived copy of the database to the level of the last completed transaction by applying recovery procedures (and using the journals for database activity information). The journals (or transaction logs) are used to achieve both rollback and rollforward.

message—an object invokes an operation in another object by communicating with it through a procedure, called a *message* in object-oriented programming terminology. Note that messages are not the same as methods. Messages are used for communications between objects, while methods generally act on the attributes of an object.

metaclass is a class that has one or more derived classes and therefore describes other classes.

metalanguage is an intermediate language produced by a compiler that allows the code to be more portable across different operating systems and hardware. An interpreter is required to execute metalanguage code.

methodology is defined as the standard procedure (or the modus operandi) for performing a task such as development of an application.

methods are analogous to a routine in conventional programming. A method is the implementation of an operation for a specific class and is encapsulated within the object. Methods typically manipulate the attributes of the object.

model is a paradigm or a prototype and serves as an abstraction of something that can be used to understand it before developing it.

multiple inheritance allows combining the properties of several existing classes into a subclass. Manipulations performed on the subclass address the variables defined for all parent classes.

multiplicity defines the one to many relationship between objects (or instances) or two associated object classes.

name server is a directory maintained by a server that lists all objects on that and other servers. This allows servers to rapidly determine where a requested object resides. A name server removes the need for searching through the entire object database for an object.

networking—a major issue in distributed databases is effective and efficient use of the network. It is important to minimize the amount of data sent over the network and to use the network bandwidth effectively. If data resides on a different node than the one requested, the request node forward may the request to the server node, which will return the data directly to the client process.

normalization is the process of defining relations over simple domains that contain atomic values only. Normalization theory takes this basic concept much further by allowing database designers to recognize cases that may still possess some undesirable properties, such as one field (or data component) being duplicated or being inclusive of another field (or data component), and converting such cases to more desirable forms. Normalization theory is built around the concept of *normal forms*. A relation is said to be in a particular normal form if it satisfies a certain specified set (or level) of constraints.

object is a corporeal body or an abstraction that has well-defined constituents and interpretations. In object-oriented programming, an object is an instance of a class.

object-based query optimization—the query optimizer in a database chooses the most efficient way to execute a particular query. Query optimization plans for object-oriented systems are object based. Significant performance improvements are achieved by fast AI-based dynamic query optimizers.

object identity is the property of an object that distinguishes it from all other objects. In object-oriented systems, this property of an object is independent of content, type, and addressability. Object identity is the only property of an object maintained across structural and behavioral modifications of an object.

object management is the storage, retrieval, and archival of objects in an object-oriented database system.

Object Model defines the detailed structural and behavioral components of each object of the system.

object-oriented database is one that stores data in the form of encapsulated objects and provides an object-oriented application development interface. That is, a true object-oriented database provides object orientation in both the back end and the front end.

object-oriented database management system is an object-based database management system that provides ordered storage and retrieval of data in the form of encapsulated objects. A true object-oriented database management system provides object orientation in both the back end and the front end.

object-oriented design is a design methodology that consists of a sequence of steps that leads to the definition, classification, and organization of objects in a database. Both structural and behavioral properties of the objects are documented.

object-oriented programming language is a language that supports the object paradigm (that is, integration of structural and behavioral constructs) and provides for programming of object classes, methods, inheritance, and so on.

object-oriented system and object-oriented database have been used throughout the text as synonyms for object-oriented database management system.

on-line transaction processing (OLTP) systems are characterized by widely distributed interactive access to a common database over high-performance network protocols.

OBDMS—object-oriented database management system.

operation as defined for object-oriented programming is a function or some kind of a transformation that can be applied to the attributes of instances of an object class.

persistent objects—database objects persist either in memory or on disk beyond the lifetime of the program that creates them and are usually stored on disk in an organized manner for future use. Such objects are called *persistent objects*. In a relational database, all records are persistent because they are retained on disk in the form of database tables. In an object-oriented database with a fully integrated object-oriented programming environment, objects may be either temporary (process based) or permanent (database server or disk based). The methods defined for an object class may operate on either type. Objects can also become persistent due to the inherited attributes and methods of a class.

polymorphism is the property that an operation may interact differently with objects from different classes. In other words, objects from different classes may respond in their own appropriate manner to a common message.

postcondition is a condition that an operation satisfies, for example, by providing certain values on return.

precondition is a condition that a caller of an operation must satisfy, for example, by providing values for certain input parameters.

primary key (as used for relational databases) is a field in a table that has a unique value for each row in the table (and therefore uniquely identifies each row). We have adapted this terminology for objects where the primary key is a unique attribute.

private attributes or operations of an object are those accessible by methods in the same class only.

public attributes or operations of an object are those that can be accessed by any method in any other object.

query is a database function that returns selected values without modifying the database in any manner.

recovery—corruption of data can leave a database in an inconsistent state. A good recovery utility can verify the data structures within the database for consistency and correct any problems found during the verification. The utility may use a combination of the last backup and the transaction log (see *journaling*) for full recovery.

redefinition is frequently used to redefine the features inherited by a child class from its parent class. The redefinition is intended to achieve a different implementation from the inherited object. The redefined version of a method (or routine) has arguments that match those of the original in number and (usually) in type, but not necessarily in value or semantics.

relation defines a set of tuples and is used as a synonym for a table in a relational database.

relational database—we have used the terms relational database and relational system throughout the text as synonyms for a database that is managed by a relational database management system.

relational database management system is a set of computer programs that provides ordered organization, storage, and retrieval of data. Data is organized in tables, and a data dictionary describes the organization.

relational (or referential) integrity is an integrity constraint that implies that an object (the equivalent of a row in a table) cannot be deleted if its primary key is referenced by a foreign key in another object. Stated another way, this says that the concept of a foreign key needs to be created in object-oriented databases and automatic checks made for referential integrity before deletions. Ensuring consistency of data and preventing updates and deletions of fields or data that may cause inconsistency require special attention in the design of an RDBMS-based application. Generally referred to as referential integrity, it attempts to ensure that tables retain consistency according to the rules set up for the database. For example, a master record for a customer cannot be deleted until all detail records (for example, invoices) have been posted and archived. Said another way, referential integrity is the ability of the database to define inter-table constraints within the database. Data entered, modified, or deleted in a table cannot circumvent these constraints. In addition, there are validation rules for data entered in specific fields. Some RDBMSs provide very methodical consistency checks automatically. Others allow the developer to program the checks in the data dictionary. Still others leave it all to the programmer to build in the application. Typically, consistency information is stored in the data dictionary.

relational system—we have used the term relational system and relational database throughout the text as synonyms for relational database management system.

remote procedure call (RPC) is a function call based on standardized syntax that provides for interpretation by another node on a network that may be from a different manufacturer. RPCs allow procedures to be executed on another node.

report generation tools are a part of a tool set provided for database systems that facilitate developing reports (printed output of data stored in the database).

request packaging is the method used for packaging requests (that is, combining multiple SQL statements in one function request) sent from the front end (client) to the back end (server). Request packaging affects network performance. The least efficient way do this is to send one database command (for example, one SQL statement) at a time and receive data in return. Some databases use stored procedures to restrict the data returned to selected fields in tables.

schema is the structure of the organization of data in a database.

second normal form is achieved in a relation if and only if it satisfies all first normal form conditions and every nonkey attribute is dependent on all elements of the primary key.

semantic network is a graphical representation of a relationship between two objects. It is a labeled directed graph where both nodes and edges may be labeled. The labels of nodes are typically used for reference purposes only and are usually mnemonic names. Designed originally for representing predicate calculus for logic programming, the semantic network concept can be easily extended to represent database designs. A semantic network gives a simple structured picture of a body of facts. The basic building block of a semantic network is a structure describing a relation (or a *predicate*).

server (database) is a system in a network that hosts database components. The term server is used in general to refer to any component in a system that provides a service to another component.

services are a group of related functions or operations of an object that are available externally.

specialization is creation of a subclass from a superclass by changing some attribute or operation (method) to provide a more specialized behavior.

stored procedures are collections of precompiled SQL statements stored in a database. These procedures allow partial encapsulation of data and operations in a relational database. Faster execution and reduced network traffic are achieved as a larger set of operations is performed in the database and only the final result is returned to the user. Stored procedures can be used for performing complicated queries and updates.

structural model describes the structural properties of objects from a static perspective. These properties include the logical elements of the objects required for the application.

structured query language (SQL) is a programming language standardized for storing, retrieving, and modifying data in a relational database. Attempts are in progress to use SQL for object-oriented database manipulation also.

subclass is a derived version of another class. The derived version is redefined.

superclass is a more abstract version of a subclass.

system architecture describes the components of the system, the services provided by each component, and the manner in which these components interact.

system design describes the planned intentions for the procedures performed by each component of the system, the role of each component in these procedures, the data elements used and saved for these procedures, and the results of these procedures.

table is an ordered set of information organized in rows and columns.

third normal form is achieved if and only if, and for all time, a relation consists of a primary key value that identifies an entity together with mutually independent attribute values (columns).

transaction is an atomic database operation that may consist of one or more database accesses.

transaction management—transaction processing is at the heart of most database applications. Data is entered, updated, and deleted by many users over and over again. The ability to smoothly, reliably, and promptly handle a complex transaction consisting of a number of queries, updates, and deletes is what distinguishes a superior application development system. If any update or delete does not complete, the transaction is incomplete and the database must be restored to the state before the start of the transaction (called rollback).

transaction model describes the interactions among application objects from the user's point of view. It describes the user-level operations (such as insert, query, update, and delete) in terms of the behavioral relationships among each application object.

transaction object is created by the transaction control object on each server that participates in the transaction and it processes each application request that is a part of the transaction. The transaction object handles distributed commits and interactions with any concurrent transactions.

triggers and stored procedures provide a means of defining and coding additional referential integrity constraints. Triggers can access other records and relations to provide operations such as collateral inserts and cascading deletes. Triggers can also be used to modify or erase otherwise not updatable records resulting from multirelation views. Possible update anomalies are avoided by having triggers that specify appropriate actions for each constituent relation.

tuple is an ordered list of data values. In simple terms it can be described as a row in a table or as a flat record.

two-phase commits are used by a number of databases to update databases distributed across a number of servers. Multiple databases can be on the same node in a network or they can be distributed across a number of different nodes. Typically, two-phase commits are used when databases reside on multiple servers. Before a transaction is applied, all databases on the network that will be updated by the transaction are polled and the update is applied if all databases reply in the affirmative. If a database cannot be updated, the entire transaction is rolled back.

versioning—many database applications, such as computer-aided design, use multiple versions of the same object. Object versions are also important in databases such as accounting and financial applications that maintain historical information. For example, versions can be used to store previous-year financial information.

wide area network (WAN)—a local-area network (LAN) provides data access to applications within a site while a wide area network (WAN) provides data access to a number of geographically dispersed sites.

Bibliography and References

Agrawal, R and Gehani, N. ODE (Object Databases and Environment): The Language and the Data Model, *AT&T Bell Laboratories Technical Memorandum,* Murray Hill, N.J., 1989.

Agrawal, R and Gehani, N. Rationale for the Design of Persistence and Query Processing Facilities in the Database Programming Language O++, *2nd International Workshop on Database Programming Languages,* Oregon Coast, June 1989.

Brodie, Michael L. and Ridjanovic, Dzenan. On the Design and Specification of Database Transactions, in *On Conceptual Modelling: Perspectives from Artificial Intelligence, Databases, and Programming Languages,* Brodie M. L.; Mylopoulos, J.; and Schmidt, J. W. (eds), *Springer-Verlag,* New York, 1984.

Ceri, Stefano and Pellagotti, Guiseppe. Distributed Databases: Principles and Systems, *McGraw Hill Book Co.,* New York, 1984

Chen, Peter Pin-Shan. The Entity Relationship Model—Toward a Unified View of Data, presented at the *International Conference on Very Large Data Bases,* Framingham, Massachusetts, September 22-24, 1975. Permission by ACM, Copyright 1976.

Church, A. Introduction to Mathematical Logic, *Princeton University Press,* 1958.

Codd, E. F. A Relational Model for Large Shared Data Banks, *Communications of the ACM,* 13, 1970, pp. 377–387.

Codd, E. F. Extending the Database Relational Model, *ACM Transactions on Database Systems,* 4, 1979, pp. 397–434.

Codd, E. F. Further Normalization of the Relational Data Base Model, *Database Systems,* Courant Computer Science Symposia Series, Vol. 6, *Prentice Hall,* Englewood Cliffs, N.J., 1972.

Codd, E. F. Is Your DBMS Really Relational?, *Computerworld*, October 14, 1985.

Codd, E. F. Normalized Data Base Structure: A Brief Tutorial, *Proceedings of ACM SIGFIDET Workshop on Data Description, Access and Control*, 1971.

Codd, E. F. Relational Database: A Practical Foundation for Productivity, *ACM Transactions on Database Systems*, 1981.

Codd, E. F. The Relational Model for Database Management: Version 2; *Addison-Wesley*, 1990, Appendix A (Section A-7).

Date, C. J. Twelve Rules for a Distributed Data Base, *Computerworld*, June 8, 1987.

Fayol, H. Administration et Generale, *Paris:Dunod*, 1916, First English Translation 1929; second translation by Constance Storrs, London, *Sir Isaac Pitman & Sons, Ltd.*, 1949.

Indirizzi di normalizzazione nell'area delle technologie dell'informazione nella publica administrazione, *Gazetta Ufficiale della Republica Italiana*, Supplemento N. 38, 30 maggio 1990, pp 24–27.

Linton, Mark A; Calder, Paul R.; and Vlissedes, John M. InterViews: A C++ Graphical Interface Toolkit, *Stanford University*, Stanford, CA,

Linton, Mark A; Calder, Paul R.; and Vlissedes, John M. The Design and Implementation of InterViews, *Proceedings of the UNENIX C++ Workshop*, Santa Fe, NM, November 1987.

Vlissedes, John M.; Linton, Mark A; and Calder, Paul R. Composition Mechanism for Graphical User Interfaces, *Stanford University*, Stanford, CA.

Meyer, Bertrand. Object-Oriented Software Construction, *Prentice, Hall*, Englewood Cliffs, N.J., 1988.

Pons, Jean-Francois and Vilarem, Jean-Francois. Dynamic and Integrated Concurrency Control for Distributed Databases, *IEEE Journal on Selected Areas in Communications, 7, No. 3*, April 1989.

Pospesel, H. Introduction to Predicate Logic, *Prentice-Hall*, 1973.

Ryu, Kyung and Thomasian, Alexander. Performance Analysis of Dynamic Locking with No-waiting Policy, *IEEE Transactions on Software Engineering, 16, No. 7*, July 1990.

Smith, J. M. and Smith, J. C. P. Database Abstractions: Aggregations and Generalizations, *ACM Transactions on Database Systems, 2*, 1977, pp. 105–133.

Stoll, R. R. Sets, Logic, and Axiomatic Theories, 1960.

Suppes, P. Introduction to Logic, *Van Nostrand*, 1967.

Verheijen, G. M. and Van Bekkum, J. NIAM: An Information Analysis Method, in *Information Design Methodologies: A Comparative Review*, by Olle, T. W.; Sol, H. G.; and Verryn-Stuart, A. A. (eds.), *North Holland*, Amsterdam, 1982, pp. 537–590.

Index

3GL, 94
4GLs (Fourth Generation Languages), 2, 94, 185, 336
abstract data type, 58–62
  axioms, 62
  constraints, 62
  implementation of, 61, 62
  instance of, 61, 62
  model, 61
  pre-conditions, 62
  programming, 62
  programming in C++, 62
  rules, 62
abstract data typing:
  definition of, 89
abstract operations, 201
abstraction:
  applied to models, 230
  behavior, 221
  principle of, 233
access control lists, 269
access mechanism:
  for database systems, 88
access methods:
  B-tree (balance tree), 312
  buffered sequential, 312
  explicit relationship, 315
  hashing, 314
  indexed sequential (ISAM), 312
  sequential, 312
access name-server, 286
access optimization:
  for distributed object oriented database, 357, 358
  manager, 357
access permissions, 269
access restrictions, 194
activity viewer, 343
advanced application builders, 337
aggregation, 138, 318, 407
  as a structural abstraction, 229
  depiction of relationships, 138, 231
animation, 358, 462
annotated code hierarchy charts, 179
annotated data flow diagrams, 179
annotated procedure structure charts, 179
application builders:
  advanced tools, 336
application servers, 323
  in networks, 327
Architectural Recommendation, 206, 207, 209, 361, 364, 376
architecture, 205
  client/server, 8, 284
  of CASE environments, 179
  of distributed systems, 284
  of networks, 284
  X Windows, 327

archival, 276, 300, 361
  of distributed databases, 378
artificial intelligence:
  for query optimization, 12
assembly structures, 148
assertion, *see constraints*
association, 407, *see also relationships*
  as a structural abstraction, 229
  for grouping objects, 248
  for indexing of objects, 319
atomic operation, 229
atomic transactions, 87
attribute, 65, 153, 154, 189, 213, 217, 253, 286, 362
  as structural component, 213
  association with entities, 217
  classification of, 153
  definition for ER diagrams, 116
  definition of, 59
  depicted in frames, 217, 385, 387
  details, 154
  in an object, 59
  in Entity Model, 216
  in Transaction Control Objects, 294
  inherited from parent, 261
  of a data entity, 109
  of objects, 154, 430
  private, 257
  public, 257
attribute domain rules, 199
attribute identification, 154
audio:
  in binary datatype, 99
authentication, 285
  of database access, 300

b-splines:
  for CAD/CAM, 349
B-trees, 312
  advantages of, 312
  used for joins, 314
backup, 361
  for system administration, 300
  of distributed databases, 378
backward chaining, 354
balanced trees, *see B-trees*
base class, 92, 269, 332
base object class:
  for transaction control, 296
  instances, 252
basic objects:
  designing, 172
behavior abstractions, 221
  definition of, 237
  examples of, 241
behavioral changes, 71
behavioral components, 174, 383
  for object design, 421
  of objects, 147, 150, 155, 157, 202, 412

behavioral frame, 156, 239, 412
  developing, 413
  example of, 390, 415
  examples of, 240
  top-level, 413
behavioral mapping, 248
  of methods, 406
Behavioral Model, 171, 213, 230, 236, 252, 362, 407, 412
  as part of Object Model, 210
  definition of, 212
  description of, 214
  prototyping of, 171
behavioral properties, 203
  as an abstraction, 230
  of database transactions, 229
behavioral relationships, 140
  decomposition, example of, 141
  example of, 140
  in Frame-Object Analysis, 140, 141
bi-modal semantic network, 129
  example, 130
binary datatype, 99, 345
  definition of, 99
binary large objects (BLOBs), 21, 58, 323, 332, 349, 462
binary search, 312
binary sentence, 126, 127
  nesting, 126
bit-mapped graphics editors, *see icon editors*
bitmaps:
  in binary datatype, 99
  in BLOBs, 58
Boyce & Cold (B&C):
  normalization, 113
breakpoint list window, 343
browsers, 342
  class inheritance, 342
  function call cross-referencing, 342
  program structure, 342
  source, 342
browsing, 342
buffered sequential access, 312
business function model, 171
business information model, 203–05, 207, 361, 364, 366, 382, 383
  components of, 207
  definition of, 212
  development strategy, 208
business model, 122, 205, 361, 364
  definition of, 212
business rules, 96, 174, 191, 194
  for design, 147, 174
  programming of, 174
buttons, 332, 337

C++ programming language, 62, 88, 94, 99, 163, 261, 332
  operator symbols, 264
C language, 336
CAD/CAM, 333, 346
  data structures, 349
  entity definitions, 349
cardinality ratio, 118
Cartesian product, 26, 28, *see also relational algebra*
cartographic systems, 345
  data structures, 351
cascading abort, 289
CASE, 176, 177, 178, 343
  integrated tools, 181
  multi-vendor tools, 181
  standards, 181
  tools, 133, 176, 336
  use of, 207, 208
circumsection, 158
class, 62, 66, 88, 90, 93
  as implementation of abstract data types, 66
  child class, 253
  class library, 55, 57, 97
  class relationships, 139
  client relationships, 94
  descriptor, 101
  ID, 91
  identifiers, 267, 269
  inheritance relationships, 94
  instances of, 65
  location descriptors, 318
  management, 318
  programming of, 66
  use of, 70, 90, 94
  use of inheritance, 69
class definition, 26, 66, 198, 199, 251, 254, 257, 426
  behavioral properties, 199
  for objects, 90
  in object oriented database, 92
  programming in C++, 63
  structural properties, 199
class hierarchy, 71, 153, 199
  class hierarchy diagrams, 71, 72, 153
  code example of, 442–44
  depicting in Frame-Object diagrams, 138, 139, 153
  depiction of, 233
  in structural frame, 408
class inheritance:
  browsers, 342
  hierarchy, 71
class method, 257, 260, 291, 419–22
  code example of, 440–60
  example of, 243
class name:
  in Information Analysis, 126
classical relational model, 462
classification, 152, 156, 407
  of objects, 151
  to create object classes, 247
classification structures:
  for attributes, 148
client, 7
client/server architecture, 282, 284, 327
  for distributed database systems, 282
client/server model, 57, 58
client/server protocols, 327

client objects, 69
clients, 42
clustered index, 316
clustering, 316
  disks, 6
  of information, 311
  of objects, 318, 319
Codd, E.F., 31, 109, 189
code generator, 177, 178
  in CASE tools, 177
cognitive concepts, 277
  hierarchy of, 277
collision detection, 289
command buttons, 327
complex methods, 264
composite abstract operations:
  as behavior abstractions, 237
computer-aided design, 93
concepts:
  definition of, 277
  in semantic networks, 130
conceptual behavioral model, 172
conceptual business model, *see conceptual schema*
conceptual data model, 171, 203, 205, 210, 212, 382
conceptual database schema, 191, 210
  combining logical data model, 192
  definition of, 191
  representation of, 193
conceptual design, 411
conceptual model, 116
conceptual objects, 117
concurrency control, 10, 25, 196
  in distributed database systems, 197, 289
  in object oriented databases, 87
concurrent transactions, 25
concurrent updates:
  of database objects, 291
configuration management, 300
conjunctions:
  depicted in semantic networks, 132
connections between objects, 147
constraints, 95, 190, 271
  in Information Analysis, 128
  programming of, 64
  relational integrity, 108
  system-defined, 36
  use of, 63
  user-defined, 96, 97
constructor method, 256, 446, 447
constructors, *see constructor methods*
control abstraction, 236, 248
  choice (or decision), 229, 236
  repetition, 229, 236
  sequence, 229, 236, 238
  use of frames for depiction, 239
conventional programming, 61, 69, 93
copy server, 304
corporate business strategy, 274
corporate hierarchy, 280
cost benefit analysis:
  as part of feasibility survey, 167
current procedures, 167
current processes, 167

data abstraction, 87
data definition language, 193
data dictionary, 46, 47, 109, 177, 189, 193, 344
  deficiencies of, 195
  definition of, 189
  distributed, 304
  for distributed databases, 194
  for object-oriented database, 197, 198
  in CASE tools, 176
  integrated, 46
  portability, 344
  role in object oriented databases, 189
  role of, 194
data encapsulation, 60
data entity, 110
  attributes, 110
data flow:
  model, 212
  modeling, 169
data flow diagram, 109, 110, 120, 235
  data flows, 122
  data stores, 122
  destination, 122
  for representing conceptual schema, 193
  limitations, 125
  processes, 122
  source, 121
  use with ER diagrams, 125
data flows, 412
  in data flow diagrams, 121
data independence, 24, 45
data integrity, 147, 288
  in distributed database systems, 288
data integrity issues, 119
data model, 111
data modeling, 336
data objects, 110
  in an information system, 208
data server, *see database server*
data storage:
  considerations for distributed databases, 379
data store, 110
  in data flow diagrams, 121
data streams:
  in data flow diagrams, 121
data structure:
  formal properties of services, 89
  modeling, 169
  services, 89
data transformation:
  in data flow diagrams, 121
data windows, 337
database:
  architecture, 308
  database engine, 308
  recovery, 348
  replication, 14
  security, 14, 285
  server, 6
  tables, 24, 110
  user configurable, 344
database browser, 163
  graphical, 339
database design, 307
  in sentence diagrams, 129
database integrity, 10
  data dictionary enforced, 194

database integrity (*cont.*)
  for distributed objects, 196
database management systems:
  hierarchical, 2
  network, 2
database object, 203
  persistent, 91
database organization, 308
  organization of objects, 310
  re-organization, 348
database schema, 106, 215
  in object environments, 215
  in relational databases, 215
database server, 58, 209, 252,
    361, 376
  location of, 209
database synchronization
  of distributed databases, 378
  of distributed servers, 379
dataflow editors, 337
datatypes, 362, 421
  arrays, 253
  binary, 345
  boolean, 253
  char, 253
  float, 253
  int, 253
  money, 253
  object list (variable length), 253
  of object attributes, 251, 442,
    444
  string, 253
  text, 345
Date, C.J., 189
debuggers, 342
decision support, 276, 279
decomposition, 120, 280
  example of, 381
  of data and methods, 138
  of functions, 222, 230
  of information system, 209
  of object class, 233, 409
DECwindows, 327, 340
deferred classes, 79, 87
  definition of, 82
deferred method, 82
denormalization, 114, 146, 307,
    316, 334
  example of, 234
  for performance optimization,
    315
  objectives of, 115
  of relational databases, 146
  use of, 114
depicting metaclasses:
  in Frame-Object Analysis
    diagrams, 139
depiction methodology, 145, 167
  Frame-Object Analysis dia-
    grams, 135, 138
  frame diagrams, 135
  success factors, 134
  use of ER diagrams, 135
  use of Information Analysis,
    135
  use of semantic networks, 130,
    134
design assumptions, 376
design depiction methodology,
    145, 167
design documentation, 170, 171
design frame:
  example of, 422–24
design life cycle, 167
design methodology, 106, 167

for object oriented systems,
    145
design specifications, 173, 203
designing database objects, 215,
    221, 430
desktop publishing, 101
destination:
  in data flow diagrams, 121
destructor method, 256, 262
  destructors, 256, 262
detail design, 412
determiners:
  in Information Analysis, 126
development life cycle, 274
development tools:
  based on expert systems, 343
diagramming techniques:
  for conveying design informa-
    tion, 167
difference operator, *see Relational
    Algebra*
digitized audio, 325
digitized voice, 325
disjunction (in semantic net-
    works), 132
disk organization, 311
  performance impact, 309
display characteristics:
  of user applications, 327
Display Postscript, 18
display systems:
  multi-media, 6
display technologies, 325
distributed:
  access, 348
  applications, 362
  architectures, 323
  CASE, 181
  data, management of, 274
  file service operations, 299
  information system, 276, 372
  network computing, 4
  network services, 300
  object-oriented data-system,
    462
  object-oriented databases, 307
  object management, 302, 320
  operations, 274
  repository, 180
  server, 379
  system administration, 300
  system architecture, 284
  systems, 276
distributed commit protocol, 10,
    290
  centralized implementation,
    290
  decentralized implementation,
    290
  for distributed systems, 14
distributed data, 10
  distributed data dictionary,
    197, 304
  server, 10
distributed database, 170, 252
  architecture, 8, 282, 348
  management, 299
  servers, 8
distributed query, 13, 286, 287
  definition of optimization, 11
  optimization, 11
distributed storage:
  for distributed databases, 379
distributed transaction, 291
  management of, 289, 293

on-line processing, 323
  protocol for management, 294
document image,
  accessing, 348
  indexing of, 347
  location of, 347
  management, 325
  scanning, 325
documentation editor, 339
domain, 111, 162, 193, 194. *see
    also relational algebra*
domain integrity, 97, 190. *see also
    integrity rules*
  rules, 34, 190
duplicated objects, 163
duplication:
  of data, 284
  of object database, 305
  of objects, 302
dynamic binding, 79–81, 87, 251
  benefits of, 81
  definition of, 81
dynamic database re-structuring,
    334
  for performance optimization,
    316
dynamic denormalization, 307,
    317
  for performance optimization,
    316
  use of expert systems, 317
dynamic locking, 289
dynamic procedures, *see stored
    procedures*
dynamic window management,
    325, 344

E.F. Codd
  foundation rules, 31
  Rule 0, 31
  Rule 1, 32
  Rule 10, 33, 37
  Rule 11, 34, 46
  Rule 12, 36
  Rule 2, 32
  Rule 3a, 32
  Rule 3b, 32
  Rule 4, 32, 46, 47
  Rule 5, 32, 47
  Rule 6a, 33
  Rule 6b, 33
  Rule 7, 33
  Rule 8, 33, 45, 46
  Rule 9, 33, 41, 46
  rules, 58
edit boxes, 337
Eiffel, 56
electronic publishing, 101
embedded systems, 162
encapsulated operations, 147
encapsulation, 13, 39, 90, 94, 96,
    138, 147, 251, 288
  benefits, 91
  criteria, 150
  definition of, 90
  example of, 461
  in object-oriented databases,
    90
  of group technologies, 356
  of inference engine, 356
  of integrity checks, 197
  of methods, 99
entity, 147, 189, 251, 412
  attributes of, 218
  characterization, 218

decomposition, 219
definition of, 116
depicted graphically, 216
depicted in frames, 218, 384–89
depicting real life objects, 216
depicting relationships, 218
hierarchy, 219
in Entity Model, 216
in relational systems, 147
in structural frame, 408–10
linking attributes to, 218
logical grouping of, 218
multi-level, 219
organization of, 189
relationships among, 219
entity decomposition
example of, 220
multi-level, 220
entity frame, 216
example of, 383
entity integrity, 36, 97, 191
as system defined constraint, 191
Entity Model, 213, 229, 362, 382, 384
as part of Information System Model, 210
definition of, 212
depicted in frames, 386
description of, 213, 215
Entity Relationship (ER) model, 116
depicted in entity frames, 219
depicted in frames, 384–86
model, 116
Entity Relationship diagrams (ER), 108, 115, 134, 218, 235
conventions, 117
drawing conventions, 118
editors, 338
for representing conceptual schema, 193
strengths and weaknesses, 120
use with data flow diagrams, 125
enumerator, 257
equi-joins, 44
error checkers
runtime, 178
static, 178
event relationships, 117
events:
in semantic networks, 130
existence relationships, 117
expert system, 343, 345, 353
for dynamic denormalization, 317
integrated into RDBMS, 353
methodologies, 110
explicit relationships, 315
exported methods, 61
extended semantic hierarchy, 230
in data abstraction model, 230
extended semantic hierarchy abstractions, 230
aggregation, 230
association, 230
classification, 230
generalization, 230
external schema, 191, 210
externals:
in data flow diagrams, 121

fault-tolerance, 323
feasibility report, 361, 364
feasibility survey, 168
fiber optic cables, 277
fifth normal form (5NF), 112
normalization, 112
first normal form (1NF), 110
flowcharts, 170
foreign key, 96, 126, 191, 193, 194
form modifiers:
in semantic network, 132
forward chaining, 354
fourth normal form (4NF), 112
normalization, 112
fragmentation:
of a database, 284
frame, 135, 251, 332
depicting objects, 254
diagrams, 134
examples of, 135, 396
hierarchical, 226
in semantic network, 130
multi-level, 230
structural, 251
use of, 407–11
used for system design, 422–25
viewed as a cluster, 319
Frame-Object Analysis, 110
Frame-Object Analysis diagrams, 134, 136, 138, 170, 202, 251, 252, 338, 378, 387, 389, 408–13, 415–21
behavioral relationships, 140
class relationships, 139
depicting aggregation, 139
depicting behavioral relationships, 140, 141
depicting circumsection, 159
depicting instance connections, 158
depicting message connections, 158
depicting metaclasses, 138
depicting multi-leg paths, 160
depicting object services, 161
depicting processes, 140
depicting structural relationships, 138
example of, 139
for conveying design information, 168
for depicting Behavioral Model, 415–21
for depicting Entity Model, 213, 216, 384–86
for depicting Object Model, 246, 408–21
for depicting Structural Model, 408–11
for depicting Transaction Model, 213, 237, 393
for modeling object oriented systems, 212
for object-oriented systems design, 145, 147
for representing conceptual schema, 193
for system documentation, 142
information depiction, 246
to describe tasks, 148
used for system design, 421
using semantic network concepts, 230

Frame-Object diagrams, *see Frame-Object Analysis diagrams*
frame analysis, 108
frame diagrams, 135
function call cross-referencing browsers, 342
function hierarchy, 230, 389
of business functions, 208
function hierarchy diagrams:
using Frame-Object diagrams, 153
function keys, 337, 389
use of, 227, 228
functional breakdown:
of application, 222
functional decomposition:
for systems analysis, 169
of systems, 146
functional expert, 169, 173
role of, 169
use of, 168
use of in knowledge engineering, 169
functional hierarchy:
in a corporation, 281
functional relationships, 117
functions, 62, 412, 413, *see also exported methods*
decomposition of, 224
hierarchical, 225
sequential, 224

Gane & Sarson model:
data flow diagrams, 337
example of, 122
for data flow diagrams, 121
generalization, 147, 150, 152, 247, 318, 407
applied to attributes, 153
as a structural abstraction, 229
genetic class, 254
geographical information systems (GIS), 100, 323, 345
data structures, 349, 351
tiling GIS data, 352
graphical database browser, 339
graphical editing, 340
editors, 337
forms editors, 337
graphical schema generator, 339
graphical source level debugger, 339
graphical user interfaces (GUI), 5, 17–20, 327, 330, 340
for distributed applications, 21
graphics, 462
group technology, 346, 353, 356
encapsulation of, 356
grouping functions, 222

hash algorithm, 314
hashing, 314
advantages of, 314
characteristics of, 315
disadvantages of, 314
hash algorithm, 314
heuristics:
for query execution plans, 287
hierarchical class definition:
from aggregation abstraction, 231
hierarchical frames, 226
hierarchical relationships:
depiction of, 225

hierarchy:
of CASE components, 176
high availability:
designing for, 378
holographic displays, 333
holographic images, 325
hypertext, 102
systems, 323

icon, 327, 330
editors, 337
image, 6
as an object, 100
data storage & retrieval, 346
decompression, 325
management, 332
management systems, 345
image management, 345
use of object oriented databases, 349
implication:
depicted in semantic networks,
133
incremental compilers, 178
interactive, 340
incremental linkers, 178
indexed sequential access
method (ISAM), 312
indexes, 57, 198
clustered, 316
indexing, 308
indexing of images, 346
indexing of objects, 88, 318
role of, 311
inference engine, 353
encapsulation of, 356
inference trees, *see rules of inference*
information:
definition of, 277
Information Analysis, 109, 125,
133, 134
uses of, 133
information engineering, 106
methodology, 106
information flow, 169, 280
information groupings, 252
information management, 279
advanced system, 2, 3
information objects, 205
determination of, 208
information processing, 277
information resource, 278
centralized systems, 282
management, 274, 278
model, 279
information strategies, 274
information structure
definition of, 117
rules, 190
Information System Model, 201,
205, 210, 361, 383, 407, 421
as a specification, 203
definition of, 201, 212
description of, 213
substituting conceptual data
model, 210
information systems, 171, 412
analysis for object design, 148
Information Systems Model, 213
information systems strategy, 274
inheritance, 60, 69, 80, 81, 88,
94, 152, 153, 163, 220, 251,
253
benefits of, 69

code example of, 256, 442, 443
depiction of relationships, 339
multiple, 88, 90, 92, 251
repeated, 88
inherited methods:
use of, 70
inner join, 42
example of, 43
instance connections, 156
depiction in Frame-Object
diagrams, 157
instance method, 260, 261, 291,
417–23
examples of, 242
instance variables, 64
instantiating client objects, 68
integrated CASE, 180
control integration, 180
data integration, 180
integrated development:
development methodology,
336
environments, 336
integrated model, *see conceptual
schema*
integrity:
domain, 97
entity, 34, 97
referential, 34, 97
integrity constraints, 34, 58, 98,
108, 197
dependency constraints, 34
state constraints, 34
system defined, 34
transition constraints, 34
type constraints, 34
user defined, 34
integrity rules, 24, 34, 190
data integrity, 34
domain integrity, 34
integrity constraints, 34
relational integrity, 34
storage of, 37
user defined, 36
inter-object relationships, 155
due to behavioral components,
155
due to structural components,
155
interactive application development:
comprehensive tools, 336
interactive code generators, 338
interactive incremental compilers, 338
interactive symbolic debugger:
object-oriented, 338
interactor, 332
internal data structures, 202
internal schema, 191, 210
intersection (operator), *see relational algebra*
inverted file, 312
ISDN, 276

join, 25, 28, 42, 51, 113, 286, 307,
311, *see also relational
algebra*
equi-joins, 44
inner, 42
join fields, 42
join order, 45, 286, 317
join plan, 45
multi-way joins, 45
natural, 42

outer, 42
uses of, 42
join class, 318
in object oriented databases,
317
join methods, 44
merging scans, 44
nested loops, 44
join optimization:
for performance optimization,
316
join plan, *see join*
journaling, 50

knowledge:
definition of, 278
engineering, 169

LAN (local area network), 4, 252,
276, 376
late binding, *see dynamic binding*
link attributes, 217, 385
depicted in frames, 386, 387
link view, 218
linked objects, 261
localization, 248, 407
applied to models, 229
example of, 235
principle of, 234
localized failures, 282, 284
definition, 10
for distributed systems, 16
location transparency, 282
definition, 11
for distributed databases, 11,
194
lock contention:
performance degradation, 289
locking, 16
explicit, 16
for concurrency control, 51
page level, 51
row level, 51
table level, 51
logical data elements, 276
logical data model, 189, 192
logical decomposition
of business information, 131
of semantic network, 131
logical relationship:
in ER diagrams, 119
long haul networks, 276
lower CASE, 178, 183

master-detail tables, 315
menu hierarchy, 222, 389, 393
depicted in frames, 222
menus, 202, 327, 332
message, 61
connections, 156
as interactor, 332
between objects, 147, 155
definition of, 68
direct invocation type, 156
formats, 156
IPC type, 156
name, 156
selector, 69
type, 156
message types:
for X Windows, 328
metaclass, 71, 78, 138
method, 16, 65, 88, 173, 213,
251–53, 362, 412, 420–23
class, 420–23

code example of, 426–60
constructor method, 256
creation of, 80
definition of, 60
destructor method, 256
for programming integrity
   checks, 97
in objects, 59, 60, 147, *see also*
   behavioral components
in Transaction Control Objects,
   294
instance, 420–23
parameters, 253
post-conditions, 64
pre-conditions, 64
triggers, 261
methodology:
  for designing objects, 215
  for developing models, 215
  for monitoring performance,
   308
Microsoft Windows, 327, 330,
  340
model:
  Behavioral Model, 213
  conceptual data model, 212
  data flow model, 212
  definition of, 202
  Entity Model, 213
  hierarchical, 1
  Information System Model, 213
  network, 1
  Object Model, 213
  relational, 26, 58
  Structural Model, 213
  Transaction Model, 213
modeling, 203, 429
  advanced databases, 230
  an information system, 210
  CAD/CAM, 332
  database structures, 338
  definition of, 202
monitoring:
  of performance, 311
monotonic reasoning, 354
multi-media:
  applications, 332, 463
  coordination, 359
  databases, 325
  display, 6, 325
  electronic filing cabinet, 21
  for distributed object-oriented
   database, 357
  information, 323
  management, 360
  objects, 345
multi-media systems, 6
  image, 6
  voice, 6
multi-processor systems, 307
multi-way joins, 45
multiple data servers:
  in network, 352
multiple inheritance, 78, 87, 90,
  153, 251
  uses of, 80, 92
multiplicity:
  of object connections, 157

name-server, 15, 303
named clusters, 273
natural joins, 42
natural language interfaces, 327,
  333
  use of, 333

negation:
  depicted in semantic networks,
   132
nested methods, 16
network, 361, 376
  architecture, 284
  security, 10
  services, 286
networking protocols:
  impact of, 376
Nijssen, G.M., 125
non-uniform rational b-splines:
  for CAD/CAM, 349
normal form:
  definition of, 110
  first normal form (1NF), 110
  second normal form (2NF), 111
  third normal form (3NF), 112
normalization, 56, 109, 110, 129,
  152, 307
  equivalent in object oriented
   design, 152
  full, 113
  theory, 110
normalized tables:
  in relational database, 112
nouns:
  in Information Analysis, 126

O++ programming language,
  93, 261, 271
object, 56, 58, 147, 174, 286, 387
  abstract datatypes, 59
  attributes, 58, 59, 108
  classes, 261
  clustering of, 319
  code example of creation, 427
  code example of destruction,
   427, 428
  constructor of, 101
  creation, 90
  data encapsulation, 59
  decomposition, 136
  definition of, 58, 59, 252
  designing, 214, 430
  designing behavioral part, 215
  designing structural part, 215
  destruction, 262
  determination of, 170
  encapsulation, 251
  establishing definitions, 151
  hierarchies, 251
  hierarchy, 59
  identifers, 256
  identification, 251
  identifiers, 267
  identity, 59, 84, 85
  in Frame-Object Analysis, 138
  in Information Analysis, 125
  in relational databases, 195
  indexing of, 319
  inheritance, 251
  instance of object class, 61
  logical relationships, 110
  methods, 58, 59
  model, 88
  modeling of, 214
  naming conventions, 150
  object-oriented model, 57
  operations, 58, 59
  ordinary, 98
  permanent, *see persistent objects*
  persistence, 269
  persistence, 90, 93
  persistent, 98

pointer to, 253, 256
re-usable, 89
refining basic objects, 151
root metaclass, 71
temporary, 93
updating of, 291
used for remote file service,
  300
versioned, 98
versions, 90
object-orientation, 18, 463
  in relational databases, 99
  programming front-ends, 99
object-oriented:
  4GLs, 96
  data model, 57
  database, 56–58, 87, 88, 91, 92,
   96, 97, 100
  database (requirements), 87
  database features, 90
  database implementation, 97
  database management system,
   90
  database model, 59
  database programming language, 93
  database systems, 58, 59, 101
  design, 58, 95, 100, 160
  development environment, 93,
   96, 97
  front-ends (programming
   languages), 99, 100
  programming, 57, 60, 88–91,
   94–96, 101
  programming environment, 93
  programming language, 56, 57,
   58, 59, 88, 89
  programming methodologies,
   60
  programming techniques, 101
  relational databases, 96
  system, 58, 88, 89, 95, 96, 100
object-oriented analysis and
  design, 170
object-oriented data management, 464
object-oriented database, 56, 58,
  97, 98, 252, 286, 332, 338,
  344, 409, 461
  advanced development environments, 339
  application, 203
  architectural constructs of, 58
  benefits of, 101
  business rules programming,
   98
  design of, 430
  emulation in stored procedures, 100
  for CAD/CAM, 102
  for CAD/CAM, cartography
   and GIS, 352
  for electronic publishing, 101
  management system, *see*
   ODBMS
  post-conditions, 98
  pre-conditions, 98
  relational extensions, 96
  rules for, 88
  use of expert systems, 356
  use of group technologies, 357
  uses for, 58, 100
  weaknesses, 96
object-oriented design, 149, 160
  methodology, 147

object-oriented design (*cont.*)
  techniques, 170
object-oriented environment, 97
object-oriented information
  model, 345
object-oriented methodology, 170
object-oriented programming, 59,
  60, 69, 95, 252
  languages, 163, 252
  messages, 60
  theory behind it, 59
object-oriented systems:
  revision tracking, 101
  role for database systems, 102
object-oriented techniques, 147
object assembly structures, 151
object attribute schema, 153
object attributes, 64, 147, 203,
  254, 257
  code example of manipulation
    of, 430–56
  in Frame-Object Analysis
    diagrams, 139
object class, 60, 61, 89, 138, 230,
  243, 251, 342, 408, 418
  defining, 252, 410
  depicting links, 338
  depiction in frame, 244, 409
  depiction in semantic network,
    131
  design of, 153
  frame, example of, 420
  from classification abstraction,
    230
  implementation of, 267
  implementation in C++, 254
  in structural frame, 408
  instance of, 61, 65
object class hierarchy, 251, 431
  depiction in frame, 411
  example of, 428–31
object class symbol:
  in Information Analysis, 127
object classification, 147, 151,
  152, 165
  in Information Analysis, 126
object clusters, 92, 272
  definition of, 92
object connections, 156
object creation list, 215
object data dictionary:
  components of, 198
object definition, 147
  constraints, 65
object design, 160
  data, 173
  for performance realization,
    318
  methodology, 406
  user interface, 173
object dynamic redefinition, 81
object encapsulation, 163
object id, 91
object identification, 84, 251, 267
  for database design, 108
  for persistent objects, 84
  in Information Analysis, 126
object identifier, 84, 97, 151, 162,
  256, 269
  in Information Analysis, 126
  index, 271
object identity, 84, 303
  analogy to file handle, 84
  definition of, 84
  in networks, 85

  of copied objects, 85
  of duplicate objects, 85
  of merged objects, 84
  replicated objects, 86
  uniqueness across networks,
    86
  use of naming conventions,
    151
object inheritance, 147
object instance, 431
object methods, 64
  creation of, 260
Object Model, 202, 205, 210, 213,
  251, 253, 362, 378, 379,
  405–407, 421
  as a specification, 204
  components of, 406
  definition of, 203, 212
  depiction methodologies, 338
  substituting conceptual data
    model, 210
object operations, 160
object paradigm, 89
  in object oriented databases,
    90
object persistence:
  in memory, 162
object pointer, 156
object programming:
  techniques, 307
object relationships, 137
  behavioral (operations), 137
  depicted in frames, 247
  representation of, 408
  structural (attributes), 137
object repository, 338, 343
  management, 340
object server, 252, 260, 269, 302
  as a nameserver, 267
object services, 147, 159
  depiction in Frame-Object
    diagrams, 161
  example of frame, 161
object set:
  definition of, 92
  processing, 253
object storage optimization, 318,
  319
object versions:
  in computer-aided design, 94
ODBMS, 3, 108, 147, 253, 269,
  298, 334
OLTP (on-line transaction processing), 6, 323, 325
  performance, 58
Open Look, 340
Open Server, 285
operational control:
  of user applications, 327
operational hierarchies, 221
operational requirements:
  for an application, 168
operations, 413, *see also exported
  methods, methods*
  as behavioral components, 214
  as methods, 15, 69
  in an object, 58
operators, 24, *see also exported
  methods*
optical disk:
  for image storage, 347
  sub-systems (large data volumes), 352
optimization, 308
  of software, 307

organizational hierarchy, 280
OSF/Motif, 330, 340
outer join, 42
  example of, 43
output entities:
  depicted in frames, 221
overloading, 69, 342
owner server, 303

packet distribution network
  (PDN), 277
packet switching, 277
parameterized class:
  example of, 253
parameters:
  to procedures, 61
parent class, 253, 261
participation:
  for object linkage, 158
performance, 307
  designing for, 379
  monitoring of, 307, 308
performance optimization:
  by denormalization, 115
permissions:
  default, 269
persistence, 16, 90, 92, 94
persistent database object, 85, 92
persistent object, 251, 343
  creation of, 79
  definition of, 93
  in object oriented databases,
    87, 93
  optimization storage, 358
physical schema, 193
pictures, 463
point-and-click, 333
pointing devices, 325, 333, 337
polymorphism, 95, 163, 251
  definition of, 81
  in programming, 81
pop-up menus, 337
pop-up windows, 389
portable repository, 182
porting strategy, 209
post-conditions, 63, 80, 98, 148
  as constraints, 98
  for object services, 160
  in objects, 97
  programming of, 64
postscript:
  display, 17
pre-conditions, 60, 63, 81, 98,
  148
  for object services, 161
  in objects, 97
  programming of, 64
  uses of, 63
predicate:
  in semantic networks, 129
Presentation Manager (OS/2),
  327, 330
primary key, 97, 111, 126, 193,
  194
private attributes, 257
procedures, 60
process flows, 238, 412
process inspector, 342
process life cycle, 169
processes:
  in data flow diagrams, 121
  in Frame-Object Analysis, 140
product, 23, *see also relational
  algebra*

product (operator), *see also relational algebra*
program structure browsers, 342
project (operator), *see also relational algebra*
project life cycle, 205
project management, 167
project plan, 204
projection, 28, *see also relational algebra*
properties of database transactions
  behavioral, 203
  structural, 203
propositions:
  in Information Analysis, 126
prototyping, 109, 171, 172, 203, 226
  an object oriented system, 95
  applications, 173
  factors for success, 171
  functions, 171
  object oriented systems, 172
  of information systems, 171
  relational database applications, 172
  screen forms, 171
  user interface, 172
public database, 257
pull-down menus, 337, 389

query, 7
  execution order, 288
  execution plan, 12
  optimizers, 287
  organization, 310
query design:
  AI based, 344
query execution plan, 12, *see also query plan*
  evaluation of, 287
query optimization, 12, 286
  for distributed databases, 10
  for distributed systems, 11, 12, 13
  in distributed database systems, 286, 288
  in object-oriented databases, 288
query plan, 12, 45, 287, *see also joins*
QuickPascal, 96

RDBMS, 50, 186, 201, 332, 336, 352
re-usable objects, 64, 89
reasoning, 354
  monotonic, 354
rebinding (of objects), 97
record-based information models, 49
record identifiers:
  in relational databases, 84
redefinition, 81, 83, 220, 251, 253
  and dynamic binding, 80
  benefits for prototyping, 82
  code example of, 447
  of methods, 80
  of object attributes, 98
  of object methods, 98
  of objects, 97
  static, 79
  uses of, 80
reference information, 373, 379
reference tables, 373

referential integrity, 38, 97, 191, 195
relation, 110
relation symbol:
  in Information Analysis, 127
relational algebra, 25, 26, 346, *see also relational model*
  Cartesian product, 26
  domain, 26
  difference operator, 30
  intersection, 30
  intersection operator, 30
  join, 25, 28, 42
  join operator, 28
  product, 28
  product operator, 28
  project operator, 28
  projection, 25, 28
  select operator, 27
  selection, 25, 27
  set difference, 25, 27, 30
  set theory, 27
  tuple, 27
  union, 25
  union operator, 25
relational database, 21, 145, 195 344, 359, 409, 459, 462, *see also RDBMS*
  application, 202
  for attribute data, 352
  strengths, 96
relational database management system:
  query optimization, 288, *see also RDBMS*
  transaction management, 48
relational database system, 106, 268, *see also RDBMS*
relational integrity, 9, 36, 96, 189, 190, 193
  automatically enforced, 97
  enforced by database, 190
  in distributed environments, 189
relational model, 26, 58, 189, 462
  algebra, 26, *see also relational algebra*
  attributes, 26
  Cartesian product, 26
  definition, *see RDBMS*
  definition of relation, 25
  domain, 25
  entity integrity, 26
  extensions to, 57
  foundation rules, 31
  integrity, 26
  manipulative part of, 26
  referential integrity, 26
  relations, 26, 57
  structural part of, 26
relational model objectives:
  communicability, 24
  data independence, 24
  set-processing, 24
relational tables, 346
relations:
  as tables, 193
  between entities, 147
relationship, 189
  definition of, 117
  depicted in frames, 388
relationships, types of:
  event, 117
  existence, 117
  functional, 117

remote file service, 299
remote procedure calls (RPCs), 99
replicated objects, 162
replication, 10, 14
  for performance optimization, 310
  of data, 282, 284
  of objects, 302
reports, 202, 221
  application output, 221
repository, 180
  for CASE, 180
  for shared documents, 178
request messages:
  in distributed object oriented databases, 293
requirements analysis, 167, 170, 206
  using structured analysis, 170
reusability, 60, 153
  of software, 69
rollback message, 293
rollback recovery:
  in object oriented databases, 88
RPC (remote procedure call), 58, 252, 260, 269
  for creating control objects, 296
rules of inference, 24
  inference trees, 24
  operators, 24

schema:
  conceptual, 192
  external, 191
  graphical, 339
  internal, 191
  schema generator, 163
screen objects, 172
  for user interface, 172
scrollbars, 327, 332
second normal form (2NF), 112
security, 14, 378
select (operator), *see relational algebra*
selection, 24, *see also relational algebra*
semantic analysis, 13, 287
  depiction within Frame-Object diagrams, 156
  for distributed queries, 13
semantic data model, 193
semantic network, 107, 129, 130, 230
  characteristics, 130
  concepts, 130
  conjunction, 132
  disjunction, 132
  events, 130
  example, 130
  implications, 132
  negation, 132
  nodes, 130
  predicate, 129
  uses of, 133, 134
  value-nodes, 130
sentence:
  in Information Analysis, 126
  sentence diagrams, 127
sequential access, 312
sequential relationship, 225
server architecture:
  classes of, 308
  in database systems, 308

server degradation:
impact of, 378
services:
of objects, *see behavioral components*
provided by objects, 148
set constraints:
in sentence diagrams, 128, *see also Information Analysis*
set difference, 25, 27, *see also relational algebra*
set management, 229
Smalltalk, 56, 72, 96
software optimization, 307
sound, 463
source:
in data flow diagrams, 121
source-level debugger, 163, 180
graphical, 339
source code browsers, 178, 342
spatial pointing devices, 332
specialization, 152
applied to attributes, 153
spreadsheets:
in binary datatype, 99
in BLOBs, 58
SQL (structural query language), 2, 56, 176
procedural extensions—benefits, 59
procedural extensions to, 57, 59
storage management:
for distributed object oriented database, 357, 358
storage mechanism:
for database systems, 89
storage technologies:
for images, 346
on-line optical disk storage, 346
stored procedures, 36, 37, 53, 99, 196
for programming business rules, 98
in SYBASE, 37
performance impact, 58
use of, 39, 41
string object, 423
structural abstractions:
aggregation, 229
association, 229
generalization, 229
structural attributes, 251
depiction of, 232
example of, 233
structural changes, 72
structural components, 379
for object design, 421
of objects, 147, 149, 153, 202, 412
structural definitions, 407
structural frame:
depiction of, 408
structural frames, 156, 251
structural information, 147
structural mapping, 248
of attributes, 406
Structural Model, 213, 230, 252, 362, 406, 407, 412
as part of Object Model, 210
definition of, 212
description of, 214
example of, 232

Frame Object Analysis diagrams for, 232
prototyping of, 171
structural objects, 229
structural properties, 202
as an abstraction, 229
example of, 232
of database transactions, 229
structural relationships:
in Frame-Object Analysis diagrams, 138, 139
structural diagrams:
in Information Analysis, 127
structured analysis, 108, 109
for requirements analysis, 170
structured analysis methodology, 108
structured graphics, 332
structured query language, *see SQL*
structured system analysis, 120
structured text, 332
sub-class, 68, 89, 138, 220
code example of, 442, 443
creation of, 80
example of, 77, 381
uses of, 91
sub-clusters:
of objects, 93
sub-functions:
depiction in frames, 400
depiction of, 225
subjects:
abstract objects, 330
subroutines, 62
SunView, 340
SUNwindows, 340
superclass, 68, 78
from generalization abstraction, 232
synchronization:
of replicated databases, 291
system administration, 373
of object oriented systems, 300
system architecture, 276
system defined constraints, 36, 191
entity integrity, 36
relational integrity, 36
system design, 201, 210, 362, 421
as a specification, 203
definition of, 202
system design methodology, 201, 204, 205
definition of, 203
diagramming for object-oriented systems, 145
for object-oriented systems, 145
system documentation:
behavioral view, 142
structural view, 141
using Frame-Object Analysis diagrams, 142
systems design, 167

table, 24
in relational database, 57, 92
table scan:
impact on performance, 311
task boundary relationships, 168
task decomposition:
example of, 148
for object design, 147

task frame:
example of, 148
task services frame:
example of, 149
technology assessment, 204, 205
technology feasibility, 378
Technology Feasibility Report, 205, 206, 208
text, 463
text-retrieval systems, *see hypertext systems*
text datatypes, 346
text editors, 332
third normal form, 112
toolkits:
for GUIs, 327
top-level frame, 389, 411
example of behavioral frame, 413
top-level menu, 222, 226, 390
frame, 223
traffic analysis:
for information system, 209
transaction, 48, 50, 196, 213, 221, 224, 277, 288, 357, 418
as methods, 418
at lower levels, 224
behavioral view of, 230
classes, 252
committing of, 297
complex transactions, 48
concurrent, 25
creating control objects, 296
definition of, 291
frame, 223
in object oriented databases, 291
nested, 16
processing, 279
scope of, 230
structural view of, 230
transaction abstractions, 229, 236
insert, 236
join, 236
query, 236
update, 236
Transaction Control Object, 294, 297
transaction log, 48
after-image journal, 48
before-image journal, 48
transaction management, 10, 15, 48, 94, 279, 357
concurrency control, 48
for distributed object-oriented database, 357
Transaction Management Object, 294
transaction manager, 49, 101, 293, 357
Transaction Model, 213, 221, 223, 226, 229, 230, 362, 382, 389
as part of Information System Model, 210
definition of, 210
depicted in frames, 389, 390
depiction methodologies, 338
description of, 213
transaction object:
proposed transaction management scheme, 294
Transaction Object, 294, 297
management, 293
transforms:

in data flow diagrams, 121
transparency, 282
trigger methods, 261, 264
triggering operation, 194
triggers, 36, 37, 98, 191, 196, 198
  database enforced, 195
  firing of, 36, 98
  for programming business
    rules, 98
  once-only, 98
  perpetual, 98
  use of, 38
tuple, *see relational algebra*
two-phase commit protocol, 290,
  292
  for distributed database sys-
    tems, 294
  transaction management
    operations, 293

union, 25, 30, *see also relational
  algebra*
union (operator), 30, *see also
  relational algebra*
uniqueness constraints, 128, *see
  also Information Analysis*
update notification, 303
upper CASE, 176, 180
user callable methods, 198
user defined constraints, 98, 191
user defined functions (UDF),
  37, 99
user defined integrity, 36
user forms, 202
user interface, 380

objects design, 173
  technologies, 325
user requirements:
  analysis of, 167
user visible functions, 222
user visible transactions:
  depiction of, 225
utility class, 253
  Vec, 253

validation rules, 196
value-nodes:
  in semantic networks, 130
value added networks, 277
vector object, 256, 431
verbs:
  in Information Analysis, 126
Verheijen and Van Bekkum, 125
version control, 303
version management, 196
version verification, 303
versioning, 49, 92, 94
  definition, 94
  definition of, 86
  for distributed transaction
    management, 94
vertical integration:
  of applications, 276
vertical menus, 386
video, 462
  animation, 20
video images:
  in binary datatype, 99
  in BLOBs, 58
viewport, 332

views, 193
  interactive objects, 330
voice, 5
voice command recognition, 327,
  334
  communications, 325
  query, 334
  recognition, 325, 334
  synthesis, 325, 327, 334
volume analysis:
  for information system, 208

WAN (wide area network), 6,
  252, 276, 376
widgets, 173
windows:
  in object oriented program-
    ming, 173
  manager, 328
workstations, 361

X clients, 327
X Consortium, 17
X protocol, 327, 328
X server, 327
X toolkit, 327, 330
X Windows, 17, 327, 340
  architecture of, 327
X11 protocol, 332
Xlib, 328

Yourdon/DeMarco model:
  data flow diagrams, 121, 337
  diagrams, example of, 123